PRAISE FOR *I'M FEELING THE*

"It sounds like a heavy duty topic, and only of interest to academics, historians, anthropologists and anyone keen on Mississippi. I thought that before I got stuck in too, but it should be read by anyone with a love of music and music history. Blues fans should stick on a Robert Johnson album, pour themselves a large JD and ice, sit down with the thought-provoking little gem and make their own mind up. There have always been three Kings when it comes to the blues: Albert, Freddie and BB. Now there are four. Good job Prof."
Blues & Soul

" . . . I applaud his industry and recommend his work to anyone that abhors dishonesty and exploitation as much as I do."
Blues & Rhythm

"A groundbreaking . . . thought provoking book."
Blues News: The Bi-Monthly Heartbeat of the Blues Society of Tulsa

"There's no doubt that Stephen King has achieved something original and urgently important here. His claim about the way in which the emergent mythology of blues tourism has transformed Mississippi from a 'death place' into a 'birthplace,' airbrushing history in the process, is brilliant, memorable, and provocative. The study shines when he arrives at a history of blues tourism in the Mississippi Delta. Most readers, even those familiar with the contemporary Mississippi blues scene, and the personalities who inhabit it, will learn something new. King has assembled a believable and coherent narrative that has long needed assembling; he's the first, to my knowledge, who has done this."
Adam Gussow, associate professor of English and southern studies at the University of Mississippi and author of *Seems Like Murder Here: Southern Violence and the Blues Tradition* and *Journeyman's Road: Modern Blues Lives from Faulkner's Mississippi to Post-9/11 New York*

"What a wonderful book! Blues history has been calling for a keen and analytic historiographer, and King's willingness to honestly confront the complexity of the blues tourism industry is an excellent start."
Paul Garon, a founding editor of *Living Blues* magazine and author of *Blues and the Poetic Spirit* and *What's the Use of Walking if There's a Freight Train Going Your Way? Black Hoboes & Their Songs*

"An insightful study of the power of myth in the development of cultural tourism. King shows how the generally accepted blues origin myth—that the blues was 'born' in the Delta as a cathartic 'escape' from work and worries—is a nostalgic rewriting of Mississippi history. While this mythic narrative may facilitate the marketing of blues tourism, it may also complicate racial reconciliation in the state."
Harriet Joseph Ottenheimer, emerita professor of anthropology and American ethnic studies at Kansas State University and author of *Cousin Joe: Blues from New Orleans*

I'm Feeling the Blues
RIGHT NOW

I'm Feeling the Blues
RIGHT NOW

Blues Tourism and the Mississippi Delta

STEPHEN A. KING

UNIVERSITY PRESS OF MISSISSIPPI • JACKSON

www.upress.state.ms.us

Designed by Peter D. Halverson

The University Press of Mississippi is a member of
the Association of American University Presses.

Parts of this book were originally published in:

"Memory, Mythmaking, and Museums: Constructive Authenticity
and the Primitive Blues Subject." *Southern Communication Journal*
71 (2006): 235–50. Published by Taylor and Francis.

"Race and Blues Tourism: A Comparison of Two Lodging Alterna-
tives in Clarksdale, Mississippi." *Arkansas Review: A Journal of Delta
Studies* 36 (2005): 26–42.

"Blues Tourism in the Mississippi Delta: The Functions of Blues
Festivals." *Popular Music and Society* 27 (2004): 455–75. Published
by Taylor and Francis.

First printing 2011
∞
Library of Congress Cataloging-in-Publication Data

King, Stephen A., 1964–
I'm feeling the blues right now : blues tourism and the Mississippi
Delta / Stephen A. King.
    p. cm. — (American made music series)
Includes bibliographical references and index.
Discography.
ISBN 978-1-61703-010-9 (cloth : alk. paper) —
ISBN 978-1-61703-011-6 (ebook) 1. Blues (Music)—Social aspects.
2. Blues (Music)—Mississippi—Delta (Region)—History and
criticism. 3. Music and tourism—Mississippi—Delta (Region)—
History. I. Title.
ML3918.B57K56 2011
306.4'84243097624—dc22   2010052088

British Library Cataloging-in-Publication Data available

TO P, D, & L

[The blues is] the mother of our music and you got to take care of your mother.
> —THELONIOUS MONK JR., speaking at the dedication of a Mississippi Blues Trail marker at Dockery Farms

The average blues player you see around here is probably about like me. He is really struggling, man. You got to really, really struggle to pay your bills. Boy, you're just one level above welfare.
> —MISSISSIPPI SLIM, blues musician

CONTENTS

Preface XI

Acknowledgments XVI

Introduction 3

1. The History of the Mississippi Delta Blues 23

2. The History of Blues Tourism in the Mississippi Delta 54

3. Blues Myths and the Rhetorical Imagination of Place 78

4. Blues Festivals, Race, and the Construction of Authenticity 100

5. A Blues Countermemory
The History of Mississippi, the Story of the Delta 117

6. Public Memory, Historical Amnesia, and the Shack Up Inn 140

7. Assessing Tourism Goals
Money, Image, and Reconciliation 164

Notes 193

Bibliography 239

Selective Discography 268

Index 271

PREFACE

The modern blues world is a strange and marvelous place,
rippling with contradictions and sorely in need of honest critique.
—ADAM GUSSOW, *Journeyman's Road*

F or more than three decades, blues tourists have traveled to Mississippi in search of authenticity in the "land where the blues began." In an effort to attract even more tourists to the state, Mississippi has proclaimed itself the "birthplace of the blues," an assertion that rests largely on the fact that many of the genre's greatest and most influential blues artists were born in Mississippi (particularly in the state's Delta region) during the end of the nineteenth century and throughout the first half of the twentieth. Robert Johnson, Charley Patton, Muddy Waters, B. B. King, Elmore James—the list is long and authoritative. Alienated in part by what they consider to be the commercialization and superficiality of popular music and the blues itself, blues tourists travel to Mississippi to drink beer at "authentic" juke joints like Poor Monkey's, attend blues festivals to listen to the "primitive" sounds of blues icons like David "Honeyboy" Edwards (who played with Robert Johnson) and James "T-Model" Ford, and photograph the gravesites of Robert Johnson, Charley Patton, and other blues alumni. This ritualistic act embodies blues tourism's "cult of death," a preoccupation with the passing of a whole generation of blues musicians and the belief that the blues itself is in the latter stages of some incurable terminal illness.[1]

Driving down U.S. Highway 61, touted as the "Blues Highway," tourists are often amazed by the Delta's otherworldly qualities. Although the largely rural and underprivileged region has changed dramatically since 1941, when Muddy Waters first played his acoustic guitar for folklorist Alan Lomax, who was visiting Mississippi to record African American folksongs in Coahoma County for the Library of Congress, tourists marvel at the seeming simplicity and purity of a land that time forgot.[2] In the book *In Search of the Blues*,

blues historian Marybeth Hamilton beautifully describes the spellbinding and intoxicating powers of the Delta:

> On Old Highway 61 in Mississippi, between Lula and Robinsonville in the heart of the Delta, stands the remains of a wooden railroad bridge partially submerged in a murky swamp. The air enveloping the bridge is sticky and fetid, thick with the smell of decayed vegetation, and the dark, stagnant water stretches far into the distance, flooding the banks, engulfing the trees. To look at the scene is to peer at an eerie, apparently timeless landscape, primordial and untouched by history, the world Noah might have glimpsed after the flood. . . . I found myself wholly caught up in the pilgrimage whose mythology I had set out to debunk.

Yet, after returning to England, Hamilton's romantic and nostalgic view of the Delta was replaced by a more realistic assessment of the images that she captured with her camera. Modernity and machines painfully intruded into the dreamlike fantasy of a primitive blues Eden:

> It took several months for the spell to be broken. Over time, once I'd returned to a frenetically urban, postindustrial London, my photograph of the railway bridge on Old Highway 61 began to tell a new tale. Looking at the swamp's stagnant water, I came to recognize that the primeval scene was in fact the product of a very modern process, which had absorbed the efforts of thousands of black workers in the late nineteenth century, of draining and clearing the wetlands to open the Delta for cotton crops. . . . Every landscape is a work of the mind, shaped by the memories and obsessions of its observers. What I glimpsed was a Delta that memory had forgotten, full of bustle and noise and machines.[3]

I admit I once entertained romantic fantasies about the Mississippi Delta. In 1986, I discovered Robert Johnson when I was a junior at Boise State University. Johnson's superlative slide guitar, coupled with his anguished, tormented cries of pain and confessions of supernatural sin, were mesmerizing and unforgettable. Through Johnson's songs, I imagined the Delta as an evocative, haunting, dangerous place where the ghosts of Johnson and other blues legends played in rowdy juke joints or on mysterious rural country roads. Years later, when I accepted a tenure-track position at Delta State University in Cleveland, Mississippi, my fantasy was put to the test. I was instantly struck by the searing, unforgiving heat (and millions of mosquitoes), the bleak, monotonous landscape, the rampant rural poverty, the wide disparity between rich and poor, and the insidious racism and discrimination that continue to consume the lives of some of the Delta's inhabitants. One local white confessed to me that he often dreamed of flying over "Niggertown" with cans of gasoline and a match with plans to burn the east side of Cleveland to the ground. The racial attitude of some whites in Mississippi makes it clear that Mississippi is still, in a very real sense, a "blues" state.

In early 2001, after completing the final proofs for my book *Reggae, Rastafari, and the Rhetoric of Social Control*, I started to seriously contemplate my options for my next scholarly project. My book on reggae traced how the music and the Rastafarian movement (a social movement responsible for the direction and development of roots reggae during the 1970s) were transformed from a perceived enemy of the state—characterized by the Jamaican government and the country's national newspaper, the *Daily Gleaner*, as a violent group of dreadlock-wearing, pot-smoking revolutionary extremists—to tourism "partner." In the book, I argued that with the international popularity of reggae music (e.g., Bob Marley and the Wailers) and the growing respect for the Rastafarian movement both in Jamaica and beyond, the Jamaican government and its surrogates successfully co-opted the movement and the music, an effective strategy of social control that also enticed tourists to visit the island nation.

During this transitional period, I contemplated the intriguing parallels between reggae music in Jamaica and blues music in Mississippi: both musical forms are, in part, responses to oppression within the black diaspora; both are examples of protest music (although reggae music is certainly a more overt form of protest); both emerged from individuals and groups that occupied the lowest stratum of society (poor, black, dispossessed, exploited, powerless); both have a relatively large white consumer base and have carved out a devoted international audience; both have been used for the purposes of cultural or heritage tourism. Then the question struck me: Is (white) Mississippi in the process of co-opting the blues just as the Jamaican authorities had done with reggae some twenty years ago?

The question of whether whites in Mississippi are in the process of, or have already accomplished the goal of, co-opting the blues is a contentious one. An equally controversial debate involves the much broader issue of white appropriation and control of blues music.[4] Some of the more vocal critics have scorned white blues musicians for playing and profiting from the blues. In *Blues People: Negro Music in White America*, LeRoi Jones (Amiri Baraka) laughingly characterized the idea of a white blues artist as "an even more violent contradiction of terms than the idea of a middle class blues singer."[5] In a 1990 editorial in *Guitar Player* magazine, guest columnist Lawrence Hoffman depicted white blues musicians as nothing more than "expressive copyist[s]" who "pretend" to play the blues. Blaming record companies, radio stations, blues societies, and a misinformed public for perpetuating a system that benefits white blues musicians at the expense of the "original" black blues masters, Hoffman lamented the fate of "true living bluesmen trying desperately to compete with the white Xerox machines who have usurped the market."[6] The condemnation of the white blues tradition also parallels the entertaining, but annoying, debate over whether whites can sing, or even play, the blues.[7]

Opposing voices contend that white involvement in the blues can be traced back nearly to the creation of the genre itself. Although he argues that the blues was, in its origins, "wholly African American," blues scholar Paul Oliver argues that the blues form combines both African (field hollers, call and response) and European influences (harmonic structures).[8] Both white and black singers recorded blues music during its early years, and there was considerable musical overlap and influence among white country blues artists and their African American counterparts.[9] It is also true that whites, for at least the last forty years, have dominated the blues world as both promoters and consumers of the musical form. In turn, some have claimed that without the blues' enthusiastic and appreciative white audience, the music would long ago have perished.[10] In a 2008 interview, Mississippi blues artist Terry "Harmonica" Bean said that if "it weren't for the white people, though, it [the blues] woulda done died out. That's who keeping it going. I hate to say it, but it's true. You know, because the black peoples is not into the blues, they into *rhythm* and blues."[11]

As I considered various arguments concerning white co-optation of the blues in Mississippi, I became less and less confident in my original assumption that white Mississippians are in the process of actively defrauding the state's black population of its blues heritage. And while most blues promoters—at both state and local levels—are white, the level and degree of any co-optation process are still undetermined. It is even more unclear if whites are reaping whatever financial benefits are associated with blues tourism. Although I discuss this subject in the latter portion of the final chapter, I am generally less interested in questions of co-optation and more intrigued with rhetorical representations of the blues, which is the primary focus of this book. What rhetorical strategies are blues promoters and organizers in Mississippi (from the local to the state level) employing to attract the attention of potential tourists to travel to the Delta? How are these promotional materials portraying the Delta's blues culture and its musicians? How do cultural producers mediate between promoting Mississippi's blues culture and history and acknowledging (or forgetting) the state's historical record of racial injustice?

Having spent over fifteen years living and working in the Delta, I have obtained, in some measure, the insider-outsider perspective, a role that allows me the necessary distance to be a skeptical critic while writing from a position of *some* authority about the Delta's troublesome and wonderful culture through firsthand experience, observation, and research. It is my hope that this book is an honest and fair critique of aspects of Mississippi's blues tourism industry.

ACKNOWLEDGMENTS

"**N**o man is an island, no man stands alone," the Mighty Diamonds sang, and indeed, no author stands alone. As I search my own private memories, hoping not to make the mistake of omission, I remember how my former professors (Michael Hogan, Richard Jensen, Carolyn Calloway-Thomas, Jan Schuetz, Ben Parker, and others) demanded excellence and encouraged me to sharpen my scholarly tools, ultimately preparing me to embark on my first major postdissertation project. I would be remiss if I did not express my love to my parents, who have always steadfastly supported my academic pursuits and interests.

I would like to thank the library staff at three local libraries, the Carnegie Public Library (Clarksdale), the William Alexander Percy Memorial Library (Greenville), and the Greenwood-Leflore Public Library (Greenwood). I also relied on Delta State University's Interlibrary Loan Department. Diane Coleman, assistant librarian II, was instrumental in securing sources not available on campus. David Salinero, a reference librarian at DSU, proved to be very skillful in locating a number of government documents used for this study. I also found rare historical documents at Delta State University's Archives Department, including slave contracts dating back to the early nineteenth century. In addition, I was fortunate to be in close proximity to the University of Mississippi in Oxford. The university's Department of Archives and Special Collections (which contains the awe-inspiring Blues Archives) is a gold mine for scholars interested in studying southern culture, civil rights, and popular culture, especially blues music, among other areas of interest. When I started conducting preliminary research on this project, blues scholar Edward Komara was the curator of the Blues Archives. Later I worked with Greg Johnson, associate professor and the Blues Archives' current curator. Greg was very supportive of my research and assisted me in locating key sources for this project. I would also like to thank Jimmy Giles of Clarksdale, the organizers for the King Biscuit Blues Festival (now called the Arkansas Blues and

Heritage Festival), KFFA radio, and Mississippi Action for Community Education (MACE).

I am very fortunate to be a member of the Division of Languages and Literature at Delta State University. My many friendships there have helped to sustain my scholarship over the years, and I am lucky to have worked for two wonderful department chairs, Dorothy Shawhan (1995–2006) and Bill Hays (2006–present). Thank you for your friendship and support. Special thanks to my colleague Susan Allen Ford for fielding citation and reference questions. The university also supported my research, providing me funding to attend a variety of academic conferences both in the United States and abroad. Beyond university support, I financed the rest of the costs associated with the project.

I would like to thank David Evans, professor of music in the Rudi E. Scheidt School of Music at the University of Memphis, for his detailed comments and helpful suggestions that started the difficult but necessary revision process. I would like to thank Adam Gussow, associate professor of English and Southern Studies at the University of Mississippi, for his careful reading of the manuscript and his supportive and constructive comments that greatly improved the manuscript. A word of appreciation is also extended to a third reader, who provided helpful feedback on how to strengthen the study.

I am highly indebted to Craig Gill, assistant director and editor in chief at the University Press of Mississippi. Craig and I have known each other since 1999, when we first talked about transforming my dissertation on reggae music into a book. While I was revising this book, he was always reasonable, cheerful, supportive, and encouraging. Although I'm sure some author-editor relationships are marked by contentiousness and distrust, working with Craig has been an absolute pleasure. On that note, I would like to thank all staff members from the University Press of Mississippi, from editorial (e.g., Anne Stascavage) to marketing (e.g., Steve Yates) to design and production (e.g., John Langston), for their hard work that made it possible for this manuscript to be transformed into a book.

While writing this book, I received, to my great surprise, unsolicited correspondence from students, both undergraduate and graduate, from Mississippi, Tennessee, North Carolina, Texas, and California, who were working on similar projects. I am encouraged by this growing interest by younger scholars in an area of blues scholarship that is still relatively new and unexplored. Perhaps this book will serve as some sort of foundation for future work in blues tourism.

Another person who has devoted considerable time to this project is P. Renée Foster. When I met Renée in January 1996, I had recently been hired as an instructor at DSU and was still struggling to complete a final draft of my dissertation. After I completed the dissertation, she helped me transform it into a book. For this blues project, I relied on her as an "internal" editor: she read countless drafts, correcting errors, crossing out sentences and paragraphs, writing suggestions in the margins, with the express goal, of course, of pushing me to create a quality manuscript. Her fingerprints are literally on every page of the book. She often accompanied me as I conducted field research, visited libraries, and attended blues festivals and other tourism events. She eased the burden associated with writing this book, and my love for her is constant and boundless. Lajara, our five-year-old gray cat, who has a remarkable devotion to me, sat in a chair next to the computer desk and waited patiently for me to turn my attention away from the computer screen and pet her. Dready, Lajara's feline companion, with his never-ending demand for food, made sure I got up to feed him. By giving me time to reflect between long writing stretches, the cats helped me get the job done.

A final word: part of the book title is borrowed from a quotation from a 2008 *Living Blues* interview with longtime Clarksdale blues musicians Wesley Jefferson and Terry Williams. I liked Jefferson's phrase "I'm feeling the blues right now" because of its ambiguity and irony. I never had the chance to interview him. He died on July 22, 2009, from complications associated with lung cancer. But I did have the chance to interview a number of individuals—musicians, local blues promoters, festival organizers, Mississippi Blues Commission members, chamber of commerce officials, blues scholars, and others—and their collective voices represent joy and anger, idealism and realism, and contradiction and conflict, qualities that signify Mississippi's blues tourism industry. Their names are listed in the bibliography, and I thank each one for sharing his or her thoughts about Mississippi's blues tourism industry.

I'm Feeling the Blues
RIGHT NOW

INTRODUCTION

But just how do you attract visitors to a region famous for poverty and a violent history of racism?
—SHELIA HARDWELL BYRD, "Deltans Find Hope in Blues"

Since the 1960s, the blues has experienced numerous cultural revivals, attracting the attention of record companies, corporate sponsors, multinational companies, and a legion of new fans. Many predicted that the latest major blues revival in 2003, dubbed the Year of the Blues, would be a major success because, according to *Rolling Stone* magazine, the "blues is more important and more necessary now than it has ever been."[1] The U.S. Senate designated 2003 the Year of the Blues because the blues is the "most celebrated form of American roots music" and blues musicians are "recognized and revered worldwide as unique and important ambassadors of the United States and its music."[2] The Year of the Blues also served as a hundredth anniversary of sorts, commemorating blues musician and composer W. C. Handy's (known as the "Father of the Blues") "initial" encounter with the blues while waiting for a train at a railroad station in the small Mississippi Delta town of Tutwiler.[3] Considerable celebratory fanfare accompanied the Year of the Blues, including the release of Martin Scorsese's The Blues: A Musical Journey, a seven-part series that aired on PBS.

Meanwhile, this most recent blues revival has also stoked the vivid imaginations of tourists seeking to consume alternative forms of popular culture, an event that parallels an increasing fascination and appetite for American roots music.[4] "By going to the root of popular forms of music," argues sociologist Robert Owen Gardner, audiences believe they can "escape the commodifying and co-optive forces of mass culture."[5] Underneath the "prefabrication and formulaic sameness of so much of what we watch and listen to," enthuses music critic Anthony DeCurtis, "the blues courses like a vital stream that can be

3

tapped into for a life-affirming jolt of raw energy."[6] Searching for an authentic and pure blues experience, many blues tourists make the journey to the Mississippi Delta, often touted as the birthplace of the blues. Located in northwestern Mississippi, the Delta was birthplace and home to some of the genre's greatest musicians, from Robert Johnson to Muddy Waters to B. B. King.

As a subset of a larger international tourism industry, blues tourism encompasses a complex series of often interrelated and multidimensional public- and private-sector organizations, from blues museums to chambers of commerce to local entrepreneurs, which attempt to draw tourists to specific geographic areas (e.g., Chicago, Memphis, the Mississippi Delta) to experience the culture or heritage of the blues. As such, blues tourism has been framed as an example of cultural tourism.[7] Anne K. Soper, a tourism scholar, argues that cultural tourism includes both tangible and intangible elements, from historic homes to places of worship, folk songs to myths.[8] In turn, cultural tourism involves marketing "cultural sites, events, attractions, and/or experiences."[9] For the blues tourist, cultural artifacts may include historical markers and signs, graves, plantations, hotels, cafés, recording studios, lounges, juke joints, blues clubs, music festivals, songs, books, DVDs, and records.[10]

A variety of entities from government agencies to local entrepreneurs are actively involved in marketing and promoting Mississippi's blues heritage and culture to potential tourists. Representing official culture, the organizations responsible for marketing the Delta blues are both local (chambers of commerce) and regional (Mississippi Delta Tourism Association), as well as statewide governmental entities (Mississippi Development Authority/Tourism Division). Typically, many promotional efforts by chambers of commerce and convention and visitors bureaus target consumers who live more than one hundred miles away from a particular Delta community, especially in border states such as Arkansas and Tennessee.[11] Through a variety of promotional tools and interactive Web sites, the Mississippi Development Authority/Tourism Division's (MDA) plan also involves targeting states that border Mississippi, with a focus on appealing to a younger demographic, ages twenty-five to thirty-four, as well as baby boomers. The state's plan also includes an in-state campaign that will give "Mississippians a new reason to visit their own state."[12] In his review of heritage sites in the Mississippi Delta, sociologist Alan Barton argued that the state should work more vigorously to target its local population. In a survey he conducted of Delta residents, only 32 percent of respondents had attended at least one blues festival or visited a blues club in 2004. The percentage for repeat visitors was considerably lower, 3.4 percent.[13]

GOALS OF BLUES TOURISM

Mississippi's blues tourism industry serves at least three separate but interrelated goals. The first and perhaps most obvious is economic. Blues tourism has become, in part, a necessary response to a seemingly never-ending economic crisis in one of the country's most impoverished states. Before the economic collapse and recession of 2008, Mississippi had the unfortunate reputation of leading the nation in the percentage of individuals unemployed. For example, in December 2007, Mississippi's unemployment rate, 6.4 percent, topped the national average of 4.8 percent.[14] In 2008 the state had the lowest personal income per capita and median household income of any state in the nation. In that same year, Mississippi had the nation's highest percentage of individuals living under the poverty line.[15] In 2007 Mississippi led the nation in the largest percentage of children and families living in poverty.[16] In the area of education, Mississippi ranked dead last (with the exception of the District of Columbia) in 2008 in a variety of categories, including ACT composite scores.[17] It is no wonder that the 2008 *State Rankings* guide rated Mississippi the nation's most *unlivable* state.[18]

Arguably, the epicenter of the state's miseries can be found in its Delta region. In July 2010 only one county (Desoto, 8.7 percent) out of nineteen "core" and "partial" Delta counties had an unemployment rate below 11.0 percent (compared to the U.S. average of 9.7 percent) with some counties as high as 22.7 percent.[19] Many Delta counties have been classified as "distressed" due, in part, to high poverty rates, low average household income, and lackluster achievement in education.[20] Indeed, recurring high rates of unemployment and poverty and a declining tax base have for all practical purposes cemented Mississippi's Delta region as one of the poorest regions in one of the poorest states in the union. In an analysis of the lower Mississippi River Delta, one observer offered a sobering account of the Delta's challenges: "Persistent poverty and a lack of resources make it difficult to create positive change in the region."[21]

However, the Delta is certainly not unique in its desire to exploit tourism as a new revenue producer. Indeed, as geographers Stephen Frenkel and Judy Walton have observed: "The post–World War II era has witnessed the decline of a number of rural, resource-based economies and an increasing turn to tourism as an alternative economy."[22] Many of these rural communities have turned to niche tourism, a relatively new development that capitalizes on the increasing efforts of whole communities to accentuate their cultural heritage, "partly in bids to increase their tourism potential."[23] During the 1960s, for example, the town of Leavenworth, Washington, decided to transform itself into a Bavarian theme town.[24] Other examples include Cave Creek, Arizona, which advertises itself as a Wild West frontier town, and Canterbury, New Hampshire, a small town of less than two thousand that draws tourists to the remnants of a once thriving Shaker Village. In a 2008 interview, Wanda Clark, the project coordinator for the Mississippi Blues Trail, stated that one of the missions associated with blues tourism is to encourage tourists to spend money in smaller Delta communities, such as the tiny town of Shaw, Mississippi, that have experienced years of economic stagnation and even depression because of depopulation (particularly white flight and black out-migration) and the loss of vital manufacturing and agricultural industries and jobs.[25]

While not a panacea for the state's economic woes, tourism is perceived as an increasingly important part of Mississippi's overall economy. In 2010 the MDA's *Fiscal Year 2009 Economic Contribution of Travel and Tourism in Mississippi* claimed that tourism is a "driving force in the state's economic development" and "a key part of Mississippi's economic development engine." Still, the industry makes up a relatively small portion of the state's overall economic activity. Tourism accounted for just 4 percent of the gross state product (GSP) in 2009, ranking sixth (out of thirteen sectors) in the state in terms of direct employment (78,240) behind government, wholesale and retail trade, manufacturing, education and health services, and professional and business services.[26]

Although Mississippi's state government does not maintain records of revenue generated from blues tourism, many tourism officials, local politicians, blues organizers, and promoters recognize the potential economic impact associated with blues tourism. Claiming that Mississippi's local government entities would be "crazy not to explore the economic potential of an art form that's rooted firmly in the Delta soil," a *Clarksdale Press Register* reporter argued that, with more financial support from the state, "blues-related tourism could grow exponentially, boosting the economy of a region hit hard in recent years by the decline of rural America's manufacturing economy."[27] Local and regional headlines, such as "There are $ in Blues, Tourism," "Will the Blues Bring Bucks?," and "Music Heritage May Be Next Cash Crop," clearly suggest that blues tourism is becoming widely recognized as a potential source of revenue.[28] Mississippi governor Haley Barbour acknowledged that while "these musicians grew up in great deprivation and poverty," the state has realized "what a powerful economic development tool this music can be."[29] In June 2010, Barbour even told an audience of 120 prominent Mississippi officials and business leaders that the Delta's economic future rests in tourism, including promoting the state's blues heritage.[30] Writing in the March–June 2004 issue of *Living Blues* magazine, a former editor of the publication, Jim O'Neal, reflected on the burgeoning blues tourism industry in Mississippi:

Whatever ironies may lie in the exaltation of a music born to poverty to boost the economy of the poorest state in the union, the fact is that Mississippi has finally realized that there is something to this business of Japanese and Norwegians and Californians showing up in search of blues sites and blues artists, buying bouquets at the local florist shop to place on some forgotten grave, or wandering around "across the tracks" with guitars on their backs or cameras in their hands.[31]

As reports from local chambers of commerce and convention and visitors bureaus indicate, more and more potential visitors are seeking information about the Delta's rich blues heritage. In a 2007 interview, Kappi Allen, tourism manager of the Coahoma County Tourism Commission, noted that the number of inquiries from blues tourists seems to increase every year. Her office typically receives at least thirty telephone calls a day (and numerous e-mail messages) from potential tourists, some from Europe and Asia.[32] Carmen Walsh, executive director of the Greenville–Washington County Convention and Visitors Bureau, confirms increasing interest by tourists about the region's blues culture.[33]

To meet the rising demands of tourists who seek out the birthplace of the blues, a number of travel guides, including *Blues Traveling: The Holy Sites of Delta Blues* (2008), *Memphis and the Delta Blues Trail* (2009), *Delta Blues Map Kit* (2004), and *Lonely Planet Road Trip: Blues and BBQ* (2005), have been published.[34] In 2004, with financial underwriting from the Mississippi Development Authority, *Living Blues* magazine devoted an entire issue to constructing a traveler's guide of sorts in an effort to "encourage visitors to come to Mississippi, and to point them in the right direction once here."[35] In addition, since the mid-1990s, the number of blues festivals in the region has expanded from a handful to approximately fifty, while new blues museums have been created (or are in various stages of development) to showcase Mississippi's blues history. In 2007 the Tourism Division of the Mississippi Development Authority launched Tune In Mississippi, a twenty-four-hour Internet radio station featuring blues music.[36]

Meanwhile a variety of tour companies, including Great Britain's Roots of Rhythm tour and Nashville's Sweet Magnolia Tours, have tapped into a growing market that demands packaged tours. For example, the Delta Music Experience (DME) markets variations of a Real Deal tour, a two-week round-trip adventure that originates in New Orleans. Traveling by train and bus, tourists spend a week in the Mississippi Delta and are introduced to an assortment of highly touted blues sites, from Poor Monkey's juke joint in Merigold to the Delta Blues Museum in Clarksdale. Asserting that tourists will be immersed in the region's music and culture, Amanda Gresham, the company's founder, proclaims that the "soul of the blues lives in the delta."[37] In Greenwood, Mississippi, local entrepreneur and Baptist deacon Sylvester Hoover has created the Delta Blues Legend Tour, a three-hour adventure that includes Robert Johnson's three burial sites. For blues fans who have neither the time nor the financial wherewithal to physically travel to the Delta, there are numerous virtual tours on Mississippi Delta blues sites, including the ghoulish Dead Blues Guys, a Web site devoted to memorializing over eighty blues musicians (among them Muddy Waters, Bukka White, Hound Dog Taylor, and Stevie Ray Vaughan) through photos of graves, headstones, and markers.[38]

Sensing the lucrative possibilities, local entrepreneurs and small business owners are even getting into the act. For example, Gary Hilton and Tom Ramsey (who is no longer with the company) officially formed a cigar company in 2007, Avalon Cigars, named after the hometown of the well-known musician Mississippi John Hurt. Cigars are named after blues artists, both living and deceased.[39] Mag-Pie Gift and Art Shop in Clarksdale sells the Cross-roads Blues Tervis Tumblers, drinking glasses and mugs with the design of the crossroads (U.S. Highways 61 and 49) emblazoned on the side of the glass. Another local business in Clarksdale sells tins of assorted candy called Delta Blues and Gold. The cover of the container features a drawing of a blue guitar and golden cotton. Blueswood Arts, in Batesville, Mississippi, has developed its own unique brand of "blues furniture" with names such as "Blind Willie's Juke Joint," a liquor cabinet, and "A Devil's Shelf," where one can display "guitar strings" and "black cat bones," among other items. One inventive soul is even selling "Mississippi Delta Graveyard Dirt" on the Internet for twenty dollars per bottle.[40]

Even with the real potential to draw audiences to the region from the four corners of the globe, the state's blues tourism industry is still in its infancy, making it difficult to guarantee its economic sustainability. As Alan Barton reminds us, unless a large segment of the local population is willing to accept and embrace the influx of new tourists to the area, "it is unlikely that the region will have long-term success in the tourism business."[41] However, in a 2005 survey of residents of eleven counties in the Mississippi Delta region, Barton found strong local support for blues tourism: 71.6 percent of respondents supported the idea of tourists visiting a blues club or blues festival, and 78.3 percent supported tourists visiting a blues museum or other blues-related sites. Reflecting the trend of white interest in the blues, white respondents demonstrated a slightly higher interest than their African American counterparts in blues tourism. For example, while 76.9 percent of white participants responded favorably to tourists visiting blues clubs or festivals, only 68.6 percent of blacks favored such an activity. Barton speculates this racial difference may be due to a number of factors, including a perception among the African

American respondents that white business people profit from festivals that feature African American musicians, as well as the belief that the blues is a negative influence on the African American community.[42]

A second goal of blues tourism is related to efforts to change public perceptions about the state's dreadful historical record of racial oppression and economic exploitation. Portrayed as uneducated, violent racists, Mississippians have fought back against these negative stereotypes. One public relations campaign, "Mississippi, Believe It!," actually exploits these stereotypes to showcase the state's strengths. Rick Looser, the COO of Cirlot Agency, a Mississippi-based communications firm, started the promotional campaign after a twelve-year-old Connecticut boy asked him if he hated black people and if he "saw the KKK on the streets every day." Since 2006 the campaign has included seventeen public service announcements, and the ads themselves poke fun, for example, at the perception that Mississippians are largely uneducated and illiterate ("Yes, we can read. A few of us can even write") while showcasing the state's literary pantheon (e.g., Tennessee Williams, Richard Wright). Two ads focus on the state's music heritage. One includes the photos of eighteen famous musicians, Jimmy Buffett, Faith Hill, Elvis Presley, Robert Johnson, among others, with the headline "Y'all May Think We Talk Funny, but the World Takes Our Music Seriously." The organization hopes this strategy will help improve the state's image as well as provide local Mississippians with a "form of intellectual ammunition to defend the state any time its image is in question."[43]

Beyond this unique public relations campaign, the state hopes that blues tourism will change the public's negative perceptions of Mississippi. State senator David Jordan believes that blues tourism will help repair the state's image as well as provide a financial benefit.[44] Two of the state's most famous citizens, B. B. King and the actor Morgan Freeman (both of whom left Mississippi during the state's Jim Crow era), are now two of the state's biggest supporters. Once ashamed of his native state, B. B. King now confidently claims that "Mississippi has changed so much, more than any other state in the union."[45] To encourage skeptics to visit the state, Morgan Freeman, a co-owner of one of Clarksdale's celebrated blues clubs, proselytizes for Mississippi's unique charm:

If you haven't been to Mississippi, you've missed one of the joys of life. We're not really what you think we are. We're not what we've been painted to be. This place is like nowhere else in the entire world. We've been cultured in fire. We are the strongest steel. We've come through the hottest fire. It's a cultural asset. It's not just the blues. It's not just music. It's music that has history, heritage, meaning, depth, truth and all of us embrace it. It's an American phenomenon, but we still embody it. Oh, not only is it alive, it's thriving.[46]

It would be patently unfair to claim that Mississippi has not significantly changed over the past five decades. Lynching, once a spectator sport, is a thing of the past.[47] Gone is the White Citizens' Council, a "cleaned-up" version of the Ku Klux Klan that virtually ruled the state during the 1950s and 1960s. The Sovereignty Commission, an organization created in the 1950s to spy on the activities of communists, civil rights workers, "racial agitators," and other supposed enemies of the state, is defunct. Numerous Jim Crow laws, from prohibiting interracial marriages to a statute that allowed the governor to close down public parks to prevent desegregation, have been abolished. Public schools and the state's numerous universities have been integrated. In a state that once prohibited African Americans from holding political office, Mississippi now has the highest numbers of black elected officials.[48]

Yet one would be naive to believe that the system of white privilege and the ideology of racial superiority that tragically marked Mississippi since its inception have suddenly vanished. While Jim Crow laws no longer exist, many Mississippi communities are still segregated by race. In the Delta and other Mississippi communities, all-white private schools (sometimes referred to as segregated or "seg" academies), a symbol of the state's efforts to combat the *Brown vs. Board of Education* ruling of 1954, are still in operation. As recently as April 2010, U.S. District Judge Tom S. Lee ordered officials of a school district in Tylertown, located in southern Mississippi, to discontinue the long-term practice of allowing white students to transfer from Tylertown's public schools, where 75 percent of students are African American, to Salem Attendance Center, a school that features a predominantly white student body. The judge argued that the practice violates both federal law and a desegregation order.[49] Compared to the state's white population, African Americans suffer from higher rates of unemployment, unrelenting poverty, infant mortality, and a host of other socioeconomic problems. For example, according to the Bureau of Labor Statistics, the unemployment rate for white Mississippians in 2007 was 3.9 percent, compared to 10.5 percent for African Americans.[50] As of May 2006, the rate of Mississippi whites living in poverty was 13 percent, slightly higher than the national average of 12 percent. In contrast, 43 percent of black Mississippians lived in poverty, 10 percent higher than the national average of 33 percent.[51] Two years later, the disparity between blacks (44 percent) and whites (15.7 percent) living in poverty had barely changed.[52] In his landmark book *The Most Southern Place on Earth: The Mississippi Delta and the Roots of Regional Identity*, historian James Cobb characterized the modern Delta region (1930–90) as an entrenched caste society whereby a relatively large African American population "lived in poverty that was difficult to imagine, let alone accept, while a small, seemingly oblivious white minority enjoyed a pampered and gracious lifestyle that many found difficult to resist."[53]

Some tourism officials and blues promoters hope blues tourism will facilitate a third function or goal: racial reconciliation. James L. Gibson, a political scientist, argues that reconciliation involves a "diminution of racial animosities" where parties engage in more meaningful communicative behavior, resulting in more cultural understanding and a celebration of racial diversity.[54] John B. Hatch, a communication scholar, argues that this rhetorical process does not necessarily end conflict or create racial harmony; the rhetorical process of reconciliation "unmakes and refashions the identities and laws of a social order in such a way that the grounds of violence are transformed into common ground for debate and dialogue."[55] These examples represent one type of reconciliation, writes David A. Crocker, which allows for a mutual coexistence and a willingness not to resort to violence to solve problems. He argues that more "robust" forms of reconciliation range from forgiveness to mutual healing to harmony.[56]

Blues promoters argue that awards ceremonies (e.g., the Peavine Awards), fund-raisers (e.g., the Blues Ball), blues markers, and the designation of occasions to remember individual blues artists demonstrate how blues music has fostered dialogue, cultural understanding, and empathy through aesthetic communication. It is argued that through the blues, white Mississippians who may otherwise have been ignorant of, or even hostile to, the African American community have come to appreciate black culture. White audiences who express genuine admiration for African American blues musicians, racially diverse blues musical groups, and local and national blues organizations that feature a membership noted for their cultural and racial heterogeneity are just a few examples, according to blues promoters, of how blues music bridges the stubborn and resistant racial divide. Noting that the blues was born out of a "vexed and painful relationship between blacks and whites in the segregated South," blues researcher Adam Gussow observed that the blues has "transmuted the mixture of fear, despair, fury, heartache, and restlessness that were their founding racial impulse into a powerful urge toward compassionate brotherhood, a brotherhood that yearns . . . to undo the spiritual and material conditions responsible for precipitating those blues feelings in the first place."[57]

A PROFILE OF THE BLUES TOURIST

With Mississippi's blues tourism industry still in early stages of development, the region mostly attracts what scholars have called the noninstitutionalized tourist.[58] As opposed to the institutionalized tourist who usually finds himself or herself immersed within the tourism industry's predictable and protective environment, noninstitutionalized tourist roles range from the "explorer," who seeks some autonomy from the tourism industry, to the "drifter," who "goes native" by immersing himself or herself in the world of a new host country.[59] In *Dark Star Safari*, Paul Theroux sums up the philosophy of the noninstitutionalized tourist: "The best travel is a leap in the dark. If the destination were familiar and friendly, what would be the point of going there?"[60] Many of the individuals interviewed for this project—chamber of commerce officials, museum curators, entrepreneurs, and musicians—claim that tourists do not want the Delta region to be transformed into a predictable and protective tourist environment. When I interviewed Kappi Allen, she observed that most tourists who travel to the Delta

> *don't want bright lights, big city, they want to come to Clarksdale and experience what it was like to walk on Issaquena Avenue and to see the places where the blues was born. And they don't want it jazzed up. They seem to want it just the way that it is. And, you know, many of the individual blues travelers, they don't want a tour guide either. They just kind of want to meander.*[61]

As numerous observers have testified, most blues tourists tend to be baby boomers, well-educated, middle- to upper-class whites, a trend that has its antecedent in the 1960s, when black interest in the blues started to wane.[62] Explanations for why African Americans, particularly younger blacks, abandoned the blues vary. First, the blues reminded African Americans of a difficult past—slavery, sharecropping, suffering—a past many would just as soon forget. Second, the blues was denigrated as "Uncle Tom" music, too passive and assimilationist in nature, especially at a time when the civil rights movement was calling for major reforms, including the abolition of legal segregation, and the shift from the philosophy of nonviolent resistance to armed militancy.[63] Third, the blues was never fully embraced in the black community in the first place—it was often debased as the "devil's music."

Some white promoters seem genuinely perplexed over the loss of the African American blues audience, while some African Americans place the blame squarely on the shoulders of an apathetic black population who are largely ignorant about their cultural heritage: "They [African Americans] look down on the blues like they're looking at a pile of garbage," said blues singer Koko Taylor. "And then our people are the first to say they [whites] took our music. Nah, they didn't take it. We give it to them."[64] However, Scott Barretta, former editor of *Living Blues* magazine, argued that expecting young African Americans to be supporters of the music is both unrealistic and unfair:

> *People [say], "Why aren't the young African American interested in this?" My standard answer is: Why aren't young white people interested in Bing Crosby?*

[They will say] "Well, Bing Crosby isn't as big as Robert Johnson." Well, Bing Crosby is as big as Robert Johnson. Why should young black people be any different than other Americans in remembering something that happened in the 1930s or the music of their great grandparents?[65]

Many of the early white consumers of the blues eventually became part of the folk revival movement that helped launch the 1960s blues revival, resurrecting the careers of blues musicians such as Son House, Bukka White, and Mississippi John Hurt. Sociologist David Grazian confirms this observation when he argues that since the 1960s, white interest in the blues has intensified because of the folk revival movement in the 1950s and 1960s, the appropriation of blues by rock-and-roll bands such as the Rolling Stones, and the "heightened visibility of black culture in the wake of the post–civil rights era."[66]

One should also credit the Blues Brothers phenomenon for helping introduce the blues to larger white audiences. Starring white comedians Dan Aykroyd and John Belushi, the Blues Brothers band also included members of the Saturday Night Live band, Booker T. and the MGs' guitarist Steve Cropper, and bassist Donald "Duck" Dunn, along with top-notch session musicians. The band's debut album, *Briefcase Full of Blues* (1978), sold an estimated 3.5 million copies, one of the highest-selling "blues" albums of all time (many of the songs are actually R&B and soul hits). In a 2007 interview, Aykroyd attributed the success of the album to both historical context and audience needs: "It was just at the end of disco, people were tired of disco. New wave was just about coming on, but it hadn't caught on, and the punk movement was just beginning. And we just slipped in there under the door, or over the transom if you want, with the 'Soul Man' cover. And that went to number one and basically established the band."[67] In the movie *The Blues Brothers* (1980), Elwood Blues (Aykroyd) and Jake Blues (Belushi), both dressed in the now-iconic identical black suits and dark sunglasses, are sent on a "mission from God" to raise money to save an orphanage. While the two comedians were the stars of the movie, Ray Charles, Aretha Franklin, James Brown, and other noted musicians made cameo appearances. The band and the movie can be credited for exposing black performers to new white audiences (and perhaps reviving some careers in the process), as well as giving unknown session musicians well-deserved public exposure. Yet some critics found the whole Blues Brothers concept appalling. Mark Coleman, a reviewer for *Rolling Stone*, lambasted the movie for "reducing this emotionally resonant music into a blaring frat-boy party soundtrack, and for reaping sizeable profits off it."[68] Other critics, such as All Music Guide critic Fred Beldin, condemned the band for spawning "thousands of terrible white R&B cover bands."[69]

The blues tourist profile also includes a variety of international travelers, especially from Europe and Asia. For example, from January to October 2007, the Clarksdale–Coahoma County Chamber of Commerce's guestbook included tourists representing eleven countries. In 2009 Clarksdale's Juke Joint Festival attracted tourists from seventeen countries.[70] The universal themes of the blues, human suffering and joy, are often credited for the music's global popularity. Blues scholar David Evans argued that although blues songs express the experiences of African Americans, the themes of conflict, tension, and worry are universal in nature, and as a result, the blues has "spread around the world and been enjoyed by most people who have come in contact with it."[71]

While this may be true, there are other reasons why foreign interest in the blues has continued unabated since the 1960s. For example, historian E. Taylor Atkins argued that Japanese interest in the blues can be traced to a number of factors: in the late 1930s, Japan experienced its first blues craze because the music seemed to convey the feelings of sadness and despair that accompanied a country at war with China; during the 1960s some Japanese felt that they, along with American blacks, shared the common experience of oppression by white European imperialism and, consequently, perceived the blues as an "artistic language of resistance"; concerned about their own inability to play authentic black musical forms, some Japanese musicians have sojourned to the United States to see and experience "real" jazz and blues, one of many "authenticating strategies" employed to "counter powerful psychological, institutional, and sociological forces that have continually cast doubt on the authenticity" of Japanese jazz and blues.[72] The search for authenticity evidently played a role in Tada Ikemasu's decision to move the United States in 1990. The Japanese-born guitarist lived in Alabama and New York and traveled extensively throughout the country before moving to Memphis in 2000. "I wanted to get close to the Mississippi River, the Delta," he told a reporter for the *Commercial Appeal.* "I thought I needed to live here to be a real blueman."[73] For Ikemasu, it seems the South—and Mississippi and Tennessee in particular—represents an opportunity to listen to the "real" blues. Japanese blues fans also hope to see and experience authentic blues in the music's supposed birthplace.

DESTINATION DELTA

The Mississippi Delta lacks the equivalent of a Beale Street, a centralized and commercialized blues tourism infrastructure. Given the Delta's relatively large geographic landscape and the dislocation of the region's blues heritage sites,

Blues Traveling: The Holy Sites of Delta Blues and other blues tourism guides are essentially written for noninstitutionalized tourists whose primary mode of transportation will be the automobile. In other words, tourists who hope to experience the totality of Mississippi's blues culture will inevitably travel on various "blues highways" (Highways 61 and 49) to visit gravesites and blues museums, attend blues festivals, and sleep in blues-oriented lodging establishments such as the Riverside Hotel and the Shack Up Inn. The following excerpt typifies the free-form approach of most blues tourists who visit the Mississippi Delta:

> *My wife, Julie, and I made a quick and thoroughly enjoyable trip through Memphis and the Mississippi Delta in October 1992, and I highly recommend the trip for any blues fan. We flew to Memphis and began our trek by driving south on Highway 61, armed with Robert Palmer's "Deep Blues," notes from John Hammond's "Search for Robert Johnson" video, a couple of old blues issues of Guitar Player magazine and a few other sources for historical reference, along with plenty of Delta blues cassettes to set a proper mood and supply an appropriate background for the video footage we could shoot within range of our rental car's stereo.*[74]

In recent years, an increasing number of Delta communities have made a concerted effort to highlight and promote existing blues artifacts (e.g., gravesites, juke joints) and develop blues attractions (museums, festivals) in the hope of cashing in on tourist demand. In Greenville, for example, Walnut Street serves as a blues strip that contains the Walnut Street Blues Bar and the Blues Walk of Fame, where local Greenville musicians are honored. (Unfortunately, the city's legendary Nelson Street, which was once home to many local blues artists, is too infested with crime, drugs, and prostitution and scarred by dilapidated and abandoned buildings to attract a significant number of tourists to its clubs that still feature live music.)[75] To the east, Leland's blues infrastructure includes the Highway 61 Blues Museum and blues murals that adorn a few downtown buildings. Blues tourists who enter the small town of Tutwiler seek out the gravesite of Sonny Boy Williamson II (Aleck "Rice" Miller) and the location where W. C. Handy supposedly discovered the blues while waiting for a train (the railroad station no longer exists; a concrete slab is all that remains).[76]

Of all the Delta communities, Clarksdale has been the most successful in packaging and promoting its blues heritage. Many of Clarksdale's blues attractions are located in a downtown district filled with a collection of government offices and small businesses.[77] Tourists can listen to music at Morgan Freeman's blues club, Ground Zero, and shop at several music stores (Cat

Head Delta Blues and Folk Art). In addition, downtown Clarksdale sports a number of well-established blues clubs and juke joints from Sarah's Kitchen to the classy-looking Delta Blues Room and blues-oriented lodging opportunities (e.g., Blues Hound Flat). The downtown area also includes "Blues Alley." Blues Alley includes, among other blues sites, the Clarksdale Station (former passenger depot of the Illinois Central Railroad) and the Delta Blues Museum (the old freight depot). Reflecting the dreams of some city officials and local entrepreneurs, Blues Alley is Clarksdale's most successful effort to construct and package its blues culture for its local community and tourists. The Clarksdale–Coahoma County Chamber of Commerce has developed a self-guided walking tour (Clarksdale Walk of Fame) in an effort to increase foot traffic in its downtown area; Clarksdale natives Sam Cooke and Son House, radio personality Early Wright, and playwright Tennessee Williams are featured on the Walk of Fame tour. A local newspaper is even called the "Clarksdale Blues-Star." In addition, Canadian businessman Les Barber and the Blues Hall of Fame have teamed up on a $30 million project to build the Crossroads Hotel and Entertainment Complex at the legendary crossroads (an intersection of U.S. Highways 49 and 61) where some blues promoters and tourism officials claim that Robert Johnson sold his soul to the devil in exchange for musical genius. In promoting this new venture, Barber argued that the complex will be built on "holy ground," adding that he wants to "create a place where music lovers from all over the world can come and reflect on where it all began, where they can experience firsthand the passion and the power of the blues."[78]

Since whites are the primary promoters and consumers of the blues, it is no surprise that many blues heritage sites (many of which were recently constructed) are often located in the white sections of various Delta communities. Blues Alley, for example, is located in Clarksdale's traditionally all-white downtown area. Samuel C. Adams's master's thesis includes a circa-1940 map of Clarksdale that places the Delta Blues Museum, Ground Zero Blues Club, and other blues sites in the middle of the "White Business Section," an area separated by a railroad track from the "Negro Business Section."[79] Thus much of Clarksdale's blues infrastructure is separated from various African American neighborhoods that played a role in the development of the Delta blues. In fact, a railroad track—the racial dividing line in many Delta communities—demarcates the Blues Alley district from an adjacent black neighborhood that includes the New World District, whose importance to the development of the blues cannot be overestimated.[80] In another example, the more affluent "white" section of Greenwood's downtown area includes the Greenwood Blues Heritage Museum and Gallery, Steve LaVere's visual testament to Robert Johnson.

In an effort to unify blues sites separated by space and time, the Mississippi Blues Commission, an organization comprising eighteen commissioners (and two alternates), initiated the creation of the Mississippi Blues Trail.[81] Although the Mississippi Blues Commission originally commissioned 130 blues markers, it now appears that at least 160 markers will be erected throughout the state and beyond by 2012.[82] Each marker will cost approximately $8,000, paid for by a variety of sources, including the National Endowment for the Humanities, the Mississippi Department of Transportation, Mississippi Development Authority–Tourism Division, and individual municipalities.[83] Jim O'Neal and Scott Barretta develop the written text for each site, and each marker includes photographs; markers will eventually be outfitted with audio, video, and GPS components.[84] Both Barretta and O'Neal are serious and highly respected blues scholars who do not engage in rhetorical flourishes of hyperbole often associated with tourist officials and public relations campaigns. Wanda Clark referred to the markers as "outside museums."[85] Tourists can also find an interactive map of the blues trail on the Blues Commission's Web site. The blues trail has already been extended beyond Mississippi (e.g., Memphis, Chicago), and there are plans to unveil markers in European and Asian locations that celebrate the blues.[86] The success of the Blues Trail project has even inspired Barbour and state senators to initiate plans for the development of a Country Music Trail to celebrate the state's contribution to country music and to pay homage to native Mississippians, including Jimmie Rodgers and Faith Hill.[87] The Mississippi Blues Trail can trace its origins back to an earlier, and much larger, effort to create sixteen National Millennium Trails in the United States. In 2000 the Clinton administration sponsored the Millennium Trail system throughout the United States to "preserve open spaces, interpret history and culture and enhance recreation and tourism."[88]

While the Delta's blues infrastructure lacks a cohesive center, the B. B. King Museum and Delta Interpretive Center, located in Sunflower County, will arguably serve as the region's (and perhaps the state's) most important tourist focal point. Located in King's hometown of Indianola, the $15 million high-tech museum opened its doors in September 2008 and reflects, in part, the vision of the B. B. King Museum Foundation and Board, a heterogeneous group made up of whites and African Americans who wanted to develop a "critical tourist destination in a struggling region."[89] Situated in an African American community and built next to a 1920s cotton gin where King worked as a teenager, the twenty-thousand-square-foot museum not only chronicles the life of the King of the Blues but contextualizes the work of King and other noted Delta blues musicians within the larger history of the Mississippi Delta itself.[90] King is reportedly very pleased with the new museum. He told one local reporter: "My vocabulary is not good enough to describe all the things I feel.

... I think that I would be feeling the same if I was holding a beautiful lady in my arms."[91] Marketing director Allan Hammons hopes the King Museum will serve as an "anchor" for the Blues Trail.[92] Craig Ray, the director of the Mississippi Development Authority–Tourism Division, believes that the King Museum is already one of Mississippi's top tourist attractions.[93] Indeed, within its first year, the museum attracted approximately thirty thousand visitors.[94] While state tourism witnessed a decline in revenue between 2008 and 2009, the opposite occurred in Sunflower County, which saw a 12.5 percent increase during the same fiscal period.[95] A vital addition to the state's blues tourism industry, the King Museum is one of a number of blues museums that have opened since 2000, including the Rock 'n' Roll and Blues Heritage Museum (Clarksdale), Greenwood Blues Heritage Museum and Gallery (Greenwood), Highway 61 Blues Museum (Leland), the Robert Johnson Blues Foundation Headquarters and Museum (Crystal Springs), Mississippi John Hurt Museum (Avalon), Howlin' Wolf Blues Museum (West Point), and the River City Blues Museum (Vicksburg).

A BLUES ROADMAP

Ironically, with all the recent attention directed at the blues, particularly its value as a tourist commodity, little critical analysis has been written on the topic of blues tourism.[96] Grazian's fascinating research on the Chicago blues tradition is one of the few book-length projects that fully explore the growing relationship between blues and tourism.[97] Yet *Blue Chicago: The Search for Authenticity in Urban Blues Clubs* focuses on urban haunts in Chicago, not the Mississippi Delta, and the book concentrates primarily on the concept of authenticity. Another important publication, *Music and Tourism: On the Road Again*, is a comprehensive examination of music tourism that crosses, according to its authors, "all continents and musical genres." While this is perhaps the first publication to fully explore the concept of music tourism, the authors pay scant attention to blues tourism in the Mississippi Delta.[98] What is missing from the extant literature is a book-length study that not only examines Mississippi's blues tourism industry but explores the nexus of authenticity, myth, and public memory.

Myth, authenticity, and memory are interconnected and mutually reinforcing concepts. As I explore in subsequent chapters, mythic representations, while not historically accurate, are often uncritically accepted by indigenous populations and consumers as unquestioned truths. The stability and perpetuation of myth often rest on issues of power and control, for it is the cultural producer, among other agents of institutionalized culture, who manages, controls, and communicates a privileged narrative that is inevitably associated with a larger collective understanding of the past and present. As a constructed phenomenon, authenticity's allure and mystique rest with its close association with myth and memory because legitimate claims of authenticity often involve a community's rearticulation or realization of its own significance (myth) that requires a historical interpretation of the past and an understanding of the present (memory). In the end, I consider myth, authenticity, and memory as three interrelated rhetorical strategies employed to market Mississippi's blues culture to both internal and external audiences.

A critical examination of Mississippi blues tourism cannot escape the real sense of irony associated with the state's determination to promote its blues culture and heritage. To be sure, the phrase "Mississippi blues tourism" can be interpreted as a bizarre oxymoron, a cruel irony that begs the question: how can a state, and its Delta region, loathed for its furious opposition to civil rights, its years of legal and extralegal means to dominate and exploit its long-suffering African American population, suddenly change in a matter of a few decades to officially embrace the blues, an African American musical form that was a symptom of oppression and exploitation and functioned, albeit implicitly, as a form of protest against the hegemony of white rule? Is this cultural embrace just another trick by whites to exploit African Americans, a twenty-first-century version of sharecropping? Or should we interpret Mississippi blues tourism as a legitimate, progressive turn by the state to finally recognize African American contributions to popular culture and beyond, a type of racial reconciliation? I argue that the promotional efforts to market blues music rely heavily on blues myths and claims of authenticity, strategies that rhetorically advance a rival story, a new positive image for the state. Promotional materials also seek to satisfy the imaginations of blues tourists who travel to the Mississippi Delta to experience and "see" authenticity (and spend money) in the birthplace of the blues. At the same time, efforts by some tourism officials and organizations to obfuscate Mississippi's past embody conscious efforts to privilege a sterilized historical narrative, a manipulation of public memory. It is hardly surprising that some tourism officials and blues promoters would seek to replace Mississippi's tragic racial history with a new sanitized version, one that denies, in many ways, the historical realities of sharecropping and segregation. Nor is it particularly surprising that the marketing of blues tourism sites would involve claims of authenticity based on the largely uncontested myth that the Mississippi Delta is the birthplace of the blues. Both the exploitation of mythic narratives and arguments for authenticity provide blues tourists compelling reasons to visit the region, while the restructuring of history may both challenge and affirm tourists' memories of Mississippi, particularly the Delta region.

This book does not attempt to cover all aspects of Mississippi blues tourism. The totality of tourism-related elements, ranging from tourists visiting the gravesites to casinos to blues museums, is simply too large in scope to be adequately covered in one book. In this book, I focus my attention on analyzing the rhetorical strategies employed to promote blues music as part of Mississippi's cultural heritage. Chapter 1 provides a brief and selective history of the Mississippi blues, focusing primarily on individuals, events, and places that would later be integrated into current efforts to promote Mississippi's blues culture. Although the blues emerged during the end of the nineteenth century, it was not until the early twentieth century that composers like W. C. Handy started to compose and sell sheet music. With the success of Mamie Smith's (the first African American recorded singing a blues song) 1920 hit "Crazy Blues," the U.S. record industry decided to categorize the blues as "race music" and market the music to a largely untapped and invisible demographic, African Americans. Although record companies were initially interested in recording Mamie Smith and other vaudeville or "classic" blues artists, a number of country blues artists from Mississippi and elsewhere—Tommy Johnson, Charley Patton, Robert Johnson—recorded songs for Victor, Paramount, and other record companies from the mid-1920s to the late 1930s. Inspired in part by the civil rights movement and the belief that the blues was quickly vanishing from its birthplace, blues promoters, enthusiasts, and record collectors traveled to the South in the 1960s to "rediscover" blues legends and purchase rare blues recordings. The 1960s blues revival also played a powerful role in discovering new blues talent, resurrecting the careers of well-established blues artists and shaping the eventual development of a blues tourism industry. In chapter 2, I provide a historical overview of Mississippi's blues tourism industry and argue that during its early years (1978–2000), it was mostly a grassroots affair, led by a group of white blues enthusiasts who immigrated to the Delta with the hope of promoting the state's rich blues heritage. By 2003, the once decentralized and largely ignored industry was finally receiving real statewide political support in the form of the Mississippi Blues Commission. It should be noted that this chapter reflects the first systematic effort to write the history of Mississippi's blues tourism industry.

Chapter 3 analyzes the use of myth as part of an overall rhetorical strategy to entice tourists to visit the region. From Web sites to brochures, promotional materials rely heavily on blues myths, including the assertion that the Mississippi Delta is the birthplace of the blues, as well as claims that Robert Johnson sold his soul to the devil at the crossroads somewhere in the Delta for fame and fortune. While these mythic representations tell a provocative and tantalizing story and recast Mississippi in a decidedly romantic light, both the birthplace and the crossroads myths have troubling implications, including the omission of the state's treatment of its African American population. Chapter 4 explores the concept of authenticity and argues that the Sunflower River Blues and Gospel Festival and other local blues festivals rhetorically construct markers of authenticity to satisfy the demands of some white blues tourists. For some of these tourists, authenticity is conceptualized as a mixture of race-ethnicity (African American), style (Delta blues), performance (solo performer), and location (noncommercialized, rustic, impoverished). While many festival organizers construct these easily consumable images of authenticity, some blues festivals target an entirely different demographic (local African Americans), who prefer, in many cases, to listen to soul-blues artists such as Bobby Rush and Nathaniel Kimble. Soul-blues, a genre popular among African Americans, particularly in the South, combines the sound of blues, gospel, soul, jazz, rhythm and blues, and hip-hop. Public memory is the topic of chapters 5 and 6. In promoting the blues, tourism officials and blues promoters have, in many respects, privileged a sanitized version of Mississippi's historical record, carefully omitting details of slavery, sharecropping, segregation, lynching, and other acts of white tyranny. To provide a point of comparison between historical reality and how the past is narrated in tourism literature, chapter 5 provides a brief historical portrait of Mississippi, particularly its Delta region, from statehood to 1955. From the cruelties of slavery to the legal practice of segregation, Mississippi's white population has historically condoned and sanctioned a variety of strategies, both legal and extralegal, to maintain its hegemony. In chapter 6, I examine current promotional efforts by Mississippi's official culture to present an alternative interpretation of the past. In this revisionist narrative, the blues is portrayed as a form of escapism, and the harsh social conditions that inspired the music are absent. Furthermore, plantation owners who profited at the expense of black laborers are portrayed as kind and benevolent. I also examine the Shack Up Inn. Located on the outskirts of Clarksdale, the inn offers tourists the opportunity to sleep in one of twelve renovated sharecropper shacks. In carefully crafting an inviting blues destination, the owners of the Shack Up Inn have radically reconstructed both the function and the form of the plantation and its physical structures from one of oppression and exploitation to consumption, escapism, and play. In the book's final chapter, I explore the challenges and potential promises of blues tourism in Mississippi. Specifically, I examine the extent to which Mississippi's blues tourism industry has achieved, or is in the process of achieving, the three goals of blues tourism discussed in this introduction. I argue that, beyond anecdotal accounts of success, there is no evidence that the rhetorical strategies have succeeded in either encouraging potential blues tourists to visit the state or changing the public's (negative) perception of Mississippi. Moreover, these strategies actually undercut the third goal, racial reconciliation.

Standpoint theory is used to explain why, despite claims of racial harmony, unresolved tension and conflict exist among blues musicians, blues promoters, and members of Mississippi's official culture. Yet because blues tourism is in its infancy, efforts to promote the state's blues heritage and culture *may*, indeed, eventually succeed in enticing a significant number of tourists to visit the region, reshaping negative perceptions of the state, and creating the mechanism for meaningful racial reconciliation.

1

THE HISTORY OF THE MISSISSIPPI DELTA BLUES

Yeah, the blues is kind of a revenge, you know. . . . We had a hard time in life and like that, and things we couldn't say . . . or do, so we sing it.
—MEMPHIS SLIM, *Blues in the Mississippi Night*

I n his excellent analysis of the origins of the blues, Peter C. Muir discovered that by 1550, the word "blues" moved beyond a simple reference to color and became associated with fear and misery. By 1616, the term "blue devil" emerged, a phrase first associated with a demon (at some later point, the plural "blue devils" became a metaphor for despondency). By the mid-eighteenth century, according to Muir, "blue devils" became "blues" or "the blues," and subsequently both terms became increasingly associated with negative emotions.[1] Thus it is not surprising that when the blues first emerged as a musical genre, it was commonly associated with emotional states such as melancholy and depression. However, this narrow understanding of the music is inaccurate, for blues singers and musicians actually express a myriad of emotions from sadness to hope to joy. Yet the tendency to link the blues to plaintiveness and anguish still, in many ways, reflects a general misunderstanding of the music. *Merriam Webster's Collegiate Dictionary*, for example, uses words such as "low spirits," "melancholy," and "lamentation" to describe the music. This erroneous understanding of the blues motivated Archie Quinn, a writer for the *Commercial Appeal*, to quip in 1985 that Memphis officials need to curtail marketing of the city's blues heritage because, among other reasons, the blues' message of "sadness" will attract only a small cult audience.[2] In response, blues scholar David Evans lambasted Quinn for writing "the most ignorant, insensitive and asinine piece of writing on the blues that I have ever read." Beyond correcting a number of inaccurate statements about the blues in Quinn's article, Evans informed the reporter that blues singers express a variety of emotions, not to say the least is joy: "In fact [the blues] relieves sadness and gets people on their feet dancing."[3]

While it is true that blues musicians expressed their despair in both lyrics and musical form, the blues is an "active agent" that gives "hope and strength to overcome disappointments," for one does not simply "wallow" in despair.[4] According to blues scholar Adam Gussow, the blues served as an important statement of "somebodiness" and "indelible individuality" in a world where African Americans were largely suppressed and despised, invisible and objectified.[5] LeRoi Jones (Amiri Baraka) claimed that the "Primitive Blues" was the "first expression of the Negro's *individuality*" after the end of slavery.[6] Indeed, the abolition of slavery made it possible for the communal slave consciousness of "we" to be transformed into the autobiographical "I," the "liberated black self."[7] Thus, while the music's protest elements are often covert in nature, sometimes communicated in coded form, it is incorrect to classify or define the blues as a passive, purely emotional, lamentable response to sorrow.

This chapter examines the development of the blues from its inception until the end of the 1960s blues revival. My primary focus is on Mississippi's blues tradition, specifically musicians and promoters who played an important role in developing what would be called the "Delta blues." Of course, I do not pretend to have written a comprehensive and complete historical treatment of the blues; the scope and breadth of the music and the limitation of space make this task impossible and unnecessary because, as many readers will already be aware, Samuel Charters, Paul Oliver, David Evans, Stephen Calt, Giles Oakley, Marybeth Hamilton, Ted Gioia, and numerous other blues scholars have already published their authoritative scholarship on the history of the (Mississippi) blues. The purpose of this chapter is to provide the necessary sociohistorical context to effectively understand and critique how blues music is used as a tourism mechanism. Many of the following individuals, places, and events not only appear in the various blues histories but reappear in tourism promotional materials, from brochures to Web sites, designed to encourage tourists to visit Mississippi. For example, the Mississippi Blues Commission celebrates Robert Johnson, Muddy Waters, Howlin' Wolf, B. B. King, Arthur Crudup, and Robert Nighthawk, among many others, in the form of individual blues markers. Through blues trail markers, museums, and festivals, tourism officials hope to convince tourists to visit the "birthplace of the blues."

ORIGINS OF THE BLUES

In recent years, the state of Mississippi has proudly promoted itself as the birthplace of the blues. The Mississippi Blues Commission's Web site invites tourists to experience the "land that spawned the single most important root source of modern popular music."[8] While this creative mythmaking strategy may satisfy the dreams and aspirations of tourism officials and blues promoters, no credible historical evidence supports this claim. Indeed, most blues scholars recognize and acknowledge the impossibility of tracing the birth of the blues to a particular moment or specific place in history. "No matter what you may have heard or read," wrote Robert Palmer, the author of *Deep Blues: A Musical and Cultural History of the Mississippi Delta*, "nobody knows where the blues began—or even if it *did* begin in a particular place, as opposed to springing up in several places more or less simultaneously."[9] Blues historian Marybeth Hamilton confirmed this observation when she argued that "no one knows who sang the first blues, or where they sang it, or when."[10]

While this may be true, most blues historians argue that the blues likely emerged throughout the southern United States during the late nineteenth century. David Evans provides perhaps the most expansive and detailed southern "birthplace map":

> No one can say precisely where the blues first came into being, but the evidence strongly suggests that it was somewhere in the vast area stretching from inland Georgia and north Florida across to Texas. This area spreads south and then west of the Appalachian Mountains, takes in the Mississippi Valley as far north as southern Illinois and the Missouri Bootheel, and runs westward, skipping over the Ozark Mountains, to include southeastern Oklahoma and east and central Texas.[11]

In his historical treatment of the blues, Giles Oakley argues that the blues emerged in the South, appearing simultaneously in Mississippi, Louisiana, Texas, and other locations.[12] Samuel Charters also articulates a "southern-born" narrative, claiming that the blues may actually have been born in Mississippi, although he is the only credible blues scholar to have made such a speculation.[13] Paul Oliver places the blues' birthplace in the rural South; he argues that the music's influence can be traced to work songs, field hollers, and chants that emanated from the region's plantation culture, a way of life that continued to persist even after the official end of slavery as an economic institution.[14] Beyond field songs, blues music was also influenced by other forms of popular culture, including folk spirituals and ballads, ragtime, southern vaudeville (featuring minstrel acts), and "coon" songs. With titles such as "The Queen of Charcoal-Alley" and "If the Man in the Moon Were a Coon," coon songs reinforced a racist image of African Americans.[15]

Anthropologist Harriet Ottenheimer has challenged the prevailing paradigm that the blues was born in the South. She argues that the blues actually originated in the Midwest, specifically in towns and cities in Missouri, Indiana, and Kentucky along the Ohio River, rather than on a southern plantation or other isolated and rural landscapes.[16] Indeed, she argues that the first documented account of "blues-like singing" could be found in St. Louis in 1892. As evidence, she cites the writing of W. C. Handy, a musician and composer, who described watching an "early blues performance" of "East St. Louis" in 1892.[17] All the earliest reports of blues music, according to Ottenheimer, took place in the Midwest, at least a decade before the first reports surfaced in the Mississippi Delta.[18] In contrast to the contention that the blues migrated from the countryside to the cities of New Orleans, Shreveport, and St. Louis before the beginning of the twentieth century,[19] Ottenheimer argues that the reverse is likely the case: the blues was actually an "urban party music" that traveled down the Mississippi River by boat to the rural South.[20] Ted Gioia acknowledged the difficulty in developing a simple and coherent birth story for the blues:

> Yet where should we begin in telling its story? With the great Mississippi flood of 1927 and the first traditional blues recordings of the 1920s? With the first published sheet music in 1912? In the Delta land of the turn of the century? Among the plantations and cotton fields of the antebellum South? On the slave ships with their doleful commerce in human misery? Or in the rich musical traditions of mother Africa? Every beginning seems to point back to an earlier reference point, every tradition to a previous one. No consensus view guides us on this matter.[21]

Since we have no consensus about the music's specific origins, perhaps the story of the blues should begin with archaeologist Charles Peabody, the first scholar to report "blues-like music" in the Mississippi Delta (although it is not clear whether Peabody actually heard blues music himself).[22] In a brief report, "Notes on Negro Music," published in a 1903 issue of the *Journal of American Folk-Lore*, Peabody described encountering the "music of Negroes" during his fieldwork in Coahoma Country in 1901 and 1902. Observing "the Negroes and their ways at close range," Peabody described the sound of voices (sometimes accompanied by guitar) as "unhappy," "primitive," "weird," and repetitive.[23]

Or perhaps the story should begin with W. C. Handy, often called the "Father of the Blues" because he was one of the first musicians to understand the commercial potential of the burgeoning musical form.[24] Born in Florence, Alabama, in 1873, Handy excelled as a musician, music teacher, bandleader, and composer, playing in minstrel bands (Mahara's Minstrels) and orchestras. After listening to a "lean, loose-jointed Negro" dressed in rags playing the "weirdest music I have ever heard," at a train station in Tutwiler, Mississippi, sometime around 1903 (he never indicated the specific date of the encounter), Handy confessed that the song "struck me instantly" with "unforgettable" effect. Around 1905 (again, Handy never indicated a specific year), at a dance in Cleveland, Mississippi, he finally realized the "beauty of primitive music," particularly the music's commercial appeal, after witnessing money rain down on the stage in front of a band led by "a long-legged chocolate boy" who stepped in when Handy's band could not play requests for "native music." Handy was transfixed and transformed:

> That night a composer was born, an American composer. Those country black boys at Cleveland had taught me something that could not possibly have been gained from books, something that would, however, cause books to be written. Art, in the high-brow sense, was not in my mind. My idea of what constitutes music was changed by the sight of that silver money cascading around the splay feet of a Mississippi string band. . . . Once the purpose was fixed I let no grass grow under my feet. I returned to Clarksdale and began immediately to work on this type of music.[25]

After this revelation, Handy started to compose blues songs and published these songs in the form of sheet music (he would not publish his first song until 1912). From the 1890s to 1920, sheet music was the primary method a composer could use to disseminate his or her material to a mass audience.[26] In 1909, Handy had composed his first blues song, "Mr. Crump"—a song written for Edward Hull "Boss" Crump's political campaign to become mayor of Memphis (Crump served as Memphis's mayor from 1909 to 1916)—which was later published as "Memphis Blues" in 1912. Although some claim that Handy's "Memphis Blues" was the first blues composition committed to sheet music, others argue that the honor should be attributed to Antonio Maggio's "I Got the Blues" (1908).[27] In any case, by 1912, a number of white and black composers were writing and composing blues songs (or at least songs that included "blues" in the title), including "The Blues" (1912), "Dallas Blues" (1912), "Yellow Dog Blues" (1912), "Nigger Blues" (1912), and "St. Louis Blues" (1914). Handy's "Yellow Dog Blues," an adaptation of the song he heard during his fateful encounter with that unknown slide guitar player in Tutwiler, helped establish Mississippi as a key geographic blues terrain. However, "St. Louis Blues" would prove to be Handy's greatest achievement, a song that would later be recorded (both as an instrumental and with a vocal track) by Handy, Bessie Smith, Louis Armstrong, Benny Goodman, Glenn Miller, and other blues, jazz, and big band musicians. Noting Handy's influence on the development of the blues, tourism officials have incorporated Handy's early encounters with the blues as part of the larger, mythical birth story. On November 26, 2009, the Mississippi Blues Commission unveiled a blues marker at a ceremony in Tutwiler that formally acknowledged Handy's achievements, as well as other musicians associated with the town, including Sonny Boy Williamson II.

THE RACE RECORD INDUSTRY, THE NEW BLACK CONSUMER, AND THE DELTA BLUES TRADITION

During the early twentieth century, U.S. record companies, largely owned and operated by whites, typically ignored both black artists and black consumers.[28] Black singers and musicians did record during this period, but their music was largely marketed to whites and mostly restricted to comedic pieces, spirituals, and coon songs.[29] For example, the Dinwiddie Colored Quartet, the first African American vocal group to make a record, recorded three songs (all spirituals) in 1902 for Victor Talking Machine Company. Although a number of vocal and instrumental blues songs were recorded by 1917, vocal blues recordings were performed exclusively by white singers.[30]

This all changed in 1920. Mamie Smith's song "Crazy Blues" sold an extraordinary seventy-five thousand copies in its first month (a single record cost approximately seventy-five cents), eventually selling, according to some unconfirmed estimates, over a million copies within a year.[31] This was unprecedented because Smith was the first African American female performer to record a blues song for public consumption. After "Crazy Blues" became a smash hit, the "race was on among record companies to record blues by black singers."[32] Between the summer of 1920 and the end of 1922, approximately thirteen record companies scrambled to record songs by African American blues musicians.[33] Initially record companies were mostly interested in recording Mamie Smith, Bessie Smith, Ma Rainey, and other (primarily) female singers who became part of the "classic" or vaudeville blues scene.

By 1922, OKeh Records and other record companies created a record series to target the new black consumer.[34] While the recordings of African American musicians were typically marketed as "race records," this was not always the case.[35] According to David Evans, a number of African American musical groups and artists, including the Ink Spots, Louis Armstrong, and Cab Calloway, were marketed in the "popular" and "general" categories. Ralph Peer, the record industry executive who claimed to have developed the race record concept, once boasted that he invented "hillbilly [music] and nigger stuff."[36] Originally, OKeh cataloged music by African American artists as "colored" music, but Peer believed that "race" was more appropriate because in the 1920s urban African American communities interpreted the word "race" as a positive statement of racial pride.[37] As a segregated music, race records were often cataloged based on a numerical classification scheme. In the case of Paramount and other companies at this time, each record was assigned a particular numerical code.[38] Although race records were primarily targeted to black audiences, some blues musicians, such as Leroy Carr, achieved somewhat of a crossover appeal during the 1930s, and white consumers, particularly record collectors, purchased race records. Race records became so popular that one writer claimed that blues music was being produced like Fords and Ivory soap.[39] LeRoi Jones argued that with profits on the rise, "it is easy to see that there were no altruistic or artistic motives behind the record companies' decision to continue to enlarge the race category."[40]

Although the vaudeville blues was an exceedingly popular blues genre during the mid-1920s, an altogether different type of blues, rural or primitive blues, largely performed by men, was quickly gaining ascendancy in the South. As early as 1923, companies dispatched mobile units to Atlanta to locate blues musicians and make field recordings of their music. By 1926, following the invention of electrical recording and the microphone, the practice of recording musicians in the field intensified as record scouts visited Dallas, Memphis, and New Orleans, among other southern locations.[41] Blind Lemon Jefferson was undisputedly the earliest, and best-known, musician to gain stardom from this country blues craze. Born around 1893 near Wortham, Texas, Jefferson learned to play the guitar at an early age and by his teens had moved to Dallas, where, for a short period of time, he supported himself as a street musician and as a wrestler.[42] In 1925, while playing on the streets in Dallas, he was discovered by a record store owner and by early 1926 found himself in a Chicago recording studio.[43] At the height of his popularity, between 1926 and 1928, Jefferson recorded a number of blues hits, including "Black Snake Moan" and "Match Box Blues," and became the "first southern self-accompanied folk blues artist to succeed commercially on records, and his success can be said to have opened the door to all the others who followed in the next few years."[44]

Meanwhile talent scouts focused their attention on recording blues artists from other parts of the South, particularly Mississippi. Some of the first recorded Mississippi blues artists played what would later be called the Delta blues, a regional style that has become virtually synonymous with the Mississippi blues, often to the exclusion of other blues styles in the state, including Jackson-style blues (Tommy Johnson), Bentonia blues (Skip James, Jack Owens), and North Mississippi blues (David "Junior" Kimbrough, R. L. Burnside). The Delta blues style achieved hegemonic status in part because it became intimately associated with blues musicians such as Robert Johnson and Charley Patton, solo performers who typically accompanied themselves with an acoustic guitar.[45] The cultural domination of this particular blues style can also be attributed to the belief among many blues fans (and tourism officials) that the music's birthplace is located in Mississippi's Delta, which represents for many a sacred place where the blues' most authentic and pure forms emerged from the region's plantation culture. Music critic Robert Palmer, for example, described the Delta blues as the "purest and most deeply rooted of all blues strains." While the Delta blues may sound simple, the music's complexities are evident in the difficulties associated with reproducing the sounds of the original black performers:

> *It seems simple enough—two identical lines and a third answering line make up a verse, there are no more than three chords and sometimes only one, melodies are circumscribed, rhythms are propulsively straightforward. Yet countless white musicians have tried to master it and failed, and Delta bluesmen often laugh among themselves, remembering black musicians from Alabama or Texas who just couldn't learn to play acceptably in the Delta style.*[46]

Actually, the label "Delta blues" is a relatively new invention. In the book *In Search of the Blues*, a beautifully written analysis of the role whites played in creating colorful and romantic blues myths, Marybeth Hamilton contends that the Delta blues was actually the invention of white enthusiasts who were obsessed with discovering the lost, passionate, and primitive "uncorrupted black singers, untainted by the city, by commerce, by the sights and sounds of modernity." Admitting that her book is "not a conventional Delta blues history," Hamilton persuasively argues that the term "Delta blues" (and the belief that the Delta is the birthplace of the blues) was coined by white enthusiasts during the 1960s blues revival, including members of the so-called Blues Mafia, a collection of fanatical record collectors. James McKune, one of the more prominent members of this group, was an alcoholic loner who spent countless hours in his rundown New York YMCA room, intently listening to old 78 records of "rough-hewn voices" of black blues singers "supercharged with raw emotion." Before the adoption of the term "Delta blues," the music had previously been labeled folk blues, country blues, or primitive blues.[47]

Charley Patton, Son House, Robert Johnson, David "Honeyboy" Edwards, and other Mississippi blues artists did not initially call their own music the Delta blues. Yet their music shared common musical and thematic elements, a product of proximity, influence, and interaction. Charley Patton's wild showmanship, vocal prowess, and guitar virtuosity inspired a legion of fellow blues musicians, Howlin' Wolf and Bukka White, among others; Robert Johnson claimed his idol was Son House.[48] Robert Johnson and Johnny Shines played together for a spell, and Son House, Willie Brown, and Charley Patton played together in a 1930 recording session for Paramount Records. Musicians liberally borrowed—or stole—lyrical and musical themes from each other; Robert Johnson's 1936 recording of "32-20 Blues" would remind listeners of Skip James's "22-20 Blues," recorded five years earlier.[49] The Mississippi Sheiks' 1930 hit "Sittin' on Top of the World" would later be recorded by Howlin' Wolf, who assumed authorship of the song.

Mississippi native H. C. Speir, who was honored with his own Mississippi blues trail marker in 2011, was perhaps the most important promoter of early country blues in Mississippi. It was Speir who first discovered and promoted early Mississippi Delta artists such as Charley Patton. In 1925 Speir decided to purchase a furniture and music store in Jackson's black downtown district because he wanted to attract a new black consumer base. According to Speir, "Negroes out-bought whites in record consumption 50 to one."[50] A year later, Speir began a career as a "talent broker," a record scout who traveled throughout Mississippi, Tennessee, Alabama, Louisiana, and Kentucky, even to Mexico, to find new talent for record companies (Victor, Paramount, OKeh) interested in exploiting the popularity of country blues.[51] Speir even helped organize the first recording "expedition" in Mississippi in late 1930.[52] In some cases, Speir paid his own traveling expenses to attend (and sometimes help produce) recording sessions in Chicago and Wisconsin. To be sure, his interest in promoting and preserving the blues was largely financially motivated. Yet it was his obsession to record commercially successful blues songs that drove Speir to be extremely attentive to detail:

> No altruistic ideals motivated his activities, yet he did more than any single individual to promote and preserve the music of the Delta region. He dressed like a banker, and thought much like one, too. For Speir, black music was a business, plain and simple. Even if he liked a singer's material, he refused to arrange for a record session unless he thought it would sell. And Speir's preeminent talent, in his own mind, was that he knew what the market wanted. . . . But the broker's practical mind-set made Speir attentive to details that a more altruistic man might have missed. He had fastidious ideas about the right tone for a guitar, the right setting for the microphone, the right shape of a room for recording, even how much shellac to put into a disk. . . . Whatever role he needed to play to ensure a successful record, he filled it with diligence and doggedness.[53]

The talent broker set up an ad hoc recording studio in his music store in Jackson and cut rough demos that he would use to persuade record companies to record a specific blues artist. In a 1966 interview, Speir recalled receiving a standard rate for providing musical talent to a record company. However, he claimed he was virtually coerced into purchasing five hundred copies of a record, a negotiation that served as "proof to the company that he had confidence in the record's sales potential." During the interview, Speir intimated that the requisite volume purchase was unfair, especially for recording "some nigger."[54] Until he retired from the music business in 1935, Speir made "test recordings"[55] of Charley Patton, Son House, Willie Brown, Tommy Johnson, Skip James (Nehemiah Curtis James), Ishmon Bracey, Bo Carter, William

Harris, and many other Mississippi artists. Gayle Dean Wardlow, who along with David Evans was one of the few blues scholars to have interviewed Speir, acknowledged his extraordinary contributions to preserving the Delta blues tradition: "If Speir hadn't been there, the greatest of the Delta blues singers would probably have never [been] recorded."[56]

With Speir's influence and perseverance, Mississippi blues artists (or artists who played in the Delta style) started to be recorded. As early as June 1926, Freddie Spruell recorded "Milk Cow Blues" for OKeh.[57] Two years later, in January and February 1928, Tommy Johnson and Ishmon Bracey recorded songs for Victor.[58] In 1929, Charley Patton entered a recording studio in Grafin, Wisconsin, to record for Paramount. A year later, Patton, Son House, and Willie Brown would record together for another session for Paramount. The Mississippi Sheiks also started recording in 1930.[59] Some of these blues recording sessions occurred in company-owned studios, while others were conducted in temporary studios in hotel rooms and radio stations. In all, from 1926 to 1930, record companies issued approximately two thousand country blues songs.[60]

To be sure, Mississippi blues artists did not get rich from selling records. Most musicians never received a royalty check. Instead, a single payment, sometimes as low as fifteen dollars, was commonplace (some musicians preferred immediate cash), and few retained the copyright to their own work.[61] Many musicians were illiterate, poorly educated, and lacked business acumen, setting up a precarious condition ripe for exploitation. In a 1969 interview with *Rolling Stone* magazine, Son House remembered a 1930 session where he received a cash payment, along with some whiskey:

> *Ooh, gee, my dammit, along with me and Charlie Patton, Willie Brown and Blind Lemon [Jefferson], 'long in them days we wouldn't get nothin'. Nothin', man. We'd get thirty or forty dollars, we had a couple of drinks of that bad old corn whiskey or something. The fact of the business is that we didn't have no sense, nohow. Didn't know nothin' about it. They just worked us, you know? They got it out of us.*[62]

The charge of economic exploitation is an overly familiar refrain in the music world, serving as a constant source of tension and resentment for musicians who believe they have been financially undermined.[63] Bessie Smith, Willie Dixon, Skip James, Leadbelly (Huddie Ledbetter) and many other musicians (blues or otherwise) claimed to have been ripped off in one way or another. Clarksdale, Mississippi, native John Lee Hooker, who engaged in subterfuge himself by recording under a number of pseudonyms for different record companies, summed up his contentious relationship with the music business: "Most of the record companies I'd been with were like a sack of snakes—they got rich quick, and I got poor quick."[64] Yet despite the exploitative nature of the music business, not all record producers and executives can be accused of defrauding their artists. In a 1985 interview in *L.A. Weekly*, John Hammond, a former music executive and record producer for CBS who was responsible for preparing Robert Johnson's album *King of the Delta Blues Singers* (1961) for public release, comes across as a rare individual who nurtured, rather than exploited, musical artists:

> *I always felt that it was obscene to make money off of other people's work. If there was a Billie Holiday coming along, I didn't want to cut in on anything that she could do for records. In those days, I felt the record business was bankrupt completely. There was no way that you could make a living making records, anyway, and recording was just an opportunity to hear an artist.*[65]

From 1927 to 1930, the first wave of Mississippi blues artists had satisfied their ambition to record songs for public distribution, although many were never recorded. However, the Great Depression devastated the record industry. By 1931, race recordings sold a meager one-tenth of what was sold in 1927.[66] Inevitably, record companies began to fold. For example, from 1930 to 1932, Paramount "limped along," barely breaking even.[67] At the end of 1933, the company closed its doors, and many of its lower-level employees were fired at a company Christmas party.[68] At the beginning of 1934, only three major race record labels (Decca, Vocalion, and Bluebird) remained.[69] But by the mid-1930s, the record industry was beginning to recover financially; in 1937, thirty-seven million records were sold, roughly six times more than in 1932.[70] In 1933 record companies released, on average, approximately three blues and gospel records per week; that number tripled by 1937.[71] While many Delta blues artists would continue to record (e.g., Charley Patton, Robert Johnson, and Tommy McClennan), by the early 1940s, record companies started to record artists who represented a newer, urban, electrified form of the Delta blues. It was also during the early 1940s that radio stations in the South started to include blues music as part of regular programming.

KING BISCUIT TIME, THE SOUTHERN BLACK DISC JOCKEY, AND THE DELTA'S MUSICAL MIGRATION

During the early years of commercial radio in the United States, radio stations occasionally played blues music, although preference was usually given to other musical forms, including jazz, big band, and country music.[72] The introduction of the *King Biscuit Time* program proved to be a watershed in blues programming. In November 1941, three white entrepreneurs helped finance the creation of KFFA, the first radio station to appear in Helena, Arkansas.[73] Known as an important blues city, Helena is located in Arkansas's Delta region on the Mississippi River, approximately thirty miles from Clarksdale, Mississippi. Shortly after the station went on the air, Max S. Moore's Interstate Grocer Company (IGC) sponsored *King Biscuit Time*, a fifteen-minute radio program (weekdays from 12:15 to 12:30 p.m.) featuring two blues musicians, Sonny Boy Williamson II and Robert Jr. Lockwood. IGC specifically targeted the large African American population of Helena and the Mississippi Delta with the hope that live blues music would inspire black customers to purchase King Biscuit flour.[74] "We were going pretty good and gettin' a lotta work and jobs off the air," remembered Lockwood. "Mr. Moore was paying us $10 a week for the five shows, but we made good at night."[75] Guitarist Houston Stackhouse, who joined *King Biscuit Time* in the late 1940s, remembered having to supplement his tiny salary from KFFA with live gigs:

> *Oh, they was payin' us a dollar a day for the 15 minutes, you know. That's all he ever paid me, a dollar a day. . . . [Mr. Moore] was real cheap. I reckon he thought that was enough for 'em for 15 minutes. But where we was makin' our money at was when we'd go out playin' dances every night somewhere. . . . They'd pay us good, too. Around 70 or $80 a piece, sometime 100.*[76]

Although *King Biscuit Time* targeted black listeners, the show became popular with some whites as well. At the 2005 Living Blues Symposium, "Sunshine" Sonny Payne, one of the station's first announcers, remembered that some whites, particularly women, found the show irresistible. Yet, reflected in the strong social norms against "race mixing," female callers would request that they remain anonymous: "They would call in and say, 'Ask Sonny Boy to play so and so. Don't mention my name. My husband would kill me.'"[77]

The show was an "absolute sensation."[78] Sales of King Biscuit Flour increased dramatically, and soon the company advertised Sonny Boy White Corn Meal, which was named after one of the show's stars.[79] The company even distributed cards to customers that read: "Now, if you want a photograph of Sonny Boy Williamson and Robert Lockwood, Jr. your favorite Radio Stars, please send your name and address to KING BISCUIT TIME." By 1942, the program's success led to the creation of a full-fledged blues band, the King Biscuit Boys, an extremely popular act in Arkansas and Mississippi throughout the 1940s and 1950s.[80]

For many African Americans, *King Biscuit Time* created an "enormous sense of racial pride in hearing black performers on the air in the South."[81] Calvin "Fuzz" Jones, a bass player who became a key component of Muddy Waters's rhythm section in the 1970s, fondly remembered the King Biscuit show:

*I'd run home from the fields to hear Pinetop Perkins and Sonny Boy William-
son on King Biscuit. I was sure enough gonna make it home to hear them. Being down on the farm you didn't hardly see or hear nothing so the show was
a treat, a big deal. Their music was the real blues. I looked forward to King
Biscuit. It would take your mind off what you be doing in the fields. For 15
minutes you could be happy.*[82]

During the Arkansas Blues and Heritage Festival (formerly called the King
Biscuit Blues Festival), tourists will find the elderly Sonny Payne holding court
at the KFFA studio located at the Delta Cultural Center in downtown Helena. Except for the six-year period from 1980 to 1986 when *King Biscuit Time*
was off the air, Payne has served as the program's main announcer since 1953.[83]
The Delta Cultural Center also contains a small museum featuring an exhibit
about the radio program. Four Mississippi Blues Trail markers mention the
radio show, including a marker titled "Mississippi to Helena" (located in Helena); a separate tourism project, the Arkansas Delta Music Trail: Sounds from
the Soil and Soul, honored the program with the dedication of a King Biscuit
Time marker on December 10, 2009.[84]

During the 1940s, at least five other radio stations, WROX (Clarksdale,
Mississippi), WGRM (Greenwood, Mississippi), KWEM (West Memphis,
Arkansas), WDIA (Memphis), and WLAC (Nashville) played a role in dis-
seminating the blues to a larger audience. (Both WROX and WGRM have
been recognized with individual blues markers.) For example, according to the
Clarksdale Daily Register and Daily News on February 9, 1948, WROX's play-
list included a number of fifteen- to thirty-minute blues shows including *King
Biscuit Time, Sonny Boy Williamson, Five O'Clock Blues*, and *Night Hawks*. The
Night Hawks were a band starring Robert Nighthawk Jr. (Robert Lee Mc-
Collum).[85] Since WROX aired *King Biscuit Time*, both KFFA and WROX
"effectively blanketed the upper Delta" until 1950.[86] A blues trail marker titled
"Broadcasting the Blues" recognizes the importance of radio to the develop-
ment of the blues throughout the South.

The "Broadcasting the Blues" marker also recognizes how WDIA in Memphis changed how broadcasters would perceive potential audiences. Historically, radio station managers and national advertisers had underestimated the
spending power of the black consumer, creating what *Sponsor* magazine called
the "forgotten 15 million."[87] For the most part, radio stations, particularly in
the South, ignored the black consumer because of the racist assumption that
blacks lacked spending power. During the first year of its existence, WDIA followed the racist traditions of the day, airing what *Time* magazine called "good-
music" to its targeted white audience.[88] However, the station was struggling.
In 1948, under pressure to increase ratings and remain financially solvent, Bert

Ferguson and John Pepper, who both owned and managed the station, decided to hire Nat D. Williams, a high school teacher, journalist, civil rights activist, and popular black personality in Memphis, to host a morning and afternoon show (Williams's first show aired on October 25, 1948).[89] Featuring one of the South's first African American disc jockeys, Williams's show (called *Tan Town Jamboree*) predictably drew a sharp rebuke from members of Memphis's white community who believed that African Americans should have no place on the airwaves. Yet, according to Cantor, for "every irate white who complained, hundreds of blacks immediately expressed delight."[90]

The show's initial success finally persuaded management to experiment with different types of black music. While WDIA's playlist emphasized spiritual and gospel music, the station also played some blues music, including a 12 p.m. to 1 p.m. slot featuring Delta-born "Bee Bee King" and "Sonny Williamson."[91] As one of the first blues musicians to be employed at the station, B. B. King was afforded a fifteen-minute segment (part of Williams's *Tan Town Jamboree* program) to play live in the studio; soon, King's popularity led the management to offer the blues singer his own show.[92] By early 1949, WDIA became the nation's first radio station to direct all its programming to an African American audience (five years later, WOKJ in Jackson would be the first station in Mississippi to move to all-black programming).[93] Subsequently, WDIA became the number-one station in Memphis and the first radio station in Memphis to gross over one million dollars in a single year.[94] By 1954, WDIA was upgraded from 250 to 50,000 watts, a decision that allowed the station to reach an estimated 500,000 homes in the Delta region and as far south as Mississippi's capital city, Jackson. In all, the station reached an estimated 1.5 million African Americans, or 10 percent of the nation's black population.[95]

Meanwhile, another important radio personality was revolutionizing blues radio programming. For fifty-one years, Early "Soul Man" Wright worked at WROX in Clarksdale, Mississippi. Wright was the first black DJ in Mississippi and, like Williams, one of the first black disc jockeys in the United States.[96] Wright certainly deserved the title "Early." For example, the first of Wright's two morning shows started at 4:45 a.m.[97] "No one in his right mind wanted to get up . . . on Sunday to do this," recalled former WROX general manager Tom Reardon. "But Early did."[98] In 1993, Wright wrote a brief autobiographical statement that was used to publicize his being named one of the winners of the Award of Distinction from the University of Mississippi, providing a chronology of events that precipitated his decision to join WROX:

> *In the early part of his adult life he formed a quartet by the name of the Four Star Quartet. He went through out the Delta singing God's praise. He later started broadcasting on KFFA with his Four Star Quartet. Then later he*

[started] broadcasting with WROX on Delta Ave. The manager, Mr. Buck Himman [sic] heard the broadcast and asked him if he wanted to be a D. J. It took several weeks to make up his mind to become a D. J. In the late 40's [1947] his mind was changed and [he] became the first black D. J. in the South. He kept God by his side and made a sussuful [sic] living for his family.[99]

A deeply religious man, Wright's daily shows consisted of both gospel and blues music (as well as a diverse assortment of other musical genres) and featured blues musicians, including B. B. King and Little Milton, who would frequently visit Wright at the studio.[100] Apparently WROX placed few restrictions on Wright. According to his widow (Wright died in 1999), Wright's on-air commentary and musical selections were never censored.[101] For a number of years, WROX practiced a financial arrangement between the station and the disk jockeys called the "brokerage system," a financial arrangement that enabled disc jockeys like Wright almost unfettered access to the airways.[102] Under this system, DJs purchased airtime from station management and then were responsible for reselling airtime to advertisers and sponsors to hopefully make a small profit.[103] Today Wright's name and memory are evoked in promotional materials, travel guides, local blues festivals, museums, and buildings. Since 1991 the organizers for Clarksdale's annual blues festival, the Sunflower River Blues and Gospel Festival, give the Early Wright Award to "successors who have continued their outstanding contributions to preserve, perpetuate, and promote blues and gospel music."[104] His name frequently appears in tourism guides, including *Blues Traveling: Holy Sites of Delta Blues*. The WROX museum, located in downtown Clarksdale, is a virtual shrine to his memory. Musician Jimbo Mathus and his uncle Guy Malvezzi have converted a former WROX studio into a recording studio, an important stop for blues tourists and musicians alike.

By the time Williams, Wright, and other black disc jockeys started to be heard on the airwaves in the South, many of the region's blues musicians had already left or were in the process of leaving the South for the northern cities of Chicago, St. Louis, and Detroit. This departure was part of the Second Great Migration (1940–60), an event triggered by a number of factors including the advancement of new agricultural technology (tractors and cotton pickers) and oppressive labor practices. Muddy Waters and Howlin' Wolf helped transform the largely acoustic Delta sound into the Chicago blues, a new, raw, and heavily amplified musical form. Other blues musicians (e.g., Willie Foster) decided to return home after a stint in Chicago or other blues centers in the North. And some Mississippi blues musicians, Son House and Skip James, decided to retire from playing music until they were rediscovered decades later as part of the 1960s blues revival.

Major record labels (ABC-Paramount and Bluesway), independents (Chess, Trumpet), and blues specialty labels (Delmark) tapped into this new market. Chess Records eventually became one of the most successful independent record labels in the history of popular music. After successfully managing a number of bars and clubs on the south side of Chicago, Leonard and Phil Chess decided to dabble in the record industry, investing in a struggling independent record company, Aristocrat Records, in 1948 with the company's co-founder, Evelyn Aron.[105] Within a year, Muddy Waters recorded one of Aristocrat's first major hits, versions of two "down-home" Delta blues songs ("I Feel Like Going Home" and "I Can't Be Satisfied") that sold out within hours of their release, mainly to African Americans in Chicago. One observer believed that Waters's early success was due in part to nostalgia, for the songs appealed to the thousands of immigrants from the Mississippi Delta who "grasped on to the old familiar sounds of home."[106] During the 1950s and 1960s, the label produced some of the most memorable and commercially successful hit songs of the decade (many written by Willie Dixon), including those by Waters ("Mannish Boy"), Wolf ("Smokestack Lightning"), Little Walter ("Juke"), and Koko Taylor ("Wang Dang Doodle").

By the early 1950s, white adolescents began to find rhythm and blues appealing.[107] Although the black market represented only 5.7 percent of domestic record sales in 1953, the music industry was "beginning to realize the potential of Negro music and styles for at least a segment of the white market."[108] Realizing that white audiences were larger and more lucrative than their black counterparts, Chess and other record companies started to promote African American musicians (Chuck Berry and Bo Diddley) as crossover artists, subsequently contributing to Chess's decision to retain only its major blues singers.[109] Meanwhile a small but devoted group of young whites were becoming increasingly interested in discovering a much older form of black music: the primitive blues.

THE 1960S BLUES REVIVAL

Blacks create and then move on. Whites document and then recycle.
—NELSON GEORGE, *The Death of Rhythm and Blues*

Centered in the United States and Europe, the 1960s blues revival was an outgrowth of the U.S. folk and jazz revivals that can be traced to the late 1930s. Although African Americans did participate in the blues revival, it was essentially young whites—folklorists, record collectors, music fans, and others—who spearheaded this blues renaissance. Although the events that transpired during the 1960s blues revival are not immune to critique, it is clear that without the efforts of dedicated blues researchers and fans, seminal blues recordings by Charley Patton and Son House, for example, might have been lost or reached only a cult audience, while the biographies of some blues performers would have been reduced to highly entertaining but wholly inaccurate romantic musings. The blues revival helped discover and ignite the careers of unknown blues musicians such as Fred McDowell, while early recording artists such as Son House, Skip James, and Mississippi John Hurt were offered a second chance to perform and receive belated recognition for their body of work, an event that Ted Gioia calls one of the most surprising events in modern American music, because career resurgences are rare, especially for elderly black musicians living on the margins of society in the rural South.[110]

Arguably, the 1960s blues revival portended the emergence of blues tourism, for the preservationist impulse embedded in the revival parallels cultural or heritage tourism, an industry steeped in the "preservation ethic," an indispensable component in informing tourists about the past.[111] The blues revival also significantly widened the music's consumer base while influencing the music's growing domestic and international popularity. Writing in 1993, blues historian Jim O'Neal correctly asserted that the blues "owes its present state of wide acceptance to many seeds that were planted in the 1960s."[112] In turn, the 1960s blues revival created the conditions for whites in Mississippi to play a dominant role in blues tourism because by the 1980s and 1990s, the music's primary advocates were white (sans African American blues musicians), and the blues had achieved newfound respect and social acceptance. In other words, without the 1960s blues revival, it would have been unlikely that white Mississippians would have had any interest in promoting their state's black cultural heritage.

What motivated young whites to be the new guardians and stewards of this "exotic" black subculture? For some blues revivalists, including folklorist Samuel Charters, the blues was intimately connected to political struggle and civil rights. Although it is impossible to attribute the blues revival to a singular event, Charters's landmark book of 1959, *The Country Blues* (and the accompanying LP featuring blues songs from the 1920s and 1930s), was a catalyzing event for the 1960s blues revival.[113] Charters was no doubt influenced by the pioneering work of John and Alan Lomax, the father-and-son team who started recording blues artists in 1933 and 1934. Claiming that his book was a "political act," Charters argued that the book's often criticized romantic style expressed his desire to combat many of the social ills that cast a pall over the United States in the 1950s. In particular, Charters wanted to dismantle the apparatus of white supremacy and racial discrimination by offering its citizens an "alternative consciousness." "I felt that much of what was stifling America was its racism," Charters explained, adding that America needed "to be forced to see that the hypocrisy of its racial attitudes was warping the nation's outlook on nearly every other major problem it was facing." By exposing white America to minority discourse, Charters believed that whites "might begin to see them as human beings, and not as stereotypes."[114] Charters hoped to play a role in "lifting the veil of fear that hung over every African American I met in the South."[115] In the preface to a 1975 edition, Charters elaborated on his rationale for writing the book:

> *If my books from this time seem romantic it's because I tried to make them romantic. I was trying to describe black music and black culture in a way that would immediately involve a certain type of younger, middle-class white American. They were the ones most ready to listen, and they were the ones, also, who could finally force some kind of change. . . . What I was doing wasn't academic, and it wasn't scholarly, but it was effective. I left the United States for more than a year after it was published, and when I returned there were people already out in the South doing the necessary work.*[116]

Although certainly not a monolithic group, other white blues enthusiasts were sympathetic to the issue of civil rights. According to folklorist William Ferris, "My work on the blues as a folklorist was directly connected to my protesting racial conditions and to try to give a voice to people that had been denied a voice."[117] As Davis has pointed out, the first blues revival was "political in implication" because its emergence coincided with acts of dissent and civil disobedience such as the Freedom Rides and coordinated efforts to register black voters in the South.[118]

Similarly, young whites enjoyed listening to the blues because they perceived the music as a powerful indictment of white middle-class values.[119] In *Robert Johnson, Mythmaking, and Contemporary American Culture*, Patricia R. Schroeder argued that many liberal middle-class whites—who rejected traditional cultural and social values—assuaged their alienation with a search for "wholeness, or authenticity, which became associated with 'alternative' cultural practices like blues and jazz."[120] Rejecting conventional values, many alienated whites believed the blues gave them an alternative value system, one that rejected materialism, artifice, traditional sexual mores, religious conventions, and other markers of middle-class conformity.[121] In *The Country Blues*, Charters observed that while white culture developed a "defensive hypocrisy" to a variety of behaviors, including sexuality, black culture provided young whites with a "directness, an openness, and an immediacy," typically not found in white culture.[122] African American blues musicians, in the eyes of their white admirers, were rebels who rejected traditional morality, monogamous romantic relationships, and the tedium of the forty-hour work week. Dick Spottswood, an avid record collector, radio disc jockey, and early proponent of country blues, noted that his initial enthusiasm for the blues was a rejection of his white (racist) identity:

> *I had grown up in Washington [D.C.] with plenty of country music on the radio but all of it was of the Hank Thompson, Ernest Tubb . . . kind of thing which is a far different kind of country music than which I have since learned to love. But I did not at all like it at the time. It just seemed like just some kind of shit from the other side of the tracks or something. And, whereas, I could naively identify with the black people that I perceived as having made this ancient blues and jazz music, the hillbillies were something else. I mean, because I sort of despised them because I was actually or nearly one of them.[123]*

Many of these white blues admirers enjoyed listening to the blues in the comfort of their own homes or in a nearby public setting, while others decided to travel to the South to find the source of this music. Some of these blues preservationists were record collectors. Record collectors passionately believed that discovering and purchasing old blues records were acts of cultural and historical necessity; many viewed their activities as a mission to save valuable blues artifacts from the ravages of time and apathy and to recover authentic blues voices that were doomed to be permanently silenced. Born in Texas and raised in Louisiana and Mississippi, Gayle Dean Wardlow became one of the earliest and most successful collectors of early blues records. Starting in 1961 and continuing into the 1980s, Wardlow would canvass black neighborhoods (and occasionally junk stores) hunting for rare copies of early blues records. Although he encountered some resistance, including a drunken man who threatened him with a butcher's knife, Wardlow developed a persuasive sales pitch that netted him copies of a number of rare recordings by blues and nonblues artists.[124] For example, in 1963 Wardlow discovered a copy of Son House's "Dry Spell Blues," a record so rare that Wardlow claimed it was the only known copy to have survived. The owners of the record were unwilling to sell it to Wardlow at an "affordable price" (Wardlow usually paid between twenty-five cents to a dollar for one record). In the end, another record collector, Bernard Klatzko, wired Wardlow twenty-five dollars to purchase the record for him.[125] In a 2001 interview, Cheryl Line, tourism manager for the Cleveland–Bolivar County Chamber of Commerce, claimed that record collectors were largely successful in their pursuit of buying old blues records and other memorabilia because many Deltans did not recognize the cultural and historical value of these artifacts: "Actually, people have been coming into the Delta taking things away from us since the sixties and seventies. [They] really came here in the seventies, collecting records, collecting anything they could get their hands on. And so they've taken a lot away from us that nobody here paid any attention to."[126]

Other blues preservationists (who were also record collectors) traveled to the South to rediscover early Delta blues musicians, although it was unclear whether these musicians could be found or were even still alive.[127] Initially many blues preservationists were interested in discovering and promoting rural country blues singers because these musicians were perceived as authentic representatives of a dying art form. In 1963 blues fan Tom Hoskins drove to Avalon, Mississippi, the hometown of Mississippi John Hurt, and was surprised to find the singer alive. In 1928 Hurt had recorded "Avalon Blues," a song that provided some indication of where the singer might be located. Although Hurt was initially suspicious of this white stranger, believing him to an FBI agent, Hoskins eventually convinced the singer to move to Washington, D.C., the so-called hotbed of the blues revival, to resume his music career.[128] In another example, following a tip from blues musician Bukka White, Nick Perls, Phil Spiro, and Dick Waterman left the Northeast in 1964 to search for Son House, who had recorded for Paramount in 1930 and the Fisk University/ Library of Congress project in 1941 and 1942. The trio stopped in Memphis and asked the Reverend Robert Wilkins, a blues and gospel musician, to join them as their guide on their excursion to the Mississippi Delta. According to one account, Wilkins assisted the travelers by "interrogating the delta Negroes in their search for Son House."[129] Unfortunately for Waterman and his group, House had left the Mississippi Delta sometime during the 1940s and was living in Rochester, New York. After learning House's permanent address, the three drove nonstop to New York and to House's front door. At the time, House had effectively stopped playing music. For a while, House lived with Waterman, and after prompting and encouragement from a small but devoted group of blues enthusiasts, House regained enough of his musical abilities to play at the 1964 Newport Folk Festival.

Meanwhile three California blues fanatics, including the musician John Fahey, went on a similar quest to find Skip James. For the blues purist, James remained "the last great prize to be found."[130] When the trio found James, he was in a hospital in Tunica, Mississippi, recovering from surgery. After being discharged (the three blues seekers paid his hospital bill), James stopped by his shotgun shack, gathered a few possessions, and joined the trio for their trip to Washington, D.C.[131] On July 13, 1964 *Newsweek* rejoiced over the discovery of House and James, claiming that the search for "lost" Delta blues musicians had an air of "urgency" to it. The Delta blues represented "our finest and oldest native-born music," one marked by a "Negro and a guitar lamenting misery, injustice, but still saying yes to life."[132] Interestingly enough, both

James and House were "discovered" on the same day, and both played at the Newport festival, an event that Waterman called the "greatest gathering of rural bluesmen . . . who represented the greatest Delta blues from the 1920s and 30s."[133] Besides James and House, other recently rediscovered musicians such as Sleepy John Estes played at the event. Scholars and fans alike also discovered new blues talent, including Robert Pete Williams and Fred McDowell, in 1959.[134] Steve LaVere remembered the blues revival as a golden opportunity to rediscover African American blues musicians who were, in many ways, disparaged in their own community.

> [It was] a time of discovery. It was just wonderful. What a great thing for a person raised essentially outside the black culture to be able to find people in that culture that other people didn't know anything about other than people in their own culture. Papa Lightfoot, for instance. We heard these early Imperial records and we said, "God, who is this guy? I wonder if he's still alive?" And to actually find him and make a record with him was just so wonderful. It was really a time of discovery. And, of course, all the great Mississippi (not that Lightfoot wasn't Mississippi, he was) Delta blues artists like Son House, Skip James, Bukka White, and John Hurt and so many others. It was really wonderful to find those people again.[135]

There is no doubt that the blues revival played a positive role in reviving the flagging careers of older black country blues artists, some of whom had not recorded since the 1930s or had stopped playing music altogether. Marybeth Hamilton put it correctly when she observed that a majority of blues artists "welcomed the attention and performed with dignity" while simultaneously "drawing new listeners to the blues who might not have taken an interest before."[136] In a 1966 interview with *Jazz Journal*, blues guitarist Fred McDowell commented on the benefits associated with the blues revival: "It makes me feel good 'cause since I've been recording these songs and goin' around all these different places they've been tryin' to help me. Things sure have changed around here and I really appreciate it to the highest."[137]

It is also true that some of these new discoveries found the unexpected attention disconcerting and bewildering. Playing for white audiences was almost too much for Skip James, who described the experience as one of heightened uneasiness, especially when whites stared at him like a strange, exotic zoo creature.[138] Indeed, Hamilton characterized the worst excesses of the blues revival as nothing more than a "circus sideshow."[139] Whites revered the performances of the elderly blues musicians even though many of their performances and recordings captured the artists well past their musical prime, due largely to advanced age, ravaging addictions to alcohol, and failing health. By all accounts,

Son House was a hopeless alcoholic who found it difficult to travel or perform onstage without frequent gulps of wine.[140]

Both House and James were managed by Dick Waterman, one of the first blues booking agents to appear on the scene, who also managed the careers of Mississippi John Hurt, Robert Pete Williams, Fred McDowell, and Buddy Guy, among a roster of other blues artists. A former journalist, Waterman became a booking agent, manager, and president of Avalon Productions. Waterman has been praised by William Ferris, Peter Aschoff, and other blues scholars for being fiercely protective of his musical stable, negotiating fair contracts, and recouping lost royalties for blues musicians such as Arthur Crudup, who were often treated shabbily by record companies.[141] Ted Gioia commends Waterman for reviving Son House's career and keeping the singer alive despite his severe health problems.[142] A reporter for the *Clarion Ledger* claimed Waterman was the "best friend a bluesman ever had."[143] Reflecting on his career, Waterman boasted to an audience at the University of Mississippi in 1984 that he was "responsible for the 'care and feeding of the bluesman.'"[144] Yet Skip James's biographer Stephen Calt has criticized Waterman's paternalist tendencies and his role as the "caregiver" to indigent blues musicians, accusing Waterman of deliberately creating a dysfunctional relationship with his clients, one based on dependence and mistrust:

> *Waterman gave the impression of someone who wanted to have blues singers dependent upon him. . . . He [Skip James] constantly complained that Waterman was not finding enough work for him. When James and other acts in Waterman's retinue found themselves on the same bill together, a good part of their time was spent comparing sour notes about their dealings with him. He was roundly accused of being a thief. One Chicago bluesman greatly gratified James by confiding that he was going to arrange for a local lowlife to "take care" of Waterman. . . . Waterman would attempt to mollify his semi-starving artist [Skip James] by paying effusive compliments to his art. In general, he tried to give the impression of being on a mission of love for blues, a posture that only instilled mistrust in James.[145]*

Despite Waterman's contentious relationship with some his clients, he successfully booked James, Hurt, and other blues acts to play on college campuses and at coffeehouses and festivals. Without a doubt, festivals served as an important performing site to reactivate older blues musicians and to initiate the eventual internationalization of the blues.

First staged in Paris in 1961, the American Folk Blues Festival (AFBF) was one of the most important festivals to showcase American blues music to a new international audience. Unlike most festivals, which are staged in one location, the AFBF traveled to different European cities.[146] Two German fans, Horst Lippmann and Fritz Rau, who cofounded the event, believed that the main purpose of the AFBF was to present a variety of blues styles to European audiences.[147] Chicago blues songwriter Willie Dixon, who along with Memphis Slim helped recruit musicians to play at the AFBF, remembered receiving attention, adulation, and financial rewards rarely accorded to blues artists in the United States. Moreover, compared to his experience with white racism in the United States, Dixon found Europe to be a beacon of racial tolerance and harmony:

The people are beautiful and they have their traditions and they couldn't live life as it's lived in America because America has had 400 years of slavery. Any country in the world that had 400 years of 15 million people working for free or practically nothing had to be one of the richest countries in the world so that's what America is.[148]

Echoing Dixon's resentment of U.S. racial policies, several European blues organizers and writers expressed dismay over the poor treatment blues musicians received in their country of origin. For example, the 1965 AFBF guide contained a grainy black-and-white photo of blues guitarist Big Bill Broonzy leaning over a decrepit piano. The photo is accompanied by a stinging indictment of the United States, a wealthy nation that allows its largely ignored blues artists to live in filth and squalor: "All of these BLUES players and singers would be real glad to hear something good done for them right NOW and not after they's dead." At the same time, the guide romanticized mythical images of the dispossessed blues artist, a wandering pauper singing songs of lament amid grinding poverty. In their opening statement in the guide, Lippmann and Rau remarked that the AFBF festival

opened up a whole new world for us—a world full of genuine artistic potency, full of plain, honest humanity, expressed in the simple 12-bar form which is known as the Blues. Here was the fascination of a real message, born of the want and the suffering of the singers' environment, of the daily happenings both great and small, of the joys of an evening well spent, or the tears shed over a lost love.[149]

Throughout the 1960s, the AFBF repeatedly labeled itself as an "authentic" blues festival. In describing the musical lineup for the 1966 festival, Lippmann and Rau argued that the diversity of musical styles, from acoustic Delta blues to the more amplified Chicago variation, would provide audience members with a "valid basic introduction" to the blues, especially for those "confronted with the authentic blues for the first time."[150] In the 1968 festival guide, the two organizers claimed that one of the event's headliners, Big Joe Williams, was the "most authentic Mississippi Country Blues artist alive" and argued that the "authentic" blues had achieved a cultural apex because, in the words of the musician Kenny Burrell, the blues had "crossed geographic, and political, boundaries to become something of a common language throughout the world."[151]

The distinction between the authentic and inauthentic played an important role in reshaping how blues musicians were packaged and sold to white audiences. Since the 1960s blues revival was based initially, in part, on rediscovering the original black masters of the country blues, "blues authenticity" became associated with the racial marker of blackness. Blues preservationists did not search for white faces but looked for the putative originators of this musical form—Son House, Skip James, Sleepy John Estes—black men who embodied the "earthiness" of black folk culture and the social experience of what it meant to be black in white America.[152] Many of these white admirers believed that age (elderly), physical disability (blindness), affliction (alcoholism), and social standing (poor) added an extra measure of authenticity, often a product of racial stereotyping rather than talent. It was also clear that for some blues purists, authentic blues musicians were men; women were excluded primarily because most of the country blues artists were men, and women like Bessie Smith and Ma Rainey were associated with the classic or vaudeville blues, a genre noted for its jazzy sound and urban sensibilities.

For some blues purists, it was the mode of delivery, the acoustic guitar and the rough, often coarse, emotional singing style of the confessional songwriter, that became associated with authenticity.[153] For these purists, blues music was a folk art, the product of earthy, emotional spontaneity, and for a time the primitive country blues artist was heralded as playing the real blues. In contrast, Muddy Waters, John Lee Hooker, B. B. King, and others who played amplified music were viewed with some disdain by purists who criticized this type of blues as both "professional" and "commercial."[154]

Rolling Stones guitarist Keith Richards remembered the hostile reaction Muddy Waters received in the early 1960s when he decided to play electric blues for an English audience who viewed electric instruments as anathema to black authenticity:

Muddy came on, acoustic guitar, Mississippi Delta stuff, and he played a magnificent half an hour. And then there was an interval and he came back with an electric band. And they virtually booed him off the stage. . . . Muddy and the band were playing great. . . . But for this audience, the blues was only blues if somebody got up there in a pair of old blue dungarees and sang about how his old lady left him. None of these blues purists could play anything. But their Negroes had to be dressed in overalls and go, "Yes'm, boss." And in actual fact they're city blokes who are so hip it's not true.[155]

Even before the 1960s blues revival, a few urban musicians, including Big Bill Broonzy, who were playing an electrified form of the music, were now encouraged to play the acoustic guitar and changed "their diction a bit to fit the new roles demanded of them." These musicians were rebranded as country singers, folk singers, or primitives.[156] This marketing effort led many young white musicians, such as Eric Clapton, to initially believe that "black music was acoustic and white rock and roll was electric."[157]

The release of several country blues albums (compiled from a collection of songs previously recorded on 78s) during the 1960s also underscored the idea that the acoustic blues was more real, more authentic. Robert Johnson's *King of the Delta Blues Singers* (1961) provides one vivid example. The front cover of the album featured a drawing of a lonely solitary figure strumming his guitar while sitting in a white chair. The image of this tragic, solitary figure, singing songs about a deceitful lover ("32-20 Blues"), alienation ("Last Fair Deal Gone Down"), and the supernatural ("Me and the Devil Blues"), captured the imagination of blues enthusiasts who, in turn, developed or perpetuated powerful mythic blues narratives. The authentic blues artist came to be recognized not only as the downtrodden country blues singer but the alienated rebel, an individual who lived outside the constraints of society, rejecting the traditional mores and values of both white and black society. The album's highly colorful, but often inaccurate, liner notes, which described in some detail Johnson's lawbreaking, womanizing behavior, supported this highly romanticized image.[158]

Charles Keil's book *Urban Blues* (1966) was one of the first to critique and admonish blues scholars, music critics, and fans alike for romanticizing the blues and stereotyping "real" blues artists as "old," "blind," and "toothless."[159] Written at a time when the call for black liberation was becoming more insistent and more radical, *Urban Blues* criticized whites for being starstruck by older black musicians:

An affair I witnessed in London featured an array of elderly bluesmen, a few of them quite decrepit; one scheduled performer had just been shipped back to the States with an advanced case of tuberculosis, another's appearance was little more than an exhibition of incipient senility, and some "stars" had all they could do to stave off the effects of acute alcoholism.[160]

While the mostly white crowd listened in "awed silence," the same performance, according to Keil, would undoubtedly produce "hoots of derision, catcalls, and laughter" from black audiences in Chicago. Keil dismissed the performance, calling it a "third-rate minstrel show."[161] In the black community, the popularity of a blues artist has less to do with a musician's status as a "cultural artifact" and more to do with demonstrating the ability to be a popular entertainer.[162]

Certainly many young white blues fans in Britain and the United States did not associate poverty or acoustic music with authenticity. Muddy Waters, Freddie King, B. B. King, and Bo Diddley, among others, played an electric urban blues and adopted a regal appearance that included expensive suits, watches, jewelry, and other material status symbols. B. B. King is on record opposing the stereotypical image of the dispossessed blues musician:

> *A bluesman is suppose to be some guy slouched on a stool, a cigarette hanging from his lips, his cap falling off his head, his overalls ripped and smelly, a jug of corn liquor by his side. He talks lousy English and can't carry on a conversation without cussin' every other word. Ask him about his love life and he'll tell you he just beat up his old lady. Give him a dollar and he'll sing something dirty. He's a combination clown and fool. No one respects him or pays him no mind. I resented that. Still do.*[163]

Whether dressed in overalls or in a suit, black American blues musicians seemed to captivate the attention of young white Europeans, who often were stunned at the emotional resonance of the music. As a child who suffered from parental abandonment and neglect, Eric Clapton attributes his lifelong obsession with the blues to his ability to identify with the music's expression of pain, dignity, and courage.[164] As a teenager, Robert Plant was enamored of Sonny Boy Williamson II, and in November 2009 he visited Tutwiler to celebrate the unveiling of a blues marker dedicated to blues musicians who are associated with the small town, including W. C. Handy and Williamson. Plant has visited the Mississippi Delta on numerous occasions, and a 1998 album he recorded with former Led Zeppelin band member Jimmy Page is called *Walking into Clarksdale*. In a video interview, Plant described the power of Mississippi's blues tradition and the allure of the Delta:

> *There's a magnetism and a draw, which considering I'm, you know, European—English—I have no real explanation for. I think it's just it was such a profound effect on me when I was younger and right the way through my career, but through my life more so, through my life, just the music and the power, and the intensity of the music and the lyric, and the directness. . . . But I just keep coming back to reconnect. It's a very, very peculiar phenomena.*[165]

Although Elvis Presley and Carl Perkins were certainly influenced by early blues records, it was the British Invasion in the mid-1960s that clearly illustrated the impact the blues had on young whites, particularly in England. From the Beatles to the Animals, Fleetwood Mac to the Yardbirds, British bands were certainly influenced by American blues music. In 1965, Eric Clapton joined forces with the British blues musician John Mayall to record *Blues Breakers: John Mayall with Eric Clapton*, an album that showcased the work of Bukka White, Otis Rush, Freddie King, and Robert Johnson and helped launch "a multitude of guitar oriented bands that looked to Clapton and his influences for inspiration and ignited a new stage of the revival."[166] British musicians were enamored with American blues music and awestruck when they met (and sometimes played with) Muddy Waters, Sonny Boy Williamson II, and other black artists who played in London in the late 1950s and 1960s. The reverence and hero worship that many white blues musicians showed their African American counterparts showcased a genuine level of cross-cultural awareness and empathy in an era when racism was very much entrenched both in the United States and in parts of Europe.

Of all the British groups, the Rolling Stones were perhaps the most indebted to the blues. The band's early albums, especially *The Rolling Stones (England's Newest Hit Makers)* (1964), comprised a number of cover versions of blues songs. In December 1964 the band scored a number-one hit in England with Willie Dixon's "Little Red Rooster," a song noted more for Brian Jones's outstanding slide guitar playing than Mick Jagger's attempt to imitate a black blues singer. In a 1968 interview with *Rolling Stone* magazine, Jagger claimed that although the members of the Rolling Stones were early converts to the blues, the band's decision to play American blues music was motivated largely by a need to spread the blues gospel to American audiences who were unaware of their own blues culture:

> *They never knew anything about it, and that's why we stopped doing blues. We didn't want to do the blues forever, we just wanted to turn people on to other people who were very good and not carry on doing it ourselves. So you could say that we did blues to turn people on, but why they should be turned on by us is unbelievably stupid. I mean, what's the point in listening to us doing "I'm a King Bee" when you can listen to Slim Harpo doing it?[167]*

In the United States, white American musicians such as Mike Bloomfield and Paul Butterfield sat in with, and were tutored by, black musicians in the clubs on the south side of Chicago. While many African American blues artists welcomed both white U.S. and British musicians, some were critical of the inability of these musicians to express the emotional impulse of the music. In a 1970 *Living Blues* interview, blues slide guitarist Hound Dog Taylor observed that most white musicians "ain't got that 'oomph.' They know all the right things to do, but it's got to be inside you, too."[168] Expressing a similar concern, Muddy Waters argued that many white musicians simply did not have that "soul down deep in the heart like I have."[169]

With the increasing white interest in the blues, it would be easy to forget that African Americans still listened to the blues, although in steadily decreasing numbers compared to previous decades. Contrary to white preservationists who predicted that the blues needed to be saved from extinction, Charles Keil argued the blues was very much a living art form, especially in urban centers such as Chicago, St. Louis, and Memphis, and that blues performers such as B. B. King and Bobby Blue Bland played to loyal black audiences.[170] Music critic Michael Erlewine claimed that "modern electric blues was very much alive and well in cities across the United States, only separated from white America by a racial curtain."[171] O'Neal's assessment of the 1960s blues revival rendered essentially the same conclusion:

> *Contemporary blues within the black community was barely acknowledged by the mass media; if so, it was likely to be pronounced dead, dying or disowned. But blacks did constitute a huge segment of the blues audience of the 1960s, an audience that was not a part of the blues revival as such. In the home territory of the blues, the music didn't need to be revived or rediscovered; it was there, in countless local bars, juke joints, and nightclubs.*

O'Neal argues that while many middle- to upper-class African Americans publicly rejected the blues because of the music's "unsophisticated" sound and identification with the poor black communities, many still bought and listened to the blues within the privacy of their own homes.[172]

At the same time, a prominent number of black scholars, writers, and poets championed the music. Amiri Baraka (LeRoi Jones) was perhaps the strongest and most vocal advocate for the blues. His book *Blues People: Negro Music in White America* (1963) was a seminal publication, for it was the first serious attempt to move beyond narrowly confining the blues as a genre or art form to contextualizing the blues as a musical "score" for the "history of the Afro-American people."[173] Baraka, who became associated with both the Beat Generation and the Black Power movement, should be considered, according to one observer, as Paul Oliver's "only peer in masterfully depicting the social milieu of the blues."[174] Baraka, along with Larry Neal, Val Ferdinand (Kalamu ya Salaam), Jayne Cortez, Stanley Crouch, and others were major figures in the black arts movement or what Larry Neal called "the aesthetic spiritual sister of the Black Power concept." One of the major goals of the black arts movement was the creation of a black aesthetic that would, according to Neal, lead to the eventual "destruction of the white thing, the destruction of white ideas, and white ways of looking at the world."[175] Through poetry, essays, music, drama, and other creative endeavors, many members of the black arts movement embraced African American artistic forms, especially blues and jazz, as part of the larger black experience in America. This black embrace of the blues was, of course, not universally supported by all members of the movement. In his essay "Black Art: Mute Matter Given Force and Function" (1968), Maulana Karenga claimed that while the blues represented a "very beautiful, musical and psychological achievement of our people," the music was "invalid" because it teaches "resignation" and fails to "commit us to the struggle of today and tomorrow, but keep us in the past."[176]

It was perhaps for this reason that younger African Americans gravitated to more aggressive forms of black popular music, including soul music.[177] Black audiences dismissed some blues musicians for playing anachronistic "Uncle Tom" music. In an interview with *Living Blues* magazine, guitarist Jimmy Dawkins berated Howlin' Wolf for playing the role of a black clown, rolling around onstage for the pleasure of whites:

Well, the Wolf is an old man. In his day and age when he was growin' up, comin' up, doing whatever he did to get up—Uncle Tom and lookin' to the white man. 'Cause in the South, you had to look to the white man to keep your money. If you had $300, you didn't keep it at home, you carried it down to the big house and he kept it for you. And you always can get your 10 or 12 dollars when you need it. . . . They just get on the stage and make a monkey out of themselves. Take T-Bone Walker, he had the splits. This was good in the '30s and '40s, but today it's looked upon as Uncle Tommism. We just don't cater to that no more.[178]

B. B. King painfully described the humiliation he experienced after a largely young black audience booed him before he even played a single note.[179] Before 1968, King played to mostly black audiences on the Chitlin' Circuit (a series of black clubs and taverns located in the South) and was viewed by many black audiences as a "has-been," according to King's close friend Little Milton, a blues artist.[180] Reflecting on his career in the 1960s, B. B. King summed up the predicament he faced by not conforming to a particular image, ultimately disappointing both young black and white fans: "Funny, though, because while young black fans were thinking we were too old-fashioned, white scholars were thinking we were too modern."[181]

King's fortunes would dramatically change. In 1968, during a scheduled stop to perform at the Fillmore, a white rock-and-roll venue in San Francisco,

King was surprised to find white hippies "covering every inch of the place" and a "cloud of sweet-smelling marijuana [hanging] over the room." After promoter Bill Graham's now-famous introduction, "Ladies and Gentlemen, the Chairman of the Board, B. B. King," King was astonished to discover that

> *every single person in the place was standing up and cheering like crazy. For the first time in my career, I got a standing ovation before I played. Couldn't help but cry. With tears streaming down, I thought to myself, These kids love me before I've hit a note. How I can repay them for this love? The answer came in my music. I played that night like I've never played before. . . . It was hard for me to believe that this was happening, that the communication between me and the flower children was so tight and right. But it was true, it was probably the best performance of my life, the one performance that showed me I was finally moving in a new direction.*[182]

Indeed, the careers of King, Junior Wells, Buddy Guy, and other electric-based black musicians were moving in a new direction. Little Milton concluded that King's success not only exposed the blues to a whole new audience but opened the doors for blues artists who had previously been ignored: "I think that it's a matter of survival and if you can be accepted into this, this is beautiful."[183] Once dismissed as "inauthentic," the electric urban blues now enjoyed a brief period of popularity that lasted until the early to mid-1970s. Although the blues had gone electric in the 1940s, the June 24, 1968, issue of *Newsweek* heralded this development as the "New Blues."[184] Echoing the advent of the folk-blues revival in the early 1960s, white musicians—this time American and British blues-rock acts, from Janis Joplin to Creedence Clearwater Revival to Cream—helped expose black blues musicians to wide-eyed white audiences.[185] In turn, the blues became, for many white rock fans, a new religious experience. "For these young people, the music is more than a music and the rock hall more than a hall," wrote one *Newsweek* reporter. "These pop palaces serve as secular churches where the truth is unleashed in 100-decibel thunder."[186] Even more important, for many young consumers, the electrified blues served as an alternative, a seemingly more authentic choice, to the white rock world, which was becoming, in the eyes of many, more and more contrived and uninspiring.

By the late 1960s, the blues was largely controlled and managed by whites. Blues festivals (as opposed to folk festivals) were held with some regularity in Michigan and California, Chicago and Memphis. Supported in part by blues societies and college students, the musicians (primarily African American) played to mostly white audiences.[187] Touted as the "first major national all-blues festival," the 1969 Ann Arbor Blues Festival (later renamed the Ann Arbor Blues and Jazz Festival) is considered by some to be another watershed event in the decade-long displacement of the blues from its black origins to its new white venues.[188] Featuring both acoustic and contemporary electric blues, the nearly all African American musical lineup played to thousands of cheering white blues fans. Also, several blues movies were released during this time; perhaps the most influential production was Les Blank's *The Blues Accordin' to Lightnin' Hopkins* (1967), a short film about the Texas blues musician. A number of blues periodicals, published in the United States and Great Britain, also appeared, including *78 Quarterly*, *Blues World*, *Living Blues*, and *Blues Unlimited*. First published in 1963, *Blues Unlimited* is recognized as the first blues periodical.

In the end, the 1960s blues revival helped rejuvenate the careers of both acoustic blues and contemporary electric blues artists, portended the development of the modern-day blues festival, and signaled the emergence of blues societies and blues scholarship alike. Paul Oliver has been credited with producing the first "serious scholarship" on the blues,[189] and Oliver's success with *Blues Fell This Morning* (1960), *Conversation with the Blues* (1964), and *The Story of the Blues* (1969) cemented his reputation as a leading and influential blues critic. David Evans, Samuel Charters, William Ferris, Stephen Calt, Tony Russell, Mike Leadbitter, Val Wilmer, and Bob Groom were among a new generation of American and British blues scholars whose work was published widely in books, journals, and magazines like *Blues Unlimited*. The decade also signaled the transformation of the blues from a form of popular music centered in the black community to a music "by black and white Americans primarily for white Americans and Europeans."[190] By the mid-1970s, this blues revival was in decline; ironically, Mississippi would stage its first major blues festival in 1978. However, it was not until much later that government officials, politicians, tourism boards, and other entities of official culture started to realize the potential financial windfall associated with promoting the blues as part of larger efforts to position tourism as the state's new source of revenue.

2

THE HISTORY OF BLUES TOURISM IN THE MISSISSIPPI DELTA

I think what's happened is that a younger generation of Mississippians have become comfortable with the idea of their state [promoting the blues]. One of the major reasons their state is important is because of the contributions of poor black people. And I don't think that older generations really meant to have their state known for that. And I don't think it's threatening to people anymore.

—SCOTT BARRETTA, former editor of *Living Blues* magazine

B y the mid-1970s, the 1960s blues revival was quickly losing steam, leading one observer to announce that the "blues is now struggling for survival."[1] The music's temporary decline can be attributed to a number of factors: the civil rights movement, which played a role in sparking white interest in the blues during the 1960s, shifted to a less-visible, less-vocal maintenance stage; a generation of blues artists who were discovered and rediscovered during the blues revival had either died or were inactive; and African American interest in the blues, which had started dissipating during the 1960s, declined further with the emergence of new black musical forms such as funk, disco, and rap.[2]

Ironically, at the end of the decade, grassroots efforts by white blues enthusiasts as well as a Greenville-based group, Mississippi Action for Community Education (MACE), portended the development of the state's blues tourism industry. MACE is an African American organization that emerged out of the civil rights movement of the 1960s. While MACE played a central role in organizing and promoting the state's first major blues festival, a small, dedicated group of young, white, blues-loving idealists struggled to construct a blues tourism infrastructure in downtown Clarksdale. Not surprisingly, this group faced a largely skeptical and indifferent local population, as well as local and state political leaders who, with a few notable exceptions, failed to recognize the aesthetic, cultural, and financial value of the region's blues heritage. To put it simply, many Mississippians did not understand the rationale for preserving and promoting the blues.

Adding to the strain, the promotion of the blues would also be marked by decentralization and fragmentation as individual communities competed for tourist dollars. However, the blues revival of the 1990s, influenced in large measure by the success of Robert Johnson's CD box set and the realization that tourism could be a new source of revenue, convinced some tourism officials and politicians that the blues should be promoted and that such an effort required a more centralized regional and state strategic plan. Early in the first decade of the new century, with the development of the state's first blues commission, blues tourism assumed a more coordinated structure, exemplified by the ambitious plan to erect blues trail markers throughout the state to provide tourists with a more visible and coherent "blues roadmap."

MISSISSIPPI BLUES TOURISM: THE EARLY YEARS

It is impossible to state with any degree of certainty when the first blues tourist visited the Mississippi Delta, but the event mostly likely occurred during the late 1950s or early 1960s. However, because a blues tourism infrastructure did not exist at that time in Mississippi, blues tourists, playing the noninstitutionalized roles of "explorer" or "drifter," rarely visited the state or the Delta region. It was also dangerous for whites, especially nonsoutherners, to socialize with blacks, a direct violation of Jim Crow laws. Local whites were highly suspicious of these "foreign agents," believing in some cases that these individuals were associated with the labor movement or the Communist Party, or just plain troublemakers who wanted to stir up racial discontent.[3] Even nontourists like folklorists Alan Lomax and William Ferris, both born and raised in the South (Ferris is a Mississippi native), encountered white hostility while conducting field research in the Delta.[4] Most of the blues tourists who did visit the Delta during this time were Europeans. Kinchen "Bubba" O'Keefe, a native of Clarksdale and the owner of the WROX museum, remembered witnessing his first (British) blues tourist in the 1960s:

> I can remember when I was in the fifth grade [or] sixth grade, picking up my first tourist in Clarkdale as vividly as I'm sitting here talking to you. He was going down the street, with a backpack and he had a British flag on the back of his jacket and I said, "What is that guy doing?" and I ran in and got him (and that's when the bus station was down here on Issaquena) and I said, "What ya

doing?" And he told me and I took him home on the back of my mini-trail and gave him a sandwich and took him back and he caught a bus out of here.[5]

Mississippi's nascent blues tourism industry emerged in the late 1970s, and until the mid- to late-1990s, this mostly grassroots movement occurred primarily in Clarksdale and Greenville. If we examine closely the development of Mississippi's blues tourism, we can identify five events as catalysts for what is now an officially sanctioned, legitimate tourism industry: (1) the creation of the state's first major blues festival, (2) the opening of the state's first blues museum, (3) the renovation of Beale Street in Memphis, (4) the pioneering work of William Ferris, the scholar who legitimized the blues as an area of cultural study, and (5) the formation of Malaco Records, a company that became an influential, independent blues record label.

Arguably, one of the first significant events that heralded the development of a blues tourism industry was the creation of Mississippi's first major blues festival, the Mississippi Delta Blues Festival, in 1978 (the name later changed to the Mississippi Delta Blues and Heritage Festival). The Mississippi Delta Blues and Heritage Festival was initially held in a tiny, impoverished rural community located approximately fifteen miles southeast of Greenville. In 1966 several poor homeless black families were involved in a sit-in at an abandoned air force base outside Greenville. After being evicted from the site, the families, along with a number of philanthropic groups, including the National Council of Churches' Delta Ministry, purchased four hundred acres of farmland and dubbed the new community Freedom Village.[6] MACE, the principal organizer during most of the festival's forty-three-year history, later characterized Freedom Village as a place that "showed what was wrong with poverty and the programs designed to remedy poverty."[7]

Although the festival is now touted as a source of revenue for Greenville, the festival's main function during its early years was, according to MACE, to preserve indigenous African American culture and the artists who practiced the craft:

> *While millions of dollars are spent yearly on developing and preserving the various exponents of elite, European music abounding in American culture, indigenous American artists such as the Delta Blues masters, cannot find enough work to support themselves and their families. The Delta Blues Festival strikes at the heart of this problem by creating an economic mechanism (in the birthplace of the blues) to promote these artist[s] and their work which is so valuable to us all.[8]*

Folklorist Alan Lomax served as the master of ceremonies at the first festival. His narrative on the development of the blues was intermixed with music from local blues musicians such as James "Son" Thomas and Sam Chatmon who played acoustic guitars to a crowd of approximately two thousand. Complementing the festival's accent on down-home blues, the performers played on the back of rusty flatbed trailer truck.[9]

The festival drew the attention of local newspapers, such as the *Delta Democrat Times* and the *Clarion-Ledger*, as well as national news outlets such as the *New York Times*. Writing for the *Washington Post*, for example, freelance writer Ellen Douglas (herself a native of Greenville) described a lively and harmonious setting, one seemingly devoid of racial animosity and bitterness:

> *The children are eating caramel apples. Beat-up pickup trucks and new Oldsmobiles are parked side by side. Earnest academic types, garden-club ladies, and old-line civil rights activists sit side by side in the grass. The beat picks up. Rural [R. L.] Burnside is playing now, a jump tune, and people are beginning to dance on the stubbily grass, kids, 8, 10 and 12 teenagers, and old folks.*[10]

Describing the mood of the first Mississippi Delta Blues and Heritage Festival as "relaxed," Douglas observed "blacks and whites mingling and greeting each other like old friends."[11] In his review of the same festival, Jim O'Neal observed that it has "probably done more to achieve real social integration in the state than any court order ever did."[12] Malcolm Walls, a former MACE representative and an organizer for the festival, believed the event served as a "welcome mat" to the United States: "There's a different kind of harmony here. The blues music of the festival transcends all the ethnic barriers and people transcend their economic condition, their problems."[13]

It should be noted that during the festival's early years, the audience was mostly drawn from the local population, although some blues tourists did attend the event. Low tourist turnout can be attributed to a number of factors: weak or nonexistent promotional and marketing efforts, lack of access to immediate information (pre-Internet era), no recognizable blues revival to inspire blues tourists to visit the area, and the festival's isolated setting.

Although the Mississippi Delta Blues and Heritage Festival is recognized as the state's first major blues festival and the oldest ongoing blues festival in the nation, additional blues festivals emerged in the state during the late 1970s and early 1980s. In 1978 the small town of Bentonia, home of blues musician Skip James, promoted its blues heritage with the Bentonia Blues Festival. In 1980 the Department of Music at Rust College, located in Holly Springs, sponsored the Northeast Mississippi Blues and Gospel Music Folk Festival. African American ethnomusicologist Sylvester W. Oliver, who was one of the primary organizers of the festival until its demise in the mid-1990s, stated that the purpose of the festival was to "promote the oral folk music traditions among the region's black population."[14] In the early 1980s, Charles Evers, a

civil rights activist and younger brother of the slain civil rights leader Medgar
Evers, established the Blues Homecoming Festival in Fayette.

The second important event in the development of the state's blues tourism
industry was the opening of the Delta Blues Museum in Clarksdale in 1979.
Sid Graves (who moved to Clarksdale in 1975) became the city library's fourth
director as well as the first director of the museum.[15] "The blues were indigenous to this area," Graves told a reporter for the *Clarksdale Press Register*, "and
frankly I couldn't believe someone hadn't already opened a museum here."[16] At
this time, Graves was one of the few individuals interested in preserving blues
artifacts, for according to Graves's successor John Ruskey, "No one was paying
attention to it around here in that kind of way [from an academic perspec-
tive]."[17] Today Graves is recognized as a blues "visionary" who is credited for
resurrecting interest in the blues in the Delta. William Ferris called Graves a
"national treasure."[18]

For the next several years, the Delta Blues Museum struggled to remain
financially solvent. The museum averaged between thirty and forty visitors a
month during its first year.[19] According to O'Keefe, Graves might have only
one tourist a day, but "he was always faithful to the cause."[20] Patty Johnson,
an early supporter of Clarksdale's blues tourism industry, noted Graves's drive
and determination to keep his dream of showcasing Clarksdale's rich blues
history alive:

> He recognized the cultural and historical importance of the musical legacy of
> this area. And he did that on his own. It was first housed at Myrtle Hall [the
> former Colored branch of Clarksdale Carnegie Public Library] . . . and he
> would have to gather up the collection every night. I mean, there was no secu-
> rity. It was not a museum as such. It was a collection. But he needed the Delta
> Blues Museum, and he would take those things home and then bring them
> back every day and set them up. Even at the time that we first visited the Blues
> Museum, it was housed in the Carnegie Public Library, upstairs, and there was
> no general access, there was no one actually showing things. If one wanted to see
> those items, one would ask a librarian—if he or she had time to open the door.
> And we would go upstairs and see it, and that was it.[21]

Receiving no city, county, state, or federal funding to meet its operating
costs,[22] the museum relied on grants and private donations and the help of local musicians, including Wade Walton, who donated photographs and recordings to the museum's growing collection.[23] While visiting Clarksdale, John
Ruskey, who would become the museum's curator during the latter half of the
1990s, toured the Delta Blues Museum and was impressed with its offerings.
In a letter to the *Clarksdale Press Register*, Ruskey applauded Clarksdale for
celebrating the life of one of its own, Muddy Waters:

I wanted to write and thank you for bringing us to the Delta Blues Museum you all have down there. We did enjoy it, and I am so happy that Muddy Waters' hometown has honored him because he has done so much in American music. He, and all the blues musicians from the Clarksdale area, are as great as any art or culture America has produced, and I love the music, just love it.[24]

The costly renovation of Beale Street in Memphis during the 1980s was a third event that showcased the potential of marketing the region's blues culture to tourists. Touted in promotional materials as the "street where the blues was born," Beale Street was originally an affluent white residential area.[25] Although Memphis was saved from the widespread destruction that was visited on much of the postbellum South, the city experienced periodic outbreaks of yellow fever. A major outbreak (1878–79), which eventually claimed the lives of nearly six thousand, forced the affluent white population to flee the city for the countryside as Memphis turned into a "nightmarish plague city."[26] By the turn of the century, Beale Street was an important hub for black commerce as banks, dentist offices, restaurants, concert halls, saloons, gambling dens, and prostitution houses lined the street. Many of the most famous and influential African American musicians, from Duke Ellington to Louis Armstrong, W. C. Handy, and B. B. King, played on what was described by one writer as the "Harlem of the South."[27] As Nat D. Williams asserted in a 1976 interview, "Well, you name them, and if he was famous and if he was known, he came to Beale Street."[28]

By the 1960s, Beale Street had declined as the center of African American commerce, but it was not dead. Robert Gordon's book *It Came from Memphis* describes Beale Street and the surrounding neighborhood as a cultural meeting place where black musicians and a growing, mostly white, counterculture movement intersected; Furry Lewis and Bukka White, whose careers were resurrected as part of the 1960s blues revival, found themselves playing in coffeehouses and sharing the stage with young white musicians such as Sid Selvidge.[29] However, by 1973, the city of Memphis decided to raze the street, as rows of empty buildings had turned the once famous area into a pitiful eyesore. A reporter for *Rolling Stone* vividly described the death of Beale Street:

Although it's actually been dead for quite a few years, they're just getting around to burying Beale Street. With bulldozers and wrecking cranes for pallbearers, the famous blues street is being put in the ground. It's going to be a lonely funeral; most of the street's friends have either died or been pushed away by the metal and concrete hands of urban renewal. . . . The saddest part, however, is that Beale Street, which for years cut a mighty fine strut through downtown Memphis, is going out quietly.[30]

By the end of the decade, the city's plan to turn Beale Street into a glitter-ing new landscape to attract new businesses was taking shape. Some observers, such as Jim O'Neal, editor of *Living Blues*, reported that the renovations also represented new efforts to turn the street's blues legacy into a tourist attrac-tion.[31] This effort started in earnest in 1983 with a $13.5 million project to re-store, according to one reporter, "the glory of the world-renowned street that is recognized as the home of the blues and the one-time center of black culture in Memphis."[32] The Rum Boogie Café was one of the first blues clubs to open after the start of the renovation, and although the club struggled during its first few years, by 1995 its annual sales topped $2.5 million.[33] The club's finan-cial health symbolized the success in transforming the once nearly abandoned site into a tourist haunt. Although a number of former blues establishments were destroyed as part of Beale's resurrection, tourists can visit a number of musical venues, including Blues City Café and the B. B. King Blues Club, the most celebrated blues club on the strip.[34] The memory of W. C. Handy is ever present on Beale Street; tourists can tour his shotgun house (where he wrote "St. Louis Blues" and other blues hits) or spend time in Handy Park. Beale Street is now a highly commercialized and flashy blues attraction and serves as a gateway for tourists interested in visiting the Mississippi Delta.

Any discussion of the history of Mississippi blues tourism is incomplete without acknowledging the influence of William Ferris in legitimizing the blues as a serious cultural artifact, one worthy of scholarly study and preserva-tion. Born in Vicksburg in 1942, Ferris developed a passion for the blues at an early age:

> *I grew up on a farm south of Vicksburg and basically everyone in that commu-nity was black. I went to a little black church as a child and the music of that church was very important in shaping who I was. And, as a teenager, I listened to blues on [the radio program] Randy's Record Shop and danced to it and then got involved in civil rights and continued to see blues as kind of a reflection of what I was and what I wanted to be. . . . All my life has been connected to the blues as long as I can remember.[35]*

After receiving his doctorate in folklore studies at the University of Penn-sylvania in 1969, Ferris, who has written and produced numerous articles, books, and documentary films on the blues, taught at Jackson State University and Yale University before assuming the position of director of the Center for the Study of Southern Culture at the University of Mississippi in 1979, a new-ly formed program that had officially opened its doors in 1977.[36] During his tenure, Ferris helped create what is now the blues archive at the University of Mississippi (arguably the finest blues-related archive in the world), sponsored educational classes on the blues, hosted domestic and international tourists and blues scholars, and honored blues musicians like B. B. King, among his other accomplishments at the center. Ferris's work with the Center for Southern Folklore, located in Memphis, is another important factor in the emerging legitimization of the blues.[37] Scott Barretta asserted that Ferris was the "face of the New South . . . who did a whole lot to help legitimize" the blues in Mississippi.[38]

Ferris also credits Malaco Records with playing an important role in the emergence of a state blues tourism industry. In 1962, Tommy Couch, a student at the University of Mississippi, started his career as a musical entrepreneur by booking bands for on- and off-campus parties.[39] After graduating from the University of Mississippi in 1965, Couch moved to Jackson and formed a partnership with Mitchell Malouf (his brother-in-law), calling their new booking agency Malaco.[40] By 1967 the partners opened a recording studio in Jackson and started recording musicians (Malaco would not be known as a significant blues label until the late 1970s). Since 1967, Johnnie Taylor, Bobby "Blue" Bland, Little Milton, Denise LaSalle, and even Paul Simon have recorded songs on the Malaco label.[41] Music critic Peter Guralnick characterized Malaco as an "old fashioned 'hit factory' built around a stable rhythm section and a stable of songwriters in the Southern pop tradition" of Stax and Muscle Shoals.[42] For many years, the small, independent recording company struggled financially until the surprising success of Z. Z. Hill's 1982 album *Down Home*, which featured the hit single "Down Home Blues." While Malaco targeted black record buyers, other blues-oriented record labels (e.g., Alligator Records, Rooster Blues Records, Fat Possum Records, High Water Records) generally catered to white consumers.[43] In all, these record labels are largely responsible for promoting the blues through the recording of artists who would otherwise have gone unrecorded.

EARLY POLITICAL SUPPORT, INCREASED MEDIA COVERAGE, AND AN EMERGING BLUES FESTIVAL CIRCUIT

Although it would take years for widespread political support of blues tourism to emerge, select members of Mississippi's political establishment realized the importance of the state's rich blues heritage. Former governor William F. Winter was arguably the first Mississippi politician to publicly express his support for blues tourism. In 1981, Winter designated September 19 as Delta Blues Festival Day. Acknowledging that Delta blues music played an "important role in the lives of countless Mississippians," the governor proclaimed that numerous musical groups "rendered outstanding service to the people of

Mississippi" through participating in this "wholesome activity."[44] Mississippi governor Ray Mabus and Clarksdale mayors John Mayo and Henry Espy were other notable political figures who provided early support for blues tourism.

Local press coverage of blues increased during the 1980s. The *Clarksdale Press Register*, for example, saw an increase—albeit uneven—in the number of articles the paper published on blues music from twenty-nine (1983) to fifty-three (1990). Panny Mayfield, former lifestyles editor and an award-winning photographer for the *Clarksdale Press Register*, wrote numerous articles on the blues. According to Skip Henderson, an early supporter of the blues, Mayfield was "using her position at the paper to try and convince not only the outside world of Clarksdale's supposed progressive attitude about the blues and how valuable the blues was, but she was also trying to educate Clarksdale itself into what it actually had, the people who actually lived there."[45] Moreover, Jackson's *Clarion-Ledger* and Greenville's *Delta Democrat Times* and other local papers wrote favorable feature stories on blues artists such as B. B. King, Houston Stackhouse, and Wade Walton, a local barber who was known as the "singing barber of the blues."[46] The lure of the Delta blues also attracted the attention of nationally recognized journalists who traveled to the area to experience the blues.[47]

In 1986 the creation of the King Biscuit Blues Festival (now called the Arkansas Blues and Heritage Festival) served as a new major tourist draw to the Delta region. Similar to the Mississippi Delta Blues and Heritage Festival, the King Biscuit Blues Festival has been called an authentic blues festival because of its geography (near the banks of the Mississippi River) and Helena's historical ties to the development of Delta blues. For example, the festival guide *Music Festivals: From Bach to Blues* describes the King Biscuit Blues Festival as the "real thing."[48] Although the festival is held in a neighboring state, I have included the King Biscuit festival because of Helena's close proximity to the Mississippi Delta, as well as the city's contribution to the development and preservation of the Delta blues. In the early twentieth century, Helena was known as a "wide-open" town where bootlegging, prostitution, and gambling mixed with the sound of blues music played by a host of Mississippi blues icons from Robert Johnson to Howlin' Wolf. The festival is now one of the largest blues festivals in the South, typically attracting over a hundred thousand visitors during the three-day event.

Meanwhile, ZZ Top's high-profile visits to Clarksdale in the late 1980s generated more local and national interest in Mississippi's fledgling blues tourism industry and created much-needed exposure for the Delta Blues Museum. Billy Gibbons, the guitarist from ZZ Top, first visited the Delta Blues Museum in 1987. Subsequently ZZ Top became one of the museum's biggest supporters, launching a campaign to raise a million dollars for the museum. In April 1988,

ZZ Top visited Clarksdale to kick off a million-dollar fund-raising drive for the creation of a permanent Muddy Waters exhibit that band members hoped would be the centerpiece of the Delta Blues Museum. Although the band was in Clarksdale for only a few hours, the buzz "left the small Delta town in a frenzy."[49] While in Clarksdale, the band presented a "Muddy Wood" guitar, an instrument that was fashioned out of cypress wood from Muddy Waters's cabin that suffered damage in a 1986 storm.[50] Governor Ray Mabus was so impressed with the fanfare over ZZ Top's visit that he proclaimed April 21 Delta Blues Museum Day.[51]

In 1988 Clarksdale held its first blues festival, the Sunflower River Blues and Gospel Festival (originally named the Sunflower Riverbank Blues Festival). "Downtown Days" served as the inspiration for the festival. Patty Johnson, one of the original organizers of the festival, ran a small booking agency in California at the time and helped book blues talent for Downtown Days, an annual event to provide support for local businesses.[52] O'Neal, who moved to Clarksdale in 1988, recalled in a 2008 interview that the Downtown Merchants Association, not surprisingly, believed that the main purpose behind a blues festival would be to draw Deltans to the city's downtown area to shop. In other words, the festival was not generally viewed by the business establishment as celebrating Clarksdale's blues heritage or even as an event that would draw the attention of tourists. With support from the Downtown Merchants Association, the local Chamber of Commerce, and the Mississippi Delta Arts Council, a handful of volunteers worked to create the festival on a shoestring budget.[53] Despite the recent celebration over ZZ Top's visit, O'Neal noted that some viewed the festival with a real sense of trepidation:

> *There was always a lot of resistance and skepticism in some quarters. You know, there were some people who were really behind it and others who just thought that people wouldn't come anyway. The blues couldn't be a tourist attraction like that. . . . Then when they did start coming they [the skeptics] were kind of disturbed that the tourists were going to the black parts of town and [the] pictures they were taking were of some of the rundown areas and not the nicer homes of Clarksdale.*[54]

At the first festival, the Clarksdale police department made its presence known during the one-day event. Because the city did not grant the organizers a beer permit and because of the city's open-container laws, festival attendees who possessed alcohol were relieved of their intoxicating substances. Frank Ratliff, owner of the Riverside Hotel (one of the few hotels operated by a black owner during Mississippi's long period of segregation), confirmed reports of police surveillance during the first festival.[55] Although some believe the local police were simply performing their duties and enforcing the laws, others have a contrary perception, one that suggests that the police were highly suspicious of the whole cultural event.

The 1989 festival was marred by inadequate funding because the event's sponsors (e.g., the Downtown Merchants Association) backed out two weeks before the event, and the organizers had to resort to an impromptu fund-raising campaign that netted approximately $750.[56] The money was used to pay the musicians because, as O'Neal told the *Clarksdale Press Register*, "We can't ask the musicians to volunteer their services."[57] With a musical lineup including Johnnie Billington, Wade Walton, and Blind Mississippi Morris and the Backwoods Blues Band, the festival, according to Panny Mayfield, "reaffirm[ed] the city's status as the birthplace of the blues."[58] There were reports that spectators were arrested for possessing alcohol, and others were ticketed for parking their cars in Clarkdale's downtown area.[59] One spectator, Dok Summer, found the police presence to be "intimidating": "The cops were perched up on Sunflower glowering down at the grassy knoll with guns at the ready."[60] In another column, Summer provided more details about the 1989 festival:

> *The 2nd fest was held in what is now called Martin Luther King Park. . . . That was a good time. People brought their own beer in and the police watched like prison sentrys from above. I've always thought the City was afraid it was going to turn into one of those Civil Rights marches from 20 years before. Maybe even a riot.*[61]

Some observers were unhappy with both the behavior of law enforcement and the general lack of community support for the festival. In an editorial published in the October 21, 1989, edition of the *Clarksdale Press Register*, Andy McWilliams, a local disc jockey and one of the original organizers of the event, believed that public apathy, combined with lack of interest by local business owners, contributed to the festival's lackluster beginnings. At the conclusion of his editorial, McWilliams's rhetorical question reflected the simmering frustration of festival organizers and the volunteers who dreamed of creating a regionally recognized blues festival: "So, Clarksdale, I ask you: why isn't there a King Biscuit/Delta Blues Festival in Clarksdale?"[62]

In 1990, Howard Stovall moved to Clarksdale and served as president of the Sunflower River Blues Association, a role that allowed him to promote the city's annual blues festival.[63] Stovall spent his early years living "at the end of cement" on the family plantation.[64] The Stovall family's association with the Mississippi blues tradition is well-known. From 1915 to 1943, Muddy Waters worked as a sharecropper on the Stovall plantation; it was a Stovall employee, an overseer by the name of Ellis Rhett, who denied Waters's request for a raise (from twenty-two cents to a quarter), a decision that inspired Waters to escape the plantation to seek his fortunes on the South Side of Chicago.[65] Apparently Stovall was not exposed to the blues as a child; oddly enough, he first discovered the blues by listening to early records by the Rolling Stones and other white rock-blues-based bands.[66] In 1983, while attending Yale University (he graduated in 1984), Stovall met Muddy Waters during the singer's last tour. Stovall asked the stage manager to be introduced to the ailing Waters: "I wouldn't have been surprised at all if he been like, 'Man, the last thing I want to do is talk to a Stovall.' But he was exactly the opposite."[67] Since returning to the South, Stovall's passion for promoting the blues has been multifaceted: he appeared in Robert Mugge's film *Deep Blues* (1991), played keyboards for the Clarksdale-based Arthneice Jones and the Stone Gas Band from 1990 to 1996, served as executive director of the Blues Foundation in Memphis from 1997 to 2002, produced the Blues Hall of Fame induction ceremony at Kennedy Center in 1998, joined forces with Morgan Freeman and attorney Bill Luckett to open Clarksdale's blues club Ground Zero in 2001, and co-founded the Resource Entertainment Group, a Memphis-based entertainment company.[68]

In another significant move for Clarksdale's growing blues tourism industry, in 1988 Jim O'Neal and Patty Johnson opened Stackhouse Mississippi Arts and Gifts / Delta Record Mart, a combination recording studio, headquarters for O'Neal's record label, Rooster Blues Records, and record shop in downtown Clarksdale. O'Neal's initiative to secure financial assistance to support the blues was met by indifference and rejection as local banks refused to support his new business:

> *Patty Johnson and I approached the local banks when we decided to set up business in Clarksdale. We had a business plan to start her chiropractic practice and to open the Stackhouse. But the banks would not loan us any money. After that, the mayor (John Mayo, was supportive of what we were trying to do), had a meeting with us and said he wanted to look at some other sources of funding "before y'all go to Greenville," which of course was a possibility since Greenville was the other town that was showing some support for the blues. But nothing ever worked out for local financial support.[69]*

In a 2008 interview, Patty Johnson, who is currently the owner of Delta Chiropractic, believed that the lack of funding had more to do with the novelty of blues tourism than with a particular bias against "outsiders" promoting the blues. After all, the Delta's economy was largely staked in agriculture and manufacturing, although both economic sectors were in decline:

I think they were looking for people to come in here who were ready to invest in Clarksdale. Obviously, we needed some help to get some of this stuff off the ground. This was a burgeoning idea about really helping to boost the tourism industry in Clarksdale. It is not surprising that they, at that time, did not understand what this could, and possibly would, mean. I think it is an entirely different situation right now. But I think it's a matter of understanding. I don't think it was about the blues. I don't think it was about us personally. I think they were looking for investors to come in and, you know, kind of spur the economy of Clarksdale.

Despite the lack of funding, Stackhouse became, in the words of Johnson, Clarksdale's blues "information resource center." Inquisitive individuals, newspaper and television reporters, and film companies from around the United States called Stackhouse for information about the region's blues culture. "It wasn't very long before we had blues buses and we were then guiding tours," recalled Johnson. "We were the ones that were giving out all the information. There was no other resource. We were the ones."[70]

After ten years of active blues promotion, Mississippi's blues tourism industry, such as it was, was still largely a grassroots efforts mostly organized and sustained by white and black blues enthusiasts. For the most part, city governments, chambers of commerce, and other institutional entities showed little interest in promoting the blues as part of the region's cultural heritage. John Ruskey observed that in Clarksdale "there wasn't any promotion, period, from the Chamber of Commerce to city government, period, except any institutional promotion that was only happening through the public library [which housed the Delta Blues Museum]."[71]

The lack of financial and moral support from Clarksdale's official culture was also clearly evident in the fact that Clarksdale's white blues enthusiasts were viewed, according to some sources, as eccentric oddballs. Official culture is made of individuals and groups in positions of power and authority that desire "the continuity of existing institutions, and loyalty to the status quo."[72] Sid Graves, who is now fondly remembered as a blues pioneer, was widely viewed by Clarksdale's elite, according to Skip Henderson, as a marginalized figure:

I remember hanging out with Sid in Madison Square Garden, backstage at Madison Square Garden where they had this tribute to John Lee Hooker. And Sid was treated as royalty. Here's the man, you know, this is the guy, the Delta Blues Museum, this is the real guy that's saving the real music in a real place. And then to see him in Clarksdale and people looking down at him 'cause he's hanging out with black people. And he should be taking care of the business of the library because you have to remember he was the director of the library. But all he wanted to do is deal with these blacks and this museum. They thought he was devoting too much time to the museum and to black people and to black culture.[73]

In contrast, Patty Johnson argues that the small group of white blues enthusiasts were not marginalized as much as viewed with a certain amount of skepticism because tourism was a completely new economic vehicle in the Delta. At the same time, blues tourism promoted interracial gatherings, forcing Clarksdale to come to terms with the unwritten rules of segregation that have governed social life since the city was founded:

I don't know if people looked at [us] as invaders as much as: "What are they really doing here and what do they think this is going to do?" . . . We were making some changes. We had an interracial musical event at the city auditorium where some of the older folks—the "elite" if you want to call them (I certainly wouldn't characterize everyone as elite). They were being put through some changes here. This was stuff that hadn't happened. There were receptions at the blues museum where, I think, there was a Clarksdale Hall of Fame that was briefly done and there were two African Americans who were honored and two white people that were honored. This was a socially changing thing as well an economic thing. I didn't feel that marginalization. I knew we were up against changing some minds.[74]

In 1990 the release of Robert Johnson's successful CD box set *The Complete Recordings* signaled a new direction for the state's blues tourism industry. The set sold an estimated 350,000 copies during the first two years of its release and eventually sold over a million copies.[75] This newfound appreciation of Johnson's work sparked a blues revival in North America and Europe. O'Neal believes that Johnson's box set, along with the 1986 movie *Crossroads* (much of which was filmed in Mississippi), encouraged a new flood of tourists to visit the Delta in search for the crossroads.[76]

Deep Blues: A Musical Pilgrimage to the Crossroads (1991) was another significant blues film that fueled the blues revival of the early 1990s. Directed by Robert Mugge and narrated by the late music critic Robert Palmer (the author of the book *Deep Blues*), the ninety-minute documentary highlighted blues artists living in the Delta, Roosevelt "Booba" Barnes, as well as R. L. Burnside and David "Junior" Kimbrough who lived near Holly Springs, Mississippi. Burnside and Kimbrough were the "leaders" of the North Mississippi blues tradition, a regional blues subgenre characterized by repetitive, droning electric guitar.[77] The movie, shot on location on Beale Street in Memphis, northeastern Mississippi, and the Delta region, turned some of the movie's most obscure blues artists into celebrities. Arguably, it was Junior Kimbrough's mesmerizing performance that received the most praise by music critics, and as a result, Kimbrough's recording career (which had been confined to a few obscure singles) blossomed. Fat Possum Records took advantage of Kimbrough's growing stature and released *All Night Long* (1992) and *Sad Days Lonely Nights* (1994) to critical acclaim. The Rolling Stones, U2, and other notable musicians visited Kimbrough at Junior's Place, his juke joint in Chulahoma, Mississippi. For many blues fans, including Roger Stolle, the owner of Cat Head Clarksdale's premier blues music and folk art shop, the film was a revelation, a reminder that Mississippi still possessed a rich, thriving, living blues culture.

With this surge of newfound interest and popularity of the blues, Mississippi's official culture began to make tentative steps to actively promote and market the music. These institutional efforts reflected more mediated, structured, and organized endeavors to target the tourism industry, what Jeff Todd Titon refers to as the "New Blues Tourism." The New Blues Tourism emerged to compete with the traditional low-key and informal processes that had characterized blues tourism up to this point. Since its inception in 1993, for example, the Coahoma County Tourism Commission has promoted the city's blues culture and, realizing the potential financial impact of the blues, doubled its efforts in 1998.[78] Cheryl Line, tourism manager of the Cleveland–Bolivar County Chamber of Commerce, recalled that her organization first started to promote the blues in the mid-1990s.[79] At the same time, the region's convention and visitors bureaus started to promote the blues. It should be noted that, with a few exceptions, the bureaus did not emerge in Mississippi until the gaming industry found a new home in the state in the early to mid-1990s.[80]

Reflecting growing institutional efforts to market the region as a blues destination, the state of Mississippi and Memphis expanded efforts to promote the blues as part of the region's tourism industry. In 1995 the Memphis Convention and Visitors Bureau formed a partnership with the Mississippi Division of Tourism to promote "America's Blues Alley." Exploiting Northwest Airlines/KLM's nonstop route from Amsterdam to Memphis, America's Blues Alley attempted to target Europeans who were desperate to visit the "motherland" of blues and rock and roll.[81] Apparently, tired of visiting Disneyland and the White House, European tourists were eager to see "real America."[82]

By 1999, Mississippi's official culture began to seriously consider the real economic potential associated with promoting its blues history and culture. The Mississippi Division of Tourism and the Mississippi Arts Commission hired the North Carolina–based Randall Travel Marketing group to conduct the first comprehensive study of blues tourism in Mississippi. The study's specific goal was to "develop a research based marketing plan that will effectively position the Mississippi Millennium Blues Trail as a heritage and cultural tourism destination." Released in 2001, the study, while complimentary of some of the efforts by the local communities to promote the blues and the region, outlined a number of deficiencies, ranging from a lack of upscale lodging to inadequate signage to assist travelers in locating blues-related sites. While some of the study's sixteen strategic initiatives have yet to be implemented, Luther Brown, director of Delta State University's Delta Center for Culture and Learning, believed that it represented a turning point in the marketing of the blues in the region: "It did do something really good in that it really did focus attention for the first time on blues tourism in particular and heritage tourism in [a] more general sense."[84]

A GROWING INDUSTRY: INSTITUTIONALIZING BLUES TOURISM

Since its inception, blues tourism in Mississippi has been marked by decentralization, fragmentation, and competition. Billy Johnson, director of the Leland Blues Project, pointed out that the different Delta communities "never have gotten together and worked towards promoting the blues together."[85] Nancy Kossman, former proprietor of Dela's Stackhouse (no longer in business) in Clarksdale, claimed that she has "never known an area where people have more trouble working together."[86] Luther Brown argues that despite efforts by organizations such as the Mississippi Delta Tourism Association to discourage competition in favor of a more regional perspective, the state's blues tourism industry is marked by decentralization and competition because the Delta itself is a "very fractured place."[87] Blues historian Steve LaVere traces the competitiveness to the Delta's plantation culture:

> *That's just a carryover from the times when all the little feudal plantations were trying to do the best they could to capture as much of that cotton money as possible. And they didn't care what the next guy did. They were worried about their own crops. And so that philosophy kind of carried over into the towns because after all, the towns were built up to serve the plantations. And so there's 150 years of philosophy that has to be counteracted and to a large extent that has happened.*[88]

Local blues promoters, especially juke joint operators, also have to compete, to some extent, with the state's casino industry. The Horseshoe Casino in Robinsonville, Mississippi (in Tunica County), features a blues-themed entertainment venue. From the exterior, which sports wall sculptures of blues musicians (Robert Johnson, Howlin' Wolf, Albert King), to the interior, adorned with blues imagery such as guitars, pictures of blues musicians, and bars that are shaped to resemble instruments, Bluesville is a large, flashy, state-of-the-art venue that takes advantage of the region's blues culture and heritage. While the casino occasionally attracts blues musicians such as Robert Cray, most acts play anything but the blues; the nightclub has attracted a variety of country (LeAnn Rimes), rock (Black Crowes), and pop (Chris Isaak) artists, as well as comedians (Jay Leno). When Bluesville opened its doors in 1998, David Simmons, the founder of the club, told *Living Blues* magazine that he hoped to hire local blues musicians to open up for national acts, although he conceded he will "avoid soul/blues stars such as Bobby Blue Bland and Bobby Rush because he does not like their music."[89]

There is debate about the extent to which casinos have impacted the livelihood of local juke joint owners in Mississippi. The movie *Last of the Mississippi Jukes* argues that the proliferation of casinos in Tunica County has jeopardized the survival of some juke joints and small clubs in the Delta region. Yet critics reject the implications of the documentary's title, declaring that while the casino industry has had a detrimental impact on local businesses and entertainment venues, "real juke joints have survived because their clientele still appreciates the kind of downhome neighborhood ambiance and musical fare that can't be experienced at Harrah's or the Gold Strike."[90] Nevertheless, with Mississippi's casino industry firmly entrenched as one of the state's major revenue providers, local musical venues will continue to be impacted, to some degree, by the further confluence of the area's gaming organizations.

The blues tourism industry has also had its share of internal, intracity conflict. In particular, Clarksdale is well known for its infighting, backbiting, and divisiveness. Local blues musicians blame festival organizers and club owners for not paying them a living wage. Blues entrepreneurs blame the city of Clarksdale and the Coahoma County Tourism Commission for not providing sufficient financial resources to promote the blues. In turn, the Tourism Commission claims that it simply does not have the necessary funding to fully support promoting the blues. Criticizing the Tourism Commission's controversial decision to fund a bluegrass festival in 2004 at the expense of other, seemingly more profitable ventures, a writer for the *Clarksdale Press Register* blasted the commission's perceived arrogance and incompetence:

> While the Sunflower River Blues and Gospel Festival struggles along with a paltry $5,000 of support from the Tourism Commission—with the Tennessee Williams Festival in the same boat—and while the Delta Blues Museum has to literally beg for support funding for nationally marketable exhibits, the

Tourism Commission seems to be ever more intent on finding new projects at which to throw money. In the meantime, those new projects suck the lifeblood out of events with a track record of attracting tourists to Clarksdale. There is no questioning the need for diverse entertainment to attract tourists. There is a great deal to be said, however, about the virtue of fully developing what Clarksdale is best known for—our blues music heritage, our literary heritage and our agrarian and river culture.[91]

Since 2000, local and state organizations have emerged to begin the slow and tedious process of coordinating and centralizing the state's blues tourism industry. In 2000, Clarksdale and Tunica formed a tourism partnership to coordinate a two-way flow of tourists from Tunica's casinos to Clarksdale's blues sites.[92] Regional tourism officials also decided to create the Mississippi Delta Tourism Association (MDTA).[93] Based in Greenville, the MDTA was founded in 1994, but it was not until 2000 that the organization gained considerable footing as an active tourism entity; in that year, the Mississippi Development Authority (MDA) provided the organization with much-needed funding ($250,000 over a three-year period). Bill Seratt, president of the MDTA and a member of Mississippi Blues Commission, discussed in a 2008 interview why the state of Mississippi was willing to provide the group with start-up funding:

The state [of Mississippi] was so willing to work with us [the Mississippi Delta Tourism Association] because we had immediate international branding. No matter where you are, if you say, "The Mississippi Delta" or "Delta blues," it conjures up some kind of image for just about anyone. And it may be about music, it may be about the mystique of fancy houses and ball gowns, or it may be about the horrors of slavery and civil rights. Some image comes up when you say the words "the Mississippi Delta" to just about anybody on Earth. I was standing on a pyramid at Chichen Itza, and when I said to this young man who spoke no English, and my Spanish is pretty rusty, and we were trying to figure out where each was from, and I said "the Mississippi [Delta]" and he got a grin on his face and he said "Sonny Boy" [Williamson]. So, there standing in a middle of a jungle, we were able to communicate through the blues.

As Seratt's story suggests, the Mississippi Delta evokes strong visual, often contradictory, images in the minds of tourists, the romanticism and mystique of the Old South (plantation mansions) and the gruesome institution of human bondage. And while the Delta may be remembered as a place of unspeakable horrors (slavery, lynching), the region's identity over the last forty years has been increasingly associated, both domestically and internationally, with the blues. Because of the region's strong association with the blues and the music's ability to communicate to a global audience, Mississippi officials seem to be increasingly convinced that marketing the state's blues heritage will ultimately reap great rewards.

Seratt describes the MDTA as an "information, navigation organization that sells the Mississippi Delta from the Tennessee line to Vicksburg."[94] Until recently, the MDTA's Web site claimed that the Delta is much more "than a region or a feature on a map"; it is "a land unto itself." The site included various proposed self-directed tours with names such as "The Mississippi Delta: Where the Music Meets the Soul" and an entertaining travelogue (written by an anonymous source) filled with a colorful account of the region's wonder and "mystique."[95] These promotional vehicles have been replaced by brief descriptions of each Delta community (seven towns and two counties), a short statement about the region's "uniqueness," and an appeal for tourists to "find out what's changed—and what thankfully hasn't—in this authentic slice of Americana."[96]

In another example of increased centralization, the Blues Highway Association held its first meeting on September 3, 2002, at Delta State University. The primarily white association of twenty-three individuals described itself as a "loose-knit, democratic association of people"[97] who realized that while a variety of "existing organizations serve a portion of the blues providers group . . . none represent the entire group."[98] The Blues Highway Association's agenda was ambitious, with efforts directed at solving a number of problems, including the need to increase signage in the area, develop blues maps and travel guides, and transform the Delta into a federal heritage area. Headed by Luther Brown, the organization first attracted the attention of museum curators and blues academics. Soon it attracted a broader coalition, including chambers of commerce representatives and tourism officials, who helped bolster the membership to include a total of 220 individuals and organizations.[99] By 2004, interest in the organization started to wane. While not defunct, the Blues Highway Association could best be described as an inactive organization.

In 2002, Roger and Jennifer Stolle opened the Cat Head Delta Blues and Folk Art store in Clarksdale, a move that helped centralize the promotion and marketing of the blues. Similar to the role that Stackhouse played in promoting the blues years earlier, Cat Head serves as a blues clearinghouse of sorts, providing tourist information and selling a variety of items from CDs to videos, books to artwork, by local artists, including blues musician Pat Thomas, whose cat head art served as the inspiration for the store's name. After visiting the Delta over a period of years, the Stolles (now divorced) decided to quit their corporate jobs in St. Louis and set up shop on Delta Avenue in downtown Clarksdale. When Roger Stolle first arrived, he was dismayed at the lack of coordinated promotion in Clarksdale:

> *Nobody was here promoting live music. You'd come into town and nobody could tell you. The museum [Delta Blues Museum] practically couldn't even tell you where the gigs were going to be. Ground Zero was still relatively new at that time. They didn't have everything there totally together there either—it wasn't booking solidly, they weren't marketing as much as they are now. So, you really think that it is dead and the blues has died in the land where it began like people have written.[100]*

In addition to managing a new business, Stolle books musicians at Ground Zero and other clubs and juke joints, has served as a volunteer at the Sunflower River Blues and Gospel Festival, hosts a blues radio program for WROX, helped create Clarksdale's successful Juke Joint Festival, organizes overseas tours for local musicians, started a record label, and has produced two blues documentaries, including *M for Mississippi: A Road Trip through the Birthplace of the Blues*, a winner of a 2008 *Living Blues* award. Most important, however, was Stolle's weekly *Cat Head Update Newsletter*, which was e-mailed to throngs of subscribers and also appeared on the company's Web site. The newsletter provided information about live blues music and upcoming blues festivals and often contained articles written by Stolle and excerpts from newspapers and other sources about blues artists and blues-related activities. Before this point, information about the state's blues events had not been disseminated in this manner; instead, each community would often promote it own blues events. Arguably, Stolle's newsletter has been more effective in disseminating blues-related information to a mass audience than the state's tourism organizations.

Perhaps the most significant development in the centralization of Mississippi's blues tourism industry was the creation of Mississippi's first blues commission.[101] Inspired in part by the Year of the Blues campaign, former Mississippi governor Ronnie Musgrove played a significant role, along with others including state senator David Jordan (who envisioned the need for such a commission), in organizing a state blues commission. It was officially established by gubernatorial decree in 2003. A year later, Mississippi's new governor, Haley Barbour, received legal approval by the state's legislature to officially sanction the commission with the hope of developing a comprehensive plan to market Mississippi's historic blues sites.[102] (In March 2010 the Mississippi Legislature passed a bill that would allow the Mississippi Blues Commission to raise private funds to provide financial assistance to Mississippi blues artists mired in debt and struggling to make a living.)[103] During the signing of Senate Bill 2082, according to a reporter for *Jet*, Barbour and other supporters of the bill "wore sunglasses to produce a 'blues musician' attitude."[104] This comical attempt by Barbour and others to play homage to John Belushi's and Dan Aykroyd's white hipster personae as Jake and Elwood in *The Blues Brothers* both signifies white control of the blues and, arguably, reflects an insensitivity to the underlining racism that permeates the film. (At the fifth annual Peavine Awards ceremony in 2002, an annual event to celebrate Mississippi blues artists, the owners of the Shack Up Inn, a white-owned blues hotel located on a plantation on the outskirts of Clarksdale, appeared on stage in Blues Brothers–inspired outfits to accept an award for "preserving the romanticism of the South for all the world to enjoy.")[105]

According to Bill 2082, of the eighteen commissioners, the governor of Mississippi is responsible for appointing seven members, one of whom serves as the commission's chairperson.[106] Although the majority of the commission is made up of white members, several African Americans are members of the board. In a 2006 interview, Luther Brown argued that although the commission is always concerned about "appropriate representation," the decentralized process by which commissioners are selected makes it virtually "impossible to have a fifty-fifty split."[107] At the same time, Brown clarifies the mission of the Blues Commission as essentially inclusive in nature:

The commission does not want the blues trail or anything else about the blues to be something, you know, taken away from one group and controlled by another group. What the commission is trying to do is to honor the blues and make it accessible, make the stories of the blues accessible not just to visitors but to local people, too.[108]

One of the Blues Commission's main goals is to develop Mississippi Blues Trail highway markers. In collaboration with blues historians, music experts, and blues enthusiasts, the commission has crafted detailed criteria for selecting who will be honored and where the blues markers will be placed. Alex Thomas, music development program manager of the Blues Trail, and a small committee are responsible for the daily operations of the project and coordinate with members of the Blues Commission. Although some critics initially claimed that a state-organized blues trail project would unnecessarily commercialize the blues, the project has met with little public resistance or controversy.[109] Instead the unveilings of these markers have become major local events attended by politicians, blues musicians and their family members, and members of the local population.[110] The unveilings are also notable for the interracial composition of the audiences. On February 13, 2008, two blues trail markers were unveiled in Clarksdale to celebrate the musicianship of harmonica player James Cotton and drummer Sam Carr. A *Clarksdale*

Press Register reporter quoted an exuberant Cotton, marveling at his good fortune: "I have been all over the world and to come back to here to this spot. . . . I'm just the happiest man in the world."[111] Nearly three months later, Greenwood, Mississippi, honored one of its own, guitarist Hubert Sumlin, whose seminal guitar style helped Howlin' Wolf gain blues prominence in the 1950s and 1960s. At the ceremony, Willie Perkins, a member of the Mississippi House of Representatives, noted that although the blues has been characterized as "downtrodden" music, "Mississippi and the world have finally recognized that the blues is about hope." David Jordan, president of the Greenwood City Council and a member of the Mississippi Senate, said that Sumlin, who left the Delta decades before, had returned to Greenwood and found a "complete change in his hometown." Although African Americans have been an oppressed people, he continued, that part of Mississippi's history is "over." Sumlin, who was nearly overwhelmed with emotion, said little other than expressing his gratitude and appreciation. Many of the recipients honored by a blues marker received the recognition posthumously, as in the case of the Nesbit, Mississippi, native Joe Callicott, who died in 1969 at the age of seventy. At the ceremony on March 11, 2010, Velma Brown, Callicott's daughter, told the crowd: "This is a great honor for my dad. He was a country boy that loved playing the blues. It was his passion and all he ever did."[112] As of October 1, 2010, approximately 115 markers have been unveiled in Mississippi;[113] musicians (Howlin' Wolf, James "Son" Thomas, Charley Patton), places (Dockery Farms), and roads (Highways 10 and 61) have been honored. In a 2008 interview, Alex Thomas described the unveiling ceremonies as an emotional event, an opportunity for Mississippi to officially recognize musicians who were once viewed as outcasts:

> *One of the things that I've been able to notice is, you know, honoring somebody like Honeyboy Edwards, who is ninety-three years old, and he comes home and the mayor gives him the key to the city, and he looks up and this marker has images of him. You know, these guys have been all over the globe, they've been in all the little countries around the globe, and there's something about being recognized by your home folk, the state that you came from, and that's what they all tell me.*[114]

The popularity of the Blues Trail has inspired individuals and organizations from throughout the state to send e-mails to Jim O'Neal and other members of the Blues Trail committee, requesting information about specific blues artists who were born (or lived) in a specific Mississippi community. For example, Gay Barnes, a member of the Forest Area Chamber of Commerce, e-mailed O'Neal asking for more information about blues artist Arthur "Big

Boy" Crudup and inquired about the possibility of erecting a marker to honor the musician in conjunction with the town's annual blues festival.

> *We have a festival here in Forest, that's about 4 years old called the Wing Dang Doodle. When coming up for the idea for the festival a few years ago, it was right about the time the legislature got behind marketing the blues as a cultural/tourism/economic development tool, and our thought process was to promote Mississippi's largest agricultural product, chicken, and Mississippi's largest cultural product, the blues together with a chicken wing cooking contest and blues festival. The name, of course, comes from the Willie Dixon tune "Wang Dang Doodle."*[115]

This inquiry clearly suggests that Mississippi communities, once unwilling to promote the blues, are increasingly convinced that blues tourism can be profitable, no matter the tenuous relationship between a community and its specific blues history. Barnes's e-mail also suggests that some tourism officials view blues tourism as working in concert with other marketable Mississippi products. Changing the name of a famous Willie Dixon song to sell chicken may seem laughable at first, but this strategy of cross-promotion is not new. For example, blues festivals highlight the state's best-known agricultural product (Cotton District Arts Festival) and its river culture, the Mississippi River (River to the Rails, Vicksburg Riverfest). Blues tourism has been and will likely to continue to be tied to other marketable products from Mississippi: food (chicken, barbecue), agriculture (cotton), the land (Mississippi River), and history (civil rights). Tourism officials, including Bill Seratt and Cheryl Line, believe that Mississippi needs to market its entire culture heritage, from sharecropping to civil rights.[116] At one level, marketing strategies that associate, for example, the blues with cotton make intuitive sense: many Mississippi blues artists worked as sharecroppers picking cotton and sang about their experiences in song. On the other hand, some of these associations are deeply ironic: the blues was, in part, a response *against* oppressive economic conditions such as sharecropping, where laborers would spend twelve to sixteen hours a day picking cotton under the burning sun. It is doubtful that many tourism officials will recognize this ironic association, promoting instead a narrative that weaves the blues and cotton into a single, seamless narrative.

In the end, the Mississippi Blues Trail symbolizes in a very real way the dramatic changes that have occurred during blues tourism's relatively brief history. Initially viewed with skepticism and indifference, and largely promoted by MACE and a determined group of white blues enthusiasts, blues tourism is now recognized as an important type of economic development and is financially supported by state government, politicians, and other legitimate institutional bodies. The Blues Trail also symbolizes how blues tourism has shifted from a bottom-up approach that encouraged fragmentation and decentralization to a top-down model that favors more coordination between the state, local chambers of commerce and convention and visitors bureaus, and local communities. Without a doubt, many Mississippi communities, once ignorant of their own blues heritage, are now actively promoting the music, hoping that tourist dollars will mitigate the financial exigency and economic stagnation characteristic of many Mississippi communities. As we will see in the next chapter, promotional materials rely heavily on blues myths and seem to be a strategic effort both to project a new, more positive image of Mississippi to the world and to minimize or even erase Mississippi's uncomfortable past.

3

BLUES MYTHS AND THE RHETORICAL IMAGINATION OF PLACE

That stuff Robert [Johnson] done more than fifty years ago, it was a hit with the people, but he didn't get nothing much out of it. Now he's dead and people are making money off his music, trying to get everything they can. The man is dead and people are trying to dig up everything they can dig up about him. It's money they're making off of it or they wouldn't fool with it.

—DAVID "HONEYBOY" EDWARDS, blues musician

After decades of failing to properly appreciate and celebrate the state's blues culture and heritage, Mississippi communities are clamoring to be officially recognized as contributing to the music's long and convoluted historical legacy. For example, Clarksdale has longed proclaimed itself to be both home and birthplace of the blues, an argument largely based on a historical narrative that places many of the genre's most revered blues musicians in the city's juke joints or on the plantations that encircled the area. In contrast, other Delta towns' claim on the blues is more limited, focusing on well-known blues musicians such as Robert Johnson, who died near Greenwood, and B. B. King, who was born near Itta Bena but claims Indianola as his hometown. Even the city of Cleveland, not normally associated with the blues, has deliberately placed itself on the "blues map" by associating itself with W. C. Handy, who around 1905 saw the commercial potential of the blues while performing at a dance in Cleveland.

Mythmaking is an important rhetorical strategy to draw tourists to the region and the state. This is not surprising, since the blues and myth have had a rather interesting and historic relationship. For example, since the 1950s, if not before, some white urbanities (e.g., record collectors, blues fans) who discovered the blues of the 1920s and 1930s rhetorically reimagined popular blues entertainers as "primitive voices from the dark and demonic Delta,"[1] an invention of imagination based largely on a racial mythology that depicts African Americans as emotional and childlike, poor and illiterate. In turn, blues music itself was divested of its complexity and characterized as a "natural outpouring of a simple people" who produced a "charming" and "heartfelt" music rooted in "emotion rather than the product of talent and craft."[2] This racial myth, the blues artist as simple, downtrodden tragic figure, was promoted by record companies, journalists, and blues fans alike. Other myths emerged, including the romanticist vision of the wandering, lone blues musician, alienated and disconnected from society, and the music's association with the occult. Even the musicians themselves constructed and promoted their own myths as a marketing tool to boost their own prominence within the blues community and increase record sales. As blues writer Robert Palmer stated: "Early bluesmen such as Tommy Johnson, Son House, and Muddy Waters knew that invoking hoodoo not only played to the beliefs and fears of their audience in the joints, it was image-making that sold records."[3] There are so many myths associated with the blues that the magazine *Juke Blues* publishes a column called "Blues Facts, Fables, Folktales and Fibs."

Mississippi tourism officials and blues promoters have marketed the myth that the state is the "birthplace of the blues." Promotional materials consistently remind readers that the Mississippi Delta is a timeless, sacred place where the blues was first conceived. An equally compelling story is the crossroads myth, the story of a young man who bargained with the devil to achieve his greatest ambition, to become a world-class musician. Of course, organizations such as the Mississippi Blues Commission did not create these myths; they simply capitalized on preexisting stories to attract tourists to the state. The birthplace myth serves to transform and reimagine the Delta as a holy site. The myth functions to change negative public perceptions of the state while obscuring the same historical realities that led some at one time to call Mississippi the most dangerous state in the union. While the crossroads myth similarly works to transform place, characterizing the Delta as a land of mystery and legend, the racist imagery—black is evil—has largely been ignored for the sinister appeal of the myth itself.

MYTH

In *Mythologies*, Roland Barthes defines myth as a "type of speech," a symbolic message that includes written discourse, photography, and the cinema.[4] In his survey of how scholars have defined myth, William G. Doty emphasizes the narrative or storytelling aspect of myth, characterizing myths as "*complex narratives*, not simple folktales or song-texts."[5] Myths are shaped by the

narrative form, writes Doty, and the story may be constructed as prose, poetry, dialogue, or some other conventional format specific to a culture's literary or oral tradition.[6] Arguing that human beings are, in essence, storytelling
creatures, Walter Fisher defines narration as "symbolic actions—words and/
or deeds—that have sequence and meaning for those who live, create, and interpret them."[7] Myths possess a temporal sequence (a beginning, middle, and
end), major and minor events, and a recognizable theme (e.g., good and evil),
among other narrative elements.

As powerful narratives, myths often involve heroic characters situated in a
significant place and time.[8] Set in the distant past or the future, myths typically take place "outside of the normal world or in a real place possessing
special symbolic power."[9] The Greek myths of the origins of the universe, for
example, exemplify how some stories are situated outside the normal world,
while the American Revolution is an example of an actual historical event
transformed into a mythic story.[10] Set in the future, movies such as *Star Wars*,
with characters like Luke Skywalker and Princess Leia, showcase how mythic
narratives include heroes that vanquish evil and, in turn, act as a "model for
social action."[11] Perhaps because myths embody these narrative and structural
qualities, the term is often commonly associated with pejorative terms such as
"fantasy," "unreal," and "false."

Yet as one scholar correctly noted, myths are not necessarily falsehoods.[12]
At the same time, myths are not the literal historical truth.[13] As Robert C.
Rowland argued, while the "details of the narrative may not reflect historical
events . . . the story is still accepted as 'true' in a larger sense by the culture
in which it is told."[14] Doty argues that through the process of retelling and
repetition, myths often become so internalized within a culture that the narrative's fictional inventiveness is lost, replaced with new, more rigid, qualities
associated with "literal" and "truth."[15] Enacted in rituals and ceremonies, these
powerful stories often produce an emotional audience response, an event that
ensures that myths become "unquestionable truths."[16] Thus both producers
and consumers of myth are complicit in legitimating and perpetuating a culture's most powerful stories.

As many scholars have observed, myths emerge to satisfy human needs. Barthes reminds us that humans "do not have with myth a relationship based on
truth but on use."[17] Doty argues that myths are never trivial stories but instead
involve "perspectives, behaviors, and attitudes that a society considers central
and essential."[18] Myths, for example, perform rhetorical and sociological functions by defining a culture's identity,[19] beliefs, and values,[20] and by validating
an existing "moral order."[21] At the same time, myths function at the psychological level, helping human beings negotiate life crises or personal upheavals,
and at the cosmological level, providing a framework for understanding one's

place in the universe.[22] In all, myths are an essential part of a culture and individual's survival, for as one observer notes: "Myths are needed for society to function and for individuals to find a sense of significance."[23]

BLUES MYTHS

Birthplace of the Blues

One of the most enduring and ubiquitous blues myths is the origin story: the Mississippi Delta (or, alternatively, Mississippi) is the home or birthplace of the blues. In *In Search of the Blues*, Marybeth Hamilton argues that the birthplace myth emerged during the 1960s blues revival as more and more whites became fascinated with the region's blues tradition and history. In an attempt to isolate the cultural boundaries that created the "country blues" (later relabeled as the Delta blues), Hamilton credits the record collector James McKune and later the folklorist Samuel Charters for spreading the gospel about the music's supposed birthplace.[24] While it is certainly true that many of the genre's most impressive and legendary artists, from Muddy Waters to B. B. King, were born or raised in the region, this often-uncontested claim is undercut by at least two problematic issues. While many blues historians will agree that the blues emerged somewhere in the South during the end of the nineteenth century, few will make the definitive claim that the blues originated in the Delta or even in Mississippi.[25] Second, other blues meccas, including Memphis and Chicago, have long claimed to be the "home of the blues." Even Mississippi's neighbor Arkansas promotes *its* Delta region, which includes a key "blues city"—Helena—as the literal birthplace of the blues.[26]

Contrary to the existing scholarly evidence, the state's blues organ, the Mississippi Blues Commission, promotes Mississippi's exclusive claims of the music's birthplace.[27] Similarly, a Mississippi Blues Trail slogan encourages its audience to "experience the blues where they were born." The Mississippi Blues Trail Web site also promises the "casual traveler" or even "die-hard" blues aficionados an informative and enlightening adventure, resulting in "a new appreciation for the area that gave birth to the blues."[28]

Alex Thomas, music development program manager of the Mississippi Blues Trail, defends the birthplace claim, arguing that the most influential blues musicians of the twentieth century were born in Mississippi. He contends that while Memphis, Chicago, and St. Louis, for example, can claim to be the "home" of the blues, where blues musicians lived and called home, *only* the state of Mississippi can make the definitive case of the music's birthplace:

True enough, I can't say I read anywhere that it gave birth in Mississippi. Chicago calls itself the "home of the blues," Memphis, Helena, Arkansas, they all say that they're "home," and I don't have a problem with [what] their saying they're the home of it, but realistically when you look at the origin of the musicians, if you look at the origin of the influential musicians, every birth certificate says Mississippi. So . . . my argument is that they were born in Mississippi, so quite naturally what they learned, what they taught others, what came out of musical genre was born in Mississippi. . . . Look at the most influential blues artists to date, and if you trace the origin from where they came from, it was from Mississippi, and that's why, I personally would stand behind saying that it is the birthplace.[29]

Yet promotional materials rarely distinguish between "home" and "birthplace," sometimes using the two terms interchangeably, and the various descriptions of the birth of blues describe the state not as the "birthplace of the most influential blues musicians" but as the literal spot where the blues originated—where it was conceived and born. There is a significant difference between the two claims, one that arguably most blues tourists will not understand or even care about. Instead the birthplace myth is rarely contested by consumers because it underscores an equally powerful and compelling argument about the region's authenticity.

Meanwhile, the state has gone beyond simply making claims about the blues' birthplace. Mississippi, according to some, "birthed" not only the blues but America's popular music. The Mississippi Development Authority/Tourism Division offered an audacious claim about the state's cultural legacy: "From blues legends Robert Johnson, Muddy Waters and B. B. King to the king of rock 'n roll, Elvis Presley, to the father of country music, Jimmie Rodgers," Mississippi is "the *only place* you'll find the history, heritage, legends and folklore that surround the sounds of America's music" (italics mine).[30] In May 2009, Haley Barbour unveiled new state welcome signs, "Birthplace of America's Music," which have been placed in a variety of locations, including the Mississippi Welcome Center in Vicksburg and on U.S. Highway 61 in DeSoto County. "I dare say, no state has a greater claim on the slogan 'Birthplace of America's Music' than Mississippi," proclaimed the governor, "and no state's governor could be as proud as I am . . . with this recognition."[31]

Whether promoting itself as the birthplace of the blues or the birthplace of American music, tourism officers and blues organizers never let potential visitors forget about the origin story. The brochure "The Mississippi Delta: Where the Music Meets the Soul" encourages the reader to "give in to it. Your yearning to see where it started. . . . Follow the beat of your heart to the land of the blues." The brief textual narrative is surrounded by a variety of color photos, including a predictable and romantic image of a musician play-ing an acoustic guitar in the middle of a railroad track, his face masked by shadows from a setting sun.[32] "These music pioneers put their lives to music," claims the "Greenville on the Mississippi" brochure, and they gave "birth" to the blues, "laying the cornerstones of jazz, rock and roll and many other original American music forms."[33] In another example, a colorful brochure (with a drawing of Muddy Waters in the foreground and the Hopson Planta-tion in the background) claims Clarksdale and Coahoma County as "the land where the Blues began."[34] Erroneously claiming that Muddy Waters was born in Clarksdale (he was born in Rolling Fork, Mississippi), another advertise-ment claims that blues singing "comes naturally to most folks here" because Clarksdale is both "THE crossroads" and the "land where blues began."[35] As visitors approach the outskirts of Clarksdale on Highway 61, they see a water tower with the message: "Come to the Crossroads—Birthplace of the Blues." Playing up the birthplace myth, Morgan Freeman, Bill Luckett, and How-ard Stovall were inspired to name their Clarksdale blues club "Ground Zero" because, according to the promotional materials, "it all started here."[36] In his foreword to *Highway 61: Heart of the Delta*, Freeman elaborates on why he believes Clarksdale is the "legendary home of the blues":

> *The Delta blues actually originated right here. This is where Robert Johnson supposedly sold his soul to the Devil one dark night at a crossroads near High-way 61, and that was the beginning of the modern blues. But the blues really started a hundred or two hundred years ago. When European orchestras were playing Beethoven and Bach in opera houses, a beautiful thing, the blues, was created right here at the same time, in back rooms, under shade trees, beside cotton gins, and in little juke joints all over the Delta.[37]*

Promotional materials even employ agricultural metaphors as proof that the Delta is the literal root of the blues. For example, a brochure from the Greenville-Washington County Convention and Visitors Bureau explains that the "fields of the Mississippi Delta gave birth to the music known as the Blues and to dozens of musicians who have taken the music from these fertile fields to the far corners of the world."[38] Claiming that Coahoma County is the home of "more blues musicians per capita than any other place on earth," another guide unequivocally states that the blues was born in the cotton fields of the Mississippi Delta.[39] And contending that the Delta is the "cradle of the blues," the Greenville-Washington County Convention and Visitors Bureau promotes Greenville's annual blues festival, the Mississippi Delta Blues and Heritage Festival, by claiming that the festival celebrates the blues "in the fields where it was born."[40] Finally, the Clarksdale Downtown Development

Association uses the roots metaphor to tell the story of the music's birth: "Clarksdale is the place to explore the history of the Blues, from the cotton plantations where it found its roots, to the local juke joints where it first was heard."[41] In all, tourism officials would like visitors to believe that the blues literally emerged from the ground, a seed once planted and now ripe for harvest and consumption.

The birthplace myth has gained further credibility from local and national media sources. For example, Victoria Pope, a reporter for *U.S. News and World Report*, claims that the "blues came out of the Delta plantations when cotton was king and thousands of blacks toiled on flat, fertile farms that went on for miles."[42] Reporting in Clarksdale, Jay Brakefield of the *Dallas Morning News* suggested to readers that "if you could pick a spot where the blues began, it would be right around here."[43] *San Francisco Chronicle* writer Douglas Cruickshank called the Mississippi Delta the "fountainhead" of the blues, "the place where it all began."[44] The *Mississippi Business Journal* referred to Clarksdale as the "cradle of the genre" and to Mississippi as the birthplace of the blues.[45] Headlines such as "Don't Miss Mississippi Delta, Birthplace of Blues," "Blues Had Birth in Mississippi Delta," "Tour Map Marks the Spots Where Blues Was Birthed," and "Guiding Pilgrims to Holy Land of the Blues" all signify how the birthplace myth has impressed the imagination of journalists, who are themselves seeking to catch the attention of interested readers.[46]

The birthplace myth is often supported by the romanticized story of W. C. Handy discovering the blues at a train station in Tutwiler sometime around 1903; in around 1905, Handy claimed to have heard the blues again at a dance in Cleveland, Mississippi. As the story goes, an audience member requested that Handy and his band, after failing to impress the audience with a request to play some "native music," take a short break to allow a "long-legged chocolate boy" and his band to play a type of music, characterized, according to Handy, as "primitive."[47] A brochure from the Cleveland–Bolivar County Chamber of Commerce claims that it is "*highly likely* that Charley Patton and Willie Brown were in this trio of musicians" (italics mine).[48] This is highly doubtful and a vivid example of how some tourism officials resort to skewing truth to captivate the feverous imagination of tourists. Elliott Hurwitt, a music historian who has spent fifteen years researching W. C. Handy, is skeptical that Patton or Brown were the musicians who showed Handy the commercial possibilities of blues music. Hurwitt argues that while it is possible that Patton could have been one of the musicians mentioned in Handy's autobiography, the identification of Patton smacks of historical convenience, for Patton has been identified (incorrectly) as the musician who serenaded Handy at the Tutwiler train station.[49] For example, Richard Carlin claims, without providing any evidence, that Charley Patton's performance "intrigued" Handy about this musical form.[50] According to Hurwitt, "People always want to pin a famous name on an incident or anecdote, because it's more satisfying to tie things up in a neat bundle, and then say, 'that's it.'" In 1905, Brown was four or five (he was born on August 16, 1900), making his participation, for all practical purposes, impossible. In his research, Hurwitt found a draft of Handy's memoir *Father of the Blues*, which identifies one of the musicians, a local band leader by the name of Prince McCoy (the name was excised from the published version). Hurwitt is skeptical that McCoy was actually present that night because McCoy was not a poor, illiterate musician: "The trouble is that Prince McCoy led a respectable brass band in the Delta region, just as Handy did. He does not at all sound like the illiterate bumpkin in rags described by Handy in the book and elsewhere." He concedes that without additional reliable and verifiable documentation, blues historians may never know the identities of the three musicians.[51]

In one of Cleveland's few claims to the blues, the city erected a historical marker of the event and celebrated the new memorial with an unveiling ceremony in April 1998. Yet it is important to point out that Handy first heard the blues in St. Louis in 1892, roughly a decade before he supposedly discovered the blues in Mississippi.[52] Based on her research, Harriet Ottenheimer concludes that all the pre-blues or blues music sightings in the Delta occurred after 1900.[53] Moreover, according to other blues scholars, the blues was heard in Alabama, Louisiana, Missouri, and other locations during the early twentieth century. As blues writer Francis Davis put it: "The blues turn[ed] up in too many other places around the same time to support the theory that this music was once exclusive to Mississippi."[54] Regardless, like other Delta towns, the city of Tutwiler has made efforts to claim its authority by erecting a mock train depot with the sign "The 'Home' of the Blues."

Other blues promoters have made even more fantastic claims concerning the exact location of where the music was born—Dockery Farms—located on Highway 8 between Cleveland and Ruleville. Will Dockery established the farm in 1895. By 1937 the responsibility of managing the plantation had passed to his son, Joe, who in turn managed the farm until 1982 (the farm is no longer in operation). At one point, approximately four hundred families lived on the plantation, including the highly religious Patton family, whose rebellious son, Charley, became one of the early stars of the down-home blues.[55] Other blues musicians, from Willie Brown to Howlin' Wolf, also worked at the plantation from the 1920s to the 1940s.[56] With the number of blues musicians who worked on the plantation and the erroneous claim that Charley Patton invented the blues, there is little surprise that Dockery's stock has risen with blues tourists, particularly since the advent of the 1960s blues revival. The Dockery Farm Web site perpetuates the birthplace myth:

The migration of whites and blacks to the Delta to cultivate cotton created a culture which in turn gave birth to the Blues. By the 1920's Dockery Farms had grown to a community of several thousand workers and it was home to a number of Blues pioneers, among them Henry Sloan, Charley Patton, Willie Brown, Tommy Johnson, and Roebuck "Pop" Staples. It was at Dockery that these musicians lived and learned from one another. . . . Their songs would influence the development of popular music all over the world.[57]

Many blues promoters and tourism organizations have claimed that Dockery is where the blues originated; some qualify the assertion by arguing that the Delta blues, a subgenre of the blues, was born at Dockery. Sweet Magnolia Tours, for example, claims that Dockery is known throughout the "Blues World" as the "true birthplace of the Blues."[58] The Blues Highway Association claims that since a number of blues "originators," including Charley Patton, Son House, and Willie Brown, lived at Dockery, the former plantation is "the birthplace of the Delta blues."[59] Claiming that Dockery Farms is "really [the] only *one* blues site," Curtis Hewston, the creator of the Web site The Blues Highway, argued that during the period when Charley Patton, Willie Brown, and others lived at the plantation, "the beginning of the blues as we know it" emerged at Dockery Farms.[60] The "Roots of Rhythm," a British-based tourism operation, claimed that plantations like Dockery are "where the blues grew up."[61] In April 2006, when Dockery was inducted into the National Register of Historic Places, a local TV anchor from WXTV, a Greenville station, claimed that Dockery was where "the blues was born."[62]

The myth surrounding Dockery has captured the imagination of tourists and musicians, who have reported visiting one of the shrines of the blues. In his Web diary, Glenn Gass, professor of music at Indiana University, narrated his 1992 journey through the Delta, a "mesmerizing landscape of haunted towns, plantations, roads, rivers, and railroad lines." Gass described Dockery Farms as the place where "Charlie Patton grew up and learned to play and, for all intents and purposes, the Delta blues was born."[63] When Dutch musician and television celebrity Cor Bakker and a film crew visited the Delta in early 2001 to shoot footage for the television special *Cor on Tour*, he toured Dockery and told a *Bolivar Commercial* reporter that "it was great—just great to be where the blues started."[64] On the Web site Voodoo Girls' Blues Pilgrimage, two women chronicled their experience traveling throughout the Delta in search of Dockery Farms:

Well, well, well,......the days have become a blur. What day is today??? Blue Friday. Yesterday we passed through the land of Colt 45 and Heaven Hill Whiskey and we have it on good authority that this is what the real blues people

drink so for authenticity we have started to drink it too. We got off Hwy 61 and
on to Hwy 8 in search of where it all started. . . . Dockery Farms.[65]

The Mississippi Blues Trail project has provided a much-needed and important correction to the Dockery myth and, implicitly, to the contention that the blues was born in Mississippi. On April 19, 2008, the Dockery blues trail marker was unveiled on the hallowed ground of the old plantation in front of an enthusiastic audience of mostly white spectators. The marker's signature line, "Birthplace of the Blues?", clearly signifies (with a question mark) the impossibility of linking the music's origins to Dockery. Yet while acknowledging that the "precise origins of the blues are lost in time," Jim O'Neal and Scott Barretta (who are responsible for crafting the text for each individual marker) contend that Dockery was "one of the primary centers" for the blues.[66]

Although Dockery is a private residence (private tours of the property are available), it will be become an increasingly public tourist destination. Led by William Lester, a Delta State University art professor emeritus and executive director of the Dockery Farms Foundation, the former plantation is undergoing a much-needed makeover, with plans to open Dockery to the public in 2011. In March 2010, the National Park Service of the U.S. Department of the Interior awarded the Dockery Restoration Project a $177,000 matching-funds Save America's Treasures grant. The money will be used to renovate a number of buildings on the former plantation, including the service station that was built in the 1940s but has since fallen into disrepair. Eventually the service station will include a classroom (for education programs) and a café for tourists. A parking lot will be built to accommodate tour buses. Lester hopes a restored Dockery Farms will showcase the region's blues heritage as well as the Delta's agricultural (cotton) culture.[67]

Beyond serving as an origin story, the birthplace myth also reinforces the image of the Mississippi Delta as the last vestige of an "unpolluted" and "pure" blues culture, a region of the country that has seemingly remained unchanged for decades. Tourism officials and blues promoters often frame the Delta as a timeless and sacred place. A Mississippi Blues Trail advertisement urges tourists to "go back in time and experience the worlds of dozens of blues legends."[68] The Greenville–Washington County Convention and Visitors Bureau invites tourists to experience the "mystique" of Greenville, where the "culture and heritage of the past still thrive in a timeless land."[69] Greenwood's Convention and Visitors Bureau describes Sylvester Hoover's Greenwood-based Back in the Day Museum as a place where Hoover takes "you on a trip back in time as he leads you through the life of blues legends such as John Hurt and Eddie 'Guitar Slim' [Jones]."[70] As historian John Bodnar pointed out, cultural authorities rearticulate the past "on an abstract basis of timelessness and sacredness."[71]

Yet since the 1920s and 1930s, when Mississippi's blues culture was a thriving, innovative musical force, the region has undergone significant economic and cultural changes. Even scholars at that time recognized the inevitability of impermanence. In 1941, Alan Lomax collaborated with Lewis Jones and Charles Johnson, two African American sociologists from Fisk University, to document, through an extensive ethnographic study, African American folksongs in Coahoma County. Contrary to the prevailing narrative, one that still exerts a powerful influence on the imaginations of tourists and cultural producers alike, the Delta was not a rural backwater area isolated and frozen in some feudal past but rather "fast-paced" and "worldly," particularly in comparison to that state's other decidedly conservative regions.[72] In a 1947 article published in *Social Forces*, sociologist Samuel C. Adams Jr. explained the reasons for the rapid cultural changes in the Delta:

> *This [change] has come about as a result of the breakdown of isolation, increase in literacy, in the growing importance of the press and other printed matter; the awakening interest of the people toward the movies, the radio, the juke box, and general city ways. . . . The tales which flourish today on the plantation are mainly the worldly stories. These stories have their place in the new scheme of living, peculiar to the younger generation. The fact that on the plantation the stories about Hitler and the other international characters exist, shows clearly that [the] plantation is no longer an isolated world.*[73]

To be sure, the Delta has experienced significant social and cultural changes: depopulation (largely a result of agricultural mechanization), changing racial demographics (growing Hispanic population), economic stagnation, new industries (gambling), white flight, and racial integration (although many Delta communities are mired in a type of de facto segregation). Moreover, this blues haven has witnessed the death of a number of blues musicians and the destruction of numerous blues sites. Although the title of Steve Cheseborough's travel book, *Blues Traveling: The Holy Sites of Delta Blues*, accentuates the image of the Delta as hallowed ground, he has no illusions about the Delta, for he hopes to help tourists find "what *is* left in the Mississippi blues world."[74] According to another observer, blues tourists travel to the Delta to "look at things that aren't there anymore."[75] Still, according to Jim O'Neal, the Delta's flat, monotonous, largely agrarian landscape provides the illusion of time standing still, a product of willful imagination:

> *There's some romanticism about the blues in the minds of tourists, I guess, and readers from afar who imagine it [the Delta] just like it used to be. And you*

can drive through the Delta and think, wow, it must have been like this for decades and decades. . . . Things do change slowly, but the thing that's really different is that during the period when all the blues was developing when you looked out across those plantations you would see lots of houses out there and now they're empty. And the downtowns would be thriving, those little towns, every little town would have something going on Saturday night. And now it seems more desolate, you know, and more vacant, but that's a bluesy image, too. Some people probably think it has always been like it is now.[76]

In all, tourism officials seek to promote the Delta as the birthplace of not only the blues but America's popular culture. The birthplace argument is further supported by depictions of the Delta as a timeless, permanent, "holy" place where blues music has not been infected and diluted by the ills of contemporary life: a disposable culture based on rampant commercialism and consumerism, mass production and duplication. This provides relief and comfort to blues fans who are repelled by the more curious and commercialized aspect of blues entrepreneurship, including the bar-restaurant chain House of Blues. Created by Isaac Tigrett (the owner of the highly successful franchise, the Hard Rock Café), the House of Blues serves not only to celebrate southern culture and the contributions of African Americans to the arts but to "celebrate the diversity and brotherhood of world culture" and "promote racial and spiritual harmony through love, peace, truth, righteousness and nonviolence."[77] Despite Tigrett's supposed allegiance to this traditional African American musical form, the House of Blues is a study in contrast and irony, for the bar's flashing lights and mostly white clientele subvert the owner's attempt to "recreate the ambiance of a funky Southern juke joint."[78] In contrast to the crass commercialization of the House of Blues, the Mississippi Delta is the "real deal," to quote the promotional materials, a place where the blues has been preserved, a place waiting to be discovered, admired, and eventually consumed.

Many Mississippians take pride in knowing that their state has been widely acknowledged as the birthplace of the blues. The birthplace myth clearly indicates that the state now celebrates and embraces a cultural product that had once been dismissed as a pathological response by black poverty culture. Only in recent years has the state actively engaged in advertising itself as the "birthplace of the blues"; in fact, some local whites and African Americans expressed skepticism about the importance and relevance of promoting the music as part of the state's overall tourism strategy. To be sure, some skepticism still exists today, but more and more Mississippians are aware that promoting the blues, if nothing else, can produce an important stream of revenue. As Ted Gioia argued, "Blues music, so despised by the masters of the region in earlier years, looms larger and larger in the region's self-identity and economy with each passing decade, until it has come to represent the most promising substitute for the riches no longer given up freely by the soil."[79]

The birthplace myth also works to challenge competing, depressing stories about Mississippi's tragic and brutal history of racial oppression and enforced segregation, as well as contemporary perceptions of the state as a home to racism, poverty, unemployment, illiteracy, teenage pregnancy, and other social ills. In contrast to the images of racial terror and death (lynching) so commonly associated with Mississippi, the "hospitality state" is now widely recognized (especially by blues fans) as having given birth to the blues and American popular music, a highly significant and positive contribution to the performing arts. The state portrays itself in a radically new and different way; the positive, life-affirming birth metaphor confounds stereotypes and attempts to reframe and reconstitute long-standing and habitual, negative perceptions. The "deathplace" is now the "birthplace." Concerned about the state's racist image, it is no wonder that skeptics who challenge the birthplace myth are often met with a verbal challenge, a dismissive response, even ridicule.

Yet, as discussed earlier, the central component of the birthplace myth—the story of how the blues was born—all but ignores the material conditions that served as the impetus for the development of the blues. In promotional materials, not surprisingly, the history of slavery and its terrible aftermath—lynching, convict leasing, Jim Crow laws, sharecropping—remain conspicuously silent, lost, and forgotten. In this mythic story, the roots metaphor is particularly troubling. Tourism narratives recast the field—the site where exploited farmhands toiled for minimal financial rewards under the watchful eye of the bossman—as the earthly mother who gave birth to the blues. This revisionist historical account fails to highlight the region's ideology of white supremacy, its exploitative and brutal employment practices, and the agents of oppression (white planters, politicians) responsible for vigorously supporting the Delta's way of life to satisfy their insatiable need for personal entitlement and class privilege. Since the field gave birth to the blues, and not the black underclass, the birthplace narrative often fails to properly acknowledge the black community's significant role in the creation of one of the United States' first original musical forms. In turn, this strategy of omission allows the rhetorical space for Delta whites to claim some legitimate ownership of the blues based on proximity. That is, the blues was born in the fields and thus became property, like cotton or soybeans, for those who owned the land. When African Americans do appear in the narrative, their occupation is often depicted in neutral or positive terms, as workers or farmers rather than an exploited underclass. Similarly, the narrative fails to acknowledge the difficult working conditions and abject poverty experienced by the black sharecropping class who gave birth to the blues. In all, the birthplace myth privileges a historical memory that favors the perspective of the ruling white class, one that ultimately denies the region's historical record of exploitation and brutality, absolves the economic system (and its agents) that created the region's disparity between the wealthy and the poor, and minimizes the active role African Americans played in the creation and development of the blues.

The Crossroads Myth

There has probably been more romantic foolishness written about the blues in general, and Robert Johnson in particular, than about any other genre or performer of the twentieth century.
—ELIJAH WARD, *Escaping the Delta*

The story of Robert Johnson selling his soul to the devil at the crossroads is a popular and ever-present myth that tourism officials and blues organizers enjoy using as much as, or even more than, the birthplace myth. The original crossroads story, rooted in West African cosmology, did not include the menacing underworld figure of Satan but was about a trickster figure called Esu Elegbara, a powerful West African deity.[80] Esu's predominant role is to serve as a mediator, "the guardian of the crossroads," between the sacred and profane, because Esu "interprets the will of the gods to man" and "carries the desires of man to the gods." As the creator of speech and language, Esu's interpretations are fraught with irony, uncertainty, and indeterminacy.[81] While Esu exploits the ambiguity of language as part of his trick, he also makes mystical and sacred knowledge accessible to humanity. Situated within the African cosmological frame, Esu is not a demon or the devil but rather, as one observer characterized, a "musical instructor," a mentor who encourages the musician to become the "voice of his people or grants the young man access to musical knowledge."[82] Through the lens of a white Christian worldview, however, the rebellious African deity was transformed into the more recognizable, more comfortable, image of Satan. In his book *Blues and Evil*, Jon Michael Spencer argued that the "demonization" of African gods like Esu was an unfortunate by-product of the "imposition of Christianity's bifurcating worldview (the sacred versus the profane) on the holistic cosmology of this people of African origin."[83] It should also be noted that many black Christians swallowed this Western characterization of Esu, firmly believing that the blues was the "devil's music" and the crossroads a literal place of human decision and eternal damnation. Biographies of Son House, Howlin' Wolf, and Skip James, for example, illustrate both parental disapproval of the blues and the musicians' own ambivalence and fears about playing secular-based music.

By the nineteenth century, the crossroads myth was already a well-established story within African American folklore, particularly by practitioners of voodoo-hoodoo, a folk-magic religion largely practiced by African Americans.[84] Although the crossroads myth has been retold with variations over the years, the story basically involves a black musician who, desperate to unlock the mystery of his guitar and achieve worldly fame as a result, encounters Satan (who is also black) at a crossroads on a deserted country road at midnight and agrees to exchange his soul for newfound musical powers. While that story has been most often attributed to Robert Johnson, there is no credible evidence that Robert Johnson ever claimed he sold his soul to the devil. It was, in fact, Tommy Johnson (no relation) who made claims that he made a pact with Satan.[85] A contemporary of both Robert and Tommy Johnson, Peetie Wheatstraw (William Bunch), also made allusions to the occult, calling himself the "Devil's Son-in-Law" and the "High Sheriff of Hell." Barry Lee Pearson and Bill McCulloch, authors of *Robert Johnson: Lost and Found*, a critical examination of the Johnson myth, cite other blues performers (Lonnie Johnson, Charlie Jordan, Tampa Red, Bessie Smith) who—while never proclaiming to have fallen under the spell of Satan—sang about hell and the devil. During the 1930s and 1940, a number of songs referenced the devil, leading Pearson and McCulloch to claim that "there was a minicraze of devil songs" during this period.[86] One would, of course, be hard pressed to believe any of these claims of soul bargaining because, among other reasons, it is clear that blues musicians employed satanic imagery to promote themselves, motivated by prestige and profit. As Gioia effectively argued: "Just as satanic rockers would find their niche market a half century later, a group of early blues singers embraced the harshest attacks their critics leveled at them—deviltry, blasphemy, apostasy, call it what you will—and tried to turn them into marks, if not of distinction, at least of notoriety."[87]

Although Robert Johnson was certainly not the first blues musician to have alluded to a bargain with the devil, the Faust story is most intimately associated with him, and so a brief biographical sketch is in order. Born in Hazlehurst, Mississippi, in 1911, Johnson was the illegitimate child of Julia Major Dodds and a farmhand named Noah Johnson (her other ten children were sired with Charles Dodds).[88] Johnson and his mother moved to Memphis to join Dodds, who, in 1909 or 1910, had moved from Hazlehurst to Memphis because of a dispute with a white landowner; Dodds also lost his farm in foreclosure.[89] The marriage soon ended. By all accounts, Johnson despised working in the fields and believed that he could make a living as a musician. In 1930, while living near Robinsonville, Mississippi, Johnson met Son House and Willie Brown, a meeting that fueled his musical ambitions. However, Johnson's musical career seemed doomed because he simply lacked the technical ability to play the guitar, let alone sing and write his own songs. Son House remembered Johnson's painful attempt to play the guitar, as told to a reporter in 1968 for the *Saturday Review*:

> *Sure I remember Robert. Originally he was a good mouth-harp player. When he was about sixteen or seventeen, I guess, he used to sneak out to try to play with me and Willie [Brown]. He used to follow us around and he didn't like to work. Especially in the fields. He used to sit and watch my hands, like I did with Willie Wilson, when I played. When we were playing and took a break he'd pick up my guitar and try to play it. He made some pretty awful sounds. I used to tell him to stop before the people got mad and run us all off.*[90]

A few years later, Johnson stunned House and Brown with his guitar virtuosity while playing at a juke joint in Banks, Mississippi. While the devil-dealing tale has been exploited to explain Johnson's sudden musical transformation, a more compelling reason may be Johnson's considerable work ethic. After being rejected by fellow musicians and jeering audiences, Johnson returned to his birthplace, Hazlehurst, during the early 1930s and studied under Ike Zimmerman. Zimmerman, who had a local reputation as a stellar performer and a skilled guitarist, invited Johnson to live with him for a short time, and guitar lessons occurred in a cemetery.[91] After he left Hazlehurst, Johnson spent the rest of his life visiting different parts of the United States, playing on street corners and at juke joints, eventually recording for the American Record Corporation in November 1936 and June 1937.[92] These sessions produced all Johnson's most memorable songs, "Cross Road Blues," "Terraplane Blues," and "Hellhound on My Trail." Claiming Johnson's music to be "ageless," one music critic argued that no other blues musician can "match the vividness of Johnson's explications of a world where all options have been closed out, where the last fair deal has gone down."[93] Johnson's options closed forever when he died in 1938 at the age of twenty-seven near Greenwood, Mississippi. Ever the womanizer, Johnson's glass of whiskey was supposedly spiked with poison by an unidentified man who was angry that the blues musician was flirting with his wife.

Since Johnson's death in 1938, the devil myth has been propagated by a number of sources, including Johnson's own work. In "Cross Road Blues," Johnson sang about his trip to the crossroads (although he never indicated in the song that he sold his soul to the devil). The singer's early death seemed to suggest, at least to some, the completion of the supernatural bargain. In 1966, Son House supposedly told journalist Pete Welding that Johnson did indeed sell his soul, although subsequent efforts to confirm the veracity of House's testimony were unsuccessful.[94]

Some members of the African American community, mostly ministers and concerned parents, have longed associated the blues with Satanism. In 2004, for example, the majority of the members of the Little Zion Missionary Baptist Church were appalled that their pastor, McArthur McKinley, did not block efforts to honor Johnson at the church; it is believed that Johnson is buried in the church's cemetery. One outraged member told the *Greenwood Commonwealth*, "The blues and the church are separate, and they should not be mixed."[95] Arguably, the film *Crossroads* (1986) moved the Johnson myth into the cultural mainstream. In the movie, a young white boy, played by Ralph Macchio, enlisted the help of a veteran blues musician, Willie Brown, to find a lost blues song. In turn, Brown asked the young man to travel to the crossroads to help him redeem his soul from the devil. Blues researcher Gayle Dean Wardlow believes that because of the movie, the crossroads story has been transformed in the minds of many from legend to fact.[96] Finally, record companies, music journalists, white blues fans, and even some blues scholars have mythologized Johnson's supposed dealings with the underworld to sell more records or further ingrain in the public consciousness a romanticized vision of the blues.[97]

Fortunately for the city of Clarksdale, a crossroads (the intersection of U.S. Highways 49 and 61) is located within the city limits. The city has erected a monument of sorts at the supposed crossroads, a sign that contains "61" and "49," three blues guitars, and the words "The Crossroads." Brochures, guides, and other promotional items highlight Clarkdale's commercialized crossroads site. The Mississippi Tourism Association plays up the crossroads connection by stating that "bluesman Robert Johnson is said to have lost his soul here."[98] The Coahoma County Tourism Commission's Web site encourages those who believe in the crossroads story to travel to the sacred spot where the "dubious deal was deemed to have been devined."[99] In another brochure, Clarksdale advertises itself as the "#1 stop on the Blues Highway . . . where the best of the Delta comes together at the Crossroads."[100] "The Path Finder" brochure changes course slightly as the writer highlights the supposed "original Crossroads" (the intersection of Martin Luther King Drive and East Tallahatchie Avenue where old U.S. Highway 61 crosses old U.S. Highway 49), a place where it is the tourist's "best bet for authentic 'Crossroads' experience."[101] Without hesitation or qualification, the Mississippi Development Authority/ Tourism Division advertises the crossroads as the literal spot where Johnson made his pact with Satan:

> *When you arrive in Clarksdale, start at the crossroads—literally—the famed crossroads of Highways 49 and 61 which is the site of where legendary blues man Robert Johnson sold his soul to the devil in order to master the guitar. A*

large sign with crossed guitars marks the spot of this diabolical deal in Delta lore. Highway 61 runs north to south and is often referred to as the "Blues Highway."[102]

The crossroads sign is perhaps the most emblematic, certainly one of the most pictured, iconic images that appears in promotional materials about the Delta blues. The Coahoma County Tourism Commission has purchased a number of promotional products, from small picture frames to plastic CD holders, that feature the image of the Highway 61/49 sign. These items are often mailed, along with brochures about the area, to inquiring potential tourists. The sign is, of course, shown in isolation, separated from its commercial surroundings, to make it appear more authentic than its present location would suggest. The commission's Web site takes this visual strategy one step further: a cropped image of the crossroads sign is juxtaposed against another image of rows of brown, harvested cotton fields.[103]

In another example, a brochure titled "Chasin' the Ghost of the Crossroads" shows an image of the crossroads sign located in a deserted countryside, a cotton field in full bloom. Underneath the sign is an African American (presumably Robert Johnson) holding an acoustic guitar and looking into the distance, apparently waiting for Satan to materialize.[104] These mythic representations of the crossroads dislocate the sign in time and space, turning the sign's commercialized surroundings into a far more enjoyable tourist fantasy.

Other blues organizations and attractions exploit the crossroads myth for economic gain. Because of Robert Johnson's connection with the small town of Rosedale (he mentions Rosedale in "Traveling Riverside Blues"), Rosedale's blues society calls itself the Crossroads Blues Society, and the city's blues festival is, predictably, named after the famous crossroads. In Greenwood, two museums (Back in the Day and the Greenwood Blues Heritage Museum and Gallery) are dedicated to Robert Johnson. A multi-million-dollar crossroads theme park and entertainment complex is currently being planned for Clarksdale. The Delta Blues Museum's permanent exhibit contains several examples of crossroads imagery, including a colorful painting of a traveler (perhaps Johnson himself) dancing in the middle of a highway (the crossroads?) under a full moon. The African American male is holding a snake, a common image associated with Satan in the Bible, blissfully unaware of the reptile's (or Satan's) deadly reputation. In another example, the owners of the Shack Up Inn—who had at one time referred to themselves as the Shackmeisters—described the birth of their blues-oriented lodging attraction. The Shackmeisters

wound up at midnight, on the same night, at the same crossroads. There the deal was made. As lightning flashed in the delta skies and thunder rolled across the moonlit cotton fields, the five shackmeisters, cypress prophets all, forged a bond stronger than old oak and new rope. Their mission, to bring the blues home to the cradle and rock the tourists in the process. Like hellhounds on their trail, the shacks have overtaken the Shackmeisters, to the benefit [of] millions of blues lovers from around the world.[105]

While the sinister and mysterious crossroads myth may be titillating to tourists, the actual crossroads may be a disappointment. The mythical intersection is located not on some backwater, isolated country road but on Clarksdale's busiest thoroughfare, a street that contains gas stations and fast food restaurants, including Kentucky Fried Chicken, Burger King, and Mc-Donalds. One writer lamented that the "mystic significance" of the famed crossroads has been reduced to the "corporate semiology of golden arches."[106] The crossroads sign is located across the street from a convenience store (Double Quick) and next to Abe's, a locally owned restaurant known for its barbecue sandwiches and ribs. According to Steve Cheseborough, if "Johnson or any other bluesmen sold their souls to the devil at the crossroads, they probably would have picked a more remote location."[107] Tourists may also be dismayed to learn that the "crossroads," Highways 61 and 49, intersect more than once, including seventeen miles north of Clarksdale.

Four Delta counties (Coahoma, Bolivar, Sunflower, Copiah) are laying claim to possessing the definitive crossroads site.[108] The Mississippi Development Authority/Tourism Division speculates that Johnson sold his soul near Dockery Farms, some forty-five miles south of Clarksdale.[109] As Bill Seratt, a member of the Mississippi Blues Commission, put it: "You know damn good and well that Highway 61 and 49 are not the crossroads. Clarksdale laid claim to being the crossroads about thirty years ago so, therefore, a lot of not very deep blues enthusiasts really think they're at the crossroads. But we all know they're not."[110] Instead, as geographer Robert N. Brown asserts, it is Hazlehurst (Johnson's birthplace), not Clarksdale, that "has the geographic credentials to make such claims to mythic landscapes . . . because it is that region [located approximately fifty miles south of the Delta] to which Robert Johnson retreated for the few years in which his talents blossomed."[111]

Moreover, Johnson's association with the devil has been, to say the least, overplayed. In an analysis of Johnson's recording sessions and the twenty-nine songs he recorded over four days in 1936 and 1937, blues researcher Elijah Wald discusses a number of themes in Johnson's music (e.g., women,) but rarely mentions Johnson and the devil. In a separate analysis by Pearson and McCulloch, only one song ("Me and the Devil Blues") makes specific reference to the devil.[112] One other song title includes the word "devil" ("Preachin' Blues [Up Jumped the Devil]"), but the song itself does not mention Satan, and Wald speculates that Johnson was not aware of the parenthetical addition—possibility drummed up by a music executive who wanted to attract the attention of fans of Peetie Wheatstraw.[113] The song "Cross Road Blues," often referenced as evidence of Johnson's supposed deal, never mentions the devil or the soul sale, although Johnson pleads with the Lord to "save poor Bob, if you please." In "Hellhound on My Trail," Johnson sings about being pursued by "hell hounds" while the blues is "falling down like hail." Pearson and McCulloch argue that the song is actually a "blues poem" about the life of an itinerant blues musician and his transitory relationship with women.[114] After meticulously examining Johnson's body of work, Pearson and McCulloch conclude:

> *Taken individually or as a group, the twenty-nine recorded songs offer no verifiable information on which to base a claim that Johnson was paranoiac, tormented, self-destructive, disillusioned, or any of the other dark characterizations that have been put forward. . . . Nor do the song texts offer evidentiary support for claims that Johnson believed he had sold his soul to the devil, that he was "drawn to the texture" of being in league with Satan, or that he encouraged people around him to believe that he had made a pact with the devil.*[115]

Finally, Johnson's fellow blues musicians have almost uniformly rejected Johnson's involvement with the devil. David "Honeyboy" Edwards, who occasionally performed with Johnson, seems to suggest in his autobiography that if Johnson visited the crossroads, he did so for musical inspiration rather than any desperate attempt to trade his soul for musical genius.[116] Robert Jr. Lockwood's (Johnson's stepson) empathetic denial is particularly powerful:

> *And all that bullshit about him selling hisself to the devil, that's bullshit. 'Cause if he's sold to the devil, I'm sold to the devil. As far as you selling yourself to the devil, you already sold to the devil if you don't pray. [If] you don't put forth a good effort to redeem yourself, you already sold.*[117]

Yet there is no doubt that the tale possesses its own intrinsic and extrinsic pleasures for tourists and the general public. George Lipsitz is not surprised that the Mississippi blues tourism industry exploits the crossroads myth, for the "story has proven its extraordinary appeal and exceptional commercial value over and over again."[118] Beyond the commercial appeal, Johnson's devil story reimagines the Delta in much the same way as the birthplace myth depicts the Delta as a timeless world, the last vestige of a pure, unpolluted blues culture. The crossroads myth depicts the Delta as a land of intrigue, a place where shady deals go down on back roads at midnight. Tourism officials are certainly aware of the power of this depiction, as the Delta is often promoted as a land of mystery and magic. For example, the Mississippi Delta Tourism Association's Web site once featured an uncredited tourism writer confessing his or her fascination with the Delta: "In my mind, it always seemed larger than life—a deep, mysterious place of gravel-voiced Bluesmen, southern culture, riverboat gamblers and vast fields of cotton that stretched out of sight."[119] Mississippi, and the Delta in particular, is a foreboding land, shrouded in secrecy, a place that both repels and invites. For the blues tourist hoping to add a little excitement to the trip, the crossroads is an attractive destination.

While the crossroads story is both lively and inventive, the myth regrettably reinforces the unfortunate connection between blackness as a racial category and evil. In *Blues and Evil*, Jon Michael Spencer argued that "identifying 'blues' as evil is like identifying 'black' as evil."[120] With the preeminence of European colonialism, blackness became associated with evil and wickedness, while whiteness with honesty and desirability.[121] Reminding us that angels are pictured as white and Satan as black, Robert Moore argues that the "symbolism of white as positive and black as negative is pervasive in our culture."[122] For example, there are a number of black-coded words and phrases, "black sheep," "black ball," "blackhearted," and "black eye," just to name a few, that signify negativity. Although rhetorical scholar Michael Osborn does not specifically explore the link between race and the light-dark archetypical metaphor, he clearly suggests that light (white) is associated with sight, freedom, truth, and life; in contrast, dark (black) is linked with blindness, captivity, ignorance, and death.[123]

The association of black with the negative is so embedded in Western culture that many fail to appreciate its racist implications. That both Robert Johnson and the devil are black reinscribes, rather than rejects, traditional and ideologically driven understandings of blackness. (Imagine the incongruous image of a white blues musician selling his or her soul to a white devil at the crossroads.) Rather than critiquing the story for containing racist imagery, the narrative is widely interpreted as romantic, mystical, and colorful. Rather than being rejected for its unappealing color symbolism, the story has become a ubiquitous part of the Delta's grand narrative. While tourism officials and blues promoters are obviously guilty of perpetuating the blues-devil narrative, Spencer places at least some of the blame on white blues scholars for celebrating the myth of the tragic hero, blues artists who "played like the devil and died like dogs." According to Spencer, blues scholars, including Paul Oliver, have reveled in an escapist narrative that has distracted from the real work of dissociating blackness and African American people from the concept of evil.[124] While lambasting white scholars for perpetuating the "blues-as-evil" theme, Spencer undervalues the role that the African American community, particular the black church, played in first creating, then emphasizing, the re-lationship between blues music and the underworld of Satan and hell.[125]

As we have seen, the birthplace and crossroads myths are powerful stories that take place in the distant past in a special symbolic space, the Mississippi Delta. While both stories are not historically accurate, myth resides in a sym-bolic landscape between literal historical fact or truth and outright falsehood. Of the two myths, the birthplace narrative appears to be the most successful and powerful rhetorical claim, a story that is constantly retold and recon-firmed by numerous sources, from journalists to local chambers of commerce to the blues musicians themselves. The birthplace myth serves to tell the ori-gin story of the blues while depicting the Delta as a timeless, unchanged, holy blues oasis, the antithesis of the most commercialized aspects of blues tourism. The birthplace myth functions at the rhetorical level by obfuscating a past that most Mississippians would rather forget, replacing negative images of Missis-sippi with a positive rival counterstory and reimaging a new landscape where the blues, an internationally cherished art form, was conceived and born.

The crossroads myth, the transformation of Robert Johnson from an in-competent amateur musician to an extraordinarily gifted musical soothsay-er imbued with supernatural powers, is repeated with as much frequency as the birthplace narrative, but with a twist of playfulness and humor. While the Johnson story has all the characteristics of a mythic narrative, the issue of truth comes into question. Without a doubt, some blues tourists believe that Johnson sold his soul to the devil; others, however, take a more skepti-cal stance, only half believing the story's veracity. Still others believe the story is an ingenious hoax. In his assessment of Robert Johnson's crossroads story, communication scholar Eric Rothenbuhler argues that "few contemporary American listeners could consider the story true, but very many of them con-sider the story to be a good one, worth talking about," because, he argues, myth operates at the level of "imagination" and "possibility."[126] In other words, the truth of the crossroads myth rests at the level of *possibility* (what if Rob-ert Johnson actually sold his soul to the devil?). The possibility is fueled by Johnson's stunning transformation as a musician, his strategic exploitation of satanic imagery, and the mystery surrounding his death and the exact location of his gravesite. The romantic possibility is good enough, as evidenced by the never-ending interest of tourists to visit the mysterious crossroads. The next chapter explores how these two myths of the Mississippi Delta are enforced by equally vocal claims that the area is the site of authentic blues music.

4

BLUES FESTIVALS, RACE, AND THE CONSTRUCTION OF AUTHENTICITY

We're the only festival [Juke Joint Festival] in the world where some raggedy old Blues clubs are as important as the festival's big headliners. We offer the music, culture and history that no other Blues event outside of the Delta can match. Honestly, you could say it's one of the world's most authentic Blues fests.

—ROGER STOLLE, cofounder of Clarksdale's Juke Joint Festival

For some blues tourists, traveling to the birthplace of the blues and visiting the famed crossroads (among other blues attractions) embodies a much larger search for authenticity. Reminiscent of the white researchers and fans who traveled to the South decades earlier, hoping to discover the music's origins and authentic representations of a vanishing folk culture, today's blues pilgrims hope to find similar representations of authenticity. Tourism officials and blues promoters are certainly well aware that tourists are often on a quest for authenticity. The Mississippi Blues Commission advertises Mississippi as a "destination for seekers of authentic experiences."[1] The Mississippi Development Authority/Tourism Division encourages tourists to "revisit the roots of American music and listen to the pure blues."[2] The same organization states that "fans come from around the world to sit down front and see the real thing—live and a-live, as we say . . . from the birthplace of American music."[3] "Whether it's a taste of Delta Cuisine, exploring the Robert Johnson mystery, or an evening filled with authentic Delta Blues music," declares an advertisement by the Greenwood Convention and Visitors Bureau, "Greenwood is . . . Blues, alive and well!"[4] In all, authenticity is evoked by words such as "real," "true," "pure," and "deep."

Although the term "authenticity" has been used to market and promote a variety of blues attractions from juke joints to blues hotels, it is often used to describe the music itself. In other words, promotional materials promise tourists that they will have the unique opportunity to listen to authentic blues music. While clubs and juke joints are obviously key venues for the consumption of authentic blues music, this chapter will examine Mississippi's blues festivals, annual cultural performances where authenticity is on display for tourists' enjoyment. Festivals are also a source of revenue for many communities struggling to survive. MACE, the organization responsible for organizing Greenville's annual festival, claims that the two-day festival pumps approximately three million dollars into the local economy.[5] Although data are not readily available regarding the economic impact of Clarksdale's Sunflower River Blues and Gospel Festival, the *Clarksdale Press Register* notes that the "economic impact of thousands of visitors converging on Clarksdale for a weekend of music and frolic can't be ignored."[6]

Unlike most blues festivals, which attract a predominately white audience, Mississippi's blues festivals attract a relatively large local African American audience.[7] At the same time, many of the tourists who attend these blues festivals are white. Kappi Allen, tourism manager of the Coahoma County Tourism Commission, claims that while Sunflower is marked by racial diversity, a noticeable number of white tourists attend the festival.[8] Some performance settings are specifically constructed to satisfy the expectations of some of these white tourists who seek out representations of blues authenticity, based largely on cultural-specific memories. Some whites have come to define blues authenticity in often rigid ways: an authentic blues artist must be African American playing acoustic blues (e.g., Delta blues), preferably in a rural or rural-like setting. Poverty, an ever-present reality in the Delta, completes this authentic blues setting, since it has been intimately associated with deprivation and hardship. At the same time, the inclusion of soul-blues acts, popular within the African American community, may seem incongruous to some tourists whose notion of authenticity is more restricted.

It is important to note, however, that some blues tourists may have no interest in issues related to authenticity. In his article "A Phenomenology of Tourist Experiences," Erik Cohen argues that it would be more accurate to describe the tourist as "tourists" because "different kinds of people may desire different modes of touristic experiences." As such, Cohen developed five different touristic experiences. Tourists who occupy the "recreational mode" view tourism as an opportunity for pleasure and entertainment and have little interest in experiencing or discovering authenticity. Likewise, "diversionary" tourists view travel simply as an escape from the boredom and monotony of daily life rather than a spiritual quest for authenticity.[9] Various blues cruises (Portland, Oregon's Delta Blues Experience Blues Cruises, for example) will most likely attract the recreational and diversionary tourists, because these tourists are probably more interested in sailing and partying on a "blues boat" than in engaging in an intense search for authenticity. Other modes (experiential, experimental, and existential) are positively correlated with varying degrees of interest in authenticity.[10] In sum, while Mississippi blues festivals may attract tourists who are more interested in authenticity than their "blues boat" brethren, it is also reasonable to conclude that not all blues tourists who travel to the Mississippi Delta are searching for authenticity.

AUTHENTICITY

"Authenticity" is a problematic term, "a polyvalent concept, presenting different meanings to different people."[11] Indeed, as Taylor has noted, there are "at least as many definitions of authenticity as there are those who write about it."[12] A brief survey of the literature on authenticity confirms this observation.[13] Sociologist Ning Wang concluded that much of the conceptual confusion rests on the inability of scholars to distinguish between "toured objects" and "tourist experiences."[14] In the first sense, authenticity is linked to its association with museums, where curators decide whether objects are "genuine" or "fake." In its second usage, authenticity is an ontological problem concerning one's state of being or existence. In other words, individuals question whether their experiences are "real" or "authentic," and much of the early literature on the subject bemoans the loss of authentic experiences in an increasingly "plastic," "superficial," and "image-conscious" world. For example, in *The Image: A Guide to Pseudo-events in America* (1961), historian Daniel J. Boorstin contended that tourists, unlike travelers of old who once desired authentic experiences, are satisfied with consuming inauthentic experiences or "pseudo-events," nonspontaneous events planned or staged for an audience. Citing improvements in air travel, the invention of package tours, and the development of Western tourist enclaves in developing countries, Boorstin criticized tourists' experiences as "diluted, contrived, prefabricated."[15]

From this distinction, scholars have conceptualized three different types of authenticity—objective, experiential, and constructive. While objective authenticity refers to the "authenticity of originals," or whether objects are genuine or fake, experiential authenticity focuses on "tourist experiences," or how specific activities can activate the personal feelings of tourists. Thus tourists who engage in tourist activities (e.g., participating in a traditional dance ritual) will subjectively evaluate their experiences as authentic based on the degree to which they are "engaging in non-ordinary activities, free from the constraints of the daily." Reflecting a postmodern perspective on authenticity, experiential authenticity, according to Wang, "can often have nothing to do with the issue of whether toured objects are real."[16] However, only the last type, constructive, conceives of authenticity as a purely rhetorical construction. "Things appear authentic," according to Wang, "not because they are inherently authentic but because they are constructed as such in terms of points of view, beliefs, perspectives, or powers."[17] For example, travel brochures and other textual artifacts present an "alternative, distorted view of people and place . . . designed to appeal to and attract tourists."[18] As a result, tourism intermediaries construct unrealistic expectations and easily ready-made stereotypes of the "native" and the host environment. For example, tour operators market certain images of indigenous populations in developing countries to "cater to certain images within Western consciousness about how the Other is imagined to be."[19] These indigenous populations are typically represented as static, passive, primitive, exotic, and, above all, authentic.

In response to the contention that authenticity is rooted in truth or objectivity, constructivists argue that all authenticity is, in one sense or another, an invented and manufactured phenomenon. As Wang put it: "There is no absolute and static original or origin on which the absolute authenticity of originals relies."[20] From the constructivists' point of view, authenticity is actually a "shared set of beliefs about the nature of things we value in the world," which are typically "reinforced by the conscious efforts of cultural producers and consumers alike."[21] As one observer noted, authenticity is a "claim that is made by or for someone, thing, or performance and either accepted or rejected by relevant others."[22]

Current scholarship on authenticity and its relationship to music acknowledges the concept's constructed, rhetorical nature.[23] Armstrong, for example, argued that authenticity is not "inherent in the object designated as authentic" but a "socially agreed-upon construct" that binds audiences and performances.[24] Auslander dismissed an essentialist notion of authenticity, declaring that the "creation of the effect of authenticity in rock is a matter of culturally determined convention, not an expression of essence."[25] In his study of Chicago blues clubs, Grazian lamented that his search for authenticity was doomed to fail because "my very definition of authenticity was, like *all* definitions of authenticity, based on a mix of prevailing myths and prejudices invented in the absence of actual experience."[26] Barker and Taylor noted that because the search for authenticity is a "quest" for the "absolute," it inevitably is "a goal that can never be fully attained."[27] Even alternative and contradictory depictions of authenticity are "idealized representation[s] of reality" and thus act as "a set of expectations regarding how such a thing ought to look, sound, and feel."[28] Although some tourists visit the Delta to *experience* authenticity, this chapter will focus exclusively on constructive or rhetorical authenticity, analyzing and evaluating how blues promoters and blues tourists project their beliefs, attitudes, and values onto toured objects (e.g., juke joints) and toured others (e.g., musicians).

BLUES FESTIVALS

Festival promoters and organizers frequently employ the term "authentic" or make allusions to the concept in advertisements and other promotional materials. The "Greenville on the Mississippi" brochure informs tourists that they will experience "fantastic festivals that thrive all year-round, authentic Delta Blues and so much more."[29] The Greenville–Washington County Convention and Visitors Bureau claims that Greenville's annual festival, the Mississippi Delta Blues and Heritage Festival, is a place where audiences can experience the "true blues."[30] The Sunflower River Blues and Gospel Festival has long claimed to offer "America's purest blues in the land where it was born."[31] The "Clarksdale and Coahoma County" guide informs tourists that the festival is known for its "authentic Delta Blues line-up each year."[32] Nat McMullen, who co-chaired the thirteenth annual Sunflower, claimed that "our attraction is our authenticity; people want to see the real deal—not a Disney version."[33] In 2008, *USA Weekend* named Sunflower as one of the top events that offered "authentic American music."[34] Similarly, the Juke Joint Festival, a relatively new event that emerged in Clarksdale to celebrate the spring season in the Delta, encourages tourists to watch pig races, sample the local cuisine, and listen to the "real blues." The festival also promotes itself as "combining the family fun of a small-town fair with the international tourist appeal of a real-deal blues festival."[35] In Rosedale, the Crossroads Blues Society promotes it own blues festival as authentic: "We are authentic; we promote local blues artists, and we are in the heart of where the blues was born."[36]

Not surprisingly, these promotional materials fail to define authenticity. Yet a closer examination reveals that authenticity is, in part, rhetorically grounded in the authentic image of the archetypical Mississippi blues artist: an African American (preferably old) musician playing in the traditional Delta style, a single performer accompanied by an acoustic guitar. This image of authenticity also is noted for its almost complete exclusion of women, with the exception of Jessie Mae Hemphill, a singer and electric guitarist who grew up in Mississippi's hill country. Race is often paramount to perceived blues credibility because, as David Grazian noted, "blackness may very well be *the* dominant signifier of authenticity in the blues."[37] As discussed in chapter 1, authenticity became an increasingly salient concept during the 1960s blues revival, as white folklorists and blues fanatics alike descended on the South, Mississippi in particular, to rediscover uncorrupted, authentic black practitioners of a supposedly dying art form. Beyond issues of perceived originality, this constructed notion of authenticity was also grounded in an essentialist view that African Americans were more adept at singing and performing the blues than whites; African Americans possessed the "blues gene," and the sociocultural conditioning of the oppressive South gave rise to an emotional insight, a sorrowful and angry cry that whites could never possess. Whites were by and large the antithesis of blues authenticity, mere imitators and copyists. This perspective was perhaps most succinctly expressed by Ralph Gleason, cofounder of *Rolling Stone*: "The blues is black man's [and women's] music, and whites diminish it at best or steal it at worst. In any case, they have no moral right to use it."[38]

Most contemporary scholars who study race reject the essentialist argument, arguing that race is a sociopolitical concept, rather than a biological one. For example, European immigrants (e.g., Irish, Italians, Germans) were not racially classified as white until the 1920s and 1930s, when these groups became assimilated (descended into the metaphorical melting pot) as white. Racial categories are human constructions, widening and contracting, shifting from inclusivity to exclusivity over time. Reflecting this anti-essentialist position, Grazian argues that "it cannot possibly follow that a musician's race *causes* their artistic efforts to become more authentic and expressively rich," because "race alone makes for a fairly poor predictor of *any* type of inherent talent or ability, including those related to music and the arts."[39] Still, many blues fans associate blackness with authenticity. Although local Delta blues festivals hire both African American and white musicians to perform (sometimes on the same stage), it is not surprising to find that white tourists, according to the African American blues performer Mississippi Slim (Walter Horn), are simply not interested in watching white musicians perform:

> A lot of people come from different states and stuff, and they come to hear the Delta blues. I tell you what, I say this: A lot of your white audience, people that come to hear the Delta blues, they don't want to see white guys. When they come down, they want to see like the original deal, like where this stuff started from and what they're looking to see, man. They don't care if the black guys that's doing it, they don't have to be all that good. But it makes them feel better if they're seeing this because it makes them feel like they're seeing the real thing, the roots of this thing.[40]

White audiences, as Mississippi Slim suggests, often watch with an uncritical eye as African American blues musicians perform onstage, and grant them a kind of privileged legitimacy and authenticity, often tone deaf to their level of musicianship. White blues musicians, regardless of skill, are often viewed with more skepticism, as imitators, not the originators of this musical form.

Some white tourists also hope to find authentic African American musicians playing in the acoustic blues style of Mississippi's past masters, Charley Patton and Robert Johnson. In an interview, Jim O'Neal discussed the expectations of tourists who visit the Delta:

> I think a lot of people have come to the Delta thinking that they were gonna hear the acoustic blues, the guy sitting on his front porch, and of course, that hasn't been the norm for Delta blues in a long time when they went to the juke joints and turned electric and all that. I can remember there was a TV crew from Germany doing a documentary, and they wanted to film some Delta blues, so I got Frank Frost, Lonnie Pitchford, and Sam Carr together [to play electric blues]—okay, this is a dream band, right [laughter]. And they were playing in this little joint in Helena [Arkansas], and the producer looked at me kind of really disappointed and said, "This is not blues" [laughter].[41]

Festival programs accentuate the relationship between race, musical style, and authenticity. For example, the front cover of the 2006 Mississippi Delta Blues and Heritage Festival program features an illustration of an African American dressed in a white shirt and overalls, playing an acoustic guitar on what appears to be a wooden stage or perhaps the porch of a sharecropper's shack. Since organizers typically dedicate a festival to a notable blues musician (sometimes deceased), festival programs for the Highway 61 Blues Festival have included drawings of David "Honeyboy" Edwards and Charley Patton playing an acoustic guitar.[42] While musicians who play traditional acoustic blues still perform (albeit infrequently), their numbers have dwindled significantly over the years; the blues heard today in Mississippi and enjoyed by black audiences is generally an amplified music.

To further inculcate the memory of these Delta blues legends in tourists, street vendors and store owners sell T-shirts featuring images of famous (and often deceased) African American blues musicians. At the 1999 King Biscuit Blues Festival, a T-shirt read "A Pact with the Devil / Robert Johnson, 1911–1938." Next to the inscription was a drawing of the famous blues crossroads (the intersection of U.S. Highways 61 and 49) where Robert Johnson allegedly sold his soul to the devil in exchange for his musical genius. At the 2000 Crossroads Blues Festival, an annual event held in Rosedale, Mississippi, vendors sold T-shirts that featured the lyrics of one of Johnson's most famous songs, "Traveling Riverside Blues." In the song, Johnson references the town of Rosedale, where Johnson would occasionally perform while taking a respite from the road. The shirts were sold to raise funds to support the festival.

To satisfy the need among some tourists to watch a "real" Delta blues performance, the Sunflower River Blues and Gospel Festival features at least one small, intimate stage setup, often called a juke or acoustic stage, where musicians play acoustic-based, down-home Delta blues. The festival traditionally showcases acoustic performances on Saturday morning at the Othar Turner Acoustic Stage, located inside the Clarksdale Station. Built in 1926 and recently renovated as part of the city's Blues Alley development, the Clarksdale Station was the site where Muddy Waters purchased his train ticket to Chicago in 1943.[43] Playing to a virtually all-white, older audience, the primarily African American musical lineup (Tater Foster, Eddie Cusic, Terry "Harmonica" Bean, Pat Thomas, and others) is often accompanied only by an acoustic or electric guitar, and most of the musicians play in the traditional solo style (although some performances have included more musicians). At the 2007 festival, Pat Thomas—son of legendary blues artist James "Son" Thomas—announced to the audience that he would play some "down-home Delta blues." The Saturday-morning event typically concludes at 1:30 p.m., when Shardee Turner and the Rising Star Fife and Drum Band march from the Clarksdale Station to the festival's main stage. Shardee Turner is the granddaughter of Othar Turner (he died in 2003), who was one of the last practitioners of the fife and drum tradition that could be found in Mississippi's hill county.[44] As one of the few contemporary female blues musicians native to Mississippi performing today, Shardee (who was already an expert fife player) decided to preserve her grandfather's musical legacy. The festival also includes a small outdoor stage where performers, some on acoustic guitar and others on electric guitar and drums, play on the back of a flatbed truck or on a small wooden stage to a small group of admirers.[45] Fans flock to hear the musicians play in this intimate environment, sometimes sitting at the feet of the performers. The Sunflower River Blues and Gospel Festival offers these local African American blues artists, who typically receive little support by local blacks for their type of blues music, an opportunity to perform in front of grateful, admiring audiences.

The Mississippi Delta Blues and Heritage Festival has a similar set construction called the Jukehouse Stage, in addition to a gospel and a main stage. The Jukehouse Stage is constructed of exposed wooden two-by-fours enclosed with tin roofing for walls; organizers typically hire both traditional acoustic blues performers (Eddie Cusic) and electric blues bands (John Horton) to play on the wooden stage. Grazian observed a similar Juke Joint stage at the Chicago Blues Festival.[46] The Highway 61 Blues Festival sports a smaller second stage (called the Scratch Ankle Stage) for performers and audiences who desire a more intimate, folksy setting. In fact, most local blues festivals have a secondary stage or alternative stages (sometimes called a "heritage" stage) that feature musicians who often play in a close approximation of the Delta style. Amateur musicians who are not hired to play at the festival often turn themselves into street performers, playing on a street corner or a sidewalk for tips.

Mississippi blues festivals feature a variety of different musical styles, including blues–southern rock, soul-blues, rhythm and blues, rock and roll, and gospel music, an important and thriving genre in many black communities.[47] Festival organizers, blues critics, and blues musicians have been critical in the past of efforts to provide fans more musical diversity. For example, by the early 1980s, the scope and direction of the Mississippi Delta Blues and Heritage Festival were changing. In a bid to make the event more commercially successful, organizers decided to hire more nationally recognized acts, whose electric, urban blues strayed from the festival's original aim of being "folk-authentic." For example, from 1980 to 1990, Muddy Waters, John Lee Hooker, Albert King, Robert Cray, and Bo Diddley agreed to headline the festival. Folklorist Worth Long, an early supporter of the festival, acknowledged that commercially oriented urban blues is an integral part of the black community, but he also lamented the festival's new direction: "I'm afraid this is becoming more and more electric."[48] Worse, at least according to one critic, the Mississippi Delta Blues and Heritage Festival was beginning to feature more and more non-blues artists to attract a wider audience. In a *Living Blues* review of the 1988 festival, blues scholar Peter Aschoff dismissed soul-blues acts like Betty White and felt personally insulted that the Fabulous Thunderbirds, a white rock-and-roll band, was the headline act. Unless MACE enacted corrective measures, Aschoff predicted the demise of the festival as a blues event:

> *MACE can't do much about the heat, and they can't do much to motivate the acts to give their best, either. But they can do a better job of determining what acts they book and how they schedule them. I hope that the festival is not losing its original vision, and that it is not sacrificing "real" blues in pursuit of a broader audience. If it is, we can look forward to the gradual demise of the Delta Blues Festival; it will become the Delta Music Festival.*[49]

With his decidedly narrow definition of what constitutes the "real blues," Aschoff would be appalled if he attended the Mississippi Delta Blues and Heritage Festival today (he died in 2002). The festival features a variety of musical styles, including southern soul music or soul-blues. As a relatively recent addition to the blues family, soul-blues artists such as Bobby Rush, Marvin Sease, and Nathaniel Kimble play an eclectic musical mix of blues, funk, soul, R&B, and rap. This form is more popular with black audiences today than more traditional forms of the blues. Some local African American blues musicians have complained about the decision of festival organizers to hire more and more soul-blues acts. In his critique of the festival, guitarist Dave Thompson complained: "I think when you say a 'blues festival,' I feel like it should be lots of blues, it should be some real blues, more real blues than all this soul stuff, you know."[50] Terry "Harmonica" Bean revealed in a 2008 interview that he has been pressured by African Americans to play soul-blues, a form that he does not consider "real blues": "You know when they have a rhythm and blues festival, they calling it a blues festival. But it's not. It's a soul music festival what it is. But they're calling it blues, but it's not blues, so they just don't know. When you heard the blues, you know it."[51]

Some blues festival organizations have debated which blues form should take precedence. Roger Stolle, a former member of the Sunflower River Blues Association and one of the primary organizers of Clarksdale's Juke Joint Festival, has observed disagreements between some of the organization's African American committee members, who favor more soul-oriented musicians, and their white counterparts, who push for more traditional blues artists. The Sunflower River Blues Association, a nonprofit organization, was created in 1990; comprising a racially mixed group of volunteers, the organization claims that it has "retained its unique individuality and laid-back, informal hospitality that has remained a trademark."[52] Reaching a compromise of sorts, the festival's soul-blues lineup on Friday is intended to target the local African American population, while Saturday's musical roster aims for the mostly white tourist population.[53] For example, at the 2008 festival, soul-blues artist Latimore (Benjamin "Benny" Latimore) headlined Friday night's lineup; in 2009 soul-blues artist O. B. Buchana headlined on Friday.

A frequent performer and headliner at Mississippi blues festivals, Bobby Rush is one of the most popular performers of the soul-blues tradition, heralded by *Living Blues* magazine as "the king of soul blues."[54] Born Emmet Ellis Jr. in Homer, Louisiana, Rush moved to Chicago in the early 1950s and was part of the Chicago blues scene along with Muddy Waters, Howlin' Wolf, Little Walter, and other blues notables. By the early 1970s, Rush changed his musical direction from traditional Chicago blues to a music that incorporated the blues with R&B and soul. Based today in Jackson, Mississippi, Rush's riveting stage act, featuring three "booty-shaking" hoochie dancers, frequent costume changes, and comedic routines, is carefully choreographed and rehearsed. For some blues tourists, Rush's live performances are the direct antithesis of the "real blues." Even Rush admits that "when I'm on the stage it's not that I'm trying to get the blues across. I'm trying to get Bobby Rush across. And getting the blues across, that's a plus."[55] While Rush is mainly known for his soul-blues recordings, he has on occasion recorded more traditionally oriented blues albums, including *Folkfunk* (2004) and *Raw* (2007).

It should be noted that some festivals cater to the local African American population. The Shaw Blues Festival typically drew an almost exclusively African American audience and featured soul-blues acts from both the local area (Mississippi Nuo Nuo) and outside (Jessie Clay from Chicago). The small town of Stephenville also established a similar festival, the Willie Clayton Homecoming Festival, named after a Mississippi-born artist who since 1969 has released a handful of albums ranging from the Al Green gospel-soul sound to southern soul music. Both festivals are now defunct. Billy Johnson, director of the Highway 61 Blues Museum in Leland, Mississippi, observed that "if you have a soul blues festival, you're not going to draw many white tourists or any blues tourists to it. But you will draw a lot more African American locals."[56]

While some white tourists (and the occasional down-home Mississippi musician) may discount soul-blues musicians as not playing the real blues, many are still satisfied with listening to African Americans play the blues in a new and exciting cultural context, another key rhetorical ingredient of authenticity. As discussed in chapter 3, tourism officials claim that the Mississippi Delta is the birthplace of the blues, an unpolluted blues culture rooted in purity, simplicity, and primitiveness. Thus, to see and experience the real blues, one must return to "where it all started." In his music festival guide, Tom Clynes makes this point clear when he uses the birthplace metaphor to describe the Mississippi Delta Blues and Heritage Festival:

> Greenville, in the heart of the Delta from which the blues sprang, is in many ways the perfect place for one of the nation's most authentic blues festivals. The land here is steeped in memories—many joyful, many sobering. Slaves weren't allowed to talk while working, but they could sing, and the blues eventually developed out of their melodic, African-inspired work songs. The festival spotlights their old instruments—jugs, harmonicas, and primitive slide guitars—and although several high-powered, electrified performers are always in evidence, "unplugged" sets are most common.[57]

The organizers of the Mississippi Delta Blues and Heritage Festival usually develop a specific theme for each year, and many of their slogans reflect a rhetorical strategy to emphasize the area's authentic roots. Slogans such as "Da' Blues Is Like Comin' Home!," "Taking It Back to Where We Started," and "Come Home to the Blues—It's Better Than Ever!" clearly play on the geographic argument for authenticity. But what exactly does "home" look like? Festivals programs suggest that home is rooted not in the present but in a distant, timeless past. For example, the front cover for the 2001 festival program sports a drawing of a transient 1920s "blues family" in motion. In the foreground, a family of three is pictured walking down a dirt road. The father is dressed in overalls with a guitar strapped to his back. The mother is carrying a basket, presumably filled with food and water. Walking between them, a young boy is holding the hands of both parents. In the background, many of the images found in Delta blues songs are present: a large field and a fast-moving train. The festival theme is positioned underneath the drawing, accentuating the relationship between authenticity and a Delta that, in many ways, no longer exists.[58] The 2008 festival poster, "Roll'in Goin Home to Da Blues!!!," features an exuberant African American blues band standing on a wooden stage playing to a (mostly black) audience (some are enjoying the music from the comfort of their pre–World War II automobiles). Set in the 1930s or 1940s, the festival scene is the countryside, one that includes histori-cally familiar images of a cotton field, dirt road, and a sharecropper shack. The organizers of the Sunflower River Blues and Gospel Festival also recognize the power of the birthplace myth, urging tourists that they should be "comin' home" for the 2004 festival, "in the land where it was born."

However, for many African American tourists, home takes on an entirely different meaning. Home is not the mythical birthplace of the blues but the actual home where their extended families reside. Since the 1980s, more and more African Americans have returned from the Southern Diaspora (Chicago, St. Louis, etc.) to Mississippi for family reunions. Blues festivals provide the opportunity for the extended family to enjoy a cultural outing in the country. These temporary sojourns parallel a larger, more permanent black in-migra-tion back to the South. Since the early twentieth century, whites have returned to the South in much greater numbers and with greater frequency than their black counterparts, while black migration back to the South started to accel-erate only during the mid- to late 1970s, an upward trend of return migration that has not abated.[59] Between 1965 and 1970, 114,296 southern-born blacks living in the North and the West returned to the South. Thirty years later, the number had more than doubled, with 232,985 southern-born blacks returning to the South between 1995 and 2000.[60] Black in-migration has several causes: the need to escape increasing black violence in the urban ghetto, globalization and the steady erosion of manufacturing jobs, the desire to reconnect with extended family members, and the realization that the most egregious forms of white supremacy in the South have been dismantled through civic activism and legal statutes.[61]

Since the blues was born in the fields of the Mississippi Delta, as promo-tional materials suggest, festival organizers have decided to hold the events primarily at outdoor venues, in parks and open fields. For example, the Mis-sissippi Delta Blues and Heritage Festival is usually staged in an open field. As discussed earlier, it was originally held in the middle of a cotton field in the small hamlet of Freedom Village, fifteen miles from the port city of Green-ville. Since the inception of the festival in 1978, the organizers have believed that the cotton field is an appropriate location for a blues festival because, according MACE's former executive director Charles Bannerman, "Country people won't come to fancy places. Blues isn't meant for the cocktail circuit."[62] Echoing this sentiment, festival organizers believed that an "open field" was a "perfect setting" to stage a Mississippi blues festival because the "blues grew out of hard times." An air-conditioned auditorium "would have been too much of a contrast."[63] Similarly, the Highway 61 Blues Festival is held at an outdoor venue, the Railroad Park in downtown Leland. The open field, a scattering of trees, and a string of stationary railroad cars that line the side of the park complete the image of the "authentic" Delta blues setting. Not only did Mississippi blues musicians employ agricultural images (mules, sun, cotton fields, and insects) as lyrical devices to describe their sharecropping experience, but they also mentioned the railroad, a symbol of liberation and escape. Other local blues festivals, such as the B. B. King Homecoming Festival and the Crossroads Blues Festival, are held at outdoor locations.

While many blues festivals are situated in a rural or a rural-urban (a park buttressed against a downtown street) setting, some are staged in a more urban area. Although Clarksdale once held its annual festival at the Martin Luther King Jr. Park, the festival is now located in Blues Alley, an area that contains the Clarksdale Station (formerly the passenger depot for the Illinois Central Railroad), the Delta Blues Museum (the former freight depot), and a bar and restaurant called Ground Zero. This area has a historical relationship to the blues because it served as one of the staging areas for African Americans to join the South's great out-migration. Unlike festivals held in rural settings, the authenticity of the Sunflower River Blues and Gospel Festival is enhanced by its relationship to Blues Alley, as well as its close spatial relationship to a number of other blues businesses and attractions, including museums, music stores, clubs, and juke joints. Thus tourists are able to leave the festival site temporarily and explore other sites, such as Ground Zero Blues Club, that act as supportive cast members in an area that, ironically, was historically reserved for whites during Clarksdale's Jim Crow era.

Because of Ground Zero's close proximity to the festival site and its high profile and popularity among blues fans, it is appropriate to devote some time to analyzing the club's claims of authenticity. Owned by the Hollywood actor Morgan Freeman, Bill Luckett, a local attorney, and Mississippi native and business executive Howard Stovall, Ground Zero Blues Club, which opened in 2001, advertises itself as a wholly authentic blues establishment. Claiming that Clarksdale is the "epicenter" and "ground zero" for blues music, Luckett told CNN iReporter Neal Moore that the decision to create a new blues club was responding to a need to offer tourists a greater opportunity to find live blues music in Clarksdale. Tourists were "looking for live blues music, and they really couldn't find it on a routine basis." Luckett claims that Ground Zero has played an important role in a new blues "cultural renaissance" in Clarksdale and has inspired the reopening of existing juke joints and even the creation of new juke joints in Clarksdale.[64] With a Hollywood star as one of its co-owners, the establishment has had its share of headlines, since celebrities have frequently visited the club since it opened in 2001. It should be pointed out that Bill Luckett, a member of the NAACP, belongs to Clarksdale's white elite and one of Clarksdale's most venerated families. Luckett is the great-nephew of Semmes Luckett, a lawyer and arch-segregationist who served on the State Sovereignty Commission Board and vehemently opposed the *Brown v. Board of Education* decision.[65] Reiterating the birthplace myth, Ground Zero's Web site elaborates on its institutional mission:

> *Clarksdale, Mississippi has long been described as "Ground Zero" for blues aficionados from around the globe. It all started here. That's why Ground Zero Blues Club was created—to celebrate the area's rich blues heritage and to pro-vide a forum in which it can continue. . . . Ground Zero Blues Club is the place for anyone looking for an authentic Delta Blues experience.*

Although Ground Zero officially identifies itself as a blues club, the own-ers have decorated the club with all the exotic trappings of what some tour-ists might expect to see in an authentic juke joint—wooden walls and floors, photos of blues musicians, well-worn pool tables, graffiti, and other iconic symbols of a "pure" blues establishment. Although Ground Zero occasion-ally features national acts, the Web site stresses that "visitors are more likely to find the 'real deal' at Ground Zero Blues Club—those musicians who live in the Mississippi Delta and continue in the tradition of their musical forefa-thers Charley Patton, Muddy Waters and John Lee Hooker."[66] Patrons even have the opportunity to sample the restaurant's down-home cooking, which includes both local Mississippi cuisine, fried catfish, for example, and "blues food," including the Voodoo Burger, the Crossroads Burger, and the Highway 61 Burger. A brochure developed by the Clarksdale Downtown Development Association claims that patrons will "eat soul food and juke 'til you drop to authentic down home blues at Ground Zero Blues Club."[67]

The allure of Ground Zero has hoodwinked some observers into believ-ing that the club is actually an authentic juke joint. According to a Cana-dian reporter, "Ground Zero is a throwback to the era when the blues rivalled cotton as king of the Delta. . . . Ground Zero is a rarity in the Mississippi Delta—a traditional juke joint where an itinerant bluesman can still show up unannounced and play for pay."[68] *Southern Living* referred to Ground Zero as a "juke joint," a place where Morgan Freeman can be found "dancing on a plank floor."[69] A local Clarksdale publication, *Here's Clarksdale!*, referred to Ground Zero as a "contemporary" juke joint.[70] Even Morgan Freeman has called his establishment a "little funky juke joint."[71]

In reality, Ground Zero is not a juke joint but a hip blues club. The differ-ence is not simply semantic. Jim O'Neal notes that while it is "fashionable for upscale venues to use the term 'juke joint' or to appropriate the folksy style of décor," there are distinct and important differences between a club and a juke joint. For example, while clubs are often managed as full-time businesses, juke joints are run "by proprietors who may have other jobs or incomes, and hence may not be open every night, but possibly just on weekends or at the owner's discretion."[72] Although Ground Zero uses a neon sign to identify itself, juke joints typically do not bear formal signs, a pattern that developed as a form of protection during the era of segregation, when law enforcement and other agents of the South's white power structure would view the gathering of African Americans to be a threat; the lack of a clearly identifiable space would serve as defense against white invasion and violence.[73] Ground Zero, however, has one characteristic that is common to juke joints. Historically, juke joints inhabit a building originally used for other purposes; J.J.'s, a juke joint in Clarksdale, was originally a café and a grocery store.[74] Ground Zero occupies a building that was previously used to class and grade cotton. Overall, however, one would be hard-pressed to classify Ground Zero as anything but a blues club, although the choice to refer to the establishment as a juke joint is an effort to bolster the club's credibility as an authentic blues destination.

While some tourists believe they have discovered the real blues at Ground Zero, others dismiss the blues club for its crass attempt to look like a traditional juke joint, and embark on a quest for a more intimate juke joint, some of which are located in the downtown area and across the railroad tracks in the neighboring black community. Red's Lounge, a juke joint that is seemingly always on the edge of financial ruin and in a perpetual state of disrepair, is a revelation for blues tourists searching for the real-deal blues in an authentic setting. "Exact opposite of the Ground Zero blues club chain," writes one tourist who found Red's to be an "authentic" juke joint where "real blues artists [are] playing in a hole in a [sic] the wall joint."[75] According to another tourist named "Nicholas":

> The first day of the festival, Friday, there wasn't much on the main stage that we were interested in, so we spent a lot of time trying to stay cool (temps were typically 100F, with humidity from 94–100%), but we meandered over to Red's at about 10:00 and stayed for a few hours. Red's is a true juke joint. The roof leaks, the bathrooms are atrocious, and the doorman has a gun. But the beer comes in 24 ounce cans (their standard size—no bottles for safety reasons) and the music is often quite good.[76]

For this blues tourist, at least, Ground Zero is the antithesis of a real juke joint, since it fails to meet the several tests of authenticity, including the fact that whereas Ground Zero's symbols of poverty are contrived, Red's dilapidated and unrefined state is uncontrived. This distinction signifies another symbol of authenticity—poverty—based on the premise that authentic blues musicians lived in a world largely absent of material prosperity. Unfortunately, festival organizers (or juke joint operators) do not have to stage the poverty. A regrettable facet of the Delta's geographic authenticity is its crushing poverty, which is neither to be underestimated nor to be romanticized. Until recently, the small Delta town of Rosedale held its annual festival in its ramshackle downtown area. Filled with abandoned buildings, gang graffiti, and streets choked with weeds and broken glass, Rosedale is a sad testament to the economic decline witnessed by many small Delta communities. Blues festivals held in Shaw, Drew, and Marks, Mississippi, offer similar images of poverty and despair. Although the Sunflower River Blues and Gospel Festival is held in Clarksdale's Blues Alley area, tourists who drive to the festival site cannot escape the city's depressing level of poverty. There are multiple points to access the city's downtown area (and Blues Alley), although many tourists—after exiting either Highway 61 or the newly built bypass—drive on Sunflower Avenue, Madison Avenue, or another side street. These streets are part of a largely impoverished African American residential area that suffers from high rates of unemployment, decaying housing, crime, gang activity, and other socioeconomic problems associated with poverty and neglect.

Similar to Clarksdale's Blues Alley project, the city of Helena, Arkansas, has renovated sections of its downtown area, believing that problems with drugs, crime, and public drunkenness needed to be addressed and solved for the city to attract a substantial number of blues tourists to its annual blues festival. In one of the few studies of blues festivals, Rotenstein explored how cultural authorities have eliminated the "rough spots" to make Helena safe for tourists. While providing a boon to the economically depressed area, the festival organizers encouraged community leaders to sanitize and repackage the community. By reconfiguring Helena's famous blues street, Cherry Street, city officials unwittingly assisted in the disappearance of "much of the 'local color' that made Helena a blues city." Rotenstein was amazed by the seemingly overnight transformation of Helena: "The juke joints that I visited three years ago are gone, replaced by parking lots full of blues ghosts."[77] Efforts to clean up downtown Helena reveal a controversial element in cultural tourism, the transformation of whole communities into commodities. Yet, similar to Clarksdale, Helena has not been able to gloss over the city's economic despair. As tourists drive into Helena's downtown district to attend the festival, visual representations of Helena's stark economic realities, abandoned factories, closed businesses, and crumbling public housing, are a sad reminder of a city in decline.

In sum, Mississippi Delta blues festivals rely heavily on race, musical style, geography, and history to support claims of authenticity and to satisfy the demands of white tourists whose notion of authenticity is largely a product of culturally derived public memories. At the same time, however, festival organizers realize the demands of other audiences, particularly the local African American population. Authentic blues festivals must also be situated in either rural areas that emphasize familiar blues themes (cotton fields, railroad tracks) or staged in downtown areas that do not (or cannot) disguise high unemployment and a crumbling infrastructure, shattered spaces bereft of hope. The result is that the Mississippi Delta is seemingly trapped in irresolvable contradiction. Economic progress and growth, the by-products of a robust tourism industry, should ideally begin to dismantle the physical signs of poverty and decay, but paradoxically the iconic images of poverty are keys to the region's authenticity.

Popular notions of authenticity characterize the term from an objectivist perspective, an epistemological position that suggests that objects, individuals, and performances are somehow infused with a genuine essence of authenticity. Yet, as I have maintained, objective authenticity does not exist. Instead, all authenticity is, in one form or another, a rhetorical construction. Blues festivals are rhetorical constructions of authenticity; a number of key organizational decisions, from the hiring of musicians to the type of blues music performed to the location itself, are motivated, in part, by a need to satisfy tourist expectations and demands for authenticity. In the end, blues festivals serve both to perpetuate the myth that Mississippi is the birthplace of the blues and to reaffirm, in some ways, a narrow and restrictive understanding of authenticity.

5

A BLUES COUNTERMEMORY
The History of Mississippi, the Story of the Delta

Hence I have no mercy or compassion in me for a society that will crush people, and then penalize them for not being able to stand up under the weight.
—MALCOLM X, *The Autobiography of Malcolm X*

They treated us like we was property. Come all through slavery time and they still wanted us to be slaves.
—DAVID "HONEYBOY" EDWARDS, *The World Don't Owe Me Nothing*

The process of rhetorically packaging Mississippi's blues culture and heritage involves efforts by official culture to privilege a particular understanding of the past. As we will see in chapter 6, blues promoters and cultural producers promote a revisionist history of the state, and the Delta region in particular, to sanitize a history of race relations that one observer correctly characterized as "awful."[1] Thus, while promotional materials highlight the Delta as the birthplace of the blues and spotlight the region's rustic and authentic blues culture, there is, not surprisingly, precious little information about Mississippi's depressing record of state-sponsored oppression of African Americans.

The purpose of this chapter is to provide a blues countermemory, a historical corrective to tourism narratives that deliberately downplay or obfuscate Mississippi's past. Since the promotional materials discussed in chapter 6 focus largely on representing Mississippi's blues culture before the conclusion of the Second Great Migration (1940–60)—an event that witnessed the exodus of many of the state's blues musicians to northern cities like St. Louis and Chicago—this selective historical treatment will cover the period from the early 1800s to 1955. Special attention will be placed on the sharecropping industry, the narrative scene of many promotional materials, and one that most Mississippi blues artists knew intimately, since employment opportunities for blacks were severely limited. Through the use of illustration and testimony, Son House, Willie Dixon, Memphis Slim, B. B. King, and others speak about the sharecropping system, lynching, legalized segregation, and other forms of oppression that Mississippi's official culture would prefer to forget. It should be noted, however, that there is no evidence that authorities singled out blues musicians for special persecution. According to James B. Stewart, during the early part of the twentieth century, blues musicians were "subjected to the same forms of social control that were directed at other African Americans."[2] While Mississippi blues artists have provided compelling narratives about the inhumanity of white supremacy, these narratives could easily have come from the mouths of nonmusicians. In fact, it can be argued that because some whites enjoyed listening to the blues, blues musicians sometimes enjoyed special privileges. For example, African American musicians were hired to perform at white private parties. In this role, blues musicians would occasionally engage audience members in casual conversation or engage in other forms of social interaction typically not available to other blacks at the time.[3] This chapter begins with two contradictory images of the Mississippi Delta, hospitality and hostility, the latter often excised from tourism brochures and other promotional materials.

THE DEADLY DELTA: DISEASE, SLAVERY, AND KING COTTON

Reviled and revered, the Mississippi Delta personifies a peculiar mixture of human graciousness and unforgiving cruelty. For many of its white residents, the Delta embodies idealized southern virtues of piety and pride, gregariousness and generosity.[4] Writing in 1923, Walter Sillers Sr., a landowner and Delta politician, claimed that Delta people were "real gentlemen and ladies, because God and environment made them so, and the colleges, fine libraries and lovely Christian women did the rest."[5] In his 1935 autobiography, the writer David L. Cohn characterized the people of the Delta as "kind, gregarious, and genuinely hospitable."[6] Yet the region's history of enforced servitude, hysterical bigotry, political corruption, insatiable greed, and human suffering cannot be ignored. Indeed, as historian Clement A. Price concluded, since the nineteenth century, the entire state of Mississippi has been a "uniquely racially charged society."[7] Highlighting this remarkable contradiction, one scholar accurately noted that in the "Old South, good manners often honey-coated a brutal reality."[8]

The origins of the Delta's paradoxical nature began with the expansion of white settlers into the area. First designated by Congress in April 1798, the Mississippi Territory would eventually consume an area as wide as present-day Mississippi and Alabama.[9] Before white settlement in the early 1800s, the Delta had been largely occupied by a number of Native American tribes, including the Choctaw Indians. After Mississippi achieved statehood in 1817, the Choctaw signed three separate treaties between 1820 and 1832, allowing for white settlement of the area.[10] Virtually from the start, the white planter class—many of whom had relocated to Mississippi from other parts of the South—viewed the Delta, with its rich fertile soil, as the "only hope of maintaining the accustomed standard of living."[11] As the region's emerging new landowners, white planters hoped to transform the Delta into one of the largest cotton-producing regions in the world.

These new settlers struggled. The area was practically a Wild West frontier, filled with sycamore trees, vines, thick brush, swamps, and game. These conditions, coupled with intemperate weather patterns, created a region rife with disease. Many of the Delta's early settlers suffered and died from a host of diseases from malaria to yellow fever.[12] These settlers also faced the additional hardship of surviving frequent floods, a result of waters overflowing the banks of the Mississippi River. Staking one's claim in the Delta was equivalent to taking a "long shot for big stakes," because the Mississippi River, without a levee system, often destroyed the planter's "growing cotton, drowned his cattle, and swept away his cabins."[13] As one observer aptly put it: "The Delta was founded and wrought in pain."[14]

Although Mississippi was a slave state, the Delta's slave population was miniscule by comparison with the rest of the state because large tracts of the region had yet to be cleared for farmland.[15] In 1840 some Delta counties—Leflore, Quitman, and Sunflower—did not have any slaves, while the slaveholdings in other Delta counties (Tunica, 251; Coahoma, 524; Bolivar, 971) were miniscule in comparison to other parts of the state. In 1840, Adams County, which includes the city of Natchez, had the largest slave population (14,241) in the state.[16] John Stauffer, an African American studies scholar, called Natchez the "pride of the cotton South and an *entrepôt* in the Atlantic and domestic slave trade." Franklin, Armfield, and Company, one of the nation's leading slave-trading firms, established one of its central headquarters in Natchez (the other was located in Washington, D.C.).[17]

By the 1850s, plantations were emerging near the Mississippi River area. As a result, between 1850 and 1860, the number of slaves in the Delta rose dramatically. For example, the total slave population in Coahoma County increased from 1,391 to 5,085, a 266 percent jump. A neighboring Delta County, Bolivar, saw its slave population grow by 316 percent, from 2180 to 9,078. By 1860, Yazoo County had 16,716 slaves, the most of any core or partial Delta county. However, the largest slaveholding counties existed outside the Delta because, despite the growth of plantations, only 10 percent of the Delta had been cleared by the beginning of the Civil War. In 1860, Hinds County—an area that includes the capital city of Jackson—was the largest slaveholding county in the state, with 22,363 slaves.[18]

Under the watchful eye of the overseer, slaves were largely responsible for planting and harvesting of cotton, as well as other crops. Other forms of labor-intensive work included chopping firewood, clearing fields, housekeeping, and preparing meals. Uncooperative slaves were whipped, beaten, starved, and subjected to other forms of barbarity. Charlie Moses, a former slave from Brookhaven, Mississippi, bitterly remembered how his master, Jim Rankin, mistreated him and fellow slaves, even taking the extraordinary measure of killing one slave:

> *Oh, Lordy! The way us Niggers was treated was awful. Marster would beat, knock, kick, kill. He done ever'thing he could 'cept eat us. . . . He whipped us 'til some jus' lay down to die. . . . If one o' his Niggers done something to displease him, which was mos' ever' day, he'd whip him 'til he'd mos' die an' then he'd kick him 'roun in the dust. He'd even take his gun an', before the Nigger had time to open his mouth, he'd jus' stan' there an' shoot him down.*[19]

In many cases, slave contracts amounted to nothing more than a hand-written statement. Sometimes whole families were sold to the same buyer, as documented in a contract, dated December 7, 1858, that revealed that one "certain Family of Negro[e]s" was sold for $2,250.00.[20] Since Mississippi slave owners wanted to increase their pool of labor to match the state's agricultural expansion, many slaves who were transported to the state stayed on a more or less permanent basis, thus alleviating the misery of forced separation from loved ones.[21] In other cases, however, entire families were divided and their members parceled out to interested parties. Writing on October 27, 1853, slave owner A. J. Bass scrawled transfer of ownership of a young African American female to a fellow slave owner:

> *I have this day sold to James H. Moore a Negro Girl named Elizabeth a [sic] for the Sum of Five hundred and seventy five dollars to me in hand paid the receipt whereof is hereby acknowledged said girl I sell as a slave for life and do by there presents Warrant her sound in mind and body.*[22]

Slave owners also advertised their human chattel in local and state newspapers. Among items of interest, C. McLaurin, for example, desired to sell 1,440 acres of land, 2,000 bushels of corn, 200 cattle, and "30 of the likeliest Mississippi raised negroes in the State."[23] On October 5, 1859, one slave owner placed an ad in the *Vicksburg Whig*, hoping to sell 192 acres of land and seventeen slaves, whom he characterized as "young and likely."[24] Another slave owner, one John Harris, advertised land for sale in the *Hinds County Gazette*. In an attempt to entice potential interested parties to respond to his ad, Harris promised to "sell three likely NEGROES with the land."[25]

With this source of labor, cotton became king in Mississippi. Indeed, as Cohn asserted, cotton was a "religion and a way of life" in the Delta.[26] Eli Whitney's invention of the cotton gin in 1793 created a "new civilization, a new empire based on cotton."[27] As a result, the production of cotton increased to the immense pleasure of white landowners. For example, Mississippi's output of cotton bales increased from 20,000 in 1821 to 387,000 in 1839.[28] By 1860, with cotton production at an all-time high, four Delta counties were named in the list of the top thirty-six wealthiest counties in the United States.[29] Although a cotton crop did not always yield a profit, some Delta planters became millionaires; others possessed an accumulated wealth of over $100,000.[30]

THE CIVIL WAR AND ITS AFTERMATH: JIM CROW, LYNCHING, AND CONVICT LEASING

With the outbreak of the Civil War, the fortunes of the white planter took a turn for the worse. Although Mississippi would be the second southern state to secede from the union, many Deltans believed that the "best hope for maintaining their wealth and status seemed to lie in remaining within the Union."[31] They were right. By 1862, the Delta lay at the epicenter of the union's strategy to "divide and bankrupt the Confederacy by exercising control over Mississippi River and Gulf of Mexico commerce."[32] Slave insurrections, the looting of personal property, the destruction of plantations and crops, and the razing of whole communities left the Delta in ruins. To add insult to injury, runaway slaves and freedmen from Mississippi joined the United States Colored Troops.[33] In the summer of 1863, this new black military regiment formed with the blessing of President Lincoln and the federal government, providing additional security along the Mississippi River. According to Jewett and Allen, "Nothing expressed the changed circumstances for former slaves more than having black soldiers guarding the river fortifications in plain sight of seething Southern slaveholders."[34] With the end of the Civil War, the "paradox of a democracy founded on slavery," wrote W. E. B. Du Bois, "had at last been done away with."[35]

To some extent, Du Bois's assessment was correct. The outcome of the Civil War and the following Reconstruction (1865–77) significantly improved the lives of some former slaves. Although the Freedmen's Bureau was limited in its success, the organization provided blacks with food and clothing, legal protection, health care, and access to public schools.[36] For the first time, former slaves enjoyed a five-day workweek. With newfound political freedom, freedmen voted in local and state elections with fervor. One scholar estimated that black turnout for many elections was nearly 90 percent.[37] In addition, 226 black Mississippians held political office during Reconstruction.

Enraged by the apparent transgressions of the North, many southern whites were terrified at the prospect of turning over their once prosperous empire to freed blacks in Mississippi:

> *These people, recently acquired from the jungles of Africa, uneducated, without preparation for the duties of government, illiterate, intensely ignorant as to the requirement of citizenship and civic duties, were given the ballot, and backed by the troops of the victors, who were stationed over the South to hold the Southern white man in subjection, while the jungle hordes took over the reins of government.[38]*

The memories of "Negro rule" belied real efforts by whites to deny African Americans their basic rights of equality. From the end of the Civil War through Reconstruction and beyond, the white response to black emancipation (ironically called "redemption") involved legal attempts by whites to regain control of the state's black labor force. For example, the Mississippi Legislature failed to ratify the Thirteenth Amendment of the U.S. Constitution on December 4, 1865. The amendment made the practice of slavery illegal. In addition, most southern states enacted "Black Codes," and in 1865, the Mississippi legislature created its own "Black Codes," a blatant attempt to "impose *de facto* slavery upon the freedmen."[39] According to Du Bois, these codes were "deliberately designed to take advantage of every misfortune of the Negro" by severely restricting blacks from carrying weapons, renting property within the city limits, occupying city streets after sundown, consuming alcohol, or even preaching the gospel.[40]

Another effective measure to restore white control of black labor came through the tenant farming system. By the 1880s, the Delta's uninhabitable dense forests and swamps were slowly being transformed into arable farmland. Personal greed and an insatiable appetite to live the good life, coupled with the culturally embedded values of progress, created the context for the deforestation of the Delta. Between 1880 and 1919, four million acres of trees were cleared, leaving in their wake a "wasteland of stumps."[41] Delta whites ruled over large tracts of farmland and black field hands, many of whom were recruited from Mississippi's hill country, a region suffering from economic stagnation and "failing soils."[42] During the 1880s, almost all Delta counties witnessed a significant increase in their black population. For example,

Washington County's black population increased from 25,367 in 1880 to 35,530 in 1890; Bolivar's black population increased from 15,958 in 1880 to 26,737 in 1890.[43]

Although there were different types of tenant-management arrangements (e.g., sharecropping, sharetenants, and renters), sharecropping proved to be the most popular with white planters. For example, by 1930, roughly 60 percent of tenant families on farms were sharecroppers.[44] Under this arrangement, laborers farmed a specific plot of land and kept half of the revenue generated from the growing and selling of crops, cotton in particular. In exchange for their labor, workers were often forced to buy goods such as farm supplies, food, and clothing on credit at exorbitant interest rates from the plantation owner.[45] Since many black field hands did not possess basic mathematical skills, plantation owners frequently "cooked the books" and shortchanged their black employees. Workers also lived in substandard housing, often in the form of a shotgun shack. In the end, many black sharecroppers barely broke even or were in debt to the plantation owner.[46] Although black field hands toiled from sunup to sundown, many whites still considered the Negro to be idle, lazy, and undisciplined. One plantation owner even chided his black tenants for not working on Sunday, the only time most blacks were afforded a day of rest from the six-day workweek.[47] With white planters as property owners and blacks as propertyless servants, the sharecropper system kept the labor force in an almost perpetual state of peonage. Son House vividly recalled the impact of the sharecropping system on the black community:

> At that time, there was mostly farm work, and sometimes it got pretty critical. Low wages and—well, people kind of suffered a little during some of those years. . . . Some of those that grew crops—if they paid their debts for the food they ate during the year, why, if they came out and cleared as much as forty or fifty dollars for a year, they were satisfied. Out of a whole year's work![48]

Forsaking plantation life, African Americans also worked in levee camps. These camps were common along the banks of the Mississippi River until the late 1930s. Adam Gussow described the camps as "notoriously murderous," as black workers were routinely gunned down by white foremen as well as black enforcers who were hired to administer a brutal form of law and order.[49] If the workers were not murdered outright, the strain of felling trees and draining swamps led many to an early grave. Blues musician Memphis Slim painfully described the misery and death that frequently visited the camps: "On the levee camps they used to say, you know, when fellers would be so tired from carrying logs or something like that, you know, clearing a new ground, he say, 'Burn out, burn up. Fall out, fall dead.'"[50]

By the early 1890s, the implementation of Jim Crow laws brought a new segregation to the South, and as a result, blacks were "pilloried in a virtual bacchanalia of racism."[51] Named after the 1828 minstrel song "Jump Jim Crow," these laws strengthened efforts to create segregated public spaces as well as deny African American males the right to vote.[52] Throughout the South, blacks were barred from occupying white trains, streetcars, restaurants, and other public spaces such as restrooms. Under these new laws, interracial relationships were strictly forbidden. For example, in 1892 the Mississippi legislature made interracial cohabitation or an act of interracial sex illegal. Punishment could include a five hundred dollar fine and ten years in prison.[53] The outcome of the 1896 *Plessy v. Ferguson* Supreme Court case added further credibility in the eyes of whites to the virtues of the illusory separate-but-equal ideology.

Whites also used extralegal, and often brutal and sadistic, tactics to control and subjugate blacks. Mississippi became known as the "lynching capital of the U.S." Since the beginning of the Reconstruction era, the practice of lynching became an alternative method for fearful whites to control the black population. In particular, planters justified such extreme measures as a vital effort to protect property and family.[54] Between 1882 and 1903, an estimated 334 reported lynchings (294 blacks, 39 whites, 1 other) occurred in Mississippi, the most of any state on record.[55] Clyde Woods claims, however, that these figures "represent a massive undercount of the deaths caused by shootings, beatings, and others forms of individual, planter, mob, and official violence."[56] In his landmark study of violence and the blues, Adam Gussow reported that in the post-Reconstruction South, some 3,220 African Americans were lynched between 1880 and 1930. These lynchings served to "terrorize black southerners, particularly men, into submitting to an emergent system of racial segregation and remaining a captive and exploited source of agricultural labor."[57] On three separate occasions, in 1922, 1937, and 1940, the U.S. House of Representatives passed antilynching legislation only to be thwarted by southern Democrats in the Senate who filibustered to kill the proposed bills.[58]

The specter of lynching certainly had its impact on the African American blues community in Mississippi and in other southern states. W. C. Handy avoided what surely would have been a lynching in Murfreesboro, Tennessee, after successfully thwarting the efforts of a white ticket agent who attempted to use an iron bar to break up an impromptu boxing match between two minstrel performers.[59] In their respective autobiographies, both B. B. King and Willie Dixon remembered witnessing the gruesome public spectacle that accompanied the lynching rituals. Whites often dismembered body parts, particularly fingers and toes, and kept them as souvenirs. In other situations, human remains were sold for profit. Blues musician Sam Price remembered a lynching that occurred in Waco, Texas, when he was a child: "They lynched this man and then they burned him and sewed up his ashes in a little cloth and *sold* these ashes to the people."[60] In *Give My Poor Heart Ease: Voices of the Mississippi Blues*, blues scholar William Ferris interviewed Shelby "Poppa Jazz" Brown, the owner of a blues joint in Leland for over thirty years. In the interview, Brown told the researcher about one particularly grisly lynching, a telling story about the fate of many African Americans who retaliated against white violence:

> *Shelby recalled a black man who killed two sheriffs in retaliation for their vio-*
> *lent acts in the black community. When the black man was captured, he was*
> *placed in a wooden box, and railroad cross ties were piled on top. Gasoline was*
> *then thrown on the box and lit. The black man managed to open the lid of the*
> *box and escape the fire, but he was caught again and hung from a bridge over*
> *the local railroad track. He was still hanging when a passenger train passed,*
> *and the railroad company sued the town for the act.*[61]

It is unclear whether the lawsuit was a response to the lynching of the black victim or the fact that the sight of a dead body hanging from a rope shocked the train passengers.

Mississippi newspapers, while not condoning lynching, certainly did not condemn the practice. For example, while acknowledging that lynching is "horrible," the *Daily Clarion-Ledger* editorialized that for "certain heinous crimes," the practice "may be excusable."[62] In a national study examining the reported causes for the lynching of African Americans during a twenty-one-year period from 1882 to 1903, Cutler found that rape was only second to murder as the primary rationale for violence against blacks.[63] Not surprisingly, the editors of the *Daily Clarion-Ledger* argued that the "heinous crime" of rape seemed to favor the rope and mob because white women were easy prey for the "black fiend":

> *No power has been able to stay their mad passion when it seizes them; the wild*
> *beast of the forest has no more control over his appetite when he smells fresh*
> *blood than these human-tigers who stalk about by night and after their ghastly*
> *orgies of blood and rape demand that the laws of the land be stayed until mon-*
> *ey and time is spent in sending them into the eternity their souls merit.*[64]

Psychologically traumatized from the threat of lynching, many black Mississippians endured further degradation and injustice. After the Civil War, many southern states, including Mississippi, developed the convict-leasing system, whereby prisoners were bound to local contractors and forced to build roads, pick cotton, or engage in other labor-intensive work. In *Slavery by Another Name*, Douglas A. Blackmon wrote that convict leasing was "a system in which armies of free men, guilty of no crimes and entitled by law to freedom, were compelled to labor without compensation, were repeatedly bought and sold, and were forced to do the bidding of white masters through the regular application of extraordinary physical coercion."[65] In essence, the convict-leasing system served as a "functional replacement for slavery."[66] While murder often led to life imprisonment or execution, lesser "crimes"—loitering, vagrancy, drunkenness, and homelessness—carried long imprisonment.[67]

The Mississippi Legislature even created the so-called Pig Law, making the theft of property—including livestock—worth more than ten dollars a criminal felony. Before the passage of this law, the theft of property valued at less than twenty-five dollars was considered petty larceny.[68] According to blues musician Big Bill Broonzy, blacks were routinely sentenced to hard labor for stealing a pig or a cow: "It would be bad if they caught you stealing a hog. They would give you two years on the farm and a hundred dollars fine."[69] As expected, the Pig Law helped replenish the pool of cheap black labor. In 1877, less than four years after the bill had passed, Mississippi's prison population increased by approximately 300 percent.[70]

Suffering from inadequate food and medical care and often forced to work in inhospitable weather conditions, many prisoners simply expired. Not surprisingly, black prisoners died at a much higher rate than their white counterparts. From 1880 to 1885, for example, 10.97 percent of all black convicts in Mississippi died versus only 5.30 percent of white prisoners.[71] This evidence reflects not only the pervasive nature of racism in Mississippi's corrections system (the majority of inmates were black) but the system's ability to provide the state with cheap labor. Prisoners who died in accidents or from disease were quickly replaced.

The Mississippi Legislature officially abolished the convict-leasing system in 1890.[72] Nevertheless local authorities continued to arrest Africans Americans on a variety of trumped-up charges (e.g., vagrancy) to satisfy labor needs, a commonplace practice until the 1940s. For example, in 1929, Willie Dixon—songwriter, musician, and composer for Chess Records—was arrested for hoboing at the age of thirteen and sentenced to thirty days on a county farm, where he toiled digging ditches and cutting weeds. In one episode, after witnessing the whipping of another inmate, Dixon himself received a beating that resulted in temporary deafness.[73] In 1931, while traveling from the Memphis area to Greenwood, David "Honeyboy" Edwards was arrested for "trespassing" when the train he was traveling on stopped in the small Delta town of Glendora.[74] Delta whites routinely forced blacks off trains to maintain a supply of cheap labor.[75] Edwards was transported to a plantation store, where he went on trial; a plantation judge (a local farmer who played the role of judge and jury) "sentenced" Edwards to two months of hard labor at a nearby plantation. "It was something like a penitentiary," recalled Edwards. "They run us from daybreak till sunset, then locked us up every night after we was done working for the day in a great big old building, a prisoner cage." A year later, the police arrested Edwards and forced him to work on reinforcing a section of the levee system during a time of potential flooding.[76] In a 1978 interview, blues guitarist Johnny Shines summed up the problems faced by blues musicians (or any African American) who had the misfortune to encounter law enforcement while traveling through the South:

> *If you were a musician walking down the highway or walking the railroad and the sheriff run down on you and you didn't have a certain amount of money in your pocket, you went to the county farm. As a matter of fact, you were taken up as an animal or something like that and leased out to these prison farms run by the big plantation owners.*[77]

While life for prisoners on county farms was dehumanizing and physically demanding, state prisons were worse. Since the legacy of Parchman Penitentiary (which was honored with a blues marker on September 28, 2010) looms large in the history of Mississippi corrections, it is appropriate to provide a brief description of the state's most infamous prison. (Sweet Magnolia Tours' blues package "Nuttin' but the Blues Vacation Holiday" promises that a tour of North Mississippi will include driving past the prison, which has the "dubious honor of being mentioned in a number of blues songs and having housed some of those very bluesman.")[78] Faced with a growing prison population and inadequate corrections facilities, the state purchased over thirteen thousand acres of land in Sunflower County in 1900 and 1901.[79] The prison opened in 1904. By 1917, African Americans constituted approximately 90 percent of the prison's population.[80] From the beginning, however, Parchman did not look like any ordinary prison; it did not have a guard tower, barbed-wire fence, or even a stockade. The prison's open fields and cotton crop resembled an "antebellum plantation with convicts in place of slaves." Indeed, Parchman served as an economic boon to the state's agricultural market. "Unlike other prison systems, which drained public coffers at an ever-expanding rate," wrote historian David Oshinsky, Parchman "poured almost a million dollars into the state treasury through the sale of cotton and cotton seed."[81]

Segregated by sex and race, the prison contained twelve camps.[82] Prisoners worked in the fields up to twelve hours a day growing and picking cotton and vegetables, guarded by both prison employees and armed convicts called "trusties." Ironically, since the majority of inmates were black, prison officials armed black convicts and encouraged them to shoot inmates who attempted to escape.[83] Prisoners who failed to work up to expectations or who were generally uncooperative were severely disciplined. Prison officials used isolation, electrical tortures, and other forms of punishment including flogging and whippings.[84] Writing in 1939, Marvin Lee Hutson observed that whippings seemed to be the preferred method of disciplining the prison population, and the number of lashes depended on the severity of the infraction. For example, criminals who failed to work hard enough were given five lashes, while inmates who acted insubordinate in front of a prison officer could receive as many as fifteen lashes.[85] Prison officials also used "Black Annie," a three-foot leather strap, to reinitiate obedience in "offending" blacks.[86] Blues researcher William Ferris interviewed a number of former prisoners (many of them nonmusicians), including James "Blood" Shelby, who told the researcher that "you had to work or get beat half to death." Another prisoner, Ben Gooch, arrived at the prison in 1934:

> *Parchman was pretty rough then. Whatever they had you doing, you had to run with it. . . . At the time when I come here, you couldn't talk on the job. You just had to sing. They didn't allow you to talk in the field. Only time you could talk was in the cage. They didn't allow you to talk at all when you was working in line. I was rode so hard that when we'd go eat dinner, I couldn't eat with a spoon. The food would shake off because I was so nervous, you know. I'd be so hot I couldn't eat. I'd just lick some of the food. But I made it. I made it through alright.[87]*

The public was largely unaware of the terror, dehumanization, and corruption that plagued the prison since its inception. J. F. Thames, president of the Mississippi Prison Board, colorfully described Parchman as a new, more humane and supportive, model for incarcerating criminals:

> *In the open air of the farm, the contact with nature, regular and reasonable hours of work, clean and sanitary quarters, and wholesome food in abundance, the physical man rapidly responds and in spite of himself he begins to feel a new zest and a new interest in life. Whatever hard and malevolent feelings he may have entertained at first are soon dissipated, and we find him gradually taking an interest in his daily tasks, and the product of his efforts, eager to learn and then in due time anxious to go back into the world and make a new start.[88]*

While many black prisoners remained silent about the horrific conditions at the prison—whether out of fear, lack of access to sympathetic media sources, or otherwise—blues musicians chronicled their experiences in song. In

1928, after shooting and killing a man who had opened fire in a juke joint, Son House was sentenced to a fifteen-year stint at Parchman. However, House was released after only spending two years in jail after a judge reviewed his case and commuted the sentence.[89] Later House went on to record "County Farm Blues," expressing his anger and sorrow for having to work for "Captain Jack." Country blues guitarist Bukka White was one of the more famous inmates at the prison. After being arrested and convicted for murder in 1937, White was shipped off to Parchman.[90] In the song "Parchman Farm Blues," White reveals the difficult working conditions at the prison: "We go to work in the morning just at dawn of day / Just at the settin' of the sun that's when the work is done / I'm down on o' Parchman Farm but I sure wanna go back home / But I hope someday I will overcome." In reality, however, White's talent as a singer and guitarist apparently saved him from most of the prison's more labor-intensive work. As White told the blues expert David Evans in 1966, "I was on easy street when I was there."[91] During the two years he spent at Parchman, the singer recorded two songs under the direction of John Lomax, who was conducting field recordings in the area. White's experience in prison was an aberration, for many of the testimonies from former prisoners paint a harrowing picture.

By the early 1920s, the small gains achieved by African Americans after the Civil War had all but evaporated. Although the Fifteenth Amendment promised to protect the voting rights of all citizens regardless of race or color, efforts to prosecute offenders of the law became difficult, if not impossible. Blacks were effectively barred from entering the voting booth. In addition, after Reconstruction, the number of blacks holding political office dwindled as whites used a variety of tactics, including duplicity and murder, to push "blacks out of the political arena while the national government acquiesced."[92] The rise of white supremacist groups such as the Ku Klux Klan further perpetuated a reign of terror in many southern communities.[93] In the end, according to historian James Cobb, "The small window of opportunity the Delta had once afforded ambitious blacks was firmly shut."[94]

A TIME OF CRISIS: FROM THE FLOOD OF 1927 TO THE GREAT MIGRATION

While blacks in Mississippi and throughout the South were alarmed at their increasing isolation, a series of events—from economic and natural disasters to sociopolitical changes—began the process of dismantling the inequities of the Old South. The Great Flood of 1927 proved to be one of the first in a series of setbacks for the Delta's white elite. This natural disaster would be chronicled in numerous historical treatments of the blues, including a Mississippi Blues

Trail marker titled "MS River Blues," which is located in Scott, Mississippi, nearly three miles from the location where the levee collapsed on April 21, 1927.[95] After months of heavier-than-expected rain during the latter half of 1926 and the early part of 1927, the Mississippi River reached flood stage in a number of areas along the levee system, from Minnesota to Louisiana. Still, federal engineers expressed confidence that "government dikes would withstand any amount of water the mighty river would send against them."[96] Two days later, however, the river overwhelmed the levee system in a small port town thirty miles south of Cairo, Illinois, flooding an estimated 175,000 acres of land. On April 21, less than a week after this initial breach, the levee system in Mounds Landing, Mississippi, collapsed under the strain of the rising tide, flooding the thriving port of Greenville, Mississippi. On the morning of April 22, six feet of water stood in downtown Greenville. The *Commercial Appeal* proclaimed there was "no hope to stop rushing waters."[97]

Greenville's population looked to LeRoy Percy, a former U.S. senator and powerful white planter, for immediate relief. For many local blacks, Percy had become a hero of sorts because of his steadfast support of black voting rights and his public condemnation of the Ku Klux Klan, which had unsuccessfully attempted to establish a base in Washington County.[98] Yet, facing the destruction of his agrarian empire and stiff opposition from a "committee" of white planters, Percy "sold out" the black community, ordering many able-bodied blacks to the levees in a futile attempt to stop the flooding. Although William Percy, LeRoy's son, quarreled with his father's plan to maintain a black workforce on the levee, the younger Percy later tempered his assessment, as described in his autobiography, *Lanterns on the Levee* (1941):

> He knew that the dispersal of our labor was a longer evil to the Delta than a flood. He was a natural gambler: he bet on warm weather and tents. Knowing that I could not be dissuaded by threats or even by his own opposition, he had accomplished his end in the one way possible and had sworn the committee [of white planters] to secrecy. Of course, none of us was influenced by what the Negroes themselves wanted: they had no capacity to plan for their own welfare; planning for them was another of our burdens.[99]

In the end, the governor supported Percy's decision, and hundreds of white citizens were evacuated to higher ground.

By this time, Greenville's black population had been more or less reduced to slaves. The National Guard and auxiliary police forces carefully monitored the work activities of blacks, who were fed limited rations only if they joined a labor organization.[100] Blacks who tried to escape the oppressive conditions were beaten, whipped, and even shot. The conditions in the makeshift levee camps were appalling:

Tents had finally arrived for shelter and the weather had turned warm, but the tents were not floored and cots had not arrived, so refugees still slept on the wet ground. There were no eating utensils or mess hall. Blacks had to eat with their fingers, standing or squatting on their haunches like animals. Beyond the line of tents, for more miles farther up the levee, were thousands of livestock. The stench was unbearable.[101]

The flood left an estimated 250 to 500 people dead and over 160,000 homes under water.[102] In all, 27,000 square miles of land were flooded.[103] The flood also served as a common topical theme for blues singers, including Barbecue Bob ("Mississippi Heavy Water Blues"), Kansas Joe and Memphis Minnie ("When the Levee Breaks"), Blind Lemon Jefferson ("Rising High Water Blues"), and Charley Patton ("High Water Everywhere I").[104]

Efforts to restore the Delta to its previous glory were thwarted by the stock market crash of 1929. As the effects of the Great Depression deepened, cotton prices fell, farm income plummeted, and farm foreclosures increased to such a significant number that one writer remarked that "on a single day a quarter of the entire state of Mississippi went on sale at auction for nonpayment of taxes."[105] David "Honeyboy" Edwards claimed that the Great Depression "equalized" Mississippi because the "banks went down and the plantations owners got broke. . . . Didn't nobody have nothing much."[106] Depression-era blues songs such as "President Blues" (Jack Kelly and His South Memphis Jug Band), "Let's Have a New Deal" (Carl Martin), "New Working on the Project" (Peetie Wheatstraw), and "Welfare Blues" (Speckled Red) reflected the psychological anxiety and social chaos of the times.[107]

It was during the Depression that dissent in the form of farm cooperatives emerged to combat the "decrepit feudal system of southern farming."[108] In late March 1936, the Christian missionary Sherwood Eddy and several other volunteers—who would eventually form the organization's board of trustees—purchased a 2,138-acre farm in Bolivar County and dubbed their new organization the Delta Cooperative Farm (DCF).[109] Twenty-nine families (nine white, twenty African American) would eventually live on the complex.[110] As outlined in the organization's manifesto, "Some Basic Principles of the Delta Cooperative Farm," the DCF envisioned a "new social order," one based largely on the principles of socialism. The DCF proclaimed its new economic scheme would eradicate the exploitative nature of capitalism and ensure "economic justice, the abolition of poverty, and a decent standard of living for all, until a socialized economy is established." Even more radical was the DCF's view of race, one that accurately accessed the long-standing efforts by white planters and race-baiting politicians to create a perpetual state of anxiety and hostility among poor whites and blacks.[111] Despite the early promise, the DCF quickly fell on hard times. In 1937 it faced a series of obstacles, including depleted soil, flooding, insect infestation, and deflated cotton prices. Meanwhile the local white power structure—fearing the social and economic consequences of a successful socialist experiment—attempted to further destabilize the DCF by stirring up rumors of a communist takeover and violently objecting to the organization's view on race. The DCF attempted to reduce its growing debt through a number of measures, including the purchase of a second farm called Providence Cooperative Farm in 1938.[112] By 1942, in debt and experiencing membership attrition, the DCF sold its original farm in Bolivar County for $34,600.[113] The remaining members soldiered on at Providence Farm until its directors, David R. Minter and E. C. "Gene" Cox were forced to leave the state in 1956, a year after critics lambasted the two at a public meeting for promoting "racial integration."[114]

The DCF's bold initiative to break the back of Mississippi's feudal plantation system reflects an important point that should be obvious but is often forgotten: a number of white Mississippians—albeit an often silent minority—did not believe in white racial superiority, approve of the state's segregation laws, or condone violence against African Americans. Unfortunately, many whites who expressed sympathy for the plight of African Americans were condemned as "race traitors."[115] Contemporary examples of race traitors, in the eyes of white racists, would include William Ferris and Panny Mayfield, two individuals who helped promote the blues in Mississippi from the late 1970s to the 1990s.

Despite the real fear of violence and retribution, some whites publicly expressed their dismay and anger over the state's and region's oppressive racial caste system. In the 1930s, for example, thousands of women joined the Southern Women for the Prevention of Lynching. Others assisted African Americans who were facing the prospect of being arrested or murdered. For example, Terry "Harmonica" Bean, a blues musician from Pontotoc, Mississippi, tells the story of his uncle, an African American sharecropper, who killed a white landlord over an argument about money during the 1940s. Afterward, the Ku Klux Klan pursued Bean's relative to enact vengeance but failed to capture him because a number of local whites living in Pontotoc helped his uncle escape to Missouri: "That just goes to show you that it was a lot of good white peoples back then that wasn't into that stuff."[116]

Although the 1927 flood and the Great Depression had forced some plantation owners to declare bankruptcy, the plantation *system* was still intact, as evident by the fact that many African Americans still worked as sharecroppers. Indeed, most blues musicians who grew up in the South lived on plantations and worked in the fields, some even before they were old enough to attend elementary school. For example, at the age of five, Little Milton would routinely work twelve-hour days as a seed boy, a position that required young Milton to place cotton seeds in the planters.[117] Similar to many African American children growing up in Mississippi during that period, blues guitarist James "T-Model" Ford did not even attend school, because his father believed his son could be more useful helping the family survive as sharecroppers.[118] Blues guitarist and singer Eddie Cusic recalled in an interview in *Living Blues* his childhood experiences working long hours in the fields:

> *I used to sing in the fields plowing mules bare-feeted. I got one pair of shoes a year and if I wore them out I went bare-feeted until the next winter and that was rough. And looked like to me I had to go from sunup to sundown follow that mule. And hot, man, it was rough. You wouldn't get no money, nothing much. Get about a dollar, if you got a dollar a day you're getting good wages.*[119]

Many Delta whites employed nonviolent tactics to control black workers, a decision motivated by the need to maintain a steady supply of cheap black labor rather than any moral imperative. Some also resorted to violence to discipline "unruly" and "unproductive" blacks. In turn, sharecroppers were forced to defend themselves, a grievous act of resistance that could have fatal consequences. While working as a sharecropper near Helena, Arkansas, drummer Sam Carr stopped the plantation owner from beating him. "I wasn't gonna let him whoop me," Carr recalled in a 2004 interview with *Living Blues*. "That was plumb out of the question. From that day on, white people called me crazy."[120] On the recording *Blues in the Mississippi Night* (1947), Big Bill Broonzy, Memphis Slim, and Sonny Boy Williamson openly discussed the racial inequities they experienced growing up in Mississippi, claiming that blacks who resisted white authority were often labeled "crazy." Pianist Eddie Boyd, who was born on a plantation near Clarksdale, bitterly recalled several incidents in which he had to defend himself against whites who threatened him for being, in his own words, a "no-good nigger." While working near West Memphis, Arkansas, Boyd stabbed his white employer with a hayfork to escape a certain beating; the singer swam across a bayou and escaped to Memphis later that day. After Boyd disappeared, the white owner called the chief of police of West Memphis, who arrived to initiate the capture of the fugitive. Described as a vicious sadist who reportedly "kicked babies out of pregnant women's stomachs," C. C. Culp (nicknamed "Mr. Cuff") and four other police officers tore up Boyd's parents' one-room shack in an unsuccessful attempt to find the musician, who was hiding in Memphis.[121] In a 1977 *Living Blues* interview, Boyd's assessment of white southern violence was blunt and stinging:

> *They would have KILLED me, man, 'cause they were always beating some black man to death down there. I went through terrible experiences here in this*

country, man. Just because I didn't buck dance and scratch behind my head when I'm looking at a white man. If a white man talked to me, he didn't want you to look him in his eye. But this was the act of a whole lot of black cats: "yessir, well, um, yessir," and he never looked in that man's eye. But when I looked at him, that make him angry. . . . Many times he told me, "You better leave here, nigger, 'cause you're a bad influence for the good niggers."[122]

Most plantation owners and overseers treated their black workers with little regard to their health or happiness. Yet this was not always the case. For example, in the early 1940s, B. B. King worked as a cotton picker and a tractor driver on a plantation near Indianola. While the work was demanding, King enjoyed working in the fields.[123] Unlike most of his contemporaries, King worked for individuals who demonstrated both a modicum of respect to their black workers and an aversion to violence. In his autobiography, King speaks highly of Johnson Barrett, a Jewish plantation boss who, according to King, "treated me like a son." Compared to "dark-hearted racists running all over the Delta," Barrett did not use physical punishment as a method to control his workers, and he even hired a black foreman—a practice unheard of in the Delta at that time.[124] In a 1999 interview, King summed up his admiration for Barrett and others who resisted traditional patterns of white racism: "They seemed to be fair people, people that if it was a black guy and a white guy doing work, whoever didn't do the work, caught the wrath of the mouth. Not just because you were black or because you're white. It's because you didn't do what you were supposed to do."[125] Yet King's narrative was hardly commonplace. Although he experienced many of the indignities of white racism, he was never beaten for insubordination and never arrested and forced to work on a county farm.

Black mobility was another strategy of resistance. The wandering, nomadic life of the blues artist served as a romantic image within the black community and a source of irritation and exasperation for white landowners who viewed such behavior as laziness or implicit rebellion against a system of enforced servitude. Despite legal efforts to ensnare mobile blacks (e.g., vagrancy laws), blues musicians took to the road to improve their craft, make a living, and perhaps secure a recording deal. In 1932, after marrying and then abandoning his second wife, Calletta Craft, Robert Johnson spent the rest of his life touring the country, playing on street corners and at juke joints, eventually recording for the American Record Corporation in November 1936 and June 1937.[126]

The road created its own set of problems. Blues singer Esther Phillips testified in a 1972 interview with *Living Blues* about the region's oppressive segregation laws: "During that time [the 1950s], there was kind of vigorous hate,

5,000 times worse than it is now. And we always had a lot of problems traveling through the South, resting accommodations and things like that."[127] In a 2004 interview, blues singer Mississippi Slim recalled how Jim Crow laws would prevent black musicians from renting rooms at white-owned hotels:

> *There was a time when the black musicians could go and play at the white vendors, but they could not live in the white hotels. You know, in other words, if you was from out of town, say you was traveling and you was from Chicago and you was playing in Jackson, Mississippi. Just say that you had an engagement in Jackson, Mississippi. So what you had to do if you was a black man, you come down here, you could probably play at the white venue, but then you would live in the black side of town that night if you had to have a hotel room.*[128]

Creative measures were used to penetrate the wall of white exclusion. At the Living Blues Symposium in 2003, Bobby Rush confessed to engaging in subterfuge to books rooms at white-owned hotels. Changing his voice and his name (to his birth name of Emmet Ellis Jr.) to sound white, Rush called a hotel and claimed he was the manager of a group of black musicians desiring a room for the night. After successfully portraying himself as a white manager over the phone, Rush would then appear at the front desk and announce that "Mr. Ellis called for some rooms for us." The trick usually worked, although it was not a foolproof scheme: "There were still a couple that put me on the spot asking to come by and pay in advance 'cause the hotel wasn't going to accept money from them black guys. You gotta do that to get a room to sleep."[129]

Located in Clarksdale, the Riverside Hotel served as the one of the few commercial lodging options for African Americans in the Clarksdale area. The Riverside Hotel was originally the G. T. Thomas Afro-American Hospital, a care center that served Clarksdale's black population. The hospital closed in 1940. Four years later, Z. L. Hill purchased the building and several surrounding lots for $15,000 and transformed the hospital into a hotel. The hotel attracted blues musicians, including Muddy Waters, Howlin' Wolf, Robert Nighthawk, and Sam Cooke. From 1944 until Mississippi's segregation laws were effectively repealed in the early 1970s, the Riverside Hotel was an indispensable source of security for blues musicians who still were struggling to build their careers, musicians who would later become international recording stars. According to the hotel's current proprietor, Frank Ratliff (the son of Z. L. Hill), the Riverside was "a starting place" for these largely unknown musical talents: "Ike [Turner] started here. John Lee Hooker had his start. He was playing around. King Biscuit Boys, Sonny Boy [Williamson II], all of them stayed here in the fifties, all them stayed right here with my mother." Ratliff's mother would cook for the musicians (when the café was still in operation) and frequently joined her musical guests for late-night talks that often lasted well into the early morning. "She always was involved with the blues, into the blues, with all the blues musicians. She met them all," recalled Ratliff.[130]

For many blues fans, the building serves as an important tourist destination because of its association with the death of Bessie Smith, widely acknowledged as the genre's greatest female blues singer. In 1937, Smith was involved in a two-car accident on Highway 61 and was transported to the hospital, where she died. After the hospital was converted into a hotel, the emergency ward was transformed into a small bedroom and christened the Bessie Smith Room. The dimly lit room contains a full-size bed, a nightstand, and a small dresser. A large painting of Smith (with "Empress of the Blues" inscribed at the bottom of the frame) hangs over the bed. On an adjoining wall, guests can view a large painting that depicts an oversized black angel hovering over two small children who are trying to cross a bridge during a storm. Guests are often denied their request to stay in the room because Ratliff believes the bedroom is a "special" place. Highlighted in numerous blues tourism guides, the Riverside Hotel is a popular tourist haunt. The Mississippi Blues Commission honored the hotel with a blues marker.

While many whites at the time disregarded the blues as "nigger music" or were simply ignorant of the state's blues culture, some genuinely appreciated the music and often hired blues musicians to play at private white parties. On the Stovall Plantation, Muddy Waters would play at white dances a few times a year: "My boss really liked that kinda carrying on. He'd give a party, and he'd get me, you know, to come do his things for him."[131] Musicians needed to develop an expansive repertoire because enthusiastic white audiences would request ragtime, country, big band, and pop songs in addition to blues standards. Eugene Powell remembered the fervent response he received at a local white dance: "One time I played for a white dance and so many whites went to dancing so hard the middle of the floor fell in."[132] White audiences also proved to be a lucrative source of income. "Sometimes we'd play for white people every night in the week down there," recalled guitarist Houston Stackhouse. "Colored people'd get mad at us, but that was where we was makin' our money! You know, colored people wasn't able to pay us that, 'cause things was kinda rough, and everything was so cheap down there."[133]

At the same time, white enthusiasm for the blues resulted in unbelievable, even comical, situations. As a young boy, Paul Jones and his father were stopped by members of the Belzoni police and transported to the local police station, where Jones entertained the crowd: "They took me to the station and I played, and they threw quarters in the hole in my guitar."[134] Whites were so enthralled with Charley Patton's skills as a musician and his wild showmanship that they sometimes invaded black dances where Patton was performing and persuaded (or perhaps forced) him to disregard his previous commitment and play for an all-white audience. Patton's treatment by whites is similar to a "white New York cop hi-jack[ing] James Brown from a show at Harlem's Apollo Theatre to perform at a policemen's ball."[135] Black musicians who did not heed the wishes of whites, however, could be severely punished. Ledell Johnson, the brother of blues artist Tommy Johnson, remembered the time Tommy was approached by a white stranger and asked to play a song. When Johnson refused to perform, the white man "took the guitar and hit Tom right on the head with it and kept trying to hit him with it until Tom got up and ran away from him."[136]

Meanwhile technological advances such as the tractor (what some blues musicians have called the "iron mule") and the mechanical cotton picker, along with the creation of powerful herbicides and pesticides, reduced the need for human labor in the Delta. This development, along with oppressive labor practices and the unfair treatment of black field hands, contributed to the Second Great Migration.[137] The First Great Migration, which started in 1915 and lasted until 1930, was a result of economic conditions in part of the South (flooding, boll weevil infestation, labor demands in the North because of World War I), as well as mob violence in Georgia and South Carolina.[138] Even after the end of the First Migration, nearly 500,000 more blacks left the South during the 1930s than moved to the South.[139] As part of the Second Great Migration (1940–60), black migration patterns peaked during the 1940s, with more than 1.4 million African Americans exiting the South between 1940 and 1950.[140] Although Mississippi blues artists had left the South before the beginning of the Second Great Migration, the deluge started after 1940: Muddy Waters left in 1943 for Chicago; Waters's rival Howlin' Wolf left a decade later.[141] John Lee Hooker left the South in the early 1940s, finally settling in Detroit in 1948. David "Honeyboy" Edwards and Little Walter Jacobs arrived in Chicago in 1945.[142] Others followed. While some Mississippi-born musicians decided to permanently relocate outside the South (some even decided to seek permanent refuge in Europe), others—James "Son" Thomas, Willie Foster, R. L. Burnside—left temporarily, returning to Mississippi to carve out a living, working a full-time job and playing music at night and on the weekends.[143] In all, from around 1910 to 1960, more than nine million people emigrated from the South to the West, North, and the upper Midwest.[144] An estimated six million were African American.

The impetus for some African Americans leaving the Delta was not the dream of freedom in the North. As the United States entered World War II, many southern blacks left for the battlefield. Elmore James, Howlin' Wolf, Jimmy Reed, and other blues artists served in the military during the war, while others such as Willie Dixon claimed conscientious-objector status and were sentenced to jail. Although the U.S. military was for all practical purposes still segregated, blacks and whites were unified against a common enemy and recognized each other's bravery and heroism. From that experience, some southern whites began to embrace the idea of racial tolerance, even believing that blacks should receive full citizenship status.[145] However, many returning white GIs wavered and then "quietly adjusted to the status quo." More significantly, however, many African Americans who fought for their country's freedom only to return home to find themselves once again enmeshed in a Jim Crow system of racial discrimination "weighed their options, impatiently waited and covertly organized for an assault on the color line."[146] Except for a vocal minority, black Mississippians did not publicly contest the state's segregation policies until the *Brown v. Board of Education of Topeka* decision of 1954.[147] In this landmark case, the Supreme Court voted in a unanimous 9–0 ruling to repeal the "separate but equal" doctrine that had previously been ruled constitutional by the Supreme Court in *Plessy v. Ferguson* (1896). The court concluded that the "separate but equal" doctrine "has no place" in the public education arena because "separate educational facilities are inherently unequal."[148]

The *Brown* case was the beginning of a series of social and cultural events that would dramatically and permanently transform the South. A year later, the gruesome death of Emmett Till at the hands of two Delta whites, along with Rosa Parks's fateful decision in December 1955 not to give up her seat on a Montgomery bus to a white passenger, catalyzed the civil rights movement. In January 1957, Martin Luther King Jr., his mentor Bayard Rustin, and two other civil rights leaders founded the Southern Christian Leadership Conference (SCLC), a civil rights group that espoused Mahatma Gandhi's philosophy of nonviolent civil disobedience. By 1960, the Student Nonviolent Coordinating Committee (SNCC) was formed to provide younger blacks an opportunity to express their rising discontent over the South's resistance to change. During the same year, the Congress of Racial Equality (CORE), which was founded in 1942, started to send college students to the South as "freedom riders" to test new laws that prohibited the segregation of interstate travel facilities.

Despite efforts by the White Citizens' Council (often simply called the Citizens' Council), formed in 1954 in Indianola, Mississippi (near the spot where B. B. King's Museum and Delta Interpretive Center currently sits), and a resurgent Ku Klux Klan to disenfranchise and intimidate the state's African American population, Mississippi witnessed some degree of social change throughout the 1960s. By 1970, the hopes of maintaining the traditions of a segregated, racially marked society were quickly fading. By the 1970–71 school year, most of Mississippi's public schools had been integrated.[149] In addition, in 1973 the State Sovereignty Commission, an organization formed in 1956 to spy on black activists and others suspected of supporting integrationist practices, was ended by Governor William L. Waller, who believed that the organization "performs no real indispensable services to the people of this state."[150] The Citizens' Council, which had achieved an extraordinary level of popular and political support in Mississippi and other southern states during the 1950s and early 1960s, was for all practical purposes defunct by 1979. It is no coincidence that at the same time Mississippi was shifting to a more socially and culturally progressive phase, the state started to recognize the need to promote its own blues heritage. In the next chapter, I explore how Mississippi's official culture employs memory as a rhetorical device to reshape public perceptions of the state while downplaying the state's historical record of racial injustice.

6

PUBLIC MEMORY, HISTORICAL AMNESIA, AND THE SHACK UP INN

Going to Mississippi was, for me, eating the fruit of the Tree of Knowledge, bitter fruit that changed my life as I became aware of things I could never again not know. What disturbed me most was realizing that Mississippi cast a large shadow over not only our history, but also our present. The straight-lined distinctions I'd always kept between past, present and future collapsed as I saw how those three strands of time crossed and snagged to form the dark weave of this country. To me, American amnesia about the past was perhaps worse than the many crimes that had been committed, because that willful refusal to confront history made impossible any meaningful action now.

—ANTHONY WALTON, *Mississippi: An American Journey*

Cultural tourism is a memory-building industry. The Mississippi Blues Trail encourages tourists to retrace, in reverse, the two Great Migration movements of the twentieth century. Blues tourists who kneel at the gravesites of Charley Patton and Sonny Boy Williamson II, visit Dockery Farms, or stand at Robert Johnson's crossroads are participating in a larger and more complex institutional effort to reconstruct the past. Institutionalized efforts to use memory to promote the blues are, however, just one example of a wider cultural practice intended to support a growing trend among various states to develop tourism as a source of revenue. Without a doubt, the South has turned memory into a tourist commodity in the form of memorials and statues to the Confederate dead, Civil War battlefields and cemeteries, and antebellum homes. Since the end of the Civil War, as historian W. Scott Poole has observed, the South has been characterized as a "culture of remembrance," for no region, with the exception of New England, "has rooted its identity so powerfully in its own historical consciousness."[1]

Official memory-building practices can be credited, in part, for changing how Mississippians view their blues heritage and the musicians responsible for shaping the music. Blues tourism has played a role in changing the attitudes of white Mississippians about the contributions of its African American population to American popular culture; African Americans, some apathetic, others opposed to the blues for religious or moral reasons, are reassessing the value of the music. Yet it is also clear that tourism officials use memory to highlight, exaggerate, and deny the region's history and heritage. Plantation owners are described as fair minded and kind, and sharecropping is depicted as fair and equitable. Slavery, political disenfranchisement, lynching, the convict-leasing system, segregation, and other past transgressions are frequently omitted from the official narrative. When past atrocities do surface in promotional materials or newspaper articles, they usually take the form of abstract generalizations or euphemisms. The blues is remembered not as a vehicle for struggle, a form of protest, but as a form of entertainment and escapism. The social conditions that gave rise to the development of the blues, and the harsh realities experienced by many Mississippi blues musicians, are conspicuously absent.

Perhaps the most peculiar example of memory building is the Shack Up Inn, a white-owned business located on a local plantation, a site where black field hands traded their labor-intensive work for inadequate housing and low wages. The Shack Up Inn demonstrates how tourism strategies in small towns often translate into the "commodification of its landscape, turning the place into something to be consumed."[2] The plantation and sharecropper shacks have been commodified for both profit and preservation, transformed from symbols of oppression into a source of pleasure for blues tourists. At the same time, the Shack Up Inn symbolizes how some white efforts to perpetuate and promote the blues are often at odds with the blues experience in Mississippi's black communities. In all, while these rhetorical strategies may alter the public's negative perceptions of Mississippi, racial reconciliation may be sacrificed as a result.

PUBLIC MEMORY

While memory is commonly understood as a process of remembering the past, public memory is a decidedly more complicated affair. The study of public memory involves, in part, understanding the temporal relationship among three interlocking and interdependent time constructs. Historian John Bodnar defines public memory as "a body of beliefs and ideas about the past that help a public or society understand both its past, present, and by implication, its future."[3] As Barbie Zelizer argues, as the past is remembered, it is intimately "woven into the present and future."[4] Public monuments, for example, not only reflect the past in memorializing a person or event but work to "preserve its memory in times to come—at the limit, times beyond measure."[5]

Scholars have differentiated public memory from other types of remembering.[6] While individual memories are characterized as unique and private, public memory is a shared group experience. Public memory occurs in a public space where individuals discuss a common topic of "concern to all who gather in a given place," a process that involves commemoration, or the act of "remembering together."[7] Any rhetorical artifact that is widely accessible to a public, including memorials (Vietnam War memorials), photographs (Twin Towers), museums (Holocaust Museum), and eulogies (Ronald Reagan) creates the opportunity for a public to remember.[8] Since memory is a function of communication, scholars have argued that memory and rhetoric are fundamentally one and the same. As rhetorical critic Kendall R. Phillips puts it: "The ways memories attain meaning, compel others to accept them, and are themselves contested, subverted, and supplanted by other memories are essentially rhetorical."[9]

As Phillips argues, because of its rhetorical nature, public memory is open to debate, revision, and rejection, an issue that causes rhetorical critic Stephen Browne to wonder whether a singular and unified public memory could ever exist: "Can we now, if ever we could, even speak of *a* public memory, for can anything so contingent and contested ever be theorized in the singular?"[10] Articulated in rhetorical practice and embodied in material objects, public memory is partial, fragmentary, unpredictable, and unstable.[11] Thus efforts to understand the nature of public memory have operated with the assumption that a singular public memory is largely a fiction because, in the words of historian Benjamin Filene, not "all the members of a given public could share [an] identical set of memories."[12]

Although a singular public memory does not exist, the struggle over which public memory becomes privileged typically occurs between vernacular and official communities.[13] While vernacular communities are "ordinary people who often oppose the representations of official culture," official communities are cultural authorities who are concerned with maintaining the status quo.[14] The struggle over how the past is remembered confirms Zelizer's assertion that public memory involves more than simply recalling the past. As a frequently contested form of discourse, public memory reflects issues of "power and authority" as competing groups struggle to create and present a particular understanding of the past.[15] Indeed, as one observer noted, "those who can create the dominant historical narrative, those who can own the public memory, will achieve political and cultural power."[16] Often legitimized by power and status, expertise and prestige, official culture has inherent advantages over its vernacular rival. For example, institutionalized stories have the power, according to rhetorical critic Barbara Biesecker, to control how people remember the past.[17] Official culture also engages in the rhetorical act of *forgetting*, for as easily as some memories can become privileged and achieve a ring of truth, others can be forgotten. "While collective memory can be about forgetting the past," argues one observer, "it often comes at the expense of a subordinate group."[18] As a result, opposing and contradictory memories produced by vernacular cultures are marginalized, dismissed, and often forgotten.

Still, the power of vernacular culture cannot be underestimated. The civil rights movement, for example, played a role in protesting present racial and class inequities and linking these policies of exclusion and discrimination to past injustices. Martin Luther King Jr.'s "I Have a Dream" epidictic speech typifies this approach, as King remembers how the framers of the U.S. Constitution wrote a "promissory note" guaranteeing *all* Americans specific and unalienable rights and freedoms. Yet systematic efforts to maintain a subservient black underclass, whether through legislative or extralegal means, demonstrated the hollowness of promise: "Instead of honoring this sacred obligation, America has given the Negro people a bad check, a check which has come back marked 'insufficient funds.'" As a result, as King sadly noted at the beginning of the speech, "One hundred years later, the life of the Negro is still sadly crippled by the manacles of segregation and the chains of discrimination." This speech would provide a powerful vernacular countermemory to the fictional separate-but-equal ideology that served to preserve the interest of white supremacy.

To understand the importance of public memory in the blues tourism industry, one needs to understand the impact and influence of memory on contemporary southern culture. The South's obsession with memory started with the Lost Cause story, a defiant post–Civil War narrative that romanticized the antebellum South, remembered its Confederate dead, and explained the South's crushing defeat at the hands of invading Yankees.[19] The Lost Cause narrative was soon embodied in material culture, for the construction of memorials became a new economic industry. By the 1890s, according to historian David W. Blight, Civil War memorials marked almost every community in the South.[20] In Savannah, Georgia, for example, all its historical squares contain at least one monument to the Lost Cause.

Memory was also central to how the South responded to economic crises and political and social unrest. For example, by the early twentieth century, many southerners fondly remembered the golden age of the antebellum era, a rhetorical response to the collapse of an agricultural empire and the deepening of rural poverty.[21] The divestment of black political power, which began shortly after the Civil War, intensified by the 1890s, and continued throughout the

1950s and 1960s, was justified by the Lost Cause story.[22] Rather than acknowledge the South's pathological racial edicts and the institutions that enforced
these policies, some white southerners believed that African Americans actually benefited from Jim Crow laws. In a 1999 interview, Charles W. Capps Jr.,
a former Bolivar County sheriff and member of the Mississippi House of Representatives from 1976 to 2005, believed that segregation created "wonderful"
racial relationships: "Everybody both black and white knew exactly what their
place was, and nobody ever got out of their place."[23]

More recently, Mississippi governor Haley Barbour claimed that his experience at the University of Mississippi during the mid- to late-1960s was "pleasant" and that his generation, unlike previous ones, did not oppose integration.[24] Barbour attended the university three years after James Meredith was
admitted. As many will recall, after initially being rejected by the university
registrar in 1961, Meredith—with the protection of 536 federal marshals—
showed up at the university on September 30, 1962, with the goal of seeking
admission and registering for classes.[25] Mississippi governor Ross Barnett, as
well as university administrators, students, and white supremacist groups like
the Citizens' Council, strongly opposed racial integration, and many appeared
on campus to voice their strong opposition. The protest, which was initially
peaceful, turned violent. During the riot, two people were killed and an estimated two hundred injured. For the rest of the semester, Meredith was under
the protection of a fleet of U.S. marshals who acted as his bodyguards, and
black students were routinely taunted and ignored by white students. Despite
the racial tensions and social turbulence that engulfed the university for the
rest of the decade and beyond, Barbour remembered his time there as a "very
pleasant experience" and claimed that he "never thought twice" about attending an "integrated" university. Verna Bailey, the first African American woman
to attend the university and a classmate of Barbour's, remembered her time
there as a period of great personal risk and claimed that her interactions with
white students were limited: "Very, very few reached out at all."[26] Based on
these conflicting memories, it is difficult to believe that Barbour and Bailey attended the same university. But it is clear that Barbour represents a generation
of white Mississippians who often engage in the practice of historical revisionism in an effort to downplay Mississippi's racist past.

Even today, many southern states remember the past by celebrating Robert E. Lee Day (his birthday is the same day as Martin Luther King Jr.'s)
and Confederate Memorial Day. Confederate Memorial Day allows state government offices in Mississippi, Alabama, and Georgia to close (typically the
fourth Monday in April) to celebrate, in the words of Robert Reames, the
commander of Alabama's Sons of Confederate Veterans, "the greatest heroes
this country has ever produced."[27] In contrast, while Mississippi celebrates

Martin Luther King Jr. Day, the state has not dedicated a day of remembrance for other important civil rights leaders, including Medgar Evers and Fannie Lou Hamer. Unlike its neighbor to the north, Tennessee, Mississippi does not even have a civil rights museum, although there are plans to build one in the capital city of Jackson. This gross omission mirrors how some tourism officials and blues promoters privilege a memory of denial.

THE DELTA BLUES AND PUBLIC MEMORY

The importance of the Mississippi Blues Trail and other institutionalized efforts to celebrate the contributions of Mississippi blues artists cannot be overstated. Until recently, the state had virtually ignored its blues heritage, although local efforts to promote the blues had been under way since the late 1970s. Through these promotional efforts, musicians such as Charley Patton and Son House have been largely transformed from despised, lazy drunkards and "field niggers" to prized, iconic music legends. Once ignored and scorned, an important part of the state's African American culture and heritage is now being recognized and celebrated. Yet while the state is engaging in a constructive memory-building enterprise by illuminating its blues culture, a careful analysis of promotional materials (e.g., brochures, pamphlets, and Web sites) suggests that the state's official culture has constructed an understanding of the past that minimizes or ignores the historical realities that served as the impetus for the blues in the first place.

Promotional materials, for example, seem to make light of the lives of Delta blues musicians, such as Muddy Waters and B. B. King, who lived in squalid conditions (no running water or indoor plumbing) and worked a demanding twelve- to sixteen-hour day, picking cotton, clearing fields, and engaging in other punishing, labor-intensive work with meager economic compensation. Others spent time on chain gangs and in penal farms or federal penitentiaries. In a brochure distributed by the Coahoma County Tourism Commission, blues musicians are referred to as "farm workers" whose lives were "hard." The music's "raw emotion" and "throbbing rhythms" are a testament to the musicians' "hardship" and their "heritage."[28] In another brochure, black sharecroppers are described as simply working the "enormous plantations of the Delta."[29] In another example, one writer characterized blues music as a music of "joy and hope to triumph over adversity" for African Americans working on farms and large plantations.[30] The Coahoma County Tourism Commission typifies this approach of minimizing the misery experienced by Mississippi's African American population while at the same time accentuating the region's alluring "mystique": "The Mississippi Delta is a land of mystery and magic where *adversity* and elation, *trial* and triumph walk hand in hand" (italics mine).[31]

If the promotional materials are to be believed, blues musicians who participated in the Second Great Migration apparently did not leave the state because of the oppressive and unfair labor practices. One brochure claims that the "Original Blues Highway" was the "route many Delta Blues musicians took to the industrial North where they went to seek work."[32] Precisely why these musicians left the Delta in the first place is not explained. Clarksdale blues singer and guitarist James "Super Chikan" Johnson provides a historical antidote to efforts to hide the past, a revealing statement that links the past to the present:

> *Well, when they call Clarksdale the "home of the blues," they wasn't talkin' about blues music. If you live around this area, you're going to have the blues. I mean, it's a blues town. It's hard work, it's sharecropping, well back in those days, so that's why most of the guys left because they were so glad to get out of the field. They didn't want to be nowhere near it. They didn't want no parts of it, so they took off up North. In fact, a whole bunch of them disowned Mississippi.[33]*

Despite evidence to the contrary, the Coahoma County Tourism Commission claims that the city of Clarksdale served as a kind of welcome center, an "urban oasis" for musicians who decided to seek their fortunes elsewhere: "At the time of the Great Migration, Clarksdale was the *first to welcome* Delta farmhands, as well as their musicians and entertainers, on their plight out of the oppressive sharecropping system of the rural plantations and farmlands" (italics mine). Clarksdale served as a "refuge" for the musicians who decided to "stay closer to home" rather than seek their fortunes in the industrialized North.[34] It is hard to image the city of Clarksdale welcoming these musicians, as the story purports to tell, and the African Americans who decided to stay in Clarksdale were virtually no better off than they were at their former jobs.

While all these promotional texts do allude to the black experience in Mississippi, language such as "worked" (i.e., slaved) and "farm workers" (i.e., exploited underclass) does not express the realities of plantation life for many African Americans. The use of "hardship," "trial," and "adversity" is a carefully crafted rhetorical device; these abstract words do not accurately convey the horrors of lynching, the isolationism of segregation, the political disenfranchisement of voting rules designed to thwart black participation in civic and political life, or the fear of encountering law enforcement. Promotional materials that fail to explain the real causes for the Great Migration or characterize the Delta as a land divided between its "liberated" urban centers and the "oppressive" rural spaces clearly demonstrate a deliberate rhetorical effort at historical revisionism.

Tourism officials also obfuscate the qualities of protest music inherent in the Delta blues. One brochure refers to John Lee Hooker and Muddy Waters as musicians who "escaped their work and worries with the haunting lyrics and melodies of their music."[35] In another brochure, blues music is described simply as cathartic dance music with lyrics that attended to the problems of lost love and wretched infidelity. "For decades the blues was all a black man might have in this world," the brochure adds, "so he put his soul into it, and it helped him make it through the next day."[36] Blues music is rarely depicted as a form of protest or dissent; rather, it is party music for tourist consumption. While there is no doubt that blues music served an important entertainment function for African American and white audiences, we should also remember that some blues songs served as a form of oppositional discourse against racism, segregation, economic exploitation, judicial malfeasance, and other forms of social control.[37] Songs by J. B. Lenoir ("Shot on James Meredith" and "Alabama Blues"), Leadbelly ("The Bourgeois Blues"), and Josh White ("Trouble," "Jim Crow Train," "Bad Housing Blues") are just a few examples of blues songs that functioned overtly as protest music.

Some promotional materials even suggest that plantation owners played a key role in popularizing the blues. The Cleveland–Bolivar Chamber of Commerce contends that the Dockery Farms plantation "provided a key asset to the Blues movement," the development of a railroad system (dubbed the Peavine Railroad) that would eventually connect the plantation to the nearby Delta towns of Cleveland, Boyle, and Rosedale.[38] While it is true that Will Dockery sent his black workers to clear land and lay railroad tracks, he did not deliberately set out to assist any supposed "blues movement." In fact, Will Dockery fired Charley Patton on a number of occasions because of Patton's freewheeling, rambling ways; Dockery's son, Joe, referred to Patton and other blues musicians as unreliable workers:

> He was quite a rounder as all blues people were. Those kind were never steady farm workers. They'd much rather be singing at a party somewhere. They had no ambition other than to sing. . . . They had fun among themselves with dances, picnics and such. Saturday night was a first-class bawl for a lot of them.[39]

The Mississippi Development Authority claims that the owners of Dockery Farms "encouraged laborers to explore their musical talents and to rely on little or no share-cropping."[40] It is hard to believe that Will Dockery or his son Joe, a former commissioner at the Parchman prison, actually encouraged their black field hands—who possessed some musical ability—to forsake sharecropping. The Dockery family was in the business of making money, not serving as music agents for a stable of blues musicians. Apparently Will Dockery disdained music in general. He felt it was morally bankrupt.[41]

Moreover, Joe—who, like his father, referred to blacks as "niggers"—was barely aware of his plantation's historic relationship to the blues until the late 1960s, thirty years after the blues scene at Dockery had more or less expired.[42] In her autobiography *Wanderer from the Delta* (2002), Joe's widow, Keith Somerville Dockery McLean, claimed that she and Joe "didn't even know about the Blues" until the late 1960s, although she admitted that Joe was slightly more attuned to his family's uneasy relationship with the music after talking with folklorist Alan Lomax.[43] Dockery also met with blues scholars Robert Palmer and Gayle Dean Wardlow.

It should be noted that, comparatively speaking, both Will and Joe Dockery had a reputation for being fair-minded and "benevolent." Dockery Farms sported a burial society, available to any worker—white or black—who ever lived on the plantation, and for a time, Will Dockery hired a white doctor to tend to the medical needs of *all* his employees.[44] Both claimed to have never cheated their workers out of their wages. And despite the Dockerys' religious conservatism, a brothel operated on the plantation.[45] Giles Oakley believes that Dockery Farms was most likely "the best kind of life available to Mississippi's illiterate black farming population."[46] Still, sharecropping, by its very nature, is an exploitative enterprise, and Joe even admitted to Robert Palmer that the whole system was corrupt: "The system was wrong. Daddy knew that, and I knew it. Everybody knew it."[47]

Other plantation owners believed that blues musicians (and all black employees) who worked on the plantation were happy and content. The following example clearly demonstrates how the memories of some white plantation owners are at odds with the realities of sharecropping. In 1989, Skip Henderson, a former social worker and vintage guitar dealer, started a nonprofit organization, the Mount Zion Memorial Fund, to memorialize blues musicians with expensive and elaborate cenotaph historical markers. More important, according to Henderson, the organization served as a "mechanism to get money into the Delta, to get money to the small church communities to protect their cemeteries," and to provide financial compensation to the surviving family members and descendants of Mississippi's blues musicians.[48] This project is particularly important, since Mississippi's white planters have had a penchant for destroying the headstones of African Americans and plowing over their graves to plant crops. Charley Patton's gravesite received a historical marker in 1991. The former plantation owner, seventy-six-year-old William T. Robinson, told a *New York Times* reporter that Patton was a "happy man":

Those people loved to sing. They were very happy. They had their own cows, their own milk and their own vegetable gardens. The work wasn't real hard. They didn't have much money, but they were well fed. They worked in the fields, where it was healthy, and they loved their churches.

In the same article, Reverend James Ratliff, who worked for Robinson as a child, bitterly remembered earning only $2.50 a day (which included lunch) for working a twelve-hour day picking and chopping cotton.[49] The gross discrepancies between these two memories are, of course, nothing new. During slavery, the white slave owner generally characterized his human chattel as "happy" and "contented" soulless creatures. Slavery, it was argued, saved the African savage from the vile wickedness of his or her native jungle and assisted in curbing the slaves' inherit primitive and uncivilized violent instincts. Robinson's memory of his black workforce is also indicative of how many white planters simply remained oblivious to, or in denial about, the inhumane economic practices associated with sharecropping.

One of the most striking examples of how some tourism officials and blues promoters manipulate memory for control and power is the slogan "No Black, No White, Just the Blues." This clever catchphrase has been used in a variety of contexts at local blues festivals; store owners and street vendors sell T-shirts, bandanas, and other items that feature the slogan (T-shirts are also available from a number of Web sites); and the public relations campaign "Mississippi, Believe It!" features an ad, "No Black. No White. Just the Blues," that includes the photos of six musicians (W. C. Handy, Little Milton, Muddy Waters, B. B. King, Howlin' Wolf, and Bo Diddley) and the following claim:

Some see the world in black and white. Others see varying shades of gray. But, Mississippi taught the world to see . . . and hear . . . the Blues. Charlie Patton, Robert Johnson, W. C. Handy, John Lee Hooker, Bo Diddley, Muddy Waters, Howlin' Wolf, Little Milton, B. B. King . . . they all travelled the most revered blues highway in the world—Mississippi's Highway 61. Mississippi. Birthplace of the blues.[50]

At first glance, the slogan plays on the supposed benefits of blues tourism for the promotion of racial harmony. Yet a closer reading suggests that "No Black, No White, Just the Blues" effectively divorces the blues from history. In this rereading of history, the blues is universal and color-blind, a music that emerged from a cultural vacuum, a music without an ancestral home. The slogan's utopian message also downplays the music's protest elements. According to blues scholar Paul Garon, the blues served as an aesthetic form of resistance against the "genocidal tendency of white culture."[51] Finally, the slogan suggests that both black and white Mississippians somehow played an equal role in shaping Mississippi's blues culture. Mississippi's claim to be the birthplace of the blues, we should remember, rests on the argument that a disproportionate number of historically important blues musicians—a list made up almost entirely of African Americans—were born in the state. In contrast, only a handful of white Mississippians, including Charlie Musselwhite, Harmonica Frank Floyd, Mose Allison, Jimmie Rodgers (a country musician who recorded a number of blues songs), and Elvis Presley, can arguably be credited for making significant contributions to the blues. In all, the slogan erases black from the blues. Cultural critic Greg Tate sufficiently frames the problem: "In a world where we're seen as both the most loathed and the most alluring of creatures, we remain the most co-optable and eraseable of cultures too."[52]

Tourism officials are certainly not alone in erasing the past through omission and silence. Journalists and local citizens have engaged in memory-building practices themselves. Harry Boschert, a contributor to Greenville's *Life in the Delta* magazine, remembered as a child watching members of the Randle family, an African American family living on his father's farm in Duncan, Mississippi, use their considerable vocal talents to turn the "drudgery" of chopping and picking cotton into an enjoyable family event: "They would sing all day long. Everyone was smiling and enjoying themselves. Their chore was transformed into a pleasant experience by singing in the field."[53] Although I have no doubt that workers were exemplary singers, it is hard to imagine the work was "pleasant." In an issue of *Delta Magazine*, Wyatt Emmerich's narrative of the Delta's racial climate during the early twentieth century typifies this approach:

> *Many of my ancestors came from the Delta. I am proud that Delta blood most definitely flows through my veins. Most Mississippians can say the same. Another critical factor, also molded by the soil, was race. African Americans were needed to pick cotton. The whites, from the very start, were a minority in the Delta. This led to a cultural mingling between whites and blacks on a scale never really experienced by the rest of the country. The ultimate manifestation of this cultural cauldron was the blues. It is important to realize that the blues was the foundation of modern day popular music. The very notes and musical scales came from the Delta. Somehow there is something in the Delta that seeped out and spread, through music, until it altered the very notes the entire world expects to hear in their songs. That's pretty amazing.*[54]

From Emmerich's description, it sounds as though this white-black cultural mingling could have happened at a cocktail party. In his description, both African Americans and whites appear to be co-owners of the blues, both groups partnered together to create a highly prized art form. Emmerich's highly nostalgic glance at the past, of course, sidesteps issues of institutionalized bigotry and racial violence. The history of slavery and its terrible aftermath is also curiously omitted.

There are exceptions to the privileged narrative of denial. The Mississippi Blues Trail contains markers that confront, rather than ignore, the state's dubious past. The "Pinetop Perkins and Hopson Planting Company" marker describes the exploitative nature of sharecropping. The marker describes sharecropping as "backbreaking work"; furthermore, as the marker indicates, musicians would make more money playing at a Saturday night dance than they would make for an entire week picking cotton and other forms of labor-intensive work. In another example, the marker for the Riverside Hotel describes in no uncertain terms how the state's segregation laws forced traveling African American musicians to seek refuge at the Riverside Hotel. The Highway 61 marker describes how the oppressive conditions of the Delta encouraged African Americans to travel the "Blues Highway" to the promised land of Chicago and other northern cities.

Other examples include promotional materials that target African American tourists specifically. In "Landmarks, Legends and Lyrics: African American Heritage Guide," the term "slave" is used in several descriptions of slave labor cultivating fields and of plantation mansions "constructed entirely of slave-made bricks." The guide also refers to "African Americans enslaved in Mississippi" who contributed to the creation of the blues and gospel musical genres (gospel and blues were actually created decades *after* the end of slavery). I did not find the term "slave" in any other tourism material I evaluated for this study. This brochure also mentions the Jim Crow era and the monumental ensuing efforts by African Americans to facilitate change:

> *However, the segregated conditions under "Jim Crow" proved to be unbearable for the African-American community, and their struggle was taken to the streets, the courts, and eventually to the voting booths as they fought for equality. The fruits of their labor were evident in the court-ordered integration of public schools, the election of black officials, and the resolution of long-awaited legal battles.*[55]

Another exception can found in a pamphlet created by an African American entrepreneur to promote his business establishment, a voice who represents vernacular culture. Jessie "Bug" Brown, owner of Bug's Blues Lounge, certainly takes a candid, "keeping it real" approach in the brochure promoting his business. The club is located in Rosedale, Mississippi, which he describes as a "sleepy, half abandoned town, that, in the fifties, was renowned for its

parties. Little is left of that period."[56] Mr. Brown also refers to the citizens of
Rosedale who are unemployed and "caught in a web of government funding
that barely reaches those who need it." This is certainly a stark contrast to
Cleveland, a town twenty miles east, which is portrayed in a brochure as "one
of the 100 best small towns in America" and a "vibrant community that keeps
in step with the pace of modern life." The "Cleveland: Crossroads of Culture
in the Mississippi Delta" brochure mentions that residents in small towns of
Bolivar County such as Rosedale "all have a story to tell and a special turn of
phrase that turns mystique into folklore." Omitting Rosedale's present-day
struggles, the brochure encourages the "adventurous" to visit Bug's Place.[57]
These examples, however, are the exception to the rule.

THE SHACK UP INN

It's hard to figure what we're doing. But we found this little niche. And
it's working and people love it. And, you know, my feelings on it are
if you don't like what we're doing, you got to be a communist. You
know, because it's laid-back and cool and calm a place as you're ever
going to [find].
　　—GUY MALVEZZI, Shack Up Inn partner

While tourists can obviously find accommodations at commercial hotels such
as the Holiday Inn and Motel 6, some have decided to seek out sites that are
themselves examples of blues attractions. Located on the Hopson Plantation
on the outskirts of Clarksdale, the Shack Up Inn offers tourists the opportunity to sleep in one of twelve renovated sharecropper shacks. Blues tourists
are interested in spending the night in old shacks because many Mississippi
blues musicians lived in these structures in both rural (plantations) and urban
(black neighborhoods) spaces. For example, Muddy Waters's formative years
were spent living in a small shack on the Stovall Plantation near Clarksdale.
In developing names for each shack, the owners of the Shack Up Inn formally
acknowledged the relationship between the blues and sharecropper shacks.
The Crossroads Shack is an obvious play on the Robert Johnson myth. The
Pinetop Shack is a nod to the plantation's former cotton-picker driver and
blues pianist, Pinetop Perkins (Joe Willie Perkins). The owners advertise the
shacks as "alternative lodging for the hip and not so famous."[58]

　　Founded by Howell H. Hopson in 1852, the roughly 3,800-acre compound
was home to both slaves and sharecroppers alike. After Hopson's death in the
early 1930s, his son, Howell H. Hopson II, took control of the plantation.[59]
The grounds were eventually distributed to descendants of the Hopson family.

Cathy Butler—a descendant of Hopson and the wife of James Butler—purchased the plantation's headquarters in 1988.[60]

The original decision to purchase and renovate old sharecropper shacks was not motivated by a desire to create a new destination for blues tourists. In the late 1990s, Tommy Polk, a singer-songwriter from Nashville (and the cousin of James Butler) believed the rustic ambience of a sharecropper shack would fuel his songwriting aspirations. Butler and other interested parties raised $400 and purchased a shack, eventually naming it the "Cadillac Shack." "The boys come on down [from Nashville] to write," remembered Butler in the November 18, 2001, edition of *Blues News*, "but it was just too small, so we went out looking for another one and found the Robert Clay shack out by Rich, Mississippi."[61] *Commercial Appeal* reporter Jennifer Spencer revealed that Polk, inspired by his shack experience, wrote "Tell Me Sweet Jesus" and encouraged other songwriters to attend informal weekend retreats at Hopson.[62] According to Talbot, the shacks were rarely occupied (except during songwriting retreats) until European tourists began to inquire about the possibility of renting the shacks for overnight stays.[63] "The Europeans walked in here saying what's with these houses?," Talbot recalled. "Could we possibly rent these houses? And we thought, ya know, pretty good idea. And it took off like a runaway train."[64]

Subsequently a partnership (Cathy's husband James Butler, Tommy Polk, Bill Talbot, Guy Malvezzi, and Jim Field) developed in the wake of increased interest in turning the property into a tourist destination. With no shortage of humor, the five owners dubbed themselves the "Shackmeisters." (In recent years, the five Shackmeisters have been reduced to three, James Butler, Bill Talbot, and Guy Malvezzi.) By 2002, the owners purchased four additional structures, moved them to Hopson, and advertised this new tourist attraction as a "six pack of shacks."[65] The six-pack shack theme complements the inn's claim that it is the state's oldest B&B (Bed and Beer). At present, there are twelve shacks on the property. The success of the Shack Up Inn has motivated the owners to develop an alternative tourist haunt called the Cotton Gin Inn. The owners have turned an old cotton gin located on the same plantation into a new lodging experience for tourists.[66] Although crops are still grown on the property, Hopson now resembles an agricultural museum. Tourists can view a rusted cotton picker and tractor as well as an old fuel tank and grain bins. According to the inn's own promotional materials, tourists will

> find authentic sharecropper shacks, the original cotton gin and seed houses and other outbuildings. You will glimpse plantation life as it existed only a few short years ago. In addition, you will find one of the first mechanized cotton pickers, manufactured by International Harvester, as you stroll around the compound.[67]

Except for some minor roofing repairs, the shacks' exteriors are in original condition. The owners even preserved old wooden outhouses, which are located near the backs of some of the shacks. Tourists who visit the Shack Up Inn's Web site will discover that the shacks' "corrugated tin roofs and Mississippi cypress walls will conjure visions of a bygone era."[68] Malvezzi hopes the decision to preserve the exterior appearance will offer tourists a glimpse of the past.[69] In a 2001 interview with National Public Radio, Talbot echoed his partner's sentiments: "Well, it—we didn't change the appearance on the outside. We just worked on the inside. And for the most part they look like they did 100 years ago."[70]

Punning on the supposed authenticity of these wooden structures, the Shackmeisters claim that the exterior has been left "au natural." Yet there have been extensive renovations to the structures' interior design.[71] The shacks have been modernized to meet local health department codes and ensure comfort for tourists. For example, the Robert Clay shack's original floor plan (two large bedrooms with a kitchen located in the back) has been reshaped to include a living room–den, kitchen, bathroom, and a back bedroom. The interior walls have been pressure-washed and cleaned; some sections were replaced with wood from moving crates, and insulation has been added to the walls and the ceiling. Moreover, the linoleum flooring was removed, revealing the original wooden floor. Signs of modern conveniences (e.g., water heater, air vents, thermostat, even electric lights) will most likely alleviate the concerns of some tourists who may find the experience *too* authentic. Before the shacks were renovated, they did not contain an interior bathroom, air-conditioning, a water heater, or even running water.

Despite its somewhat isolated location, minimal advertising, and no signs, the Shack Up Inn has proved to be a popular blues lodging attraction. In 2008 the inn attracted over ten thousand visitors.[72] The inn has attracted a diverse array of patrons, from former Mississippi governor Kirk Fordice to singer Robert Plant. Although the Shack Up Inn was open for three years before the first African American guests arrived,[73] in recent years the inn's customer base has become more culturally and racially diverse. Malvezzi explained this demographic shift: "You know, it tells them that we don't have an ax to grind. If somebody has an ax to grind over some kind of racial problem that happened in the past, they can drive it down the road. . . . We're not trying to make a buck off a part of history that was black."[74] In fact, according to Talbot, the owners of the inn have been "thanked by many a black person for preserving some of their history."[75]

Indeed, the owners of the Shack Up Inn have argued on more than one occasion that their efforts are constructive in nature, a vivid example of cultural and historical preservation, part of a larger push to safeguard Mississippi's

past. "Hopson's goal is no longer to make profits in cotton," claims the promotional material. "It now wishes to have a part in the preservation of the
culture of both the Southern United States and the Mississippi Delta."[76] There
is certainly considerable truth to this claim; without the efforts of the Shackmeisters, some of these wooden shacks would have disintegrated due to age
and weather or been destroyed by local farmers who viewed these domiciles as
an eyesore. Although all indications suggest that the owners are profiting from
the venture, it wasn't always that way, and furthermore, the Shackmeisters
have contended that profit was never a prime motivating factor. Collectively,
the owners share an "overwhelming appreciation for the Delta Blues" and an
"overpowering affection for the hospitality industry."[77] This apparent affection for the hospitality industry and the blues was perhaps one reason why
the owners of the Shack Up Inn received the Keeping the Blues Live Award in
2009, and why the Mississippi Legislature unanimously passed House Con-
current Resolution 57 praising the work of Talbot and Malvezzi in promoting
the state's blues heritage.[78]

Despite the questionable moral and ethical implications of transforming
sharecroppers' shacks into tourist haunts, most of the press coverage has been
surprisingly positive. In January 2007, for example, the Shack Up Inn was
ranked as one of the "10 Great Places to Rent a Cottage" in the United States,
according to Eleanor Griffin, editor in chief of *Cottage Living*.[79] Proclaiming
the inn as "one of the most spectacular examples of a Delta Renaissance," the
Guardian claimed that the restoration of old sharecropper shacks "is an act of
cultural reparation, part of the protracted and painful healing process of the
old south."[80] Striking a similar note, *Blues News* contended the inn is playing
a significant role in diminishing the "daunting poverty of the region."[81] In
2008 *National Geographic Traveler* evaluated properties in the United States,
Canada, Mexico, and the Caribbean and ranked the Shack Up Inn as one
of the top 150 places to stay.[82] The magazine warned tourists to "get ready
for basic shacks in high cotton."[83] In all, observers were neutral or favorably
impressed, including Bill Minor of the *Clarion-Ledger*, who expressed reser-
vations about the owners' decision to transform dilapidated, poverty-ridden
hovels into "chic hostelries for nostalgia-hungry patrons."[84]

PRIVILEGED MEMORY

Since the inn's inception, members of the Shackmeister team have occasionally been confronted with troubling questions about the premise behind their
unique blues attraction. In an effort to provide tourists with a rustic, but
comfortable and enjoyable, bluesy experience, does the Shack Up Inn end

up whitewashing the historical realities of plantation life in Mississippi: slavery, racial bigotry, white supremacy, Jim Crow, and economic exploitation? Collectively shrugging off this type of accusation, the owners have crafted a counterstory that, unsurprisingly, paints a much more positive, even uplifting, account of plantation life. For example, rather than acknowledging the plantation's role in the systematic oppression of its largely African American workforce, the Shack Up Inn highlights and emphasizes the technological innovations that took place on the plantation. In 1944, the Hopson Plantation, in partnership with the International Harvester Company, featured one of the first mechanical cotton pickers, and it was the first plantation in the world to use a mechanical picker to totally harvest a crop.[85] This technological advancement revolutionized agricultural production and undoubtedly "spelled the end of the old system and sent plantation workers off to the big cities."[86] The story of Hopson's role in transforming how crops are grown and harvested is repeated on the Web sites of the Hopson Preservation Company and the Shack Up Inn and Cotton Gin Inn. However, these sites fail to acknowledge that the invention and the eventual full implementation of the mechanical cotton picker was a response, in part, to a fear of black civil unrest and a perceived labor shortage as a result of black out-migration.[87] Indeed, the invention of the cotton picker accelerated the migration of southern blacks from the cotton fields to the urban centers of Chicago, St. Louis, and Detroit.

Similar to charitable descriptions of Will and Joe Rice Dockery, H. Howell Hopson has been described as a kind and benevolent plantation owner. Paul Oliver correctly observed that conditions on the plantations "varied widely,"[88] and Hopson was apparently far more generous than other plantation owners of his time. According to Talbot, he was one of the first owners in the area to offer workers health benefits and a retirement program.[89] Historical accounts of life on the Hopson Plantation are scarce, although the Hopson Preservation Company has published one such account on its Web site. James E. Thweatt, who grew up and worked on the plantation until he left in 1942 or 1943 to join the military, described Hopson as a decent, upright plantation owner who seemed to be respected, if not beloved, by his employees, including an elderly African American woman named Mammy Nancy Hopson (a former slave who "adopted" the Hopson name). In his plainspoken, unapologetic account of life on the plantation, Thweatt describes the "settle" (when sharecroppers received their annual payment) as a routine business transaction:

After all the cotton had been picked and ginned, about the middle of December, Mr. Hopson would "settle up" with each tenant family. . . . Some years they would get a few hundred dollars and other years they ended up owing Mr. Hopson a hundred dollars or two, and some years they would just break even. In the latter cases Mr. Hopson would give them a couple of hundred dollars and charge this against their next year's crop. If a tenant got unhappy and wanted to move to another plantation, there was an unwritten rule among the plantation owners that you would not let a family move onto your plantation without permission from the former place. Also, if they owed their plantation any money, their debt went with them so if they made any money at their new place, this plantation owner would deduct from their settlement and send to their former plantation owner. This rule kept the labor supply stable, thus insuring better crops.[90]

Rather than glossing over this highly exploitative labor practice, Thweatt's matter-of-fact description of the settle suggests that he believed sharecropping to be a mutually beneficial business arrangement. Although plantation owners would not always net a profit (crop prices, weather, and insect infestation were always a concern), black sharecroppers were obviously the real losers. After toiling in the fields for months, a tenant might only receive, at the most, a couple thousand dollars (tenants did receive, on credit, "furnishings" such as food and mules during the year). This problem was exacerbated by the fact that many black field hands and tenants were illiterate and were discouraged, even sometimes forbidden, to develop rudimentary mathematical skills. It is hard to contest the settle when one lacks a basic understanding of elementary math, and many feared retribution for openly challenging the word of a white person. Although his grandfather was apparently illiterate, blues musician Eddie Boyd learned some basic math skills and discovered the true cost of the settle:

When I got to know a little bit about mathematics and I found out, when my grandfather would clear at the end of the year 12 or $1,800, man, we had worked for 35 to 52¢ a day, all of us. That's all you got. But you get it in a lump sum, it seemed like a whole lot, you understand. But it didn't to me. I didn't like that hot sun and plowing that slow mule. That kind of obligation was too much for me. I just was born with that type of mentality. I had a lot of trouble with those plantation owners.[91]

True enough, Boyd's grandfather made a pittance, but he did not go into debt. Many did. "Clearly many 'debts' were mere fabrications of the planter or the bookkeeper," wrote historian James Cobb, "but, given the questionable wisdom of a black tenant's disputing the word of a white planter, in the Delta an imaginary debt was as effective as a real one in restricting labor mobility, although in neither case was actual or alleged indebtedness an absolute guarantee that a worker would stay put."[92] If a worker or family was allowed to leave the plantation (as Cobb noted, many left without permission), their debt would follow them to the next place of employment. Freedom of movement and economic independence were, to say the least, restricted. According to historian Ted Ownby, plantation owners justified the sharecropping system by arguing that blacks were undisciplined, willful and irresponsible spenders: "If African Americans had the chance, they would literally spend themselves into starvation." With a paternalistic eye to "protecting" blacks from their own devices, plantation owners believed that blacks should live on "narrow margins."[93] Despite Hopson's virtues as a plantation owner, even the best plantation system reinforced an asymmetrical relationship between a powerful white minority and a virtually powerless black majority.

The privileged historical memory is supplemented with personal testimonies from former inhabitants of these dwellings who have offered, more or less, their unconditional approval of the owners' decision to convert sharecropper shacks into a tourist destination. One writer, an African American who grew up in a sharecropper shack six miles from the Hopson Plantation, favorably described the Shack Up Inn as a "nostalgic, ingenious undertaking by Delta entrepreneurs."[94] Pinetop Perkins has publicly proclaimed his support for the Shack Up Inn.[95] In an interview with the *Clarksdale Press Register*, Perkins fondly recalled his experience working at the plantation: "It brings me a whole lot of memories to be here 'cause I used to have fun right around here, driving tractors and picking cotton."[96] It should be pointed out that the Pinetop Perkins Homecoming event is held annually at Hopson. As evidenced in the inn's guest books, conveniently located in each shack, some former shack dwellers have returned to the South on vacation and, curious about the Shackmeisters' cultural experiment, decided to stay at the inn. Almost without exception, these visitors have applauded the owners' decision to preserve a vanishing symbol of the South's past. One visitor left the following brief, heartfelt expression of appreciation:

> *I also grew up not far from here. As my 2 sisters previously stated, the houses we were born and raised in were not as comfortable as this "shack." We only wished and prayed that one day we would be "uptown." "Uptown" meaning indoor plumbing & central heat and air. No doubt we were materially unwealthy. We had what a lot of others wished they had. We had strong family ties that still bind us together. This is a wonderful place. Keep up the good work guys.*

Another satisfied visitor wrote:

> *The Delta is unique, and the Shack Up Inn epitimizes its uniqueness. I grew up in Coahoma County on a farm in a house just a little bit better than this one.*

This brought back the wonderful memories of my childhood—one that [was] short on material wealth but unsurpassed in family love and love of place. Staying here was a delightful experience—one that I shall never forgot.

In other cases, the owners of the Shack Up Inn actively speak for the former shack occupants. For example, James Butler described how Roosevelt Hill, a former employee of the Hopson Plantation, would fondly reminisce about his experience living on the Hopson plantation: "He's got wonderful memories which was great to hear. . . . He talked about the family unit and how strong this house was and momma, daddy, and family all living in this home and how strong that unit was."[97] When asked by a reporter for National Public Radio about the moral and ethical implications of transforming a symbol of oppression into a tourist haunt, Talbot offers a strikingly similar response:

We've had a few people that expressed a little, you know, concern about what we're doing. And questioned why. But then, you know, they're in such the minority. I mean, 99.8 percent of the people who have come here love what we've done. And even—we've had people here that grew up on the plantation that left, you know, 30 years ago, moved to California, and have come back, and loved it, and talked about what a wonderful life they had here, which really surprised me. But I think it probably goes back to the family unit. You know, they just remembered fond memories of having a wonderful life with their family.[98]

There is certainly a paradox at work here. Why would former shack dwellers deliberately choose to pay $65 to $140 a night to return "home" to stay in a "mocking" facsimile, a renovated, air-conditioned shack? Wouldn't this experience resurrect painful memories of material deprivation? Instead it seems that the Shack Up Inn provides these tourists a singularly unique opportunity to reexperience past familial memories, a nostalgic return to a simpler time. For these tourists, these shacks also mark the ascendency of time, the (long) transition from childhood poverty to some level of relative material prosperity in adulthood. For these tourists, the Shack Up Inn may indeed symbolize the great American story: personal perseverance and hard work trumps early hardships and the social barriers of inequity.

Yet the believable story of the close-knit, happy family bound together by circumstance and spatial proximity belies the inherent problem of representation. By actively presenting only one story, a story that seemingly conforms to the larger, pro-sharecropping narrative, the owners have, in essence, silenced other competing stories. Conspicuously absent are the dissenting voices of the tens of thousands of black tenants who found both sharecropping and their living conditions to be, at best, intolerable. David "Honeyboy" Edwards, Big Bill Broonzy, Son House, Eddie Boyd, and scores of other blues musicians have provided decidedly unromantic and candid accounts of living in a wooden shack. Raised on a plantation outside Clarksdale, Big George Brock remembered that his childhood home did not need windows because he "could look through the cracks."[99] B. B. King was raised in similar surroundings, as he described to a PBS interviewer: "I was born on a plantation and things weren't so good. We didn't have any money. I never thought of the word 'poor' 'til I got to be a man, but when you live in a house that you can always peek out of and see what kind of day it is, you're not doing so well. And your rest room is not inside the house."[100] David "Honeyboy" Edwards recalled that one of the only sources of heat in the wintertime was an old stove and homemade quilts.[101] As these testimonies indicate, these wooden dwellings, usually elevated on blocks or rocks, contained, at the most, three rooms and reflected the realities of abject poverty:

> *The leaky roof was made of split pine shingles or, later, galvanized iron, which turned a rusty brown after years of service. The tiny windows had board shutters or, later, sash and glass. . . . Two hundred square feet of floor space made up the average interior. The frame of the shack, often papered with newsprint, served as the wall. Most landlords furnished the shacks with beds or pallets, chairs, and a stove for cooking and heating. There was, of course, no electricity. . . . People, pets, livestock, insects, and the elements seemed to move in and out of the shack at will.*[102]

These collective narratives—revealed in biographies and published interviews—are largely absent from official representations of Mississippi's blues heritage. Moreover, there are no institutions in the state (e.g., a civil rights museum) that provide competing interpretations and representations of Mississippi's sharecropping history.

The owners of the Shack Up Inn not only gloss over the wretched living conditions that existed for many black tenants but also reject the argument that poverty was in large measure determined by race. As the Shackmeisters tell it, rural poverty was *not* a result of institutionalized racism because *poor whites* also lived in these primitive structures. In separate interviews, both James Butler and Guy Malvezzi underscored this point. As Malvezzi argued:

> *When you think of a shotgun shack you think of a black farmhand. That's what comes to most people's minds. Well, it's absolutely amazing, the white people that have been through here. Parents or grandparents lived in these things. No electricity, no running water. . . . You just associate it with just being a black thing. Poverty was rampant and it didn't discriminate through the years.*[103]

But it did. For example, in 1959, 31.8 percent of white Mississippians lived in poverty; in contrast, 84.9 percent of nonwhites were reported living in poverty.[104] A decade later, poverty conditions improved for both whites (17.9 percent) and nonwhites (64.8 percent), but the disparity between the two groups still remained strong.[105] In both years, 1959 and 1969, whites and African Americans made up more than 99 percent of Mississippi's total population. Black poverty resulted from a myriad of sociopolitical factors, including the destruction and fragmentation of the family structure, political disenfranchisement (lack of voting rights), economic exploitation (the sharecropping system), and legalized segregation (Jim Crow laws). Undoubtedly the poorest segment of southern white society did work along with their black counterparts in the cotton fields and lived in sharecropper shacks. However, the justification that whites also lived in sharecropper shacks should not erase the fact that sharecropper shacks symbolize in a very real way Mississippi's institutionalized mistreatment and exploitation of its black labor force.

As Hopson has been transformed into a tourist attraction, the symbols of oppression have all but vanished, reconstituted as tourist commodities. Tourists who have little knowledge about the history of southern plantation life may not even recognize the relationship between plantation life and social inequity or understand the connection between plantation life and the blues. For example, many tourists who visit the plantation's commissary may not associate that building with its historical role as a center of exploitation of black workers. For many black field hands, the commissary was a symbol of both survival and exploitation. Commissaries served as "early self-contained shopping malls" where members of a community, including tenant farmers and fieldworkers, collected their paychecks and purchased groceries, clothing, and other supplies.[106] Monetary practices at the plantations often included paying workers in scrip, not real money.[107] Goods were available on credit, but extremely high interest rates were charged as a means to keep workers in debt to their employers. Nowadays the Hopson commissary functions as a restaurant and lounge, and local blues bands, such as the Marshall Drew Band, will occasionally perform for guests. In a move to preserve the building, the Hopson Preservation Company was created by Clarksdale area business leaders to keep the Delta heritage "alive" because the building, and the antique farming items, continue to "create a nostalgic atmosphere reminiscent of the deep south Delta."[108]

Sharecropper shacks, once a depressing image of poverty, are now the feature attraction on a plantation that resembles a rustic blues fantasyland. To accentuate the relationship between blues music and sharecropper shacks, the owners decided to decorate the shacks with a variety of blues paraphernalia. In the Robert Clay Shack, touted as the establishment's "flagship" domicile,[109] guests can find an old red Platter Pax box that contains a collection of 78 records. Old vinyl records are displayed near the kitchen and the bathroom. Photos and drawings of blues musicians can be found in the living room and the bedroom. In the bedroom, guests can leaf through recent editions of *Guitar Player*, *Big City Blues*, and *King Biscuit Time Magazine*. The Cadillac Shack is adorned with a similar blues motif: blues festival posters, photos of blues performers (Bobby Blue Bland), and Steve Cheseborough's travel guide, *Blues Traveling: The Holy Sites of Delta Blues*. The owners even use a cotton sack as a window curtain. In addition, each shack is outfitted with a fully functioning stereo system (typically located in the kitchen) and a TV-VCR-DVD (viewers can turn on the blues channel or rent movies).

For the amateur blues musician, each shack also includes an assortment of musical instruments. Tourists can strum a guitar or pick out notes on a piano while listening to a CD of Robert Johnson or Muddy Waters, all the while romanticizing the image of a solitary, tragic blues figure creating brilliant compositions in a world largely absent of material prosperity. Or, in the case of the writer Elizabeth Hoover, one can imagine hearing the sound of Robert Johnson playing his 1936 regional hit "Terraplane Blues":

> *On a warm evening in late September, as I sat on the steps of a sharecropper shack, nursing a Corona and watching the dusk settle over cotton fields on either side of Highway 49, I could almost hear "Terraplane Blues" in the Delta breeze. Of course, I was paying for the experience, and not with hard labor.*[110]

To add to the fantasy, tourists can take a leisurely stroll through the plantation grounds and gaze at tractors, farm equipment, and grain bins, an experience that may excite many interested in finding the blues genesis, the literal "root" that served as the catalyst for much of the blues created in Mississippi before World War II. Indeed, part of the appeal and success of the Shack Up Inn is also related to its relationship with its surrounding rural landscape. The twelve shacks easily merge with Hopson's cotton gin and open fields. Cohen has suggested that the "distinguishing characteristics of covertly staged touristic attractions, however, is precisely that they are not . . . so separated from the surrounding environment—rather they are, or are made to appear, an integral part of it."[111] The ambience is enhanced by the pastoral nature of the Shack Up Inn, for it resembles, in many ways, an all-inclusive resort in which tourists are contained within a remote enclave, isolated from the surrounding community. Within this context, tourists are engaged in a form of play rather than feeling personally conflicted about temporarily inhabiting a shack that, before its technological transformation, barely provided a basic means of survival for an oppressed population. Tourists are also unlikely to critically evaluate the sharecropping system and the role of the plantation in maintaining an economically dependent, politically disenfranchised black underclass. In all, the plantation's transformation from a working farm to a tourist attraction conceals the history and memory of place by radically reconstructing the meanings of some of the establishment's more obvious symbols of oppression. From the perspective of the owners of the Shack Up Inn, the painful historical realities of plantation life are best forgotten. By creating a nostalgic, charming atmosphere that romanticizes sharecropping life, the owners have sacrificed an opportunity, perhaps even a responsibility, to engender in their visitors a healthy critique of the whole exploitative enterprise.

While not denying the importance of vernacular culture in contesting ideologically driven narratives, this chapter reveals the role of official culture in shaping a particular understanding of the past, a strategic move which "reduce[s] the power of competing interests that threaten the attainment of their goals."[112] While the Mississippi Blues Trail symbolizes important efforts to recognize and honor the state's blues heritage, the state's official culture promotes a privileged memory for tourists. Characterizing blues music as essentially escapist in nature, employing abstract language to mask the impact of white tyranny on a powerless, subjugated class of people, celebrating the plantation as the genesis of the blues, and reimagining the plantation owner as "fair" and "kind" suggest a deliberate rhetorical strategy to renarrate an understanding of the past. The Shack Up Inn exemplifies the most controversial example of this rhetorical approach. Memory, both remembering and forgetting, has implications for the present and the future. How can meaningful racial reconciliation ever materialize if the past is appropriated by Mississippi's official culture to transform Mississippi into a desired blues tourism destination? Indeed, whitewashing the past may hinder efforts to achieve racial reconciliation, one of the goals of blues tourism and the subject of the next chapter.

7

ASSESSING TOURISM GOALS
Money, Image, and Reconciliation

You mean you came all the way down here to hear a n[igger] play a guitar?
—CONVERSATION BETWEEN A WHITE CLARKSDALE BUSINESS OWNER AND
AN AUSTRALIAN BLUES TOURIST, circa 1990s

Talk about terror. People I've been terrorized all my days.
—WILLIE KING AND THE LIBERATORS, *Living in a New World*

No amount of historical amnesia or personal denial will erase Mississippi's past.[1] Following a brief period of political, social, and personal freedom during Reconstruction, African Americans experienced political disenfranchisement and were virtually reduced to their previous slave status. Ensnared in an economic caste system that benefited white planters, African Americans were further demoralized by segregation laws designed to maintain the ideological commitment to white supremacy. Lynching, police brutality, and other heinous acts of white terror created an atmosphere of high anxiety and fear in practically all black communities in Mississippi and much of the South. Even a century after Abraham Lincoln signed the Emancipation Proclamation, many black Mississippians still did not possess the full range of freedoms as established by the U.S. Constitution and the Bill of Rights. Segregation was still rigidly enforced, civil rights protesters were arrested and beaten by police, the Ku Klux Klan reemerged as a powerful force of intimidation, efforts to block African Americans from participating in political and civic life were largely successful, and black aspirations for upward mobility were still severely limited. Eleanor Holmes Norton, representative of the District of Columbia, journeyed to Mississippi in the early 1960s as a member of the Student Nonviolent Coordinating Committee (SNCC) and discovered, much to her chagrin, that Mississippi was still a "wide-open, terrorist country in the United States of America."[2]

Yet it is clear that Mississippi has, in many ways, changed dramatically since the social upheavals of the 1960s. B. B. King, Bennie Thompson, and Morgan Freeman are three black contemporaries who, despite their past experiences living under white rule, have come to appreciate and praise the state's progress on race relations. Born in 1925 on a Delta plantation, King grew up as part of a sharecropping family. As a child and adolescent, he worked the fields including picking cotton and driving a tractor. His mother died when he was nine, and he later lived alone in a wooden cabin. He suffered under the restrictions of segregation and other indignities of white racism and was, for a number of years, ashamed to be associated with Mississippi. In interviews, King has candidly discussed how his perceptions of his home state have changed over the years, partly due to hard-fought social and political changes that helped dismantle many of Mississippi's most blatant race-caste policies, and the state's decision to embrace the blues: "There were times in the early years where I wouldn't say I was from Mississippi unless you asked me. Now I say it on stage three or four times every night—'I am from Mississippi! That's my home.' To know the pride that Mississippi has taken in us, accepting us as a people, accepting us as people not just trying to help the state, but the world."[3]

Since 1993, Bennie Thompson has served in the U.S. Mississippi's House of Representatives for the Second District of Mississippi. Born in Bolton, Mississippi, in 1948, Thompson and King shared the experience of growing up in a segregated black community: "You hear stories about blacks and whites being so close down south, but Bolton was always two separate communities. I *never* had a single white friend."[4] Thompson attended an all-black segregated secondary school system and later received degrees from Tugaloo College and Jackson State University at a time when opportunities in higher education for African Americans in Mississippi were limited.[5] With an interest in political and social justice, Thompson became a member of SNCC in the mid-1960s and, in 1969, won an election for a seat on the Board of Aldermen in Bolton, despite efforts by white members of the board to nullify the election results.[6] Despite his negative experiences, Thompson decided to stay in Mississippi rather than immigrate to the North. In a 1985 interview with *Esquire* magazine, Thompson told Joe Klein why he decided to stay in Mississippi. Speaking about his hometown, he said: "There are things I just can't find words for . . . This place is important to me."[7] Apparently for Thompson, Mississippi was worth fighting for, and during his political tenure, he has improved the lives of his constituents, especially the majority of poor African Americans who make up most of his district. While the racial inequities still exist, Thompson has witnessed positive social and cultural changes in his home state.

A prominent spokesperson for the state and its blues heritage, Morgan Freeman, who left Mississippi in 1955 to join the U.S. Air Force, remembers living in an "openly segregated" Delta society, complete with "white" and "colored" water fountains and segregated public schools. He left the state with no plans to return. Yet, years later, the actor now views Mississippi as his home, claiming that living in the state provides him with a genuine sense of security and comfort.[8] He also argues that the state's history has, to some extent, been unfairly portrayed in the media and encourages tourists to visit Mississippi to experience "one of the joys of life."[9] Of course, none of these individuals actually believes that Mississippi's exclusionary norms have been fully eradicated. In 1997, Freeman attempted to end Charleston High School's longstanding tradition of holding racially segregated proms.[10] Although Freeman calls Charleston his hometown, the actor was actually born in Memphis, Tennessee. Freeman tried to integrate the prom by offering to pay for the entire event with the stipulation that both whites and blacks could attend the event. Although his initial proposal was rejected, he finally convinced school officials to break this long-standing racist practice, an event chronicled in the HBO documentary *Prom Night in Mississippi* (2009). Unfortunately, a year later, the high school once again held a whites-only prom.[11]

Set against this historical narrative, it is perhaps both ironic and fitting that Mississippi is now promoting its blues culture and heritage as a central part of its overall tourism plan. Similar to other rural areas undergoing economic transition, Mississippi has embraced the blues, a significant part of its rich cultural heritage, as a potential new source of revenue. The birthplace myth has captured the imagination of some blues tourists, who subsequently travel to Mississippi, and the Delta in particular, in the search for authenticity: "real-deal" African American blues musicians performing in authentic settings, such as a charming and rustic juke joint, on a street corner, or on a heritage stage at a blues festival. Meanwhile, official tourism narratives frequently conceal Mississippi's traumatic past, privileging a sanitized historical record that largely omits the memory of the sorrow and suffering that accompanied the experience of black life in Mississippi. To no one's surprise, it is not uncommon for tourism intermediaries to accentuate a region's positive attributes to attract more visitors to an area.

Yet the question still remains: have these promotional and marketing strategies succeeded in drawing more blues tourists to the state and, consequently, achieving the three goals associated with blues tourism? The answer is inconclusive. The economic impact of blues tourism is still largely unknown, a result of incomplete data and contradictory evidence. On the one hand, there are signs that more blues tourists are visiting the state, and the industry itself has had some economic impact on the state. In the last five years, more blues-oriented small businesses have opened in Clarksdale and other Delta communities. The B. B. King Museum attracted approximately thirty thousand visitors during its first year in operation, although it is unclear precisely how many visitors are from out of state. Blues promoters Bill Luckett, Roger Stolle, and Guy Malvezzi, among others, have witnessed more blues tourists visiting in the Delta in recent years.[12] In July 2010, CNN reporter Tom Foreman visited Clarksdale and reported a "rising tide in blues tourism." He cited plans to expand the Delta Blues Museum to twice its current size (presumably because of the increase in the number of visitors) and a significant increase (13 percent) in tourism tax dollars generated in Coahoma County for the first half of 2010 over the previous year. Blues musician Terry Williams noted correctly that blues tourism is no longer a seasonal phenomenon (May to October). Blues tourists visit the state throughout the entire year.[13]

Yet this evidence must be viewed anecdotally because there is no systematic and reliable method to gather verifiable data. For example, tourism officials do not ask visitors their specific purpose for traveling (and tourists may visit the state for multiple reasons), and local chambers of commerce and other tourism entities do not track the specific number of blues tourists who visit the state every year. Until tourism officials develop a more systematic and dependable method to track the number of blues tourists visiting the state on an annual basis, it will be impossible to make any reliable conclusion about the number of blues tourists who visit the state or the real financial impact of the state's blues tourism industry.

Furthermore, after examining economic data for the six-year period from 2004 to 2009, I found that the economic impact of tourism suggests uneven growth and retrenchment in important economic indicators. For example, the total number of visitors to the state has declined significantly from 31 million in 2004 to 19 million in 2009; the number of overnight leisure visitors declined from 11.4 million (84 percent out-of-state visitors) in 2004 to 10 million (75 percent out-of-state visitors) in 2009. Travel and tourism state tax revenue declined from $471 million in 2004 to $407 million in 2009. City-county tourism tax also fell from 2004 ($152.3 million) to 2009 ($111.7 million). Jobs directly related to tourism decreased from 2004 (92,400) to 2009 (78,240). In 2004 and 2009, tourism ranked sixth in total estimated employment.[14] Hurricane Katrina's devastation of the Mississippi Gulf Coast, as well as the onset of the worldwide recession in 2008, certainly had a significant impact on tourism. Jim O'Neal confessed that "as much as I want to promote the blues, I would have to admit it's still not an easy thing to do, make money at it in Mississippi or probably [many] other places."[15] While it is difficult to ascertain whether blues tourism is actually the cash cow that tourism officials and community leaders hoped it would be, the industry is arguably still in its infancy, and a real potential exists for blues-related tourism to become a reliable form of economic revenue.

Blues tourism is also part of a campaign to improve, in the words of one observer, the image of "our much-maligned state."[16] This campaign involves transforming the deathplace where Africans Americans were lynched into the "birthplace of the blues," a timeless, mysterious land with a notably down-played racist history. Yet the evidence that blues tourism has actually positively affected public perceptions of the state is purely anecdotal, because no system-atic study has ever been published on the subject. Still, some blues organizers and tourism officials believe that blues tourism has already made a difference in improving the state's negative image. Billy Johnson, a blues festival orga-nizer and director of the Highway 61 Blues Museum in Leland, believes that the region's music and visual arts have significantly changed the public's per-ception of the state: "Instead of viewing Mississippi as a place of racial hatred and injustice and all, people look at Mississippi as this wonderfully, culturally creative place that produced all of these artists. They want to come here, and they're intrigued by a culture that can produce so much talent."[17]

Other promoters believe that blues tourism provides a key opportunity for visitors to reexamine negative stereotypes about the state. Alex Thomas, a member of the Mississippi Blues Commission, argues that years of negative media portrayals, particularly about the state's troubled race relations, have obfuscated the "real existence of Mississippi today": "They see the relations between Whites and African Americans and how things here in Mississippi are no different then anywhere else."[18] Bill Seratt, a member of the Mississippi Blues Commission, has observed that "the perception of Mississippi is so to-tally changed after someone visits for the first time. People who visit Missis-sippi are just amazed at how progressive, and how friendly, and how eager we are to help them."[19] But until scholars more rigorously examine the degree to which blues tourism has favorably impacted the state's reputation and image, any conclusions about the success of this goal are purely speculative.

While the current promotional efforts may eventually succeed in enticing additional tourists to visit the region or reshaping the public's image of Mis-sissippi, they undercut another important by-product of blues tourism: racial reconciliation. Some of the current rhetorical strategies and practices, I sug-gest, may actually be counterproductive, perpetuating the social and political inequities that still characterize the lives of many black Mississippians. The goal of this extended discussion on racial reconciliation is not to reopen old racial wounds but to confront the ways in which race still structures social life for both whites and blacks in Mississippi (and the United States), particularly as it manifests itself in the promotion of the blues. Reconciliation involves *confronting* uncomfortable and emotional issues like race and racism rather than assuming that racism is no longer exists, an unfortunate symptom of a former unenlightened society, or believing that silence or avoidance will help raise us to some sort of mythic, postracial utopia. As an example of this tendency to avoid racial issues, in interviews conducted for this study and for other publications, both white and black respondents often avoided using specific racial designations, instead employing words such as "other group," "they," and other race-neutral terms, when speaking about power-sharing issues. It is my hope this chapter will initiate a dialogue about the degree to which blues tourism can serve as a medium for reconciliation as well as provide a theoretical lens to understand why conflict exists and the inherent difficulties involved in achieving reconciliation.

RACIAL RECONCILIATION

Although scholars have argued that the concept of reconciliation lacks uniform agreement in terms of its definition and the process needed to achieve a desired goal,[20] the concept can involve a variety of positive behaviors, including managing conflict through nonviolent means such as debate and discussion and forgiveness as well as a multitude of goals that include the attenuation of racial animosities and mutual healing. Some of the steps involved in achieving a reconciliation goal have been identified as including dialogue (a two-way process involving both speaking and listening), truth telling (historical truths are revealed), apology (on the part of the victimizer), forgiveness (on the part of the victim), and reparation or some other symbolic effort of restorative justice.[21] Communication scholar John B. Hatch argues that the process is often "messy" and "contentious."[22]

The William Winter Institute for Racial Reconciliation, named after the former governor of the state, is one of the most successful initiatives to heal the bitter wounds of racism in Mississippi. Compared to Mississippi's legion of racist and fearmongering politicians—Theodore Bilbo, James Eastland, and Ross Barnett, just to name a few—Winter was a revelation. Born in Grenada, Mississippi, in 1923, Winter graduated from the University of Mississippi with a law degree in 1948 and spent the next thirty-two years in political service as a legislator, tax collector, state treasurer, and lieutenant governor. During the turbulent 1960s, he was one of the "few Mississippi officials to urge racial moderation in the face of federal mandates."[23] For example, while speaking at All Saints' Junior College in Vicksburg in March 1963, Winter argued that the state needed to find more humane solutions to solve racial problems rather than resorting to the "bull-whip and the shotgun."[24] In 1980, Winter was elected to the state's highest office.[25] After serving as the governor for four years, he returned to practicing law and became involved in a host of social issues from education to economic development.[26]

Established by the University of Mississippi in 1999, the William Winter Institute for Racial Reconciliation emerged as an outgrowth of "One America in the 21st Century: The President's Initiative on Race," a national conversation initiated by former president Bill Clinton in 1997.[27] The institute, which has a presence in a number of Mississippi communities, is dedicated to fostering "reconciliation and civic renewal wherever people suffer as a result of racial discrimination or alienation."[28] For the institute, reconciliation involves understanding the systematic and institutional nature of racism, community building through dialogue and truth telling, and restorative justice that involves cooperation of all parties.[29] Other organizations involved in reconciliation efforts in Mississippi include Mission Mississippi, Activists with a Purpose, and the Philadelphia Coalition.[30]

While the William Winter Institute provides a roadmap to pursue reconciliation goals, one wonders whether blues tourism can serve as a mechanism to achieve similar goals. In the closing chapter of *Journeyman's Road*, Adam Gussow poses the question "Where is the love?" as a way to begin discussing the role of love (or absence of) in the development of the blues and blues communities, how blues music can serve as an anecdote to discrimination and division fostered by white racism, and how contemporary blues communities may embody Martin Luther King Jr.'s imagined egalitarian community. Gussow observed that blues "has helped erode what remains of the color line by bringing black and white musicians and audiences together into a series of local subcultural communities or 'blues scenes' governed, at their best, by mutual admiration, economic partnership, and the spirit of shared aesthetic creation."[31]

The initial moves toward racial reconciliation vis-à-vis the blues community have been under way in Mississippi at least since the late 1970s when the state began to recognize its rich blues history and culture. For example, in 1967, when B. B. King returned to Indianola, Mississippi, to play a local festival, he was denied access to white-owned hotels. Yet thirteen years later, in 1980, the city of Indianola celebrated B. B. King Day in recognition of the singer's many contributions to the development of post–World War II blues.[32] Award ceremonies honoring blues musicians, fund-raising events for destitute blues artists, and various "blues in the schools" programs demonstrate how music can foster genuine dialogue, cultural understanding, and empathy through aesthetic communication. Blues tourism endeavors have also attempted to educate local whites about the significance of the state's blues culture. Kappi Allen, tourism manager of the Coahoma County Tourism Commission, revealed in an interview that she possessed little knowledge of Mississippi's blues culture until she started working to promote the blues as part of her job responsibilities.[33] Bill Luckett, one of the partners of Clarksdale's premier blues club, Ground Zéro, makes a similar admission, arguing he was largely unaware of Clarksdale's blues heritage until the mid-1990s, when he noticed more blues tourism traffic in Clarksdale; he was also inspired to learn about his community's blues heritage after listening to Howard Stovall present a lecture on Muddy Waters's early relationship with the Stovall family plantation.[34] Likewise, blues tourism hopes to change how many religiously oriented African Americans perceive what they have longed considered a "devil-worshipping" music.

White audiences who express genuine admiration for African American blues musicians and racially diverse blues musical groups, as well as local and national blues organizations that feature a membership noted for its cultural and racial heterogeneity, are just a few examples of how blues music serves to bridge the resistant racial divide. In reflecting on his experience as a volunteer at the Sunflower River Blues and Gospel Festival, for example, Bill Gresham—who has served as the chairman for the event—recalled: "My wife and I have made some of the best friends across racial lines by being involved in the festival. . . . I've got some extremely dear friends that are black who I would not have met except for the festival."[35] Wanda Clark, trail coordinator for the Mississippi Blues Trail, believed that unveiling ceremonies associated with the Mississippi Blues Trail serve an important role in the reconciliation process, especially among in-state residents:

> Well, I would certainly hope that they see the kind of bridge building that I see with these [events]. I've never been a part of anything that's been so color-blind. I made an unbelievable number of friends, and if you go to many of these unveilings at all or see community turnouts, I mean, I can't imagine somebody from the outside coming in and viewing any kind of racial problems by seeing these [marker unveilings].[36]

While recognizing the important role that blues music has played in changing the attitudes of white Mississippi about the state's African American culture and heritage, it is clear that blues tourism is not a panacea for Mississippi's present-day racial tensions. While blues tourism can play a role in facilitating the reconciliation process, that role is decidedly limited because of temporal constraints (the fleeting nature of blues festivals and Blues Trail dedication ceremonies), the audience (the pleasure and leisure principle of tourism and tourists), and structure of the state's tourism industry (largely controlled by whites). Furthermore, as we will see, the level of anger expressed by some local African American blues musicians and promoters concerning perceived or actual incidents of exploitation by whites reflects the racial animosity that characterizes the region and the state. Well-intentioned efforts have unfortunately, in some cases, led to unforeseen consequences, exacerbating racial tensions rather than moving both communities toward reconciliation.

Arguably, some promotional strategies, including memory-building practices, may have impeded efforts at racial reconciliation. Neglecting to fully embrace and critique the important role Mississippi played in promoting the institution of slavery, the development of the exploitative economic practice of sharecropping, the ritualistic horrors of lynching, and the rigid enforcement of segregation laws that only perpetuated frustration, anger, and hopelessness in many African American communities will *not* facilitate an honest discussion and debate that symbolizes the reconciliation process. Indeed, blues promotional materials that deny historically marginalized groups their historical truths through rhetorically privileging a benign rereading and remembrance of Mississippi's past and present are counterproductive to achieving goals associated with racial reconciliation. In other words, reconciliation efforts are compromised when a dominant group attempts to privilege a particular memory to sustain a dominant ideology that perpetuates discriminatory and exclusionary social policies.

Blues musicians are certainly aware of how history has been manipulated to serve tourism goals. "Some folks like to put their head in the sand and try to pretend," Bill "Howl-N-Madd" Perry told me in a 2007 interview. "But you can't pretend over reality. And it's a part of our history, the horror, violence and all that stuff down here."[37] James "Super Chikan" Johnson agreed, arguing that while many whites would prefer to forget the past, the lingering scars of injustice and poverty make it impossible.[38] In a 2004 interview, blues singer Mississippi Slim summed up the feelings of some local Delta blues musicians: "[The past] is being completely ignored—that's the truth."[39] Ignoring the past or rewriting history may sublimate anger and resentment and give the illusion of racial progress, but this practice will not engender racial reconciliation. Not surprisingly, however, blues promoters and tourism officials engage in the rhetorical act of forgetting because remembering the past may be counter to the pleasure principle of tourism—tourists desire a fun-filled escape from the drudgery of daily routine. As tourism scholar Emanuel de Kadt observed, "For most tourists a trip is a chance to 'get away from it all,' and the last thing they want is to be confronted with anything problematic during this short period of the year when they can be essentially pleasure-seekers."[40]

Without a doubt, collective acts of historical amnesia exacerbate racial tensions, counteracting claims that blues events promote racial unity and reconciliation. Forgetting the past is a convenient strategy by some members of official culture to ignore Mississippi's legacy of racial injustice and deny the real presence of white racism in the Mississippi Delta today. Indeed, Mississippi's U.S. representative Bennie Thompson is correct when he warned blues promoters and tourism officials of the perils of obscuring or misrepresenting the African American experience in Mississippi: "I think it would be a great mistake if people promoting tourism in the Delta ignored the history of the Delta. You have to talk about slavery. You have to talk about the night riders."[41]

In all, some white blues promoters contend that blues tourism is serving an important role in promoting racial reconciliation in both the region and state through events and attractions that embrace and celebrate, rather than disparage, African American culture. Some African American musicians, on the other hand, argue that some of these promotional efforts are exploitative in nature. Standpoint theory clearly suggests why these different perceptions exist; the theory also provides an opportunity for scholars and other interested parties to discuss alternative solutions to manage or resolve this cultural conflict. For the rest of the chapter, I will use standpoint theory to examine three points of contention.

STANDPOINT THEORY

Standpoint theory is chiefly concerned with how the positioning of a group within a socially constructed hierarchy "produces shared experiences for individuals in those groups."[42] Groups can be classified in numerous ways, from class to race, gender to regional orientation. Based on common experiences, a group develops a "situated knowledge"[43] or "local knowledge systems."[44] In other words, a group's position in a social hierarchy will dramatically affect how members perceive and interpret messages and events and acquire a specific understanding or knowledge of the world. For example, standpoint theory helps us understand why African Americans, who have historically endured an indifferent and often corrupt judicial system, overwhelmingly supported the acquittal of O. J. Simpson in his much-publicized murder trial in 1995. Most whites, who generally lack this shared group experience, believed the former football star was guilty. In another example, the majority of Africans Americans blamed white racism as the precipitating cause for the slow response to assist the victims of Hurricane Katrina. The majority of whites, on the other hand, blamed the residents of New Orleans for their situation.[45] This theory does not suggest that *all* African Americans or whites will have identical perceptions, attitudes, beliefs, or knowledge; it does suggest, however, that the "social, material, and symbolic circumstances of a social group shape the standpoints of members of that group."[46]

Although each group will have differing perceptions, groups at the lower end of the hierarchy, according to standpoint theorists, will have a more complete and accurate view of society because, for example, to survive within the system, such groups need to know how elites operate.[47] In contrast, groups that occupy a position at the top of the hierarchy may be oblivious to the dehumanizing elements of the social system or engage in a collective sense of denial in order not to take responsibility for the system's tragic failures.[48] To put it another way: "In systems of dominance the vision available to the rulers will be both partial and perverse."[49] The promotion of Robert Johnson provides one vivid example of how incongruent perspectives can complicate the goal of racial reconciliation.

PROMOTION OF ROBERT JOHNSON

Robert Johnson's musical legacy, coupled with the crossroads myth, has turned a marginalized former sharecropper into a pop culture icon and a multi-million-dollar business. In Greenwood, Mississippi, Sylvester Hoover and Steve LaVere promote the musical legacy of Robert Johnson and deride each other's claims of authority. Indeed, the long-standing animosity between Hoover and LaVere exemplifies both differences in perception regarding the preservation and exploitation of the blues and, to some extent, the racial divide that has, on occasion, characterized the state's blues tourism industry. This conflict is not news. The two sides have publicly expressed contempt for each other in the *Greenwood Commonwealth* and other media outlets. (In 2009, LaVere and another blues promoter, state senator David Jordan, an African American, were engaged in a public dispute over Jordan's decision to place a Robert Johnson marker in Baptist Town. The marker states that Robert Johnson died in Baptist Town. LaVere argues that there is no factual evidence to prove such an assertion. He was quoted as saying: "There is no disagreement among people who know the facts.")[50]

Sylvester Hoover and his wife, Mary Ann Edwards Hoover, were born in Mississippi during the 1950s and worked on large plantations in the Greenwood area. Claiming to be the "keeper[s]" of Robert Johnson's legacy, the Hoovers operate out of one of Greenwood's impoverished black communities, Baptist Town. In the 1930s, Robert Johnson, David "Honeyboy" Edwards, Sonny Boy Williamson, Elmore James, and other blues musicians played on the street corners and juke joints in Baptist Town. In March 2004 the Hoovers developed the Delta Blues Legend Tour, a three and a half hour guided trip through Baptist Town and beyond, promising tourists that they will "follow the footsteps down the soulful and untouched Mississippi Delta" and "feel the essence of the Mississippi Blues history maker" Robert Johnson.[51] Nearly a year later, the Hoovers opened up the Back in the Day Museum. Mary Ann, who acts as the museum's curator, states that the museum's primary mission is to teach young blacks about the extraordinary struggles and difficulties faced by African Americans in Mississippi before the social and political progress resulting from the civil rights movement: "They can see things for themselves and lay hands on the stark realities that black children had to face during my childhood."[52]

The Hoovers represent the few African Americans who actively promote the blues in the Greenwood area and one of a handful of African American blues promoters in the entire state. Sylvester Hoover believes that other blues promoters, whose businesses are located in the more-affluent white section of Greenwood, have intentionally staked out their territorial claim on the blues and are unfairly profiting from the city's African American blues culture. Blacks, he argues, have been unfairly excluded from fully participating in promoting the region's blues culture:

> *They always got something to stop [the] normal African American from getting into it. They don't want him in it. Certain peoples want to keep it the way they got it and they ain't going to accept it any other way. They make money, they got plenty of money. And, you know, money rules. If you got a lot of money, peoples got a tendency to get in your corner and I can understand that. But I'm not mad about it. That's their problem. . . . I don't have no bad attitude about it. Just the way they're doing it is not right.[53]*

Steve LaVere's interest in Robert Johnson started in 1962 when the California teenager listened to a copy of Johnson's *King of the Delta Blues Singers*. By 1974, LaVere had entered into a consensual legal agreement with Johnson's half sister, Carrie Thompson, who was believed at the time to be the late blues singer's last remaining heir. Under the agreement, Thompson transferred the rights to Johnson's photos, songs, and other memorabilia to LaVere.[54] In return, Thompson would receive fifty percent of the royalties the materials rendered.[55] As a blues historian, record collector, and music producer, LaVere has certainly been instrumental in preserving and promoting Johnson's image and music, from copyrighting his songs (which were in the public domain) to writing about the musician's short, brilliant, and tragic life. LaVere was also instrumental in the release of Johnson's box set, *The Complete Recordings*, in 1990, which sold over a million copies and ignited, yet again, another blues revival. However, the financial success of the box set generated the first of a series of legal struggles that would last for more than a decade. Carrie Thompson died before the release of the box set, and she left her estate to her half-sister, Annye Anderson, and grandson, Robert Harris.[56] At the same time, Claud Johnson, a trucker driver, claimed to be Robert Johnson's son. By 1998, a judge named Claud Johnson sole heir to the Johnson estate, entitling him to $1.3 million in royalty money and future royalty earnings. The resulting litigation has apparently produced mutual contempt among the various parties. In a 2008 interview, LaVere claimed that the Johnson family's role is simply to collect a paycheck, not to manage or promote Johnson's musical legacy:

> *They're simply the heirs that spend the money that I make and send to them. That's the only thing they do, and that's the only thing they've ever done. And nobody ever, in that family, not one person, has ever voiced any thanks or appreciation to me for saving those songs and copyrighting them and doing the work that I did. But I keep half the money, so they don't have to thank me if they don't want to. But still it's a very poor way to exist when a great deal of what you do is dependent upon someone else and never voiced any degree of thankfulness.[57]*

In 2001, LaVere moved from Glendale, California, to Greenwood to open the Johnson-inspired Greenwood Blues Heritage Museum and Gallery. The museum is located near the upscale Alluvian Hotel, the brainchild of Fred Carl Jr., the owner of Viking Range Corporation and the former chairperson of the state's Blues Commission. In a 2008 interview, LaVere criticized Hoover, who is a deacon at Little Zion Missionary Baptist Church, as a

> *shaman [who has] no authority to be doing what he's doing. And I don't mean he needs someone else's authority. He just has no authority. He doesn't know what he's doing. He has no education. He's never studied the blues. On his Web site, he calls Guitar Slim "Eddie Guitar Slim." His name is Eddie "Guitar Slim" Jones. I don't think he knows that. His Web site is full of faux pas. He's not the "keeper" of Robert Johnson's legacy.[58]*

The controversy over whether tourists (who are part of a guided tour) should be forced to pay a fee of ten dollars per person to visit the Little Zion Missionary Baptist Church cemetery where Johnson is buried reveals the deep enmity between the two promoters. Hoover argued that the money will be used for general maintenance of the church and cemetery. LaVere, who paid approximately $3,000 for a headstone to be placed at the site of Johnson's grave, called the plan an "audacious, ungrateful, short-sighted extortion." In this bitter tit-for-tat exchange, Hoover claimed that LaVere has reaped the financial benefits from exploiting Johnson's music and image: "I and other people believe that after all the millions you've made off the man and his music, putting a headstone at the site of his grave should've been just the start."[59]

As standpoint theory clearly suggests, both men see each other through the perspective of their different socioeconomic and racial groups. LaVere, who has spent over forty years researching, studying, and promoting the blues, seems to view Hoover as an uninformed layperson who exploits his cultural background as the only source of identification with Johnson. In contrast, Hoover most likely sees LaVere as an interloper, a cultural outsider who has read and written about the blues but never worked as a sharecropper on a plantation or experienced the despair of poverty or the subjugation of white racism. "They got a lot of people promoting the blues that read about the blues, learn about it by peoples telling them," Hoover told me in a 2008 interview. "They're not doing it the authentic way."

These incompatible perspectives are also exacerbated by material inequity and physical separation. LaVere's blues museum is located on Howard Street in an area noted for its relative prosperity. In contrast, Hoover's restaurant and museum are located across the railroad tracks and east of the downtown area in a poor, all-black community called Baptist Town.[60] Standpoint theorist Nancy C. M. Hartstock argues that "if material life is structured in fundamentally opposing ways for two different groups, one can expect that the vision of each will represent an inversion of the other."[61] As a former sharecropper and lifelong resident of Greenwood, Hoover may perceive LaVere's activities as just another example of how whites have historically and systematically deprived the state's black residents a real opportunity for economic empowerment. Baptist Town, with its gang graffiti, trash, high unemployment, and poverty, is a testament, one could argue, to how whites are still largely indifferent to black poverty and the social inequities that still characterize most Mississippi communities. In contrast, LaVere would probably view his role quite the opposite. Rather than promoting Robert Johnson from his perch in California, LaVere decided to move to Greenwood to make a real difference: to provide a much-needed economic stimulus to a city that has been in rapid decline since the 1940s. (In 2010, the *Greenwood Commonwealth* reported that LaVere and his wife, Regina, are planning to move to Hawaii; his blues museum will remain open. LaVere was quoted as saying, "We've never made any money here. We've never had a month where we've at least broken even.")[62] Ultimately, it appears, both see each other as unfairly profiting from the blues.

BLUES FESTIVALS: THE ILLUSION OF RACIAL HARMONY?

Mississippi's official culture argues that blues festivals promote and create a cultural space that encourages racial harmony and social integration because these events are arguably one of the few venues in which African Americans and whites (and other racial and ethnic groups) can develop a temporary, but important, human connection. Yet opposing critical voices claim this harmony is largely illusory, obfuscating the dysfunctional racial norms that still exist in the Delta as well as the history of racial injustice that is ever present in the memory of both blacks and whites, despite the best efforts of some who would conveniently forget the past. While some of these incompatible perceptions may be attributed to the fact that whites and blacks in Mississippi generally occupy different positions on the class ladder, it is also clear that this divide can also be categorized along another power dynamic: promoter and musician. At best, musicians and promoters can establish fruitful, mutually beneficial working and personal relationships. In fact, a number of local blues promoters, both past (Jim O'Neal) and present (Roger Stolle), have promoted the music and local musicians and received comparatively little financial rewards for their efforts. At worst, however, the relationship is defined by contempt: the musician views the promoter as a parasite, a leech who financially defrauds the talent for personal gain. Inversely, the promoter views the musician as essentially ungrateful and ignorant about financial realities.

In general, local blues musicians complain about inadequate financial compensation and resent the earning power of headliner acts. These objections are certainly not unique to blues festivals or Mississippi. Historically, (blues) musicians have testified about their powerlessness, representing themselves as victims of an unethical financial arrangement that benefits the promoter at the expense of the talent. Many music festivals feature local talent and national headlining acts; the headliner commands a higher fee, while local musicians receive a relatively modest amount. However, what makes these issues especially salient is that these complaints run counter to expressed postracial themes ("No Black, No White, Just the Blues") sometimes employed to rhetorically frame Mississippi's blues festivals, and the concept of racial reconciliation, one of the goals of blues tourism. The problem of perceived financial exploitation also takes on special meaning within the historical and social context of the Mississippi Delta, a region where blacks have historically been exploited by the white ruling class.

Scholars have articulated various theories to explain how festivals act to bridge social and cultural divides between historically antagonistic groups. Folklorist Beverly J. Stoeltje argues that part of the symbolic processes embedded in the ritualistic nature of festivals involves transforming perceptions of society. Specifically, she argues that festivals act to invert the social hierarchy. "In hierarchical societies, symbolic inversion creates an upside-down world with the 'inferior' at the top and the 'superior' at the bottom, or it declares egalitarianism to be in order for the duration of the festival."[63] Although only temporary, festivals act to neutralize, or at the least downplay, racial animosity.

Mississippi blues musicians escape their status as racial and cultural others by inhabiting the role of the authentic blues sage, a role many whites admire and celebrate. James Steven Sauceda, a researcher of intercultural communication, provides another compelling explanation for the power of aesthetic communication to bridge cultural differences. He argues that the performance aspect of aesthetic communication allows individuals to "actively participate and share in another's culture." This sharing of cultures is predicated on the active involvement of both audience and performer. Rather than silently reading a poem at a library or listening to music within the privacy of one's bedroom, Sauceda insists that individuals must travel into this new and unknown culture and attend live performances; this strategy creates the opportunity for individuals to appreciate and accept cultural differences. Sauceda cites the example of an Aborigine "counterfestival" that took place in Townsville, located in a remote section of Queensland, Australia. Although the community was outraged by news that their town would host such as festival, by the conclusion of the event, the distrust and suspicion had turned to admiration because the local population had a firsthand encounter with the Aborigines' long and proud visual-arts tradition.[64]

A number of blues promoters, musicians, and other observers believe that blues festivals provide the opportunity for important intercultural exchange between whites and African Americans. For example, Mae Smith, Interpretation Specialist at the Delta Blues Museum, believes "different groups of people can come together for a function and can exist and not tear each other apart and talk to each other and share ideas."[65] Nancy Kossman, former proprietor of Dela's Stackhouse (a music store in Clarksdale that no longer exists), commented in a 2002 interview that blues festivals create an opportunity for disparate communities to enjoy a shared experience.[66] Donald E. Wilcock, the managing editor of *The King Biscuit Times*, discussed the important role that blues festivals play in disarming racial prejudice: "Blues festivals . . . bring the races together, and if they point up how we're different, that's good. We need to embrace, celebrate and flat out enjoy those differences together instead of being afraid of one another."[67] Former editor of *Living Blues* David Nelson observed that blues festivals "tend to bring tourists and less affluent residents together in positive ways."[68] Most audience members recognize the positive racial climate that permeates most blues festivals, according to Barry Bays, a local musician: "You're not worried about, 'Oh, man, there's forty thousand blacks and ten thousand whites, what if a riot starts?' That's not going to happen. I mean, if a fight starts so many people will be breaking it up, you know, not trying to egg it on."[69] Since 1996, when I attended my first Mississippi blues festival, I have never witnessed any racial tension, in the form of either verbal or physical confrontation, between whites and blacks. On the contrary, blues festivals seem, at least on the surface, to embody the *absence* of racial tension and antagonism.

Blues musicians are clearly aware of the power of music to unite traditionally segregated groups. At the 2008 Sunflower River Blues and Gospel Festival, blues musician Willie King discussed the need for "love" and "peace." During a performance at the 2002 Highway 61 Blues Festival, his song "America" expressed an urgent need to bridge the racial divide in America: "America, we've been separated too long / We all need to come together / . . . with love like that / You know, we can't go wrong." Willie Foster, who passed away in 2001 at seventy-nine, would often stop between songs to describe his birth on a cotton sack in a cotton field, preach his faith in God, and reiterate his belief that the blues is about "love," not "hate." At the 2000 Highway 61 Blues Festival, Foster urged the audience to follow the "golden rule" and "love one another." The festival's organizer, Billy Johnson, punctuated Foster's remarks with a plea for racial tolerance and love: "God did not make a black world, a red world, or a white world, just one world." During the 2000 B. B. King Homecoming Festival, King invited several children in the audience to join him onstage for a "dance contest." After a series of run-off competitions, two participants remained on the stage: an African American boy and a white girl. Although the boy eventually "won" the contest, King's "dance contest" included members who represented the racial diversity of the audience itself.

Festival organizers have occasionally used reconciliation themes to frame these cultural events, including the Sunflower River Blues and Gospel Festival's 2008 slogan, "Let's Work Together."[70] Even merchandise—from coffee mugs to hats to T-shirts—reflects themes of integration, tolerance, and love. The 1960s-inspired slogans "Make Blues, Not War," "Peace, Love, Blues," "I've Got the Blues, Brother," and the ever-popular "No Black, No White, Just the Blues" urge spectators to transcend the human failings of prejudice and discrimination.

The Sunflower festival, similar to many blues festivals in Mississippi, also serves as a bridge to mending cultural and racial conflict by providing financial assistance to elderly, and often destitute, blues musicians. The 1998 Sunflower festival program guide vividly describes the fate of many aging blues musicians who are trapped in a cycle of debt and poverty:

> *Eugene Powell is in a nursing home in Greenville. Jessie Mae Hemphill's trailer is literally eroding into the pine country soil, open to snakes and vermin. Wesley Jefferson lost most of his equipment and his van in an accident on Highway Sixty-One. Delta musicians usually have no retirement set up nor a "nest egg" locked up in CDs or saving accounts, no IRA, no stocks and bonds. . . . The little that remains for many musicians is their few (if any) recordings, their*

stories, and us—their fans. The Sunflower River Blues Association adopted by resolution the formation of "The Sunflower Musician's Relief Fund" to help delta blues musicians in needy times . . . in times of survival, when there might not be anyone else to lend a helping hand.[71]

Other blues festivals in the area provide similar relief for blues musicians. For example, the Sonny Boy Blues Society, based in Helena, Arkansas, provides funding for Blues Aid, a project designed to "bring worldwide attention and financial assistance to the plight of our aging blues musicians."[72] Referring to these musicians as "cultural resources," Bubba Sullivan, one of the founders of the Sonny Boy Blues Society, lamented that "our living cultural history is dying."[73] Impromptu concerts have also been organized to assist blues musicians who have suffered illness or needed medical attention. In 1987, after James "Son" Thomas was injured in an accident at his home, a concert was held to raise money for his medical bills.[74]

The act of honoring musicians for their achievements and other individuals who played a role in promoting the blues also seems to be another rhetorical strategy employed to invert the social hierarchy and promote a sense of racial justice.[75] For example, the 1999 Sunflower festival paid tribute to John Lee Hooker, who was born in Clarksdale in 1917. Near the conclusion of the festival each year, organizers present the Early Wright Award to a recipient or recipients who are characterized by "their outstanding contributions to preserve, perpetuate, and promote blues and gospel music." Frank Ratliff, the owner of the Riverside Hotel (one of the few African American owned hotels in the area that provided shelter for African Americans during Mississippi's Jim Crow era), and Sonny Payne, one of first radio announcers at KFFA radio, received the Early Wright award at the 2003 festival.[76] The honoring function is also displayed by dedicating festivals to the memory of blues performers who have passed away, often due to old age or inadequate medical care. Remembering the 1993 Sunflower festival, an audience member writing under the pseudonym "Fiat Lux" framed the festival as a "wake" for James "Son" Thomas of Leland, Mississippi, who died shortly before the event.[77] The 2000 festival was dedicated to the memory of three blues musicians, Frank Frost, Little Jeno Tucker, and Wade Walton, and the radio pioneer Early Wright.

In sum, one can hardly deny the positive outcomes associated with blues festivals: these cultural events do create an aesthetic space for African Americans and whites (and other cultural groups) to collectively participate in enjoying a singular music experience, an event that temporarily, at least, inverts power relationships. The star attractions are mostly African American blues musicians, not white farmers or city officials. Rites of enhancement, such as the Early Wright Awards ceremonies, and festival dedications, strategies to evoke the memory of dead and living blues musicians, would have been un-thinkable forty years ago. Efforts to provide financial assistance to struggling musicians who are caught in a cycle of poverty and dependence are com-mendable and signify, in a very real way, how blues tourism can serve as an opportunity to redress, at least implicitly, past racial transgressions. Finally, one cannot deny that blues festivals do provide local musicians with another opportunity to make a living, although there is debate as to whether the mon-etary compensation practices are, on the whole, fair and equitable.

Yet while blues festivals may provide an opportunity for African Americans and whites to find common ground through music, create the opportunity for intercultural interchange, or temporarily invert the social hierarchy whereby black performers enjoy a brief period of privilege (higher status than their white counterparts),[78] these possible outcomes do not add up to the disap-pearance of race as a social construct. Nor do these possible outcomes lead to racial harmony, because significant structural racial inequities still exist in the region. In a 2004 letter to the editor published in the *Clarksdale Press Register*, Rebecca Brandt was appalled with Clarksdale's racial-segregation practices:

> *I visited Clarksdale several months ago, for only three days, but I left with a very strong sense of injustice and moral outrage. Living in Iowa all my life, I guess I'm naive about racial issues. We have so few non-Caucasian people that segregation isn't really an issue. But in your community, I visited a public school that is almost entirely composed of black students. I was told that most white children go to private school. . . . My impression is that you've all reached a comfort level with the separateness. This makes daily life easier for both sides, but it is extremely unfair. You simply must address the issue of all-black public schools for the sake of all children. And you must purposefully reach out to each other. Segregation is not just, even if it's comfortable.*[79]

In a 2004 interview, James "Super Chikan" Johnson observed that while blues festivals provide an opportunity for whites and blacks to share a com-mon space and interact, the apparent interracial goodwill is temporary, "win-dow dressing" for tourists. "When these people [tourists] are all gone, you're back in the same damn rut. Alright, back to what you was doing. Yeah, we put on a front for the tourists and every damn body who comes here."[80] Blues singer and guitarist Bill "Howl-N-Madd" Perry agrees: "He told the truth. That's basically the bottom line. At the same time, at least there's the effort. And maybe, maybe somewhere down the line we'll get it together. The odds are that we won't."[81] For the typical tourist who might spend a weekend drink-ing beer and enjoying the sounds of "authentic" blues, Mississippi blues fes-tivals provide compelling evidence that the state has transcended its racist past. Indeed, a promoter who tried to organize an interracial blues festival in Mississippi during the 1960s would have been called foolhardy or prevented by local authorities from staging such a "reckless" and "immoral" event. For some local blues musicians, however, who *live* in a region still mired in the vestiges of Jim Crow, a region where white privilege and black poverty are ever present, blues festivals today are, at best, an inaccurate picture of the real structural and material inequities that still afflict the residents of the Delta region.[82]

At the same time, some local blues musicians are frustrated and angry about issues related to perceived financial disparity. John Sherman, a Clarksdale attorney and the co-chair of the 2007 Sunflower River Blues and Gospel Festival, noted in a 2007 interview that the festival's headliner acts (e.g., Koko Taylor) typically receive between $5,000 and $15,000, while most local acts receive considerably less money, ranging from $500 to $2,500 depending on a musician's status and popularity.[83] Approximately 95 percent of the local blues musicians who play at local blues festivals are African American males. In the April 2008 edition of *Living Blues*, Wesley Jefferson and Terry "Big T" Williams, two Clarksdale blues musicians, complained that the local musicians are receiving scant financial compensation for playing at Sunflower, while the "stars," often artists who do not live in Mississippi, receive top billing and the financial rewards associated with status. "Very little bit coming in helps the local peoples," explained Jefferson. "It's helping the club that owns it, like Sunflower River Blues, they keeping that and they a non-profit. . . . I'm feeling the blues right now but I needs the financials to help me." Williams argued that local black performers are simply viewed as "field hands," a phrase used by other blues musicians to explain their predicament:

> *Most of your supporters of our festivals . . . only support because of the publicity that they can receive as being recognized as one of the supporters. We, on the other hand, as the workers—you can call us field hands if you want—we still the buffalo soldiers. We going to rescue them, we going to come and play and make people enjoy themselves and buck jump and carry on and when we get done we still don't got nothing.[84]*

Patty Johnson, one of the original promoters of the festival, argued that the purpose and direction of Sunflower had changed to such a degree that she decided to resign in 2000:

> *The festival has totally changed, gotten away from our actual purpose statement in supporting people who play Mississippi music, and that is not what our charter states. We founded that festival to support the musicians from and*

in Mississippi, primarily the Mississippi musicians that were still here who were not out on the touring circuit, who did not have those avenues, and were not the major [stars], not the B. B. King, Buddy Guy bunch. These musicians didn't have that advantage. And we started the blues festival to support them. And when major funding was going to support musicians who had no ties to Mississippi other than playing the blues, I resigned.[85]

Local blues musicians have observed a similar disparity at other blues festivals. For example, guitarist Mickey Rogers once tried to negotiate a price of $1,800 to play at a local festival; the organizer's counteroffer of $300 was rejected because, as Rogers flatly put it: "How am I going to pay the band?"[86] Mississippi Slim, a local blues singer, provides a helpful example to depict the problem:

You bring in an act and pay them five thousand dollars. Then you got your local people around here who play and might make five hundred dollars. You see. And, boy, that's a big gap there. The other people leaving with all the money in their pockets, when you do the show, when you get done by the time you pay your light bill, or your gas bill [laughing], you know, out of that five hundred—which four people or five people [other band members] had to get paid out of—you don't have anything left, man.[87]

In contrast, some musicians have criticized their peers for, in some cases, exacerbating unfair compensation practices. Singer Barbara Looney argues that some musicians have agreed to play at festivals and clubs for minimal financial compensation, which has made it difficult for other musicians to charge a higher fee.[88] Terry "Harmonica" Bean argues that the opposite is true: some local musicians have refused opportunities to perform and earn money because the fee was perceived to be inadequate: "They get a gig, but if it ain't a big paying gig, they can hardly take it. They want more money."[89] Billy "Howl-N-Madd" Perry provides the following insight:

You want all this money. What are you going to do for it? . . . Now, it's like, if you ain't done taking the time out and respecting this enough to give it everything that you got, why would you expect someone to pay you a whole bunch of money? You know, you half-ass giving them a product. So if you're half-ass giving something, you should get half-ass pay for it. I mean, that's the way I see it. But now if you done went, besides paying your dues, and you really love what you are doing and when you walk up on that stage and you give everything that you got, you can't dig up no more, then see you should get paid for that. A lot of these folks out here don't deserve no more than they're getting. Some of them don't even deserve even that. But in their minds, I should be getting paid a million dollars a gig.[90]

Regardless of the reasons, many local blues musicians have to rely on part-time or full-time work to make ends meet, an economic reality experienced by most blues musicians, white and black. For a number of years, blues guitarist Big Jack Johnson drove an oil truck to supplement his earnings as a musician. Known as the "Oilman," Johnson named his band Big Jack Johnson and the Oilers. John Horton, a blues guitarist who lives in Greenville, works full-time in construction. Pat Thomas sells his artwork to supplement his income as a part-time musician. Terry "Big T" Williams has held various jobs, including working as a painter as well as owning a blues club. In a 2004 interview, James "Super Chikan" Johnson described growing up as a sharecropper, living under Mississippi's Jim Crow racial edicts, and working as a construction worker and truck driver, among other labor-intensive jobs.[91] Although he had recently won the Mississippi Governor's Award for Excellence in the Arts, Johnson described the difficulty of earning a living wage as a musician in the Delta. To make ends meet, Johnson sells his famous guitars fashioned from old gas cans. Since that time, Johnson has released three albums and received increased domestic and international exposure. In a 2009 CNN interview, Johnson stated that while his decision to pursue the blues as a career is "paying off," he still considers himself as a musician who inhabits the "blues world":

It's been a hard trail. Like the old blues world go, you know, you start out with nothing and you wind up with ninety percent of it left. And that's what I got [laughter]. Today I am, according to the people and fans, I'm famous and I definitely got to write a song about that. Now, they's thinkin' I'm famous. But me, until I got something to match that fame, I don't think I'm famous yet. . . . But while I'm still struggling, I'm still struggling with the blues, the blues don't let go easy. It holds on to you. From poor life up to whatever you want to call it now (I guess that's my ten percent of nothing that I got now), but the blues still hangs on to you and it's hard to shake. Even if you come out of the strain of everyday life, you got the music, so you got the blues either way you go, either way you look at it.[92]

These contemporary examples are certainly not unique. Before his death in 1993, James "Son" Thomas worked various labor-intensive jobs from share-cropping to grave digging. "Yessir, I dug graves 'til I got where I couldn't handle it," recalled Thomas in a 1988 interview with the *Delta Democrat Times*. "I got where when I digged, I couldn't walk the next day, and I was afraid, you know, to be driving that truck, because the pain hits in your back and you're gone then."[93] While acknowledging the legitimate complaints about inadequate compensation, it is also true that *any* local musician would probably find it difficult to make a living wage as a full-time musician in the Mississippi Delta. Jay Kirgis, a white blues musician who now lives in Texas, stated that it was difficult for him to survive only on income derived from playing at festivals, clubs, and other live venues in Mississippi: "I don't know too many musicians who got into playing the blues because they thought it was going to be commercial, they were going to make hundreds of thousands of dollars. . . . The blues has never been noted for making people rich, making musicians rich. So, they're pretty much there because they love [it]."[94]

Even when local blues musicians travel overseas to Europe or Asia, some have questioned whether these musicians are well compensated for their efforts, although musicians usually have their expenses paid, including airfare, food, and accommodations.[95] In a 1972 interview later published in *Living Blues* magazine, Robert Jr. Lockwood's complaint about the systematic exploitation of blues musicians served as a rationale for his decision not to accept opportunities to travel overseas to perform:

> They [music promoters] was gatherin' up a lot of dudes that hadn't ever made any damn thing and didn't even know the value of a dollar in a sense and was takin' 'em over there and givin' them 200 or 300 dollars a week when the talent was earnin' 6 or 700 dollars a week. That's why I've never been to Europe 'cause that is what was happenin'. . . . When I go over there, I want to go as Robert Lockwood Jr., and I don't want no damn body to take me. And if I can't go that way, I don't want to go.[96]

Sade Turnipseed observes that during a monthlong overseas tour, local black musicians may earn as little as a few thousand dollars. Local musicians "have been so misrepresented and abused. . . . People take them around the world, they'll be gone for a month and come back with two thousand dollars in their pocket. Hey, come on. That's so disrespectful."[97] While some blues musicians who have toured overseas live in relative comfort, many others live in rather sparse and meager surroundings. Before his death in 1993, for example, James "Son" Thomas's dwelling was colorfully described as a "battered wooden house" with a bed that was as "wobbly as Son himself."[98] When I traveled to Greenville to interview James "T-Model" Ford in 2007, I discovered that the singer lived in a rundown duplex in an economically depressed neighborhood.[99] In the film *You See Me Laughin': The Last of the Hill Country Bluesmen* (2003), Ford was living in far worse conditions: his house, where he lived with his wife and three children, was in an advanced stage of deterioration with a rotted foundation, leaking roof, and an almost nonworking plumbing system. R. L. Burnside's house in Holly Springs, Mississippi, was in marginally better shape, although the singer was so financially strapped that he did not have enough money to consult a doctor about his various health problems.[100] In a 2004 interview, blues singer and guitarist Jay Kirgis discussed the incongruity between fame and poverty:

> *You'll see somebody who seems like they're touring all the time, and playing all over the place, and their name is heard by all these people, and they're up at big, big parties up in New York for rich people, playing for the President and everything like that and then [you] go over to their house and it's a shack, a shotgun shack with dirt floor and you're thinking, "Wait a minute, there is some type of disparity here that isn't adding up."*[101]

While a blues musician's financial situation may be attributed to a number of factors, including an inability to save and invest wisely or personal vices such as alcohol and gambling, it does call into question both the difficulty of earning a living as a performer and the time-old practices of promoters who enrich themselves at the expense of the musicians who record and tour as a mean of economic survival.

If Mississippi blues musicians do achieve some sense of recognition and financial compensation, it will generally occur late in their careers when they are collecting social security checks. For example, North Mississippi blues artist Junior Kimbrough toiled in relative obscurity for most of his life until he was featured in the documentary film *Deep Blues* (1991). By that time, Kimbrough was a senior citizen. He told a *New York Times* reporter that "I always knew my day would come. I just never knew it would take so long."[102] Although Kimbrough released four albums between 1992 and 1997, including his acclaimed debut, *All Night Long*, to mostly glowing reviews and was championed by blues fans and rock stars alike as a truly authentic blues musician, he lived in a modest apartment in a housing project and suffered from several health problems before succumbing to a heart attack in 1998 at sixty-seven.

While acknowledging the pay disparity, John Sherman argued, for example, that most local festivals have limited budgets and that some festivals, like the Sunflower River Blues and Gospel Festival, do not charge an admission fee. He argues that organizers need to pay headliners a "reasonable" performance fee and that many actually agree to play for much less than their average asking price.[103] In a 2004 interview, Billy Johnson, who organizes Leland's Highway 61 Blues Festival, acknowledges the financial realities associated with organizing a blues festival: "You can put all the local musicians in a festival, and if you don't put a couple of big headliners on the top to bring the people, you're going to lose money every the time."[104]

For festival organizers, this appears to be the dilemma. As the logic goes, the inclusion of a recognizable star to headline a festival is necessary to maximize the potential audience and increase the likelihood that the event will break even or be profitable. At the same time, some local musicians believe they are being excluded from the opportunity to earn the financial rewards and the prestige associated with headliner status. Perhaps feeling slighted and unappreciated, the relatively meager financial compensation may symbolize to some performers a certain level of disrespect. Clearly these incompatible perceptions reflect a long tradition of mistrust and animosity between musician and promoter, one that is obviously not exclusive to the promotion of Mississippi's blues culture. It should be pointed out that similar complaints (e.g., inadequate compensation) have been leveled at MACE, an African American civil rights group, the organization that has been responsible for organizing Greenville's Mississippi Delta Blues and Heritage Festival.

Yet it is apparent that there is also a racial component to this conflict. The perceptions among some black musicians that they are treated as nothing more than common laborers, black "field hands," evokes the memory of sharecropping and the asymmetrical power relationship between the white plantation owner (and the overseer) and his exploited black workers. For many of these musicians, memory is based on personal life experiences, not just an abstract understanding of the past. Many local musicians grew up in a sharecropping family, picking cotton in the fields at an early age and witnessing firsthand the abusive and violent realities of white rule. Playing music at local festivals and receiving as little as $250 for their services may be akin to picking cotton and waiting for the settle. Although nearly all the blues musicians who sharecropped (or engaged in inequitable working practices) no longer work as farm laborers, those early experiences profoundly shaped their perceptions and knowledge of Mississippi's social structure in much the same way that the Great Depression shaped an entire generation's attitudes about material wealth and prosperity. To be sure, the term "field hand" is not being used irresponsibly, nor is the phrase the hysterical ravings of musicians who are exploiting the idea of race to cover over their personal shortcomings. Indeed, the phrase reflects both a historical orientation to the world and the present-day power relationships that still constitute the region's social structure.

In the end, while many blues festivals promote reconciliation themes of peace and harmony, an undeniable crosscurrent of resentment, frustration, and resignation exists. The perceptual divide between musician and promoter is further exacerbated by the historical and present-day social structure in Mississippi that benefits, to a large extent, the state's white population. A critical examination of Mississippi blues festivals reveals that these cultural events, while serving a number of positive social functions, may impede goals associated with reconciliation.

BLUES TOURISM: TWENTY-FIRST-CENTURY SHARECROPPING?

The metaphor of the black field hand certainly conjures images of a racial caste system and provides an opportunity to discuss the varying perceptions of whether white Mississippians today are exploiting the blues in the same way that sharecropping subjugated generations of black workers to a cycle of debt and dependence, providing insufficient financial returns for intense physical labor. Although whites largely control the promotion of the blues, it is unclear whether blues tourism is a profit-making enterprise. White promoters stress that many blues attractions are nonprofit entities that rely on grants, sponsorships, and other forms of financial assistance as part of their operating budgets. Some blues festivals, even the ones that charge an admission fee, barely break even; some lose money. Perhaps the only entities truly profiting from blues tourism are local restaurants and hotels, although it is impossible to ascertain how much revenue results from blues tourism. In other words, while one might claim that whites are financially profiting from blues tourism at the expense of black artists, there is no empirical evidence to prove such an assertion. In a 2008 interview, former *Living Blues* editor Scott Barretta stated that there is a perception that whites are reaping profits from blues tourism at the expense of the black community:

> I think there's a sense that this [blues tourism] is primarily benefiting the white folks who always have been making the money. I don't know if that's really the case right now. I don't really see that much money is being made. I certainly understand, particularly from a historical experience, why people feel that way and how that could be viewed.[105]

It is clear, however, that whites are largely in control of promoting and preserving the blues in Mississippi, and thus there is the real *potential* for African Americans to be financially disenfranchised. While Adam Gussow is hopeful that blues tourism will provide an opportunity for racial reconciliation and healing, he also worries that blues tourism may be nothing more than a twenty-first-century version of the Delta's feudal system of sharecropping:

> Since economic power here continues to be wielded primarily by whites, even as African American political power has markedly expanded since the end of segregation, the nascent blues tourism business may, of course, turn out to be one more way in which white capital extracts profit from black artistry without truly sharing in the wealth—which is to say, blues tourism may yet end up reinscribing the same old blues on Mississippi's black citizens, the blues of economic expropriation that generations of black sharecroppers knew so well.[106]

Indeed, from the standpoint of Mississippi's black communities, many of which are still devastated by poverty, unemployment, crime, and a real sense of hopelessness, and African American blues musicians, who themselves grew up working on white-owned plantations and experienced the discriminatory practices legally sanctioned by segregation laws, white interest in promoting the blues *may* ultimately result in the culmination of Gussow's worst fears. Given this historical context, it is no wonder that some members of the African American community complain about perceived or actual incidents of racial exploitation. In his research, sociologist Alan Barton speculated that one of the reasons why African American respondents are less likely to attend a blues festival compared to their white counterparts is the perception that "blues festivals showcase black talent but make money for white businessmen."[107] Yet whites have also expressed concerns about this issue, as indicated in a statement by Skip Henderson, an outspoken critic of Mississippi's blues tourism industry and an early blues promoter who lived at one time in Clarksdale:

> *They want blues without black people. That's what they want: they want the blues without black people. They want people to come down and say how great Mississippi is. They want people to come down and say, we had a wonderful time, it's a great culture and everything else, and, oh, there's some black people there. We liked their music, they're great. But don't give them a chance to buy into the business essentially. Don't give them a chance to own a piece of the store. They're hired hands, they're always going to be hired hands. They're replaceable, and they're expendable, and that's it, they're never given their due. And unless they win an Academy Award or become millionaires, that's the way they're always going to be.*[108]

Most white promoters reject the claim that they are exploiting the region's blues musicians or the African American community. Kinchen O'Keefe, owner of the WROX Museum in Clarksdale, told a reporter for the *Commercial Appeal* that blues festivals like Clarksdale's Juke Joint Festival do not exploit African Americans or the cultural heritage of the blues but provide an opportunity for both whites and blacks to share in a rich cultural experience.[109] "I don't want to exploit it," argued Cheryl Line, tourism manager at the Cleveland–Bolivar County Chamber of Commerce. "What I would like to do is to develop our portion of that story, so the community can be proud of that product that we end up with."[110] Bill Seratt, who has worked in tourism for over twenty years, claims that he has never witnessed the exploitation of African American blues musicians, although he acknowledges the practice does exist.[111] Bill Gresham of Clarksdale, an attorney, former chairperson of the

Sunflower River Blues and Gospel Festival, and member of the Delta Blues Museum Board of Trustees, rejects the implication that whites have exploited the blues:

> *I wouldn't say that white Mississippi or anything is trying to capitalize on it. You know, Coahoma County is a 70 percent black community. We've got a board of commissioners that is majority black, and they're the ones that [are] promoting this. It's not a white Mississippi promoting blues, its Mississippi, which in our area is a majority black.*[112]

Standpoint theorists argue that these incongruous perceptions and interpretations are not surprising because a group's material conditions structure social reality. Since African Americans and whites often occupy different locations on the social stratification ladder, their perceptions will accordingly, in many cases, be the inverse of each other. Yet as standpoint theory also clearly suggests, marginalized groups occupying the lower end of the social hierarchy often have a more complete understanding of society than elites because the struggle involved in obtaining a particular vision of social life affords the lower-status group a clear understanding of the "inherent inhumanity in the social order."[113] Thus while whites deny charges of exploitation, claiming instead that blues tourism is actually a constructive move to preserve and promote the blues, opposing, critical voices arguably provide a richer understanding of the intercultural dynamics that are at play. In other words, these critical voices provide a window into the structural imbalances that *may*, indeed, characterize Mississippi's blues tourism industry. Standpoint theory also clearly argues that elites are less likely to critically evaluate systems of domination because to do so would invite social change.

While standpoint theory is useful in understanding the intercultural communication conflict, the theory may also help to facilitate meaningful racial reconciliation. Although much of the research on standpoint theory involves understanding and critiquing patriarchy, the theory has not been used as a mechanism for racial reconciliation. Participants will first need to understand that incongruous perceptions can actually be useful as a first step to understanding, rather than discounting, the other. Individual interpretations should be viewed not as idiosyncratic but as part of a larger community's understanding of the world. At the same time, the dominant group will need to explore and evaluate their limited standpoint, perhaps eventually recognizing issues of power such as white privilege.

To be sure, racial reconciliation is a painfully slow process, fraught with cultural land mines and social barriers. Speaking at a 2004 event commemorating James Chaney, Andy Goodman, and Michael Schwerner, the three civil rights activists who were murdered near Philadelphia, Mississippi, in 1964, former Mississippi governor William F. Winter clearly expressed the hard work necessary for racial reconciliation to become a reality:

> *Because we have lived close together for so long—but too often in the past in a way that did not acknowledge our common humanity—now we can more easily realize the incredible potential that we have. But it will take a commitment that is expressed in actual deeds and not just in good intentions. It will mean reaching out beyond the old boundaries of race and class and seeking to achieve together what we cannot do separately. That will be how we most effectively justify the sacrifice of these young men whose memory we honor today. This is the torch that has been passed to us to carry and which we must pass on to another generation. It is a task that demands the best in all of us.*[114]

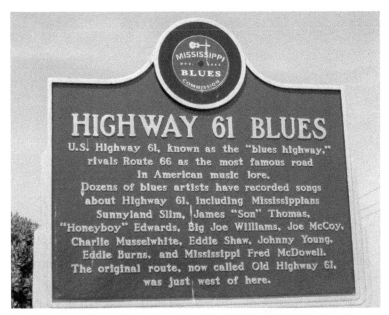

Fig. 1. Highway 61 blues marker. Sponsored by the Mississippi Blues Commission, the Mississippi Blues Trail will include approximately 160 markers. U.S. Highway 61 serves as a major thoroughfare to access blues sites in the Mississippi Delta. Welcome/Visitors' Center in Tunica County, 15 July 2009. Photo by author.

Fig. 2. Barn at Dockery Farms, 16 February 2007. Dockery Farms is located between Cleveland and Ruleville on Highway 8. At one time, the plantation was home to approximately four hundred sharecropping families, including blues alumni Charley Patton and Willie Brown. The former plantation is being converted into a tourist attraction. Photo by author.

Fig. 3. Dockery Farms blues marker, 19 April 2008. Tourists travel to the Mississippi Delta to visit the "birthplace of the blues." This marker serves as a corrective to the myth about the music's birthplace. Photo by author.

Fig. 4. Eddie Cusic, a noted musician from Leland, Mississippi, playing before a virtually all-white audience at the Sunflower River Blues and Gospel Festival, Clarksdale, Mississippi, 12 August 2006. Historically, festival organizers schedule blues performers like Cusic to play traditional blues music on Saturday morning. Othar Turner Acoustic Stage, Clarksdale Station. Photo by author.

Fig. 5. Pat Thomas, son of legendary James "Son" Thomas, playing a set of down-home blues at the Sunflower River Blues and Gospel Festival, 12 August 2006. Othar Turner Acoustic Stage, Clarksdale Station. Photo by author.

Fig. 6. Shardee Turner and the Rising Star Fife and Drum Band making the traditional walk from the Clarksdale Station to the Blues Alley Main Stage. This annual rite marks the transition from largely acoustic performances in the Clarksdale Station (scheduled on Saturday morning) to afternoon and evening performances by local and out-of-state performers on the Blues Alley Main Stage. Sunflower River Blues and Gospel Festival, 14 August 2004. Photo by author.

Fig. 7. Mississippi hill country musician Kenny Brown playing on the Blues Alley Main Stage. Brown apprenticed with a number of Mississippi blues musicians including R. L. Burnside and Fred McDowell. Sunflower River Blues and Gospel Festival, 13 August 2005. Photo by author.

Fig. 8. Blues Alley Main Stage at the Sunflower River Blues and Gospel Festival, 13 August 2005. Photo by author.

Fig. 9. Local Clarksdale musician Terry Williams ("Big T") demonstrating his instrumental prowess on the Blues Alley Main Stage. Williams grew up on a plantation near Clarksdale, and as a teenager he toured with one of the area's most famous blues bands, the Jelly Roll Kings. Sunflower River Blues and Gospel Festival, 14 August 2004. Photo by author.

Fig. 10. Greenville-based guitarist Mickey Rogers playing on the Blues Alley Main Stage, 17 April 2004. This performance was part of the Juke Joint Festival, one of Clarksdale's premier blues events. Rogers has played with Jimi Hendrix, John Lee Hooker, Howlin' Wolf, Buddy Guy, and other notable blues musicians. Photo by author.

Fig. 11. Alabama guitarist Willie King (foreground) and harpist and guitarist Terry "Harmonica" Bean entertain a mostly white audience at Acoustic Stage 2 (Delta Avenue Park), located in downtown Clarksdale. King, who died in 2009 of a heart attack, wrote songs that explicitly address sociopolitical issues such as racism and poverty, as well as songs that call for universal peace and unity. Sunflower River Blues and Gospel Festival, 9 August 2003. Photo by author.

Fig. 12. Bill Abel (left) and Cadillac John (right). Acoustic Stage 2, Sunflower River Blues and Gospel Festival, 9 August 2003. Photo by author.

Fig. 13. James "T-Model" Ford playing on Acoustic Stage 2. Ford spent his youth working as a sharecropper and at a log camp, among other labor-intensive jobs. He also spent two years on a Tennessee chain gang for murder. Sunflower River Blues and Gospel Festival, 12 August 2006. Photo by author.

Fig. 14. James "Super Chikan" Johnson playing one of his famous "Chicantars," guitars fashioned from old gas cans. In 2004, Super Chikan was awarded the Mississippi Governor's Award for Excellence in the Arts. Acoustic Stage 2, Sunflower River Blues and Gospel Festival, 13 August 2005. Photo by author.

Fig. 15. Clarksdale musician Wesley "Junebug" Jefferson (left) and an unidentified musician playing on the Blues Alley Main Stage. He grew up in a sharecropping family, and his mother ran a juke joint out of the family home. Jefferson, who was a mainstay of the Clarksdale blues scene for years, died from complications related to lung cancer in July 2009. Sunflower River Blues and Gospel Festival, 12 August 2006. Photo by author.

Fig. 16. Born in Shaw, Mississippi, in 1915, David "Honeyboy" Edwards has played with a who's-who list of blues legends including Robert Johnson, Charley Patton, and Howlin' Wolf. Here he is performing on the main stage at Highway 61 Blues Festival, Leland, Mississippi, 7 June 2008. Photo by author.

Fig. 17. Bobby Rush, the "King of Soul Blues," performing with his dancers at Clarksdale's premier blues club, Ground Zero, in June 2003. This performance was eventually released in 2003 on both CD and DVD. Photo by author.

Fig. 18. Wade Walton's Barber Shop, Clarksdale, Mississippi, 9 August 2003. Called the "Singing Barber of the Blues," Wade Walton worked as a barber for over fifty years in Clarksdale. He also played guitar and harmonica and was a featured artist in Robert Mugge's acclaimed 1991 documentary. Walton died in January 2000. Photo by author.

Fig. 19. The Robert Clay Shack at the Shack Up Inn, Hopson Plantation, Clarksdale, Mississippi, 16 August 2003. Promoting itself as Mississippi's only "bed and beer" establishment, the Shack Up Inn has become a popular lodging alternative for tourists seeking authenticity. Visitors can stay in twelve renovated sharecropper shacks. Photo by author.

Fig. 20. Robert Clay, former inhabitant of the shack. Before the shack was moved to the Hopson Plantation and renovated, Clay raised seven sons in this domicile without the benefit of indoor plumbing and running water. He died in 1998. Photo by author.

Fig. 21. During Mississippi's Jim Crow era, the Riverside Hotel was one of the few hotels in the Clarksdale area that provided accommodations for African Americans, including blues musicians. Ike Turner, Muddy Waters, John Lee Hooker, and Sonny Boy Williamson II were just some of the musicians who rented a room at the hotel. Clarksdale, Mississippi, 30 August 2003. Photo by author.

Fig. 22. Blues mural on a building in downtown Leland, 18 November 2004. Photo by author.

Fig. 23. Downtown Leland, June 2005. This photo shows clear evidence of the poverty that still plagues many Delta communities. Photo by author.

Fig. 24. Terry "Harmonica" Bean performing on the main stage at the Highway 61 Blues Festival, 7 June 2008. Bean, who is based in Pontotoc, Mississippi, located near Oxford, is a frequent performer at festivals, clubs, and juke joints in the Mississippi Delta.

Fig. 25. Greenville guitarist and singer John Horton playing on the main stage at the Highway 61 Blues Festival, 4 June 2005. Horton is a full-time bulldozer operator. Photo by author.

Fig. 26. Greenville singer Mississippi Slim (Walter Horn Jr.) playing on the main stage at the Highway 61 Blues Festival, 4 June 2005. Born in Shelby, Mississippi, in 1943, Slim moved to Chicago in 1968 and participated in the city's blues culture. He returned to Mississippi in 1994 and performed at clubs and festivals, often teaming up with John Horton. He died on April 14, 2010. Photo by author.

Fig. 27. Greenville guitarist Lil' Dave Thompson on the main stage at the Highway 61 Blues Festival, 4 June 2005. Thompson formed his first band at fourteen and was influenced by a number of Delta musicians, including the legendary guitarist Roosevelt "Booba" Barnes. He recorded four albums before his untimely death in 2010 in a vehicular accident while returning from a gig in South Carolina. He was forty. Photo by author.

Fig. 28. Rev. Slick (Daniel Ballinger) showing his guitar technique with the Soul Blues Boys on the main stage at the Highway 61 Blues Festival, 12 June 2004. Born in North Carolina, Ballinger moved to Mississippi after completing high school, studied under Othar Turner, and played with Hubert Sumlin and Pinetop Perkins, among other blues artists. He is now a gospel performer. Photo by author.

Fig. 29. Downtown Rosedale, Mississippi, 8 May 2004. Audience members enjoying performances at the Rosedale Blues Festival (now called the Rosedale Crossroads Blues and Heritage Festival). Before the festival was moved to the River Resort in 2008, Rosedale's blues festival was held in the city's dilapidated downtown area. Photo by author.

Fig. 30. Barbara Looney singing at the Rosedale Blues Festival, 8 May 2004. Looney has performed with recording legends such as Chuck Berry, Bobby Bland, and B. B. King and has served as an opening act for soul-blues stars Bobby Rush and Denise LaSalle. Photo by author.

Fig. 31. Sam Carr, tour-de-force drummer and son of Robert Nighthawk Jr., at the Rosedale Blues Festival, 8 May 2004. Born in the Arkansas Delta, Carr lived in Chicago and St. Louis before moving to Mississippi in 1960. He was a pivotal figure in the Jelly Roll Kings (with Frank Frost and Big Jack Johnson). He died in September 2009. Photo by author.

Fig. 32. Robert "Wolfman" Belfour playing on the Houston Stackhouse Acoustic Stage at the Arkansas Blues and Heritage Festival (formerly the King Biscuit Blues Festival), Helena, Arkansas, 7 October 2006. A native of Mississippi, Belfour moved to Memphis in 1959 and worked in construction for thirty-five years. Photo by author.

Fig. 33. "Sunshine" Sonny Payne holding court at the KFFA studio during the King Biscuit Blues Festival, Helena, Arkansas, 9 October 2004. In 1941, KFFA revolutionized blues programming with *King Biscuit Time*, a fifteen-minute radio program featuring blues musicians Sonny Boy Williamson II (Aleck "Rice" Miller) and Robert Jr. Lockwood. Payne was one of the station's first radio announcers. Photo by author.

Fig. 34. Thelonious Monk Jr. and an unidentified woman in front of the Dockery Farms blues marker on the day the marker was unveiled to the public, 19 April 2008. Monk served as a speaker at the event. Photo by author.

Fig. 35. Hubert Sumlin marveling at his blues marker at the unveiling ceremony, Greenwood, Mississippi, 6 May 2008. Born in Greenwood in 1931, Sumlin later relocated to Chicago and played guitar on some of Howlin' Wolf's greatest songs, including "Wang Dang Doodle" and "Killing Floor." Photo by author.

Fig. 36. A crowd waiting for the arrival of B. B. King at the ribbon-cutting ceremony for the B. B. King Museum, Indianola, Mississippi, 13 September 2008. Due to exhaustion, King did not attend the event. Note the old cotton gin in the background. Photo by author.

Fig. 37. B. B. King Museum and Delta Interpretive Center, Indianola, Mississippi, 13 September 2008. The centerpiece of blues tourism in the state, the $15 million museum opened in 2008 and attracted approximately 30,000 visitors during its first year. Photo by author.

Fig. 38. Charley Patton's headstone, Holly Ridge, Mississippi, 9 March 2003. Blues tourism involves activities such as visiting gravesites. Note the beer can by the headstone. Photo by author.

NOTES

Preface

1. Quoted in Paige McGinley, "Highway 61 Revisited," *TDR: The Drama Review* 51.3 (2007): 93. "Save the Blues" campaigns embody what Scott Barretta has called the "narrative of decline," the belief that the blues is in the process of an irreversible death. In his critique of the Chicago blues tradition and blues guitarist Buddy Guy, Carlo Rotella discusses both the narrative of decline and an opposing ideological position that articulates the ascent of the blues: "Chicago blues is in decline; Chicago blues is booming" (103). See Carlo Rotella, *Good with Their Hands: Boxers, Bluesmen, and Other Characters from the Rust Belt* (Berkeley: U of California P, 2002).

2. Lomax and John W. Work III, a professor of musicology at Fisk University, along with a group that included sociologist Lewis Wade Jones and a graduate student, Samuel C. Adams Jr., participated in field research in Coahoma County in 1941 and 1942. The project was cosponsored by Fisk University and the Library of Congress. See *Lost Delta Found: Rediscovering the Fisk University–Library of Congress Coahoma County Study, 1941–1942*, ed. Robert Gordon and Bruce Nemerov (Nashville: Vanderbilt UP, 2005).

3. Marybeth Hamilton, *In Search of the Blues* (New York: Basic, 2008) 1, 4.

4. In books including *Music: Black, White, and Blue: A Sociological Survey of the Use and Misuse of Afro-American Music* (1972) and *Everything but the Burden: What White People Are Taking from Black Culture* (2003), critics illustrate that white control of black popular culture typically involves a variety of manipulative strategies, including possessing and expunging the black presence through imitation and appropriation. For example, one critic argued that the labeling of blues as "universal" music by record companies and white journalists was a clever strategy intended to "redefine the blues in order to take it out of black culture and appropriate it for white music." Predictably, as blacks were being "written out of history," whites "were yet again making history all by themselves and writing themselves into the leading role" (Finn, 227–28). See, e.g., Greg Tate, "Nigs R Us, or How Blackfolk Became Fetish Objects," *Everything but the Burden: What White People Are Taking from Black Culture*, ed. Greg Tate (New York: Broadway, 2003) 4; Ortiz M. Walton, *Music: Black, White, and Blue: A Sociological Survey of the Use and Misuse of Afro-American Music* (New York: William Morrow, 1972); Julio Finn, *The Bluesman: The Musical Heritage of Black Men and Women in the Americas* (New York: Interlink, 1991) 227–28.

5. LeRoi Jones (Amiri Baraka), *Blues People: Negro Music in White America* (1963; New York: Harper Perennial, 2002) 148.

6. Lawrence Hoffman, "At the Crossroads," editorial, *Guitar Player* Aug. 1990: 18. See also Tony Russell, *Blacks, Whites and Blues* (London: Studio Vista, 1970), in Paul Oliver, Tony Russell, Robert M. W. Dixon, John Godrich, and Howard Rye, *Yonder Come the Blues: The Evolution of a Genre* (Cambridge, Eng.: Cambridge UP, 2001) 143–242; and Paul Garon, "White Blues," 5 Feb. 2010, http://racetraitor.org/blues.html.

7. See, e.g., Joel Rudinow, "Race, Ethnicity, Expressive Authenticity: Can White People Sing the Blues?," *Journal of Aesthetics and Art Criticism* 52.1 (1994): 127–37.

8. Paul Oliver, "Blues," *The New Grove Dictionary of Music and Musicians*, ed. Stanley Sadie, vol. 3, 2nd ed. (London: Macmillan, 2001) 730; Paul Oliver, *The Story of the Blues* (1969; Boston: Northeastern UP, 1998) 21.

9. Elijah Wald, *Escaping the Delta: Robert Johnson and the Invention of the Blues* (New York: Harper Collins, 2004) 17–22; Charles Wolfe, "A Lighter Shade of Blue: White Country Blues," *Nothing but the Blues: The Music and the Musicians*, ed. Lawrence Cohn (New York: Abbeville, 1993) 233–63.

10. See, e.g., Joy Bennett Kinnon, "Are Whites Taking or Are Blacks Giving Away the Blues?" *Ebony* Sept. 1997: 86–92.

11. Terry Bean, telephone interview, 23 Apr. 2008. Many blues artists, including Muddy Waters and B. B. King, have publicly acknowledged the financial rewards associated with white interest in the blues. When asked by a reporter for *Time* magazine in 1971 about the Rolling Stones' lucrative profits from recording his songs, Waters appeared to be unconcerned, commenting that "if they had never started taking my stuff, I don't know that I could have moved up financially. Sure they made more money than I did. So what? I'm just glad I did my thing." Quoted in "Down Home and Dirty," *Time* 9 Aug. 1971: 46.

Introduction

1. Anthony DeCurtis, "Rocking My Life Away: The Blues Will Pour Down like Rain This Year," *Rolling Stone* 30 Apr. 2003, 3 May 2003, http://www.rollingstone.com/news/newsarticle.asp?nid=17985. The Year of the Blues had its share of critics. In a 2004 editorial in *Living Blues* magazine, editor Brett J. Bonner summed up the frustration of many blues enthusiasts who had hoped this unprecedented attention to the blues would pay off: "I'm sorry to say that after speaking to folks around the industry over the last two months, it seems like that was about it. There was no boost in sales for most labels, no boost for pay at clubs for artists, no boost in signings or releases for living artists, and no groundswell of interest in the music among the masses. Not a lot to show for the 'Year of the Blues'" (2). See Brett J. Bonner, editorial, *Living Blues* Jan.–Feb. 2004: 2.

2. The Year of the Blues, "Official Proclamation," 20 Aug. 2007, http://www.yearoftheblues.org/officialProclamation.asp.

3. Although numerous sources indicate that Handy "discovered" the blues in 1903, Handy never indicated when he did so, leaving the 1903 date in question.

4. Sociologist Erik Cohen defines a tourist as a "voluntary, temporary traveler, travelling in the expectation of pleasure from the novelty and change experienced on a relatively long and non-recurrent round-trip." See Erik Cohen, "Who Is a Tourist? A Conceptual Clarification," *Sociological Review* 22.4 (1974): 533.

5. Robert Owen Gardner, "Tradition and Authenticity in Popular Music," *Symbolic Interaction* 28.1 (2005): 143.

6. DeCurtis, "Rocking."

7. In March 2009, President Barack Obama signed into law the Omnibus Public Land Management Act, which created both the Mississippi Delta National Heritage Area and the Mississippi Hills National Heritage Area. See Blues Highway Association, 11 Sept. 2009, http://www.blueshighway.org/bluesnews.htm.

8. Anne K. Soper, "Developing Mauritianness: National Identity, Cultural Heritage Values, and Tourism," *Journal of Heritage Tourism* 2.2 (2007): 96.

9. Jennifer Craik, "The Culture of Tourism," *Touring Cultures: Transformations of Travel and Theory*, ed. Chris Rojek and John Urry (London: Routledge, 1997) 113.

10. A "blues tourist" is "someone who journeys to experience blues music and, perhaps, something of the society and culture that produce it." See Jeff Todd Titon, "The New Blues Tourism," *Arkansas Review: A Journal of Delta Studies* 29.1 (1998): 5.

11. Cheryl Line, telephone interview, 3 Oct. 2007; Kappi Allen, telephone interview, 5 Oct. 2007; Carmen Walsh, e-mail communication, 15 Oct. 2007.

12. Mississippi Development Authority/Tourism Division, Marketing Plan FY 2009, 4 Oct. 2010, http://www.visitmississippi.org/resources/09_fy09_advertising_marketing_plan.pdf.

13. Alan W. Barton, *Visitation to Heritage Tourism Sites by Residents of the Mississippi Delta*, Policy Paper No. 07-01 (Delta State University: Center for Community and Economic Development, 2007) 2–4. According to Barton, 3.4 percent of respondents indicated that they had visited a blues club or attended a blues festival at least six times in 2004.

14. Mississippi Department of Employment, Labor Market Information Department, 18 Feb. 2008, p. 11, http://www.mdes.ms.gov. By August 2010, Mississippi's fortunes had, comparatively speaking, improved, as the state's unemployment rate (10 percent) was considerably better than that of Nevada, the state with the highest national unemployment rate (14.4 percent). See U.S. Department of Labor, Bureau of Labor Statistics, Unemployment Rates for States, 15 October 2010, http://www.bls.gov/web/laus/laumstrk.htm.

15. U.S. Census Bureau, "The 2010 Statistical Abstract: State Rankings," 7 June 2010, http://www.census.gov/compendia/statab/rankings.html.

16. Kathleen O'Leary Morgan and Scott Morgan, eds., *State Rankings 2009: A Statistical View of America* (Washington, D.C.: CQ Press, 2009) 521–22.

17. Morgan and Morgan 127, 129–30, 136.

18. Kathleen O'Leary Morgan and Scott Morgan, eds., *State Rankings 2008: A Statistical View of America* (Washington, D.C.: CQ Press, 2008).

19. Mississippi Department of Employment Security, Labor Market Information Department, July 2010, Unemployment Rates, 11 Sept. 2010, p. 3, http://www.mdes.ms.gov. The Mississippi Delta is composed of nineteen "core" (e.g., Bolivar) and partial counties (e.g., Yazoo), although this number is often disputed by experts.

20. Mississippi Development Authority, *2004–2007 State of Mississippi Delta Region Development Plan* (Jackson, MS: Mississippi Development Authority, 2004) 4.

21. Michele A. Morgan, "Lower Mississippi Delta," 4 Aug. 2003, p. 89, http://morgan graphicstakoma.com/T57ADeltaOverview.pdf.

22. Stephen Frenkel and Judy Walton, "Bavarian Leavenworth and the Symbolic Economy of a Theme Town," *Geographical Review* 90.4 (2000): 559.

23. John Connell and Chris Gibson, "Music and Tourism: The Blues, the Bizarre, and Big Business," *Geodate* 17.2 (2004): 1.

24. Frenkel and Walton 559.

25. Wanda Clark, telephone interview, 23 Apr. 2008.

26. Mississippi Development Authority/Tourism Division, "Fiscal Year 2009 Economic Contribution of Travel and Tourism in Mississippi, February 2010," pp. 4–5, 17, 4 Oct. 2010, http://www.visitmississippi.org/resources/FY2009_Economic_Contrib ution_Re port_and_ Cover.pdf.

27. "State Can Aid Efforts to Promote the Blues," editorial, *Clarksdale Press Register* 20 Jan. 2004: 4A.

28. See, e.g., "There Are $ in Blues, Tourism," *Clarksdale Press Register* 29 Aug. 1991: 1B; Maria Burnham, "Will the Blues Bring Bucks?," *Clarion-Ledger* 1 May 2001: 1C, 8C; Sheila Byrd, "Music Heritage May Be Next Cash Crop," *Commercial Appeal* 22 Mar. 2010; DeSoto ed.: DSA1, DSA3; Becky Gillette, "Blues Tourists Steady, Keep the Delta Green," *Mississippi Business Journal* Nov. 26–Dec. 2, 2001: 18, 28; Aimee Robinette, "Tourism Big Business in Cleveland," *Bolivar Commercial* 19 May 2006: 1, 8.

29. Quoted in Nigel Williamson, "In Search of the Blues," *Observer* 28 Jan. 2007, 22 Aug. 2009, http://www.guardian.co.uk/travel/2007/jan/28/culturaltrips.usa.escape.

30. Phil West, "Gov. Addresses Delta Summit," *Commercial Appeal* 17 June 2010; DeSoto ed.: DSA1.

31. Jim O'Neal, "The Continuing Wellspring of the Blues," *Living Blues* Mar.–June 2004: 17.

32. Kappi Allen, telephone interview, 5 Oct. 2007.

33. Carmen Walsh, e-mail communication, 15 Oct. 2007. As a result, local chambers of commerce are directing more and more of their financial resources to promote the blues. For example, Allen stated that although her budget does not have a separate line item for the promotion of blues music and culture, the "majority of the budget" is used for blues tourism. Incidentally, chambers of commerce typically receive funds from a local tourism tax. For example, the Cleveland–Bolivar County Chamber of Commerce receives 2 percent from restaurants (food and beverage) and 2 percent from lodging. The Coahoma County Tourism Commission receives 2 percent from lodging and 1 percent from restaurants. Cheryl Line, telephone interview, 3 Oct. 2007; Kappi Allen, telephone interview, 5 Oct. 2007.

34. See, e.g., Steve Cheseborough, *Blues Traveling: The Holy Sites of Delta Blues*, 3rd ed. (Jackson: UP of Mississippi, 2008); Tom Downs, *Lonely Planet Road Trip: Blues and BBQ* (Australia: Lonely Planet, 2005); Melissa Gage and Justin Gage, *Memphis and the Delta Blues Trail* (Woodstock, Vt.: Countryman, 2009); Jim O'Neal, *Delta Blues Map Kit* (Kansas City, Mo.: BluEsoterica, 2004).

35. Preston Lauterbach, editorial, *Living Blues* Mar.–June 2004: 6.

36. "Tune in Mississippi," *Life in the Delta* Nov. 2007: 38.

37. Delta Music Experience, 2 Nov. 2007, http://www.deltamusicexperience.com.

38. "Dead Blues Guys," 20 Aug. 2009, http://www.deadbluesguys.com.

39. Lynn Lofton, "Cigar Company Promoting Hand-Rolled Products, Delta Blues," *Mississippi Business Journal* 8–14 Jan. 2007: 3. Blues artists featured on the cigars (or their families and heirs) will receive 3 percent of cigar sales. "Avalon Cigars," 22 Aug. 2009, http://www.avalon.com/about.html.

40. Mississippi Delta Graveyard Dirt, 22 Aug. 2009, http://www.deltablues.net/dirt .html.

41. Alan W. Barton, *Attitudes about Heritage Tourism in the Mississippi Delta: A Policy Report from the 2005 Delta Rural Poll*, Policy Paper No. 05-02 (Delta State University: Center for Community and Economic Development, 2005) 1. Yet, ironically, the citizens of Mississippi are perhaps the last to recognize the potential economic and cultural benefits associated with blues tourism. Jimbo Mathus, a white blues guitarist who has recorded with the likes of Elvis Costello and Buddy Guy, told *Guitar Player* magazine in 2003 that while Mississippi "spawned a whole lot of music . . . people there don't acknowledge it, or even respect it." In a three part-series on the blues, a *Clarion-Ledger* writer claimed that it "looks like the rest of the world is about to expose Mississippi's own secret to itself." "Blues Joint," *Guitar Player* Sept. 2003, 15 Aug. 2003, http://www.guitarplayer.com/0903_I02.html; Lori Herring, "Mississippi Has the Blues," *Clarion-Ledger* 9 June 2002: 1A.

42. Barton, *Attitudes* 15, 22.

43. Quoted in "Mississippi, Believe It!," 15 July 2009, http://mississippibelieveit.com.

44. Becky Gillette, "Out of Suffering, the Blues Rose from the Mississippi Delta," *Mississippi Business Journal* 18–24 Aug. 2003: 8.

45. B. B. King, no title, *Living Blues* Mar.–June 2004: 11.

46. Morgan Freeman, no title, *Living Blues* Mar.–June 2004: 9.

47. Mississippi's last reported lynching occurred in 1964.

48. "Mississippi Turning," *Economist* 6 Jan. 2007: 27.

49. "Miss. Schools Ordered to End Racial Imbalance," *Commercial Appeal* 17 Apr. 2010; DeSoto ed.: DSA3.

50. U.S. Department of Labor, Bureau of Labor Statistics, "Employment Status of Civilian Noninstitutionalized Population by Sex, Race, Hispanic or Latino Ethnicity, and Detailed Age, 2007 Annual Averages," 17 July 2008, http://www.bls.gov/lau/patable14fill2007.pdf. This difference is slightly larger than national trends, 4.2 percent unemployment rate for whites compared to 9.0 percent unemployment for African Americans (June 2007). See U.S. Department of Labor, Bureau of Labor Statistics, "Employment Status of the Civilian Noninstitutionalized Population by Race, Hispanic or Latino Ethnicity, Sex, and Age," 17 July 2008, http://www.bls.gov/web/cpseea15.pdf.

51. "Mississippi: Poverty Rate by Race/Ethnicity, States (2005–2006), U.S. (2006)," statehealthfacts.org, 17 July 2008, http://www.statehealthfacts.org. These statistical data were also presented at the following lecture: Larry J. Griffin, "Race, Memory, and Historical Responsibility: What Do Southerners Do with a Difficult Past?," Sammy O. Cranford Memorial Lecture in History, Delta State University, Cleveland, Miss., 21 Apr. 2008.

52. "Mississippi: Poverty Rate by Race/Ethnicity, States (2007–2008), U.S. (2008)," statehealthfacts.org, 20 Aug. 2010, http://www.statehealthfacts.org/profileind.jsp?ind=14&cat=1&rgn=26.

53. James C. Cobb, *The Most Southern Place on Earth: The Mississippi Delta and the Roots of Regional Identity* (New York: Oxford UP, 1992) 324.

54. James L. Gibson, "Does Truth Lead to Reconciliation? Testing the Causal Assumptions of the South African Truth and Reconciliation Process," *American Journal of Political Science* 48.2 (2004): 202.

55. John B. Hatch, "Beyond Apologia: Racial Reconciliation and Apologies for Slavery," *Western Journal of Communication* 70.3 (2006): 189.

56. David A. Crocker, "Reckoning with Past Wrongs: A Normative Framework," *Ethics and International Affairs* 13.1 (1999): 60.

57. Adam Gussow, *Journeyman's Road: Modern Blues Lives from Faulkner's Mississippi to Post-9/11 New York* (Knoxville: U of Tennessee P, 2007) 157–59.

58. Erik Cohen, "Toward a Sociology of International Tourism," *Social Research* 39.1 (1972): 164–82.

59. Institutionalized tourists are to a varying degree embedded within the protective infrastructure of the tourism industry. For example, one institutionalized role, the organized mass tourist, usually remains confined to his or her "environmental bubble" of inclusive resorts, guided packaged tours, and air-conditioned buses. Ridiculed for their apparent need to consume superficial and "inauthentic" experiences, these tourists rely almost exclusively on tourism intermediaries to shield them from immediate, often unpredictable, experiences by ensuring that expectations are satisfied (Cohen, "Toward" 167–74). See also Donald L. Redfoot, "Touristic Authenticity, Touristic Angst, and Modern Reality," *Qualitative Sociology* 7.4 (1984): 291–309.

60. Paul Theroux, *Dark Star Safari: Overland from Cairo to Cape Town* (Boston: Houghton Mifflin, 2003) 18.

61. Kappi Allen, personal interview, 3 Feb. 2003. Although Luther Brown, director of Delta State University's Delta Center for Culture and Learning, has not witnessed a large number of commercial bus tours, an obvious sign of mass tourism, he notes that more and more groups are visiting the area, including a Jewish congregation from New York, university students, and workshops for teachers.

62. See, e.g., Ted Gioia, *Delta Blues: The Life and Times of the Mississippi Masters Who Revolutionized American Music* (New York: W. W. Norton, 2008) 397.

63. In *Big Road Blues: Tradition and Creativity in the Folk Blues*, David Evans discusses why blues songs do not "devote a great deal of attention to perhaps the biggest problem area of all, racial discrimination" (29).

64. Quoted in Joy Bennett Kinnon, "Are Whites Taking or Are Blacks Giving Away the Blues?" *Ebony* Sept. 1997: 92.

65. Scott Barretta, personal interview, 28 Feb. 2008.

66. David Grazian, *Blue Chicago: The Searching for Authenticity in Urban Blues Clubs* (Chicago: U of Chicago P, 2003) 20.

67. Roger Gatchet, "Interview and Review: The Blues Brothers," 10 Mar. 2010, http://www.austinsound.net/author/roger-gatchet/page/2.

68. Mark Coleman, "The Blues Brothers," *Rolling Stone Album Guide*, ed. Anthony DeCurtis and James Henke with Holly George-Warren (New York: Random House, 1992) 70–71.

69. Fred Beldin, "The Blues Brothers: Made in America," allmusic, 10 Mar. 2010, http://www.allmusic.com/cg/amg.dll?p=amg&sql=10:3ifixqq5ldhe.The Blues Brothers phenomenon served as a precursor to the short-lived 1980s blues revival. Music critic Stephen Thomas Erlewine claimed that Stevie Ray Vaughan, a young white guitarist out of Texas, ignited the 1980s blues revival. Vaughan's 1983 debut album, *Texas Flood*, was a revelation for white blues and rock fans alike, and his subsequent releases *Couldn't Stand the Weather* (1984), *Soul to Soul* (1985), and *In Step* (1989) only increased his status as one of the genre's finest (white) guitarists. At the same time, a young black guitarist by the name of Robert Cray released two important albums, *Bad Influence* (1983) and *False Accusations* (1985), that became crossover hits and established Cray as a star. See Stephen Thomas Erlewine, "Stevie Ray Vaughan: Biography," allmusic, 10 Mar. 2010, http://www.allmusic.com/cg/amg.dll?p=amg&sql=11:wzftxqegldke~T1.

70. Roger Stolle, "Juke Joint Festival," *Blues Revue* Sept.–Oct. 2010: 48.

71. David Evans, *Big Road Blues: Tradition and Creativity in the Folk Blues* (Berkeley: U of California P, 1982) 19.

72. E. Taylor Atkins, *Blue Nippon: Authenticating Jazz in Japan* (Durham: Duke UP, 2001) 12, 132–33, 252–53.

73. Quoted in Michael Donahue, "Blues Traveler: Taking the Long Road for the Real Thing," *Commercial Appeal* 5 Oct. 2003: D1, D6.

74. Glenn Gass, "A Trip through the Delta Blues," 10 Sept. 2010, http://www.music .indiana.edu/som/courses/rock/delta.html.

75. Steve Cheseborough, *Blues Traveling: The Holy Sites of Delta Blues*, 2nd ed. (Jackson: UP of Mississippi, 2004) 136.

76. Cheseborough 89–92.

77. In the 1990s, Coahoma County government and the Clarksdale–Coahoma County Chamber of Commerce purchased the Illinois Central Railroad Freight Depot, which was originally built in 1918. The museum is currently located in the Old Freight Depot. The other section of the complex is the Clarksdale Station, which, according to Cheseborough, is historically significant because it is "where Muddy Waters bought his ticket, sat in the colored waiting room, and boarded the train to Chicago in 1943. Thousands of other black Clarksdalians, probably including other blues singers, made that trip from the same spot" (71–72).

78. Quoted in Nathalie Vanderheyden, "Traveling to the Holy Ground of the Delta Blues," BlogCritics.Org, 1 Dec. 2008, 1 June 2009, http://www.crossroadshotel.tv/PDF/Dec1_08BCM.pdf.

79. Samuel C. Adams Jr., "Changing Negro Life in the Delta," *Lost Delta Found: Rediscovering the Fisk University–Library of Congress Coahoma County Study, 1941–1942*, ed. Robert Gordon and Bruce Nemerov (Nashville: Vanderbilt UP, 2005) 230.

80. Cheseborough 74–76. Handy lived in Clarksdale from 1903 to 1905 and played in bars in the New World District. It was around this time that the New World District "found itself a principal exponent of this new musical form. Hoboes and wanderers dropped off freight trains or the backs of trucks to sit on the sidewalks of Issaquena Avenue and Fourth Street, singing their plaintive tunes to the accompaniment of their dilapidated guitars." See Harry Abernathy, "'New World' Scorned by Clarksdale Elite," *Clarksdale Press Register* 14–15 Aug. 1982: 4B. According to Cheseborough, even today, despite the area's general disrepair, the New World District is still the "liveliest part of town" (75).

81. Mississippi Blues Commission, 9 Mar. 2008, http://www.msbluestrail.org/commission.html.

82. Alex Thomas, e-mail communication, 12 Oct. 2010.

83. Mississippi Blues Commission, Mississippi Blues Trail, 9 Mar. 2008, http://www .msbluestrail.org/blues_trail/; Scott Barretta, telephone interview, 28 Feb. 2008.

84. In 2008, AT&T awarded the Mississippi Blues Commission a $25,000 grant for the integration of wireless technology that allows tourists who visit the blues markers to stream audio and video content to their wireless devices. See "Blues Commission Awarded $25,000 by AT&T; Plans to Invest in Mississippi Blues Trail Mobile Technology," *Delta Business Journal* Dec. 2008: 10.

85. Wanda Clark, telephone interview, 23 Apr. 2008.

86. Luther Brown, "Guest Commentary," editorial, *Cleveland Current* 22 Mar. 2009: A6.

87. Phil West, "'Trail' to Honor Country Music Heritage," *Commercial Appeal* 13 Feb. 2009; DeSoto ed.: DSA1.

88. Millennium Trails, Program Overview, 19 May 2003, http://www.millenniumtrails .org/MT_active_pages/overview/b-right.asp.

89. Craig Havighurst, "B. B. King's Hometown Museum," *Wall Street Journal* 16 Oct. 2008: D7; Bob Mehr, "Delta and Its King Interpreted," gomemphis.com; *Commercial Appeal* 12 Sept. 2008: 8–9. Local citizens (residents and businesses) raised approximately $1.7 million, a remarkable feat considering the fact that Indianola, a town with an estimated population of twelve thousand, is not immune to the socioeconomic problems that plague other Delta communities.

90. Mehr 9.

91. Quoted in Landry Barbieri, "King of the Delta Blues Opens Doors to Museum," *Bolivar Commercial Advertiser* 16 Sept. 2008: 2.

92. Billy Watkins, "B. B. King Isn't Singing the Blues over Museum," *USA Today* 15 Sept. 2008, 29 Jan. 2009.

93. Craig Ray, "Come One, Come All," interview with Leslie Galloway, *Mississippi Business Journal* 6–12 July 2009: 50.

94. "King Museum Still Drawing Crowds," *Commercial Appeal* 13 Sept. 2009; DeSoto ed.: DSA1.

95. Byrd, "Music Heritage" DSA3.

96. Beyond my own work, only a handful of scholarly articles have been written on the subject of blues tourism: Kip Lornell, "The Cultural and Musical Implications of the Dixieland Jazz and Blues Revivals," *Arkansas Review: A Journal of Delta Studies* 29.1 (1998): 11–21; Paige McGinley, "Highway 61 Revisited," *TDR: The Drama Review* 51.3 (2007): 80–97; David S. Rotenstein, "The Helena Blues: Cultural Tourism and African-American Folk Music," *Southern Folklore* 49.2 (1992): 133–46; Titon, "New Blues Tourism."

97. David Grazian, *Blue Chicago*; see also David Grazian, "The Production of Popular Music as a Confidence Game: The Case of the Chicago Blues," *Qualitative Sociology* 27.2 (2004): 137–58.

98. Chris Gibson and John Connell, *Music and Tourism: On the Road Again* (Clevedon, Eng.: Channel View, 2005) vii.

1. The History of the Mississippi Delta Blues

1. Peter C. Muir, *Long Lost Blues: Popular Blues in America, 1850–1920* (Urbana: U of Illinois P, 2010) 81.

2. Archie Quinn, "Let's Move Beyond the Blues," *Commercial Appeal* 24 Feb. 1985: J7.

3. David Evans, "Revised History of the Blues," letter, *Commercial Appeal*, Clarksdale, Miss.: Carnegie Public Library.

4. Douglas Henry Daniels, "The Significance of Blues for American History," *Journal of Negro History* 70.1–2 (1985): 21.

5. Adam Gussow, *Seems Like Murder Here: Southern Violence and the Blues Tradition* (Chicago: U of Chicago P, 2002) 5.

6. LeRoi Jones, "Blues, Black and White America," *Metronome* Mar. 1961: 12.

7. Daniel Stein, "The Things That Jes' Grew? The Blues 'I' and African American Autobiographies," *Interdisciplinary Humanities* 23.2 (2006): 43.

8. Mississippi Blues Trail, "Experiencing the Blues Where They Were Born," 28 Aug. 2010, http://www.msbluestrail.org.

9. Robert Palmer, "Black Snake Moan: The History of Texas Blues," *Blues and Chaos: The Music Writing of Robert Palmer*, ed. Anthony DeCurtis (New York: Scribner, 2009) 53.

10. Marybeth Hamilton, "Sexuality, Authenticity, and the Making of the Blues Tradition," *Past and Present* 169 (2000): 139.

11. David Evans, "Goin' Up the Country: Blues in Texas and the Deep South," *Nothing but the Blues: The Music and the Musicians*, ed. Lawrence Cohn (New York: Abbeville, 1993) 33.

12. Giles Oakley, *The Devil's Music: A History of the Blues*, 2nd ed. (London: Da Capo, 1997) 9.

13. Samuel Charters, "Workin' on the Building: Roots and Influences," *Nothing but the Blues: The Music and the Musicians*, ed. Lawrence Cohn (New York: Abbeville, 1993) 20.

14. Paul Oliver, "Blues," *The New Grove Dictionary of Music and Musicians*, ed. Stanley Sadie, 2nd ed., vol. 3 (London: Macmillan, 2001) 730.

15. See Race Parody Sheet Music, box 1 (6–12), Blues Archives and Special Collections, University of Mississippi, Oxford, Miss. Coon songs were written and performed by both white and black artists.

16. Harriet Ottenheimer, "Blues in the Heartland: African-American Music and Culture in the Middle West," *Black Heartland: African American Life, the Middle West, and the Meaning of American Regionalism*, Occasional Papers Series, 1.2 (1997): 16.

17. Harriet Ottenheimer, "Prewar Blues in St. Louis," *Popular Music and Society* 14.2 (1990): 87–89.

18. Ottenheimer, "Blues" 16. According to Ottenheimer, freed blacks found the Midwest to be an appealing region for relocation during the 1860s and 1870s, and these new arrivals from the South brought with them African and American pre-blues styles and were subsequently influenced by European American music, especially from Germany: "The Middle West would have been a unique kind of musical and cultural mixing ground for African-Americans and it would have fallen to the next generation of musicians, the ones born free, to experiment with the new richness of musical sources" (17).

19. Evans, "Goin' Up" 34.

20. Ottenheimer, "Blues" 32.

21. Ted Gioia, *Delta Blues: The Life and Times of the Mississippi Masters Who Revolutionized American Music* (New York: W. W. Norton, 2008) 7. While recognizing that the blues is a musical genre unique to the United States, some scholars have also searched for its antecedents in the "motherland," the African continent. See, e.g., Paul Oliver, *Savannah Syncopators: African Retentions in the Blues* (London: Studio Vista, 1970), in Paul Oliver, Tony Russell, Robert M. W. Dixon, John Godrich, and Howard Rye, *Yonder Come the Blues: The Evolution of a Genre* (Cambridge, Eng.: Cambridge UP, 2001) 11–112; Paul Oliver, "Interview with Paul Oliver," interview with David Horn, *Popular Music* 26.1 (2007): 5–13; Samuel Charters, *The Roots of the Blues: An African Search* (Boston: Marion Boyars, 1981); Gerhard Kubik, *Africa and the Blues* (Jackson: UP of Mississippi, 2008); David Evans, "African Elements in the Blues," *L'Oceano dei Suoni: Migrazioni, Musica e Razze nella Formazione delle Societa Euroatlantiche*, ed. Pierangelo Castagneto (Torino: Otto Editore) 3–16.

22. Ottenheimer, "Blues" 18.

23. Charles Peabody, "Notes on Negro Music," *Journal of American Folk-Lore* 16.62 (1903): 148–52.

24. Oakley 40.

25. W. C. Handy, *Father of the Blues: An Autobiography* (1941; New York: Da Capo, 1991) 74–78.

26. Larry Starr and Christopher Waterman, *American Popular Music: From Minstrelsy to MTV* (New York: Oxford UP, 2003) 7–8.

27. Lynn Abbott and Doug Seroff, "'They Cert'ly Sound Good to Me': Sheet Music, Southern Vaudeville, and the Commercial Ascendency of the Blues," *American Music* 14.4 (1996): 405–6.

28. David Suisman, "Co-Workers in the Kingdom of Culture: Black Swan Records and the Political Economy of African American Music," *Journal of American History* 90.4 (2004): 1296.

29. Sandra R. Lieb, *Mother of the Blues: A Study of Ma Rainey* (Amherst: U of Massachusetts P, 1981) 19; Tim Brooks, *Lost Sounds: Blacks and the Birth of the Recording Industry, 1980–1919* (Urbana: U of Illinois P, 2004) 7–8.

30. David Evans, *The NPR Curious Listener's Guide to Blues* (New York: Perigee, 2005) 22; Muir 11.

31. Steven C. Tracy, introduction to *Write Me a Few of Your Lines: A Blues Reader*, ed. Steven C. Tracy (Amherst: U of Massachusetts P, 1999) 3. David Evans argues that the sales figures are likely an exaggeration because the existing empirical data in OKeh sales records do not confirm the claim. David Evans, reader's report, July 2010.

32. David Evans, *NPR* 23. As Starr and Waterman observed, some of the larger and more conservative record companies did not immediately jump on the "race record" bandwagon. For example, Victor did not create its own race record series until 1927 (Starr and Waterman 88).

33. Ted Vincent, "The Social Context of Black Swan Records," *Living Blues* May–June 1989: 34.

34. Lawrence N. Redd, "Rock! It's Still Rhythm and Blues," *Black Perspective in Music* 13.1 (1985): 34. See also David Brackett, "The Politics and Practice of 'Cross-over' in American Popular Music, 1963 to 1965," *Musical Quarterly* 78.4 (1994): 774–97.

35. David Evans, reader's report, July 2010. Record companies also created other classifications including "hillbilly" music (sometimes called "old-time music"), music mostly by white performers marketed to southern whites (Starr and Waterman 86–87). Record companies also had a foreign music series, including music from the West Indies. See John Cowley, "West Indies Blues: An Historical Overview, 1920–1950s; Blues and Music from the English-Speaking West Indies," *Nobody Knows Where the Blues Come From: Lyrics and History*, ed. Robert Springer (Jackson: UP of Mississippi, 2006) 187–263.

36. Quoted in Hugh Barker and Yuval Taylor, *Faking It: The Quest for Authenticity in Popular Music* (New York: W. W. Norton, 2007) 49.

37. William Barlow, "'Fattening Frogs for Snakes': Blues and the Music Industry," *Popular Music and Society* 14.2 (1990): 22.

38. For example, in the early 1920s, Paramount started issuing its race records under the 12,000 series. See Gayle Dean Wardlow, "Godfather of Delta Blues: H. C. Speir," interview with Pat Howse and Jimmy Phillips, *Monitor (Peavey)* 13.2 (1994): 42.

39. Guy B. Johnson, "Double Meaning in the Popular Negro Blues," *Journal of Abnormal and Social Psychology* 22.1 (1929): 12.

40. LeRoi Jones (Amiri Baraka), *Blues People: Negro Music in White America* (1963; New York: Harper Perennial, 2002) 100.

41. Robert M. W. Dixon and John Godrich, *Recording the Blues* (London: Studio Vista, 1970), in Paul Oliver, Tony Russell, Robert M. W. Dixon, John Godrich, and Howard Rye, *Yonder Come the Blues: The Evolution of a Genre* (Cambridge, Eng.: Cambridge UP, 2001) 271, 277.

42. Alan Govenar, "Blind Lemon Jefferson: The Myth and the Man," *Black Music Research Journal* 20.1 (2000): 7–9.

43. Evans, "Goin' Up" 55.

44. Evans, "Goin' Up" 56.

45. By the 1950s, the Delta blues had evolved into a music performed in a small combo context with electric guitars and drums.

46. Robert Palmer, *Deep Blues: A Musical and Cultural History of the Mississippi Delta* (1981; New York: Penguin, 1982) 18.

47. Marybeth Hamilton, *In Search of the Blues* (New York: Basic, 2008) 12, 22, 230–33.

48. James Segrest and Mark Hoffman, *Moanin' at Midnight: The Life and Times of Howlin' Wolf* (New York: Thunder's Mouth, 2005) 18.

49. Gioia 171.

50. Quoted in Gayle Dean Wardlow, "The Talent Scouts: H. C. Speir (1895–1972)," *78 Quarterly* 1.8 (1993): 13.

51. Wardlow, "Godfather" 38.

52. "Speir to Record Mississippi Talent," *Jackson City News* 30 Nov. 1930: 18.

53. Gioia 52–53. It should be acknowledged that although Speir's racial attitudes were not remarkably different from those of most southern white men at the time, he did provide a measure of compassion to black artists he was associated with. For example, after trying unsuccessfully to cash his royalty check in Jackson, Mississippi, Ishmon Bracey, a noted blues musician turned minister, asked Speir for help: "When I got my money from [a recording session conducted in] Wisconsin, a white man up here at McRae's Department Store wouldn't let me buy a new suit. Wouldn't cash my check for me. He said that [$900] was too much for a colored man to have. I called Mr. Speir and he came around and signed it and I put it in the bank." Quoted in Gayle Dean Wardlow, *Chasin' That Devil Music: Searching for the Blues*, ed. Edward Komara (San Francisco: Backbeat, 1998) 56–57.

54. Quoted in David Evans, "An Interview with H. C. Speir," *JEMF Quarterly* 8.27 (1972): 117–19.

55. Evans, "An Interview" 119.

56. Wardlow, "Godfather" 39. While Speir proved to be an important figure in the recording of the early country blues, credit must also be given to John and Alan Lomax. As native Texans, both father and son (Alan was just a teenager when he accompanied his father) started recording blues and other black-based music forms during two field trips in 1933 and 1934. As David Evans points out, while Speir was part of a commercial enterprise recording *popular* music, the Lomax team was trying to preserve *folklore* traditions (David Evans, reader's report, Dec. 2008). David Evans praised the contributions of the two folklorists, arguing that their respective field research and writings "covered nearly an entire century and nearly the entire history of the blues as an identifiable form of music." David Evans, "Alan Lomax: An Appreciation," *Living Blues* June–Aug. 2003: 50.

57. Edward Komara, "Blues," *Encyclopedia of the Blues*, ed. Edward Komara, vol. 1 (New York: Routledge, 2006) 116.

58. Dixon and Godrich 283.

59. Jas Obrecht, "Sam Chatmon: The Last of the Mississippi Sheiks," *Living Blues* Feb. 2009: 70.

60. Jeff Todd Titon, *Early Downhome Blues: A Musical and Cultural Analysis* (Urbana: U of Illinois P, 1977) 63.

61. David Sanjek, "Marketing," *Encyclopedia of the Blues*, ed. Edward Komara, vol. 2 (New York: Routledge, 2006) 654.

62. Quoted in Michael Goodwin, "Son House: 'You Can't Fool God,'" *Rolling Stone* 27 Dec. 1969: 14.

63. Barry Lee Pearson, "Wasn't Only My Songs, They Got My Music Too," *Write Me a Few of Your Lines: A Blues Reader*, ed. Steven C. Tracy (Amherst: U of Massachusetts P, 1999) 377.

64. John Lee Hooker, foreword, Paul Trynka, *Portrait of the Blues* (1996; New York: Da Capo, 1997) 7.

65. John Hammond, "John Hammond: A Life for the Record," interview with Neville L. Johnson, *L.A. Weekly* 11–17 Jan. 1985: 61.

66. Dixon and Godrich 295.

67. Stephen Calt with Gayle Dean Wardlow, "Paramount's Decline and Fall (Part 5)," *78 Quarterly* 1.7 (1992): 23–24.

68. Calt and Wardlow 23–24.

69. Dixon and Godrich 308. By the end of the 1940s, many of the major labels started to abandon their race series. In 1949 the term "race records" was replaced by a new term, "rhythm and blues."

70. Dixon and Godrich 312.

71. Dixon and Godrich 312.

72. Elijah Wald, author of *Escaping the Delta: Robert Johnson and the Invention of the Blues*, noted that while radio often marginalized blues music, it also allowed many Delta blues musicians to encounter different genres of popular music. According to Wald, radio acted as the "great leveler, allowing someone in a Delta Cabin to listen to anything from hillbilly fiddling to opera" (96).

73. Hank Harvey, "Growing Up with the Blues," *Living Blues* July–Aug. 1986: 25.

74. Oakley 202; Amy O'Neal, "King Biscuit Time 1971," *Living Blues* Summer 1971: 4. The show originally aired from 12:45 to 1 p.m. until 1945, when it was moved to 12:15–12:30 p.m. See Mike Leadbitter, "Bring It on Home," *Blues Unlimited* Jan. 1973: 5.

75. Harvey 25.

76. Houston Stackhouse, "*Living Blues* Interview: Houston Stackhouse," interview with Jim O'Neal, *Living Blues* Summer 1974: 29.

77. Sonny Payne, interview with Jim O'Neal, Living Blues Symposium, Oxford, Miss., 19 Feb. 2005.

78. Oakley 202.

79. Oakley 202. The band was also called the King Biscuit Entertainers.

80. Leadbitter 5.

81. Oakley 205.

82. Calvin "Fuzz" Jones, "Calvin 'Fuzz' Jones: I Love the Blues. The Blues Is Everything I Was Raised Up With," interview with Margo Cooper, *Living Blues* Feb. 2008: 28.

83. Steve Cheseborough, *Blues Traveling: The Holy Sites of Delta Blues*, 2nd ed. (Jackson: UP of Mississippi, 2004) 59.

84. "Music Trail Marker to Be Unveiled," *Daily World*, 10 Dec. 2009, 14 Mar. 2010, http://www.helena-arkansas.com/entertainment/x1669483201/Music-trail-marker-to-be-unveiled.

85. WROX, *Clarksdale Daily Register and Daily News* 9 Feb. 1948: 4.

86. Palmer, *Deep Blues* 187.

87. "The Forgotten 15,000,000," *Sponsor* 10 Oct. 1949: 23–24.

88. Quoted in "Biggest Negro Station," *Time* 11 Nov. 1957: 86.

89. Louis Cantor, *Wheelin' on Beale: How WDIA-Memphis Became the Nation's First All-Black Radio Station and Created the Sound That Changed America* (New York: Pharos, 1992) 29, 41.

90. Cantor 49.

91. "Today's Radio Programs and Highlights," *Commercial Appeal* 8 Nov. 1949: 12.

92. Cantor 80.

93. Cantor 86. Kathy M. Newman, "The Forgotten Fifteen Million: Black Radio, the 'Negro Market,' and the Civil Rights Movement," *Radical History Review* 76 (2000): 115. See "Broadcasting the Blues," Mississippi Blues Trail, http://www.msbluestrail .org/_webapp_1301186/Broadcasting_the_Blues.

94. Cantor, 1.

95. Yolanda Jones, "Still Wheelin'," *Commercial Appeal* 18 Oct. 2005: M4. It can be argued that WDIA's success reflected a much larger cultural phenomenon, one that witnessed the shift in radio from a national to a local medium because of the ascendency of television. As a result, advertisers focused more on local markets, initiating research efforts to gather demographic information on local audiences: "One of the findings, that did not go unnoticed was the popularity among black people of radio broadcasts featuring black music. Moreover, owners of radio stations and advertisers discovered that advertisements in black music programmes reached an audience to which other programmes had no access. Because of increased purchasing power, caused by the post-war 'boom,' the black consumer market was becoming ever more interesting for commercial purposes." Robert C. Kloosterman and Chris Quispel, "Not Just the Same Old Show on My Radio: An Analysis of the Role of Radio in the Diffusion of Black Music among Whites in the South of the United States of America, 1920 to 1960," *Popular Music* 9.2 (1990): 159.

96. Patrick Goldstein, "The Bluest Voice on the Delta," *Washington Post* 19 Mar. 1989: G1.

97. WROX, *Clarksdale Press Register* 25 June 1954: 8.

98. Quoted in "Early Wright," advertisement, *Clarksdale Press Register* 23 Feb. 1988: 12.

99. Early Wright, no title, 1993, Subject Files (Miscellaneous), no. 2423, Blues Archives and Special Collections, University of Mississippi, Oxford, Miss.

100. Cheseborough 78.

101. Greg Ellis, lecture, "WROX Early Years," Clarksdale, Miss., 8 Aug. 2003.

102. George Hines, personal interview, 18 Oct. 2004.

103. Brian Ward, *Just My Soul Responding: Rhythm and Blues, Black Consciousness, and Race Relations* (Berkeley: U of California P, 1998) 30.

104. Sunflower River Blues and Gospel Festival, "About Awards," 12 Feb. 2010, http:// www.sunflowerfest.org/index.cfm?page=awards&sub=awards.

105. Pete Golkin, "Blacks Whites and the Blues: The Story of Chess Records" (Part One)," *Living Blues* Sept.–Oct. 1989: 24; Rich Cohen, *The Record Men: The Chess Brothers and the Birth of Rock and Roll* (New York: W. W. Norton, 2004) 62.

206   NOTES

106. Benjamin Filene, *Romancing the Folk: Public Memory and American Roots Music* (Chapel Hill: U of North Carolina P, 2000) 88.

107. Charlie Gillett, *The Sound of the City: The Rise of Rock and Roll* (New York: Outerbridge and Dienstfrey, 1970) v.

108. Gillett 17.

109. Filene 112.

110. Gioia 347–48.

111. Robert J. Wallis and Jenny Blain, "Sites, Sacredness, and Stories: Interactions of Archaeology and Contemporary Paganism," *Folklore* 114.3 (2003): 316.

112. Jim O'Neal, "I Once Was Lost, but Now I'm Found: The Blues Revival of the 1960s," *Nothing but the Blues: The Music and the Musicians*, ed. Lawrence Cohn (New York: Abbeville, 1993) 387.

113. Evans, *NPR* 49. Evans also mentions other events that influenced the 1960s blues revival, including the publication of Paul Oliver's *Blues Fell This Morning* (1960), the release of the first Robert Johnson LP (1961), and the publication of *Blues Unlimited*, a British magazine. David Evans, reader's report, Dec. 2008.

114. Samuel Charters, preface to *The Country Blues*, 1959, by Charters (New York: Da Capo, 1975) ix–x.

115. Samuel Charters, *Walking a Blues Road: A Blues Reader, 1956–2004* (New York: Marion Boyars, 2004) 16.

116. Charters, *Country Blues* x–xii. Charters's book also had a tremendous impact on aspiring young white blues musicians. For example, in a December 2004 interview with *Living Blues* magazine, harp player Charlie Musselwhite claimed that historical accuracy aside, the *Country Blues* "captured the feeling" of the blues and served as a "source of a lot of information and got me inspired to go out and meet people and look for blues more, too." Quoted in D. Thomas Moon, "Part I: We and Big Joe," *Living Blues* Nov.–Dec. 2004: 73.

117. William Ferris, telephone interview, 3 June 2008.

118. Francis Davis, *The History of the Blues: The Roots, the Music, the People from Charley Patton to Robert Cray* (New York: Hyperion, 1995) 13.

119. Nick Bromell, "'The Blues and the Veil': The Cultural Work of Musical Form in Blues and '60s Rock," *American Music* 18.2 (2000): 207.

120. Patricia R. Schroeder, *Robert Johnson, Mythmaking, and Contemporary American Culture* (Urbana: U of Illinois P, 2004) 99.

121. O'Neal 378.

122. Charters, *Country Blues* ix.

123. "A Conversation on the Blues," 14 Mar. 2001, http://www.bluesworld.com/Lor nell.htm.

124. Wardlow, *Chasin'* 10–16.

125. Wardlow, *Chasin'* 14.

126. Cheryl Line, personal interview, 10 May 2001.

127. Gioia 348.

128. Gioia 355–56.

129. Bernard Klatzko, "Finding Son House," *Blues Unlimited* Sept. 1964: 8.

130. Eddie Dean, "Skip James' Hard Time Killing Floor Blues," *Washington City Paper* Nov. 25–Dec. 1 1994: 26.

131. Dean 24.

132. "Looking for the Blues," *Newsweek* 13 July 1964: 82. Some blues musicians strenuously rejected the claim that they were "lost." In 1967, Joe Callicott, a Mississippi blues artist who recorded in the 1920s, told a researcher who asked the singer about his whereabouts for the last forty years: "Been? I ain't been nowhere. I ain't been lost. I been here all along." Quoted in Margaret McKee, speech, ts., Clarksdale, Miss.: Carnegie Public Library, 20 Apr. 1983, n.p.

133. Dick Waterman, "Dick Waterman Speaks at Brown Bag Lunch," 7 Nov. 1984, Subject File (Producer), no. 2288, p. 6, Blues Archives and Special Collections, University of Mississippi, Oxford, Miss.

134. Evans, *NPR* 50.

135. Steve LaVere, personal interview, 18 Jan. 2008.

136. Hamilton 236.

137. Fred McDowell and Roosevelt Sykes, "Blues People: Fred and Roosevelt," interview with Valerie Wilmer, *Jazz Journal* 1966: 23–24.

138. Stephen Calt, *I'd Rather Be the Devil: Skip James and the Blues* (Chicago: Chicago Review, 1994): 275.

139. Hamilton 236.

140. Calt 300.

141. In his address to an audience at the University of Mississippi in 1984, Waterman claimed that although Arthur Crudup died poor, his family eventually received approximately $300,000 in royalty money that was owed to the singer (Waterman 10).

142. Gioia 374–79.

143. Joe Atkins, "Born-and-Bred Yankee in Oxford Best Friend Bluesman Ever Had," *Clarion Ledger* 16 Oct. 1994: 3G.

144. Waterman 6.

145. Calt 300, 302, 304.

146. Christine Wilson, *All Shook Up: Mississippi Roots of American Popular Music* (Jackson: Mississippi Department of Archives and History, 1995) 64.

147. *American Folk Blues Festival '65*, Subject Files (Events and Festivals), no. 7, Blues Archives and Special Collections, University of Mississippi, Oxford, Miss., n.p.

148. Willie Dixon with Don Snowden, *I Am the Blues: The Willie Dixon Story* (New York: Da Capo, 1989) 128.

149. *American Folk Blues Festival '65*.

150. *American Folk Blues Festival '66*, Subject Files (Events and Festivals), no. 8, Blues Archives and Special Collections, University of Mississippi, Oxford, Miss., n.p.

151. *American Folk Blues Festival '68*, Subject Files (Events and Festivals), no. 10, Blues Archives and Special Collections, University of Mississippi, Oxford, Miss., n.p.

152. Rudinow argues that authenticity has been defined and defended in a number of ways, including the proprietary argument (who owns the blues?) and the experiential-access argument (who can best express the blues?). Joel Rudinow, "Race, Ethnicity, Expressive Authenticity: Can White People Sing the Blues?," *Journal of Aesthetics and Art Criticism* 52.1 (1994): 127–37.

153. R. A. Lawson, "The First Century of Blues: One Hundred Years of Hearing and Interpreting the Music and the Musicians," *Southern Cultures* 13.3 (2007): 43.

154. Roberta Freund Schwartz, *How Britain Got the Blues: The Transmission and Reception of American Blues Style in the United Kingdom* (London: Ashgate, 2007) 168–69.

155. Keith Richards with James Fox, *Life* (New York: Little, Brown, 2010) 82–83.

156. Charles Keil, *Urban Blues* (Chicago: U of Chicago P, 1966) 101.

157. "Red, White, and Blues," *The Blues: A Musical Journey (Part 6)*, dir. Mike Figgis, executive prod. Martin Scorsese, PBS, Jackson, Mississippi, 4 Oct. 2004.

158. Robert Johnson, *King of the Delta Blues Singers* (Columbia, 1961).

159. Keil 34–35.

160. Keil 37. While praising the book as "thought-provoking" and "well-reasoned," Groom criticized Keil's description of white audience members and African American performers as "bitter" and "unjustified" (86). Bob Groom, *The Blues Revival* (London: Studio Vista, 1971).

161. Keil 37. While there may some validity to this critique, it is also true that black musicians often employed different repertoires for black and white audiences. See, e.g., William R. Ferris Jr., "Racial Repertoires among Blues Performers," *Ethnomusicology* 14.3 (1970): 439–49.

162. Patrick Ragains, "Blues: An Assessment of Scholarship, Reference Tools, and Documentary Sources," *References Services Review* 21.4 (1993): 15.

163. B. B. King with David Ritz, *Blues All around Me: The Autobiography of B. B. King* (New York: Avon, 1996) 126–27.

164. Ulrich Adelt, "Trying to Find an Identity: Eric Clapton's Changing Conception of 'Blackness,'" *Popular Music and Society* 31.4 (2008): 437.

165. Robert Plant, News, "Mississippi Blues Trail Marker Dedication Honoring W. C. Handy—RP Interview," 26 Nov. 2009, 15 Feb. 2010, http://www.robertplant.com/news/mississippi-blues-trail-marker-dedication-honoring-wc-handy-rp-interview.

166. Schwartz 194.

167. Mick Jagger, "Mick Jagger," interview with Jonathan Cott, *The Rolling Stone Interviews: Talking with the Legends of Rock and Roll, 1967–1980*, ed. Peter Herbst (New York: St. Martin's/Rolling Stone, 1981) 46.

168. Hound Dog Taylor, "Hound Dog Taylor," interview with Jim O'Neal and R. T. Cuniff, *Living Blues* Winter 1970–71: 6.

169. Quoted in "Rebirth of the Blues," *Newsweek* 26 May 1969: 83.

170. Keil 101–2.

171. Michael Erlewine, "Ann Arbor Blues Festival: The First of Its Kind," *Living Blues* Mar.–Apr. 2006: 37.

172. O'Neal 368–369.

173. Amiri Baraka (LeRoi Jones), "Blues People: *Looking* Both Ways," introduction to *Blues People: Negro Music in White America*, 1999, by Baraka (New York: Harper Perennial, 2002) ix.

174. Ragains 15.

175. Larry Neal, "The Black Arts Movement," *The Norton Anthology of African American Literature*, ed. Henry Louis Gates Jr. and Nellie Y. McKay (New York: W. W. Norton, 1997) 1960–61.

176. Maulana Karenga, "Black Art: Mute Matter Given Force and Function," *The Norton Anthology of African American Literature*, ed. Henry Louis Gates Jr. and Nellie Y. McKay (New York: W. W. Norton, 1997) 1976–77.

177. Although O'Neal acknowledged the Africans Americans made up a sizable segment of the blues audience during the 1960s, young blacks were not avid consumers of the blues because the music was mostly heard in adult spaces (e.g., taverns), and many

young African Americans could not readily identify with the life experiences conveyed in blues songs (372).

178. *Living Blues* originally published the interview in 1972. It was reprinted in 1978. Jimmy Dawkins, "*Living Blues* Interview: Jimmy Dawkins," interview with William Cummerow, *Living Blues* Sept.–Oct. 1978: 48.

179. King 210–11.

180. Little Milton, "*Living Blues* Interview: Little Milton," interview with Lynn S. Summers and Bob Scheir, *Living Blues* Autumn 1974: 22.

181. King 213.

182. Quoted in King 239–40.

183. Milton 22.

184. "The New Blues," *Newsweek* 24 June 1968: 112.

185. The irony of white musicians playing "funky" and "down-home" electric blues was not lost on one *Newsweek* reporter: "The pop scene has become a roaring, pulsating paradox of sound—the white man singing the black blues" ("Rebirth" 82).

186. "Rebirth" 82.

187. O'Neal 373.

188. O'Neal 373.

189. Schwartz 113.

190. Jeff Todd Titon, "Reconstructing the Blues: Reflections on the 1960s Blues Revival," *Transforming Tradition: Folk Music Revivals Examined*, ed. Neil V. Rosenberg (Urbana: U of Illinois P, 1993) 223.

2. The History of Blues Tourism in the Mississippi Delta

1. Hollie I. West, "Can White People Sing the Blues?," *Ebony* July 1979: 142.

2. Giles Oakley, *The Devil's Music: A History of the Blues*, 2nd ed. (New York: Da Capo, 1997) 238.

3. Adam Gussow, reader's report, June 2010.

4. William Ferris, *Give My Poor Heart Ease: Voices of the Mississippi Blues* (Chapel Hill: U of North Carolina P, 2009) 6–7. Alan Lomax, *The Land Where the Blues Began* (1993; New York: New Press, 2002). In 1941, Lomax was jailed in Tunica on suspicion of being an "agitator" and a "spy" after using the word "Mister" to refer to Son House, a social taboo in many southern states until the end of the 1960s. The Tunica County sheriff, whom Lomax described as "red faced" with "stern baronial manners," believed that no self-respecting southerner would ever call "a nigger Mister" (21–23).

5. Kinchen O'Keefe, personal interview, 18 Oct. 2004.

6. Ellen Douglas, "Delta Beat," *Washington Post* 23 Oct. 1978: B3.

7. Mississippi Action for Community Education, "History: Mississippi Delta Blues and Heritage Festival," 3 Sept. 2010, http://www.deltablues.org/index.php?id=9.

8. Mississippi Action for Community Education, press release, 21 June 1985.

9. Gregg B. Bangs, "Blues Festival Celebrates 'Dying Art,'" *Clarion-Ledger/Jackson Daily News* 22 Oct. 1978: 3A, 6A.

10. Douglas B3.

11. Douglas B1.

12. Jim O'Neal, "We've Got the Blues," editorial, *10th Annual Mississippi Delta Blues Festival*, Sept. 1987, n.p.

13. Quoted in "Festival Provides Showcase for National, Regional Talent," *Clarion-Ledger* 19 Sept. 1985: 1G.

14. Sylvester W. Oliver, "Local Folk Singer—an Unsong Legend," Clarksdale, Miss.: Carnegie Public Library, 1980.

15. Panny Mayfield, "Library Head Sid Graves Resigns Post," *Clarksdale Press Register* 15 Mar. 1995: 1A.

16. Quoted in Rebecca Hood-Adams, "The Delta Blues Museum: A Happy Harmony," *Delta Scene* Fall 1980: 9.

17. John Ruskey, personal interview, 20 Apr. 2001. Graves's vision has remained intact; the current mission statement of the museum encourages "visitors [to] find meaning, value and perspective by exploring the history and heritage of this unique American musical art form known as the blues." See the Delta Blues Museum, "Mission Statement," 23 Oct. 2009, http://www.deltabluesmuseum.org.

18. Laura Barnaby, "Sid Graves' Field of Dreams," *Here's Clarksdale!* Aug. 2007: 10.

19. Danny McKenzie, "Delta Blues Museum Spreads Tuneful Tale across the World," *Clarion-Ledger* 27 Mar. 1992: 1B.

20. O'Keefe, personal interview.

21. Patty Johnson, telephone interview, 29 Apr. 2008.

22. Mayfield, "Library" 2A. According to Ruskey, a former curator of the Delta Blues Museum, the museum was "self-supported" through grants, profits from the museum's gift shop, and donations from visitors and blues musicians. John Ruskey, telephone interview, 10 July 2008.

23. Jim Ewing, "Wade Walton: The Singing Barber of Blues Fame," *Clarion-Ledger/Jackson Daily News* 22 Nov. 1981: F1.

24. John Ruskey, "Blues Fan Plans to Return," letter, *Clarksdale Press Register* 2 Aug. 1990: 12.

25. Fred L. Hutchins, "Beale Street as It Was," *West Tennessee Historical Society Papers* 26 (1972): 56.

26. Larry Nager, *Memphis Beat: The Lives and Times of America's Musical Crossroads* (New York: St. Martin's, 1998) 18–19.

27. Jesse W. Fox, "Beale Street and the Blues," *West Tennessee Historical Society Papers* 13 (1959): 129.

28. Nat D. Williams, "Oral History Interview with Nat D. Williams," interview with Ronald Anderson Walter, 13 Sept. 1976, p. 7, Memphis Public Library (Central).

29. Robert Gordon, *It Came from Memphis* (New York: Pocket, 1995) 78–84.

30. Walter Dawson, "Beale Street: Memphis Razes Blues Landmark," *Rolling Stone* 2 Aug. 1973: 20.

31. Jim O'Neal, "Blues for the Tourists at Blues Alley in Memphis," *Living Blues* Nov.–Dec. 1978: 28.

32. "Home for Blues," *Commercial Appeal* 10 May 2009; DeSoto ed.: DSA2.

33. Nicky Robertshaw, "Beale Street Survivor: Rum Boogie Hangs On, Reaps Rewards," *Memphis Business Journal* 15 May 1995, 24 Feb. 1999.

34. Steve Cheseborough, *Blues Traveling: The Holy Sites of Delta Blues*, 2nd ed. (Jackson: UP of Mississippi, 2004) 24.

35. William Ferris, telephone interview, 3 June 2008.

36. Center for the Study of Southern Culture, History of Southern Studies, 10 May 2008, http://www.olemiss.edu/depts/south/history.html. Ferris held that position until 1997, when he was appointed to chair the National Endowment for the Humanities.

37. Ferris, telephone interview.

38. Scott Barretta, telephone interview, 28 Feb. 2008.

39. Peter Guralnick, "I Do Not Play No Rock 'n' Roll: Malaco Records—the Last Soul Company," *Living Blues* Jan.–Feb. 1989: 39.

40. Guralnick 39.

41. Afi-Odelia E. Scruggs, "Making Sounds in the Silence," *Clarion-Ledger* 29 Nov. 1988: 5C.

42. Guralnick 38.

43. David Evans, reader's report, July 2010.

44. William F. Winter, Mississippi Executive Department Jackson, "A Proclamation by the Governor," Blues Archives and Special Collections, University of Mississippi, Oxford, Miss.

45. Skip Henderson, telephone interview, 19 Mar. 2008.

46. See, e.g., "He's Come Home," *Delta Democrat Times* 6 June 1980: 1; Carol Taff, "Stackhouse, Friends Sing the Delta Blues Tomorrow," *Clarion-Ledger* 7 Sept. 1979: 1C.

47. See, e.g., Stephen Flinn Young, "Looking for the Blues in Iverness, Mississippi," *Southern Reader* Fall 1989: 20–25, 71–72; Bruce Nixon, "The Landscape of the Mississippi Blues," *Dallas Times Herald* 29 Jan. 1984: 13–21, 24–28.

48. Tom Clynes, *Music Festivals: From Bach to Blues* (Detroit: Visible Ink, 1996) 133.

49. Jeremy S. Weldon, "ZZ Top Kicks Off Funding-Raising for Delta Blues Museum," *Daily Mississippian* 27 Apr. 1988: 11.

50. Billy Gibbons of ZZ Top told a *Commercial Appeal* reporter about the event that inspired the creation of the Muddy Wood guitar. "It [Muddy Waters's cabin] had been hit by lightning and this big windstorm and there were some inspectors planning to take a look at it to see if it had to be torn down. When we got there there was this big pile of discarded wood from the lightning. Sid [Graves] and Jim [O'Neal] told me to take a piece of wood as a souvenir. Right there I got the idea to take this wood and see if we could make a guitar out of it." Quoted in Ron Wynn, "Museum Not Singing Blues," *Commercial Appeal* 13 Jan. 1991: G1.

51. Weldon 11.

52. Patricia Johnson, no title, *Highway 61: Heart of the Delta*, ed. Randall Norris (Knoxville: U of Tennessee P, 2008) 54.

53. Johnson, *Highway 61* 54. The festival changed locations every year until 1991. At the fourth annual festival, the event was held at the old freight depot loading dock where the Delta Blues Museum is currently located. See Sunflower River Blues and Gospel Festival, "History," 13 July 2008, http://www.sunflowerfest.org/index.cfm?page=history.

54. Jim O'Neal, telephone interview, 22 Feb. 2008.

55. Frank "Rat" Ratliff, personal interview, 30 Aug. 2003.

56. Johnson, *Highway 61*, 55.

57. Quoted in Panny Mayfield, "Blues Festival Is Saturday," *Clarksdale Press Register* 2 Aug. 1989: 3A.

58. Panny Mayfield, "Busy Weekend Includes Blues and Beauties," *Clarksdale Press Register* 4 Aug. 1989: 3A.

59. Andy McWilliams, "Why Does City Lack Major Blues Attraction?," letter, *Clarksdale Press Register* 21 Oct. 1989: 5A. In a 2008 interview, Patty Johnson disputes claims that

festival-goers were arrested. In 1990 O'Neal and Howard Stovall asked Melville Tillis, who was at that time in charge of organizing an independent gospel festival in Clarksdale, to join the festival. Thus in 1990 gospel music became part of the entertainment package of the festival. Melville Tillis, personal interview, 26 Oct. 2007.

60. Dok Summer, "Selective Memories of Festivals Past," *8th Annual Sunflower River Blues and Gospel Festival*, Aug. 1995: n.p.

61. E. H. Summer, "Shake Your Moneymaker," *The 10th Annual Sunflower River Blues and Gospel Festival* Aug. 1997: n.p. Apparently, by the third festival, the audience was more "well-behaved." According to the *Clarksdale Press Register*, "Attending policemen said large numbers were unknown locally and obviously were visitors to Clarksdale. All were well-behaved." See Panny Mayfield, "Sunflower River Blues Festival Draws Fine Music, Many Smiles and Visitors," *Clarksdale Press Register* 8 Aug. 1990: 1B.

62. McWilliams 5A.

63. Mark Jordan, "Music Notes," *Memphis Flyer* 18 Feb. 2010, http://www.memphis-flyer.com/backissues/issue416/mus416.htm.

64. Howard Stovall, MySpace, 18 Feb. 2010, http://www.myspace.com/howardstovall.

65. Robert Gordon, *Can't Be Satisfied: The Life and Times of Muddy Waters* (Boston: Little, Brown, 2002) 64.

66. Jordan.

67. Quoted in Jordan.

68. Cheseborough 84–85; Resource Entertainment Group, "Celebrity Industry Profile Featuring Howard Stovall," 18 Feb. 2010, http://www.regmemphis.com/index .cfm?page=newsArticle&newsID=13.

69. Jim O'Neal, e-mail communication, 29 Mar. 2008. Despite the lack of local assistance, O'Neal and Johnson managed to open up their respective businesses. In 1998, O'Neal moved to Kansas City and eventually sold Stackhouse in 2005 for a fraction of what it cost him. Johnson still maintains a practice in Clarksdale.

70. Johnson, telephone interview.

71. Ruskey, personal interview.

72. John Bodnar, *Remaking America: Public Memory, Commemoration, and Patriotism in the Twentieth Century* (Princeton: Princeton UP, 1992) 13.

73. Henderson, telephone interview.

74. Johnson, telephone interview.

75. David McGee, "Robert Johnson," *Rolling Stone Album Guide*, ed. Anthony De-Curtis and James Henke with Holly George-Warren (New York: Random, 1992) 376–77.

76. O'Neal, telephone interview. In *Crossroads*, a young white boy, played by Ralph Macchio, enlists the help of a veteran blues musician, Willie Brown, to find a lost blues song. In turn, Brown asks the young man to travel to the crossroads to help him redeem his soul from the devil.

77. *Deep Blues: A Musical Pilgrimage to the Crossroads*, dir. Dir. Robert Mugge (Oil Factory/Radio ActiveFilms, 1991).

78. Kappi Allen, personal interview, 3 Feb. 2003.

79. Cheryl Line, telephone interview, 13 Mar. 2008.

80. Bill Seratt, telephone interview, 17 June 2008. The oldest convention and visitors bureau in Mississippi is located in Vicksburg, which opened its office in 1983.

81. "Tourism Boost Foreseen," editorial, *Memphis Business Journal* 17–21 Feb. 1997: 4.

82. Quoted in Kris Hunter, "'America's Blues Alley' Campaign Expanding to Lure German Visitors to Mississippi," *Memphis Business Journal* 4 Mar. 1996: 40.

83. Randall Travel Marketing, *Mississippi Millennium Blues Trail: Strategic Marketing Plan for Travel and Tourism* (Mooresville, N.C., 2001) 1, 7.

84. Luther Brown, personal interview, 7 Sept. 2007.

85. Quoted in Lori Herring, "Mississippi Has the Blues," *Clarion Ledger* 10 June 2002: 3D.

86. Nancy Kossman, personal interview, 6 Sept. 2002.

87. Brown, personal interview, 20 Mar. 2001.

88. Steve LaVere, personal interview, 18 Jan. 2008.

89. "Bluesville," *Living Blues* May–June 1998: 9.

90. Jim O'Neal, *Delta Blues Kit* (Kansas City, Mo.: BluEsoterica, 2004) 2.

91. Robin Rushing, "Revisit Tourism Board's Mission," editorial, *Clarksdale Press Register* 12 Feb. 2004: 4A.

92. "Clarksdale, Tunica Form Partnership to Hike Tourism," *Memphis Business Journal* 18 Feb. 2000: 18.

93. The MDTA includes seven Delta towns and DeSoto and Yahoo counties.

94. Seratt, telephone interview.

95. Mississippi Delta Tourism Association, 16 Apr. 2008, http://www.visitthedelta.com.

96. Mississippi Delta Tourism Association, 15 Oct. 2010, http://www.visitthedelta.com.

97. The Blues Highway Association and the Mississippi Blues Commission, 20 Feb. 2008, http://www.blueshighway.org/synergies.htm.

98. Blues Highway Association, minutes from September 10, 2002 meeting, Luther Brown, e-mail communication.

99. The Blues Highway Association, 20 Feb. 2008, http://www.blueshighway.org/bha.htm.

100. Roger Stolle, personal interview, 1 Sept. 2004.

101. In my interview with Patty Johnson, she revealed that the state had flirted with the idea of a blues commission as early as 1991. Although a committee had completed some work on the project, the blues commission never made it past the formative stages.

102. Jennifer Farish, "Mississippi Looks for Ways to Cash In on the Growing Interest of Historic Music Culture," *Daily Journal* 27 June 2004: 5A.

103. Sheila Byrd, "Perhaps Fewer Musicians Will Sing the Blues," *Commercial Appeal* 5 Mar. 2010; DeSoto ed.: DSA2.

104. "Bill Creates Mississippi Blues Commission," *Jet* 17 May 2004: 15.

105. 5th Annual Peavine Awards, Delta State University, Cleveland, Mississippi, 15 Oct. 2002: n.p.

106. Other appointments are mostly based on previously held positions on tourism boards and other agencies. For example, the director of the Division of Tourism of the Mississippi Development Authority, the executive director of the Mississippi Arts Commission, and the director of the Center for the Study of Southern Culture at the University of Mississippi, among other official representatives, all serve on the board. See Blues Highway Association, Senate Bill 2082, 3 Sept. 2010, htpp://www.blueshighway.org/commissionlegislation.htm.

107. Luther Brown, telephone interview, 23 Aug. 2006.

108. Brown, personal interview, 7 Sept. 2007.

109. Wanda Clark, telephone interview, 23 Apr. 2008.

110. Brown, personal interview, 7 Sept. 2007.

111. Andy Ross, "Two New Blues Trail Markers Placed," *Clarksdale Press Register* 14 Feb. 2008: 1A.

112. Quoted in Yolanda Jones, "Nesbit's Callicott Honored with Blues Trail Marker," *Commercial Appeal* 12 Mar. 2010; DeSoto ed.: DSA1–DSA2.

113. Alex Thomas, e-mail communication, 12 Oct. 2010.

114. Alex Thomas, telephone interview, 27 Mar. 2008.

115. Jim O'Neal, e-mail communication.

116. Seratt, telephone interview; Cheryl Line, personal interview, 10 May 2001.

3. Blues Myths and the Rhetorical Imagination of Place

1. Elijah Wald, *Escaping the Delta: Robert Johnson and the Invention of the Blues* (New York: Harper Collins, 2004) 3.

2. Patricia R. Schroeder, *Robert Johnson, Mythmaking, and Contemporary American Culture* (Urbana: U of Illinois P, 2004) 100.

3. Robert Palmer, "Black Snake Moan: The History of Texas Blues," *Blues and Chaos: The Music Writing of Robert Palmer*, ed. Anthony DeCurtis (New York: Scribner, 2009) 59.

4. Roland Barthes, *Mythologies*, trans. Annette Lavers (1957; New York: Noonday, 1972) 109–10.

5. William G. Doty, *Myth: A Handbook* (Tuscaloosa: U of Alabama P, 2004) 13.

6. William G. Doty, *Mythography: The Study of Myths and Rituals* (Tuscaloosa: U of Alabama P, 1986) 16.

7. Walter R. Fisher, *Human Communication as Narration: Toward a Philosophy of Reason, Value, and Action* (Columbia: U of South Carolina P, 1987) 58.

8. Stephanie Kelley-Romano, "Mythmaking in Alien Abduction Narratives," *Communication Quarterly* 54.3 (2006): 385–87.

9. Robert C. Rowland, "On Mythic Criticism," *Communication Studies* 41.2 (1990): 104.

10. Rowland 104.

11. Rowland 104.

12. Lloyd A. Hunter, "The Immortal Confederacy: Another Look at Lost Cause Religion," *The Myth of the Lost Cause and Civil War History*, ed. Gary W. Gallagher and Alan T. Nolan (Bloomington: Indiana UP, 2000) 189.

13. Malcolm O. Sillars and Bruce E. Gronbeck, *Communication Criticism: Rhetoric, Social Codes, Cultural Studies* (Prospect Heights, Ill.: Waveland, 2001) 178–79.

14. Rowland 103.

15. Doty, *Mythography* 21.

16. Doty, *Mythography* 11, 27.

17. Barthes 144.

18. Doty, *Myth* 19.

19. Martin Barker and Roger Sabin, *The Lasting of the Mohicans: History of an American Myth* (Jackson: UP of Mississippi, 1995) 5.

20. Ulrich Gehmann, "Modern Myths," *Culture and Organization* 9.2 (2003): 105.

21. Joseph Campbell, *Myths to Live By* (New York: Viking, 1972) 215.

22. See Joseph Campbell with Bill D. Moyers, *The Power of Myth* (New York: Double-day, 1988) 31; Mark P. Moore, "Rhetorical Criticism of Political Myth: From Goldwater Legend to Reagan Mystique," *Communication Studies* 42.3 (1991): 296; Kelley-Romano 387–89; Rowland 102–3.

23. Kelley-Romano 385.

24. Marybeth Hamilton, *In Search of the Blues* (New York: Basic, 2008) 232–33.

25. See, e.g., Paul Oliver, *The Story of the Blues* (1969; Boston: Northeastern UP, 1998); LeRoi Jones (Amiri Baraka), *Blues People: Negro Music in White America* (1963; New York: Harper-Perennial, 2002).

26. Arkansas Vacation and Destination brochure, advertisement supplement, *Commercial Appeal* 30 Sept. 2007: n.p.

27. Mississippi Blues Commission, 9 Mar. 2008, http://www.msbluestrail.org/index .htm.

28. Mississippi Blues Trail, "Experiencing the Blues Where They Were Born," 28 Aug. 2010, http://www.msbluestrail.org.

29. Alex Thomas, telephone interview, 27 Mar. 2008.

30. Mississippi Development Authority, "The Birthplace of America's Music," 10 Sept. 2010, http://visitmississippi.org.

31. Quoted in "Highway 61 Scores New Name," *Bolivar Commercial* 14 May 2009, 17 May 2009, http://www.bolivarcom.com.

32. "The Mississippi Delta: Where the Music Meets the Soul," Greenville, Miss.: Mississippi Delta Tourism Association, n.d.

33. "Greenville on the Mississippi," Greenville, Miss. Greenville–Washington County Convention and Visitors Bureau, n.d. [brochure 1].

34. Clarksdale and Coahoma County, "The Land Where the Blues Began . . ." Clarksdale, Miss.: Coahoma County Tourism Commission, n.d.

35. Holli Haynie, "Super Chikan and the River Rat," advertisement, *Memphis Spoon* Spring 2010: 103.

36. Ground Zero Blues Club, advertisement, n.d.

37. Morgan Freeman, "My Mississippi Delta Story," foreword, *Highway 61: Heart of the Delta*, ed. Randall Norris (Knoxville: U of Tennessee P, 2008) xi.

38. "Greenville on the Mississippi," Greenville, Miss.: Greenville–Washington County Convention and Visitors Bureau, n.d. [brochure 2].

39. "The Path Finder: A Guide to Clarksdale and Coahoma County," Clarksdale, Miss.: Sunflower River Trading Company, 1999.

40. "Greenville on the Mississippi" [brochure 2].

41. "Clarksdale, Mississippi," Clarksdale, Miss.: Clarksdale Downtown Development Association/Memphis Convention and Visitors Bureau," n.d.

42. Victoria Pope, "Still Singing the Blues in the Mississippi Delta," *U.S. News and World Report* 23 Apr. 2001: 66.

43. Jay Brakefield, "Birthplace of the Blues Draws Tourists to Clarksdale," *Milwaukee Sentinel* 23 Jan. 1991, part 5: 2.

44. Douglas Cruickshank, "Mississippi Delta: A Trip up the Mississippi Delta, the Bittersweet and Poignantly Beautiful Birthplace of the Blues," SFGate.com, 14 Mar. 1999, 16 Apr. 2010, http://www.sfgate.com/cgi-bin/article.cgi?file=/e/a/1999/03/14/MAGA ZINE16138.dtl&type=printable.

45. Wally Northway, "Blues Continue to Draw Tourists to Towns around the State," *Mississippi Business Journal* 2 May 2005: 18.

46. Larry Katz, "Don't Miss Mississippi Delta, Birthplace of Blues," *Boston Sunday Herald* 31 Mar. 1991: 58; Carl McIntire, "Blues Had Birth in Mississippi Delta," *Clarion-Ledger* 30 Sept. 1979: 1F; Steve Walton, "Tour Map Marks the Spots Where Blues Were Birthed," *Clarion-Ledger* 30 July 1992: 3E; Rheta Grimsley Johnson, "Guiding Pilgrims to Holy Land of the Blues," *Clarion-Ledger* 20 Feb. 1995: 1D.

47. W. C. Handy, *Father of the Blues: An Autobiography* (1941; New York: Da Capo, 1991) 76–77.

48. "Blues and More," Cleveland, Miss.: Cleveland–Bolivar County Chamber of Commerce, n.d.

49. Elliott Hurwitt, e-mail communication, 7–16 July 2010.

50. Richard Carlin, "Handy, W. C.," *American National Biography*, ed. John A. Garraty and Mark C. Carnes, vol. 10 (New York: Oxford UP, 1999) 4.

51. Elliott Hurwitt, e-mail communication.

52. Harriet Ottenheimer, "Prewar Blues in St. Louis," *Popular Music and Society* 14.2 (1990): 87–89.

53. Harriet Ottenheimer, "Blues in the Heartland: African-American Music and Culture in the Middle West," *Black Heartland: African American Life, the Middle West, and the Meaning of American Regionalism*, Occasional Papers Series, 1.2 (1997): 27.

54. Francis Davis, *The History of the Blues: The Roots, the Music, the People from Charley Patton to Robert Cray* (New York: Hyperion, 1995) 28.

55. Steve Cheseborough, *Blues Traveling: The Holy Sites of Delta Blues*, 2nd ed. (Jackson: UP of Mississippi, 2004) 107.

56. For more information on the number of musicians who lived and performed at Dockery, see David Evans, "Blues on Dockery's Plantation: 1895 to 1967 [Part I]," *Blues Unlimited* Jan. 1968: 3–4; David Evans, "Blues on Dockery's Plantation: 1895 to 1967 [Part II]", *Blues Unlimited* Feb. 1968: 14–15.

57. Dockery Farms, "History," 10 Sept. 2010, http://www.dockeryfarms.org/History .html.

58. Quoted in Sweet Magnolia Tours, "Nuttin' But the Blues Vacation Holiday," 24 Feb. 2010, http://www.sweetmagnoliatours.com/P_FlyDrive_NuttinButBlues.php.

59. "Three Icons of the Delta: The River, the Plantation, and the Juke," Blues Highway Association, 10 Sept. 2010, http://www.blueshighway.org/icons.htm.

60. Curtis Hewston, "The Blues Highway," 10 Sept. 2010, http://thebluehighway.com/ links.html. According to Hewston's own Web site, the Blues Foundation awarded the Web site the Keeping the Blues Alive Award for Blues on the Internet in 1998.

61. "Roots of Rhythm," 2 Nov. 2007, http://www.rootsofrhythm.com/tours.html.

62. WXVT-TV, newscast, Greenville, Miss., 20 Apr. 2006.

63. Glenn Gass, "A Trip through the Delta Blues," 10 Sept. 2010, http://www.music .indiana.edu/som/courses/rock/delta.html.

64. Quoted in David Lush, "Pianist from Holland Fascinated by the Blues," *Bolivar Commercial Advertiser* 30 Jan. 2001: 1–2.

65. Voodoo Girls' Blues Pilgrimage, "Mississippi Delta Day 2," 1998, 15 Dec. 2006, http://www.p1.com/mp/Delta%20-%20Day%202.htm.

66. Even the Delta Blues Museum perpetuates the birthplace myth. Visitors who enter the exhibit will immediately come into contact with the museum's opening narrative,

"The Birthplace of the Blues," which, in part, states: "While it cannot be denied that the social and emotional situation in which black Deltans found themselves also contributed to the development of the Delta blues, it was the land itself—a unique geographical setting at just the right point in time—that provided the initial crucible in which African Americans in the Mississippi Delta created the artistic synthesis known as the Blues."

67. Bill Lester, "The Dockery Farms Restoration Project," First Tuesday Program, Delta State University, Cleveland, Miss., 4 May 2010.

68. "Mississippi Delta and the Blues," advertisement, *Tunica Mississippi 2009 Visitor's Guide*. Tunica, Miss.: Tunica Convention and Visitors Bureau, 2009: 19.

69. Greenville–Washington County Convention and Visitors Bureau, "Greenville on the Mississippi," 10 Sep. 2010, http://www.visitgreenville.org.

70. Greenwood Convention and Visitor's Bureau, "Back in the Day," 10 Sept. 2010, http://www.gcvb.com/back_museum.php.

71. John Bodnar, *Remaking America: Public Memory, Commemoration, and Patriotism in the Twentieth Century* (Princeton: Princeton UP, 1992) 14.

72. Marybeth Hamilton, "The Blues, the Folk, and African-American History," *Transactions of the Royal Historical Society* 11 (2001): 21.

73. Samuel C. Adams Jr., "The Acculturation of the Delta Negro," *Social Forces* 26 (1947): 202–3.

74. Cheseborough 10.

75. Mark Jacobson, "Down to the Crossroads," *Natural History* Sept. 1996: 48.

76. Jim O'Neal, telephone interview, 22 Feb. 2008.

77. House of Blues, "About the House of Blues," 10 Sept. 2010, http://www.houseof blues.com/aboutHOB.

78. Daniel Lieberfeld, "Million-Dollar Juke Joint: Commodifying Blues Culture," *African American Review* 29.2 (1995): 217.

79. Ted Gioia, *Delta Blues: The Life and Times of the Mississippi Masters Who Revolutionized American Music* (New York: W. W. Norton, 2008) 4.

80. In Haiti, the Esu character is named Papa Legba, a voodoo deity. Ayana Smith argues that trickster tales can be traced to slavery. The slave perceived the trickster character as a "folk hero" whose deviousness "presents an alternative, vicarious existence that contrasts with the strict boundaries of slave existence." Ayana Smith, "Blues, Criticism, and the Signifying Trickster," *Popular Music* 24.2 (2005): 179–80.

81. Henry Louis Gates Jr., *The Signifying Monkey: A Theory of Afro-American Literary Criticism* (New York: Oxford UP, 1988) 6.

82. Melissa J. Richard, "The Crossroads and the Myth of the Mississippi Delta Bluesman," *Interdisciplinary Humanities* 23.2 (2006): 20.

83. Jon Michael Spencer, *Blues and Evil* (Knoxville: U of Tennessee P, 1993) xii.

84. Spencer 28.

85. Gioia 115.

86. Barry Lee Pearson and Bill McCulloch, *Robert Johnson: Lost and Found* (Urbana: U of Illinois P, 2003) 66.

87. Gioia 116.

88. Wald 106–7.

89. Pearson and McCulloch 6.

90. Quoted in Lawrence Cohn, "Son House—Delta Bluesman," *Saturday Review* 28 Sept. 1968: 69.

91. Bruce Michael Conforth, "Ike Zimmerman: The X in Robert Johnson's Crossroads," *Living Blues* Feb. 2008: 72–73.

92. Pearson and McCulloch 7–9.

93. David McGee, "Robert Johnson," *The Rolling Stone Album Guide*, ed. Anthony DeCurtis and James Henke with Holly George-Warren (New York: Random, 1992) 377.

94. Pearson and McCulloch are highly skeptical that House actually told Welding that Johnson had "sold his soul to the devil in exchange for learning to play like that" (quoted in Pearson and McCulloch 89). Beyond the absence of the recorded tapes of the 1966 interview, House was interviewed about Johnson on numerous occasions but never mentioned that Johnson sold his soul to the devil. For Pearson and McCulloch's critique of the Welding interview, see pp. 88–92. See also Son House, "I Can Make My Own Songs," *Sing Out!* July 1965: 38–45. In this account of Johnson's transformation as a musician, House does *not* refer to any deal with the devil. See also Gayle Dean Wardlow, *Chasin' That Devil Music: Searching for the Blues*, ed. Edward Komara (San Francisco: Backbeat, 1998) 196–203. The chapter includes a postscript by Edward Komara (203–6).

95. Quoted in Charles M. Brown, "Little Zion Split over Johnson," *Greenwood Commonwealth* 6 June 2004: 1A, 14A.

96. Wardlow 200.

97. Julio Finn's *The Bluesman: The Musical Heritage of Black Men and Women in the Americas* (New York: Interlink, 1991) presents one of the most entertaining analyses of the Johnson myth. Claiming that "Johnson's songs present the visions of a haunted mind" that is obsessed with the consequences of his decision to sell his soul to the devil, Finn claims that "it is doubtful whether Johnson could have written the lyrics of his songs without having been initiated into the [voodoo] cult" (215, 217).

98. Mississippi Tourism Association, 10 Sept. 2010, http://www.mstourism.com/deltaregion.html.

99. Coahoma County Tourism Commission, "The Blues," 10 Sept. 2010, http://www.clarksdaletourism.com/theblues.htm.

100. "Clarksdale, Mississippi."

101. "The Path Finder."

102. Mississippi Development Authority, "Featured City—Clarksdale," 10 Sept. 2010, http://www.visitmississippi.org/features/clarksdale.html.

103. Coahoma County Tourism Commission, "Clarksdale and Coahoma County," 10 Sept. 2010, http://www.clarksdaletourism.com.

104. "Chasin' the Ghost of the Crossroads." Clarksdale, Miss.: Clarksdale Revitalization, n.d.

105. "FAQ: The Shackmeister Files," Shack Up Inn, 26 June 2007, http://www.shackupinn.com/faq.html.

106. Jacobson 52.

107. Cheseborough 68–69.

108. Luther Brown, "Blues Sites to See Before You Die," *Delta Magazine* July–Aug. 2005: 52.

109. Mississippi Development Authority, Dockery Farms, 10 Sept. 2010, http://www.visitmississippi.org/groups_marketing/Itineraries/EDTour_Delta2.pdf.

110. Bill Seratt, telephone interview, 17 June 2008.

111. Robert N. Brown, "Traveling Riverside Blues: Landscapes of Robert Johnson in the Yazoo-Mississippi Delta," *Focus on Geography* 49.3 (2006): 24.

112. Pearson and McCulloch 65.

113. Wald 267.

114. Pearson and McCulloch 83.

115. Pearson and McCulloch 86.

116. Edwards 104–5.

117. David Evans, "The Birth of the Blues," *American Roots Music*, ed. Robert Santelli, Holly George-Warren, and Jim Brown (New York: Abrams, 2001) 54.

118. George Lipsitz, "Remembering Robert Johnson: Romance and Reality," *Popular Music and Society* 21.4 (1997): 39.

119. "The Delta Communities: The Diary of a Delta Traveler," Mississippi Delta Tourism Association, 31 July 2009, http://www.visitthedelta.com/communities.

120. Spencer xvi. In the last decade, the work of Wald, Schroeder, and Pearson and McCulloch has served as a critical corrective, critiquing the Johnson myth and exposing the excesses of imagination and romanticism.

121. Finn 194.

122. Robert B. Moore, "Racism in the English Language," *Race, Class, and Gender in the United States: An Integrated Study*, 4th ed., ed. Paula S. Rothenberg (New York: St. Martin's, 1998) 467.

123. See Michael Osborn, "Archetypal Metaphor in Rhetoric: The Light-Dark Family," *Quarterly Journal of Speech* 53.2 (1967): 115–26.

124. Spencer xiv.

125. Adam Gussow, reader's report, June 2010.

126. Eric W. Rothenbuhler, "Myth and Collective Memory in the Case of Robert Johnson," *Critical Studies in Media Communication* 24.3 (2007): 204.

4. Blues Festivals, Race, and the Construction of Authenticity

1. Mississippi Blues Commission, "Mississippi Blues Trail," flyer, n.d.

2. Mississippi Development Authority, "Soulful Sounds," 25 June 2006, http://www.visitmississippi.org.

3. "Live from the Birthplace of American Music," advertisement, visitmississippi.org, *Juke Joint Festival Guide*, Apr. 2006.

4. Greenwood Convention and Visitors Bureau, advertisement, *Living Blues* Oct. 2009: 52.

5. Mississippi Action for Community Education, "History: Mississippi Delta Blues and Heritage Festival," 3 Sept. 2010, http://www.deltablues.org/index.php?id=9.

6. "Sunflower River Blues Festival Is a True Gem," *Clarksdale Press Register* 29 May 2008, 15 July 2008, http://www.sunflowerfest.org/index.cfm?page=news&newsid=52.

7. To date there has been no systematic study of the demographic makeup at Mississippi blues festivals. This demographic description is based on my own personal observations and the testimony of festival organizers.

8. Kappi Allen, personal interview, 3 Feb. 2003.

9. Erik Cohen, "A Phenomenology of Tourist Experiences," *Sociology* 13.2 (1979): 179–80.

10. Cohen, "A Phenomenology" 186–193. Cohen describes the experiential tourist as an individual who, having lost the ability to live an authentic life within his or her own society, is on a spiritual quest for meaning and uses tourism as a mechanism to enjoy

new authentic experiences. In the experimental mode, the tourist samples a wide variety of "authentic" experiences, "hoping eventually to discover one which will suit his [or her] particular needs and desires." In the final mode, existential tourism, the tourist may "switch worlds" and live in this new, authentic, spiritual center. Cohen argues, however, that a permanent move is unlikely for many existential tourists. These tourists "will live in two worlds: the world of their everyday life, where they follow their practical pursuits, but which for them is devoid of deeper meaning; and the world of their 'elective' centre, to which they will depart on periodical pilgrimages to derive spiritual sustenance" (186–90). John Ruskey and Roger Stolle might be examples of existential tourists who decided to permanently relocate to the Mississippi Delta.

11. Stephen Frenkel and Judy Walton, "Bavarian Leavenworth and the Symbolic Economy of a Theme Town," *Geographical Review* 90.4 (2000): 568.

12. John P. Taylor, "Authenticity and Sincerity in Tourism," *Annals of Tourism Research* 28.1 (2001): 8.

13. See, e.g., Edward M. Bruner, "The Maasai and the Lion King: Authenticity, Nationalism, and Globalism in African Tourism," *American Ethnologist* 28.4 (2001): 881–909; Erik Cohen, "Authenticity and Commoditization in Tourism," *Annals of Tourism Research* 15.3 (1988): 371–86; Christina Goulding, "The Commodification of the Past, Postmodern Pastiche, and the Search for Authentic Experiences at Contemporary Heritage Attractions," *European Journal of Marketing* 34.7 (2000): 835–53; Dean MacCannell, "Staged Authenticity: Arrangements of Social Space in Tourist Settings," *American Journal of Sociology* 79.3 (1973): 589–603; Philip L. Pearce and Gianna M. Moscardo, "The Concept of Authenticity in Tourist Experiences," *Australian and New Zealand Journal of Sociology* 22.1 (1986): 121–32; Ira Silver, "Marketing Authenticity in Third World Countries," *Annals of Tourism Research* 20.2 (1993): 302–18.

14. Ning Wang, "Rethinking Authenticity in Tourism Experience," *Annals of Tourism Research* 26.2 (1999): 349–51.

15. Daniel J. Boorstin, *The Image: A Guide to Pseudo-events in America* (1961; New York: Harper Colophon, 1964) 79.

16. Wang 359.

17. Wang 351–52.

18. Martin Young, "The Social Construction of Tourist Places," *Australian Geographer* 30.3 (1999): 375.

19. Silver 302.

20. Wang 355.

21. David Grazian, *Blue Chicago: The Search for Authenticity in Urban Blues Clubs* (Chicago: U of Chicago P, 2003) 12.

22. Richard A. Peterson, "In Search of Authenticity," *Journal of Management Studies* 42.5 (2005): 1086.

23. See, e.g., Elizabeth Eva Leach, "Vicars of 'Wannabe': Authenticity and the Spice Girls," *Popular Music* 20.2 (2001): 143–67; Kembrew McLeod, "Authenticity within Hip-Hop and Other Cultures Threatened with Assimilation," *Journal of Communication* 49.4 (1999): 134–50; Richard A. Peterson, *Creating Country Music: Fabricating Authenticity* (Chicago: U of Chicago P, 1997).

24. Edward G. Armstrong, "Eminem's Construction of Authenticity," *Popular Music and Society* 27.3 (2004): 338.

25. Philip Auslander, "Seeing Is Believing: Live Performance and the Discourse of Authenticity in Rock Culture," *Literature and Psychology* 44.4 (1998): 6.

26. Grazian 12.

27. Hugh Barker and Yuval Taylor, *Faking It: The Quest for Authenticity in Popular Music* (New York: W. W. Norton, 2007) x.

28. Grazian 10–12.

29. "Greenville on the Mississippi," Greenville, Miss.: Greenville–Washington County Convention and Visitors Bureau, n.d. [brochure 1].

30. Greenville–Washington County Convention and Visitors Bureau, advertisement, *Oxford American* Winter 2009: 16.

31. "The 16th Annual Sunflower River Blues and Gospel Festival," flyer, 2003.

32. Clarksdale and Coahoma County, "The Land Where the Blues Began . . ." Clarksdale, Miss.: Coahoma County Tourism Commission, n.d.

33. Quoted in Panny Flautt Mayfield, "Keeping Blues 'Authentic' Goal of Delta Music Lovers," *Clarion-Ledger* 25 Feb. 2001: 33.

34. "Travel: Ten Top Places to Hear Authentic American Music," *USA Weekend* 18 May 2008, 14 July 2008, http://www.usaweekend.com/08_issues/080518/080518summer-travel .html.

35. *Juke Joint Festival Guide*, Apr. 2006, n.p.

36. Crossroads Blues Society, 8 July 2009, http://www.rosedaleblues.com.

37. Grazian 14.

38. Quoted in Joel Rudinow, "Race, Ethnicity, Expressive Authenticity: Can White People Sing the Blues?," *Journal of Aesthetics and Art Criticism* 52.1 (1994): 127.

39. Grazian 41.

40. Mississippi Slim, telephone interview, 2 Dec. 2004.

41. Jim O'Neal, telephone interview, 22 Feb. 2008.

42. See, e.g., *9th Annual Highway 61 Blues Festival*, June 2008.

43. Steve Cheseborough, *Blues Traveling: The Holy Sites of Delta Blues*, 2nd ed. (Jackson: UP of Mississippi, 2004) 71–72.

44. "Otha Turner Kept Fife-and-Drum Tradition Alive," Blues Music Now!, 15 Sept. 2010, http://www.bluesmusicnow.com/otha_obit.html.

45. The Acoustic Stage performances typically are held from 1:30 p.m. to 6 p.m.

46. Grazian 213. In his critique of urban blues clubs in Chicago, Grazian found that many African American blues artists will develop a performance style and repertoire (which includes standard blues songs such as "Sweet Home Chicago") that are known to be pleasing to white audiences. While not specifically speaking about modern blues festivals, William Ferris argues that traditionally black performers will select songs that do not contain obscenities or overt themes of racial protest. See William R. Ferris Jr., "Racial Repertoires among Blues Performers," *Ethnomusicology* 14.3 (1970): 439–49.

47. The gospel performances usually occur on Sunday.

48. Quoted in "Fifth Annual Delta Blues Festival," *Jackson Advocate* 11–17 Nov. 1982: A8.

49. Peter R. Aschoff, "The 1988 Delta Blues Festival," *Living Blues* Jan.–Feb. 1989: 18.

50. Dave Thompson, personal interview, 22 May 2003.

51. Terry Bean, telephone interview, 23 Apr. 2008.

52. Sunflower River Blues and Gospel Festival, "History," 13 July 2008, http://www .sunflowerfest.org/index.cfm?page=history.

53. Roger Stolle, personal interview, 1 Sept. 2004.

54. "Bobby Rush: The King of Soul Blues," *Living Blues* Nov.–Dec. 2003: n.p.

55. Bobby Rush, "Bobby Rush," interview with William Cochrane, Bill Ferris, Peter Lee, and Jim O'Neal, *Living Blues* Jan.–Feb. 1989: 30.

56. Billy Johnson, telephone interview, 19 Nov. 2004.

57. Tom Clynes, *Music Festivals: From Bach to Blues* (Detroit: Visible Ink, 1996) 179.

58. *The 24th Annual Mississippi Delta Blues and Heritage Festival*, Sept. 2001.

59. James N. Gregory, *The Southern Diaspora: How the Great Migrations of Black and White Southerners Transformed America* (Chapel Hill: U of North Carolina P, 2005) 16, 330–31.

60. Gregory 331.

61. Larry L. Hunt, Matthew O. Hunt, and William W. Falk, "Who Is Headed South? U.S. Migration Trends in Black and White, 1970–2000," *Social Forces* 87.1 (2008): 96–97; Adam Gussow, reader's report, June 2010.

62. Quoted in Gregg B. Bangs, "Blues Festival Celebrates 'Dying Art,'" *Clarion-Ledger/Jackson Daily News* 22 Oct. 1978: 3A.

63. "Delta Blues Festival Set for Sept. 8," *Clarion-Ledger* 19 Aug. 1979: 3G.

64. Neal Moore, "Politics Meets the Blues with Mississippi's Bill Luckett," CNN.com, 26 Oct. 2009, 12 Apr. 2010, http://www.ireport.com/docs/DOC-346661.

65. Nicholas Lemann, *The Promised Land: The Great Black Migration and How It Changed America* (New York: Knopf, 1991) 314–15.

66. Ground Zero Blues Club, 15 Sept. 2010, http://www.groundzerobluesclub.com/home.php.

67. "Clarksdale, Mississippi," Clarksdale, Miss.: Clarksdale Downtown Development Association/Memphis Convention and Visitors Bureau, n.d.

68. Sheldon Alberts, "Delta Blues Fans Are Living the Music They Love," *Montreal Gazette*, CanWest News Service, 9 Oct. 2007, 10 Oct. 2007. For another example of how journalists describe Ground Zero, see Tim Sampson, "72 Miles to Clarksdale," *Memphis* June 2001: 43–47.

69. Farrah Austin, "A Visit with Delta Royalty," *Southern Living* Aug. 2006: 24.

70. Kinchen O'Keefe, "A Letter from Our Publisher," *Here's Clarksdale!* Apr. 2007: 5.

71. Morgan Freeman, no title, *Living Blues* Mar.–June 2004: 9.

72. Jim O'Neal, *Delta Blues Map Kit* (Kansas City, Mo.: BluEsoterica, 2004) 3.

73. Jennifer Nardone, "Roomful of Blues: Jukejoints and the Cultural Landscape of the Mississippi Delta," *Constructing Image, Identity, and Place: Perspectives in Vernacular Architecture*, ed. Alison K. Hoagland and Kenneth A. Breisch (Knoxville: U of Tennessee P, 2003) 168.

74. Jennifer Nardone, "Juke Joints," *Encyclopedia of the Blues*, ed. Edward Komara, vol. 1 (New York: Routledge, 2006) 552–53.

75. Trip Advisor, "Red's Lounge," 17 July 2008, http://www.tripadvisor.com/ShowUserReviews-g43722-d626776-r16721827-Red_s_Lounge-Clarksdale_Mississippi.html.

76. "2006 Sunflower River Blues and Gospel Festival," discussion board, nikonians.org, 17 July 2008.

77. David S. Rotenstein, "The Helena Blues: Cultural Tourism and African-American Folk Music," *Southern Folklore* 49.2 (1992): 138, 143.

5. A Blues Countermemory

1. "Mississippi Turning," *Economist* 6 Jan. 2007: 27.

2. James B. Stewart, "Message in the Music: Political Commentary in Black Popular Music from Rhythm and Blues to Early Hip Hop," *Journal of American History* 90.3 (2005): 205.

3. David Evans, reader's report, July 2010.

4. James C. Cobb, *The Most Southern Place on Earth: The Mississippi Delta and the Roots of Regional Identity* (New York: Oxford UP, 1992) 325.

5. Walter Sillers Sr., "Historical," *Imperial Bolivar*, ed. William F. Gray (Cleveland, Miss.: n.p., 1923) 9.

6. David L. Cohn, *Where I Was Born and Raised* (Boston: Houghton Mifflin, 1935/48) 17.

7. *Fannie Lou Hamer: Courage and Faith*, Mississippi Public Broadcasting, 20 Feb. 2006, exec. producer Linda C. Coles.

8. Sally Avery Bermanzohn, "Violence, Nonviolence, and the Civil Rights Movement," *New Political Science* 22.1 (2000): 33.

9. Robert V. Haynes, "Territorial Mississippi, 1798–1817," *Journal of Mississippi History* 64.4 (2002): 283.

10. J. Cobb 7.

11. J. Cobb 9.

12. John C. Willis, *Forgotten Time: The Yazoo-Mississippi Delta after the Civil War* (Charlottesville: UP of Virginia, 2000) 10.

13. Harris Dickson, *The Story of King Cotton* (New York: Funk and Wagnalls, 1937) 20.

14. Cohn 30.

15. Although the United States legally abolished the slave trade in 1807 (the law went into effect in January 1808), the internal slave trade flourished.

16. Slave Population Census (Mississippi), Geospatial and Statistical Data Center, University of Virginia Library, 1 Mar. 2010, http://fisher.lib.virginia.edu/collections/stats/histcensus/php/newlong3.php.

17. John Stauffer, "Interspatialism in the Nineteenth-century South: The Natchez of Henry Norman," *Slavery and Abolition* 29.2 (2008): 248–50.

18. Slave Population Census.

19. The Federal Writers' Project, 1936–38, *Mississippi Slave Narratives: A Folk History of Slavery in Mississippi from Interviews with Former Slaves* (Bedford, Mass.: Applewood, n.d.) 114–15.

20. No name, slave contract, 7 Dec. 1858, Bacon-Messenger Family Papers, M138, Box 2 (Folder 1), Delta State University Archives, Cleveland, Miss.

21. Clayton E. Jewett and John O. Allen, *Slavery in the South: A State-by-State History* (Westport, Conn.: Greenwood, 2004) 165.

22. A. J. Bass, slave contract, 27 Oct. 1853, Bacon-Messenger Family Papers, M138, Box 1 (Folder 1), Delta State University Archives, Cleveland, Miss.

23. C. McLaurin, "Bargains to Be Had! Sale of Land, Negroes, &C," advertisement, *Mississippi State Gazette* 27 Jan. 1858: 1.

24. D. L. Rawls, "Land and Negroes for Sale," advertisement, *Vicksburg Whig* 5 Oct. 1859: n.p.

25. John Harris, "Plantation for Sale," advertisement, *Hinds County Gazette* 14 Feb. 1855: n.p.

26. Cohn 41.

27. Dickson 6.

28. Clyde Woods, *Development Arrested: The Blues and Plantation Power in the Mississippi Delta* (London: Verso, 1998) 47.

29. Woods 59.

30. J. Cobb 31.

31. J. Cobb 31.

32. Woods 62.

33. Jewett and Allen assert that by the end of the war, an estimated 17,000 African Americans from Mississippi had joined the United States Colored Troops (166).

34. Jewett and Allen 167.

35. W. E. B. Du Bois, *Black Reconstruction in America: An Essay toward a History of the Part Which Black Folk Played in the Attempt to Reconstruct Democracy in America, 1860–1880* (1935; New York: Atheneum, 1975) 121.

36. Eric Foner, *Reconstruction: America's Unfinished Revolution, 1863–1877* (New York: Harper and Row, 1988) 142–52.

37. Foner 291.

38. William F. Gray, "Reconstruction," *Imperial Bolivar*, ed. William F. Gray (Cleveland, Miss.: n.p., 1923) 14.

39. Broadus B. Jackson, *Civil War and Reconstruction in Mississippi: Mirror of Democracy in America* (Jackson, Miss.: Town Square, 1998) 116.

40. W. E. B. Du Bois, "The Black Codes," *Race, Class, and Gender in the United States: An Integrated Study*, ed. Paula S. Rothenberg, 4th ed. (New York: St. Martin's, 1998) 409.

41. Woods 90.

42. J. Cobb 82.

43. General Population Census (Mississippi), Geospatial and Statistical Data Center, University of Virginia Library, 1 Mar. 2010, http://fisher.lib.virginia.edu/collections/stats/histcensus/php/newlong3.php.

44. James W. Loewen, et. al., *Mississippi: Conflict and Change*, ed. James W. Loewen and Charles Sallis, rev. ed. (New York: Pantheon, 1980) 203.

45. J. Cobb 55.

46. Charles E. Cobb Jr., "Traveling the Blues Highway," *National Geographic* Apr. 1999: 58.

47. Howard Snyder, "Traits of My Plantation Negroes," *Century* July 1921: 374.

48. Son House, "I Can Make My Own Songs," *Sing Out!* July 1965: 39.

49. Adam Gussow, *Seems like Murder Here: Southern Violence and the Blues Tradition* (Chicago: U of Chicago P, 2002) 217.

50. *Blues in the Mississippi Night* (Cambridge: Rounder, 2003).

51. Mary Frances Berry and John W. Blassingame, *Long Memory: The Black Experience in America* (New York: Oxford UP, 1982) 348.

52. Giles Oakley, *The Devil's Music: A History of the Blues*, 2nd ed. (London: Da Capo, 1997) 22–23.

53. Stephen J. Whitfield, *A Death in the Delta: The Story of Emmett Till* (New York: Free Press, 1988) 2.

54. James Elbert Cutler, *Lynch-Law: An Investigation into the History of Lynching in the United States* (London: Longmans, Green, 1905) 153.

55. Cutler 179.

56. Woods 107.

57. Gussow 3, 45.

58. Bermanzohn 32.

59. W. C. Handy, *Father of the Blues: An Autobiography* (1941; New York: Da Capo, 1991) 46–47.

60. Paul Oliver, *Conversation with the Blues* (1965; London: Cassell, 1967) 35.

61. William Ferris, *Give My Poor Heart Ease: Voices of the Mississippi Blues* (Chapel Hill: U of North Carolina P, 2009) 106–8.

62. "Purpose of the Law," editorial, *Daily Clarion-Ledger* 2 Oct. 1902: 2.

63. Cutler 176.

64. "The Corinth Burning," editorial, *Daily Clarion-Ledger* 2 Oct. 1902: 4.

65. Douglas A. Blackmon, *Slavery by Another Name: The Re-enslavement of Black Americans from the Civil War to World War II* (New York: Doubleday, 2008) 4.

66. Christopher R. Adamson, "Punishment after Slavery: Southern State Penal Systems, 1865–1890," *Social Problems* 30.5 (1983): 556. States such as Mississippi also used other prison reform methods, including the "state account" method, which perpetuated the practice of selling the products produced from convict laborers on the open market.

67. Henrietta Yurchenco, "'Blues Fallin' Down like Hail': Recorded Blues, 1920s–1940s," *American Music* 13.4 (1995): 453.

68. J. H. Jones, "Penitentiary Reform in Mississippi," *Publications of the Mississippi Historical Society* 6 (1902): 115.

69. Big Bill Broonzy with Yannick Bruynoghe, *Big Bill Blues: William Broonzy's Story* (London: Cassell, 1955) 13.

70. Adamson 562.

71. Jones 128.

72. David Oshinsky, "Forced Labor in the 19th Century South: The Story of Parchman Farm," p. 10, 28 Feb. 2010, http://www.yale.edu/glc/events/cbss/Oshinsky.pdf.

73. Willie Dixon with Don Snowden, *I Am the Blues: The Willie Dixon Story* (New York: Da Capo, 1989) 26–27.

74. Edwards 35–36.

75. J. Cobb 117.

76. Edwards 35–36, 49–50.

77. Barry Lee Pearson, "'If I Couldn't Make a Quarter in a City, I Was Gone': Blues Stories of Life on the Road," *Arkansas Review: A Journal of Delta Studies* 34.3 (2003): 221.

78. Sweet Magnolia Tours, "Nuttin' but the Blues Vacation Holiday," 24 Feb. 2010, http://www.sweetmagnoliatours.com/P_FlyDrive_NuttinButBlues.php. As part of developing the Mississippi National Heritage area, the Blues Highway Association lists Parchman on its blues registry. Blues Highway Association, "Registry of Blues and Blues Heritage Sites," 24 Feb. 2010, http://www.blueshighway.org/registry.htm.

79. William Banks Taylor, *Down on Parchman Farm: The Great Prison in the Mississippi Delta* (Columbus: Ohio State UP, 1999) 21–22.

80. David M. Oshinsky, *"Worse Than Slavery": Parchman Farm and the Ordeal of Jim Crow Justice* (1996; New York: Free Press, 1997) 137.

81. Oshinsky, *Worse* 139, 155.

82. Marvin Lee Hutson, "Mississippi's State Penal System," thesis, U of Mississippi, 1939: 5.

83. As the following transcript reveals, the policy of forcing black inmates to supervise part of the prison population was a surprise to Judge Hutcheson of Texas as he questioned James F. Thames, president of Mississippi's State Prison Board, at the 1925 American Prison Association meeting. James F. Thames, "The Mississippi Prison System," *Proceedings of the 55th Annual Congress of the American Prison Association, Jackson, Mississippi, November 7th to 14th, 1925* (New York: Central Office, 1925) 83.

> *Judge Hutcheson of Texas*: We have a great many negroes like you have. Do you mean you have negro guards over those negroes?
> *Mr. Thames*: Yes.
> *Judge Hutcheson*: Negro trusties?
> *Mr. Thames*: Yes.
> *Judge Hutcheson of Texas*: And you give them the inducement if a man tries to run and he shoots him down, you will pardon him?
> *Mr. Thames*: That goes to his credit in addition to his other good conduct. (86–87)

84. William J. Farmar, *The Delta Prisons: Punishment for Profit* (Atlanta: Southern Regional Council, 1968) 3.

85. Hutson 22–23.

86. Taylor 60.

87. Ferris 85–86.

88. Thames 83.

89. Jas Obrecht, "Deep Down in the Delta: The Adventures of Son House, Willie Brown, and Friends," *Guitar Player* Aug. 1992: 68.

90. According to B. B. King, who is White's first cousin, White claimed it was an act of self-defense.

91. Quoted in David Evans, "Booker White—Part 2," *Blues Unlimited* Oct. 1966: 7.

92. Berry and Blassingame 155.

93. Ironically, the Klan's presence in the Delta was never more than minimal, especially compared to the southern region of the state, where numerous Klan organizations appeared during this period. Between 1915 and 1944, Mississippi's Klan membership (15,000) paled next to that of Indiana, the state with the largest Klan membership (240,000). See Kenneth T. Jackson, *The Ku Klux Klan in the City, 1915–1930* (New York: Oxford UP, 1967) 237.

94. J. Cobb 113.

95. "MS River Blues," Mississippi Blues Trail, 28 Feb. 2010, http://www.msbluestrail.org/_webapp_2718877/MS_River_Blues.

96. "Protective Agencies Are Massed on River," *Commercial Appeal* 14 Apr. 1927: 1.

97. "Greenville Flooded When City Levee Is Topped by Torrent," *Commercial Appeal* 22 Apr. 1927: 1.

98. John M. Barry, *Rising Tide: The Great Mississippi Flood of 1927 and How It Changed America* (New York: Simon and Schuster, 1997) 308.

99. William Alexander Percy, *Lanterns on the Levee: Recollections of a Planter's Son* (1941; New York: Alfred A. Knopf, 1966) 258.

100. J. Winston Harrington, "Work or Die of Hunger Is Dixie Order," *Chicago Defender* 4 June 1927, sec. 1: 1.

101. Barry 312.

102. J. Cobb 129.

103. "Fatal Flood," *PBS American Experience*, 1 Oct. 2006, http://www.pbs.org/wgbh/amex/flood/index.html.

104. For an excellent account of the 1927 flood and flood songs, see David Evans, "High Water Everywhere: Blues and Gospel Commentary on the 1927 Mississippi River Flood," *Nobody Knows Where the Blues Come From: Lyrics and History*, ed. Robert Springer (Jackson: UP of Mississippi, 2006) 3–75.

105. Donald Holley, *The Second Great Emancipation: The Mechanical Cotton Picker, Black Migration, and How They Shaped the Modern South* (Fayetteville: U of Arkansas P, 2000) 55.

106. Edwards 21.

107. Oakley 145–205. See also Guido van Rijn, *Roosevelt's Blues: African-American Blues and Gospel Songs on FDR* (Jackson: UP of Mississippi, 1997).

108. Reinhold Niebuhr, "Meditations from Mississippi," *Christian Century* 10 Feb. 1937: 183.

109. Sherwood Eddy, "The Delta Cooperative's First Year," *Christian Century* 3 Feb. 1937: 139.

110. "Dr. Sherwood Eddy's Co-operative Farm," Jerry Dallas Delta Cooperative Farm Collection, Manuscript 109, Delta State University Archives, Cleveland, Miss. Other sources list 31 families (19 black, 12 white). See, e.g., Jerry W. Dallas, "The Delta and Providence Farms: A Mississippi Experiment in Cooperative Farming and Racial Cooperation, 1936–1956," *Mississippi Quarterly* 40.3 (1987): 290.

111. "Some Basic Principles of the Delta Cooperative Farm," Jerry Dallas Cooperative Farm Collection, Manuscript 109, Delta State University Archives, Cleveland, Miss.

112. Dallas 302–3.

113. Dallas 305.

114. Kenneth Toler, "Smoldering 'Suspicions' Flare over Farm Project Activities," *Commercial Appeal* 1 Oct. 1955: 28; Dallas 307–8.

115. Bermanzohn 35.

116. Terry Bean, telephone interview, 23 Apr. 2008.

117. Henry B. Dorris, "Little Milton: 'The Blues Is Alright,'" *Mahogany Magazine* Feb.–Mar. 2003: 18–19.

118. T-Model Ford, "I'm Hanging; I'm Happy," interview with Margo Cooper, *Living Blues* Nov.–Dec. 2006: 13.

119. Eddie Cusic, "'Sound So Good': The Eddie Cusic Story," interview with Barry Lee Pearson, *Living Blues* Nov.–Dec. 2006: 25.

120. Sam Carr, "The Drums Got to Be Heard Just Right," interview with Margo Cooper, *Living Blues* Jan.–Feb. 2004: 18.

121. Eddie Boyd, "*Living Blues* Interview: Eddie Boyd (Part I)," interview with Jim O'Neal and Amy O'Neal, *Living Blues* Nov.–Dec. 1977: 13; James Segrest and Mark Hoffman, *Moanin' at Midnight: The Life and Times of Howlin' Wolf* (New York: Thunder's Mouth, 2005) 72.

122. Boyd 14.

123. See, e.g., B. B. King's description of sharecropping in chapter 6 in his autobiography with David Ritz, *Blues All around Me: The Autobiography of B. B. King* (New York: Avon, 1996).

124. King 59.

125. "B. B. on the Blues," *Humanities* May–June 1999: 8.

126. Barry Lee Pearson and Bill McCulloch, *Robert Johnson: Lost and Found* (Urbana: U of Illinois P, 2003) 7–9.

127. Esther Phillips, "'Baby I'm for Real': Esther Phillips," interview with Jim O'Neal and Amy O'Neal, *Living Blues* Summer 1974: 14.

128. Mississippi Slim, personal interview, 2 Dec. 2004. At the same time, "Whites Only" signs on the windows of restaurants and hotels were not a problem endemic to Mississippi, Alabama, or other southern states. As guitarist T-Bone Walker and others have confirmed in interviews, black musicians who toured outside the South experienced similar prohibitive laws associated with segregation. See T-Bone Walker, "*Living Blues* Interview: T-Bone Walker," interview with Jim O'Neal and Amy O'Neal, *Living Blues* Winter 1972–73: 20–26.

129. Bobby Rush, "Blues Music Today," Blues Today: A *Living Blues* Symposium, University of Mississippi, Oxford, Miss., 22 Feb. 2003. For a similar story, see Art Tipaldi, *Children of the Blues: 49 Musicians Shaping a New Blues Tradition* (San Francisco: Backbeat, 2002) 91.

130. Frank Ratliff, personal interview, 30 Aug. 2003.

131. Muddy Waters, "Muddy Waters," interview with Jim O'Neal and Amy van Singel. *The Voice of the Blues: Classic Interviews from Living Blues Magazine*, ed. Jim O'Neal and Amy van Singel (New York: Routledge, 2002) 164.

132. Quoted in Ray Mikell, "Singing Blues No Sweat for Eugene Powell," *Delta Democrat Times* 11 Sept. 1989: 2A.

133. Houston Stackhouse, "*Living Blues* Interview: Houston Stackhouse," Interview with Jim O'Neal, *Living Blues* Summer 1974: 22.

134. Quoted in Rick Bragg, "The Blues Is Dying in the Place It Was Born," *New York Times* 22 Apr. 2001: A26.

135. David Evans, "Charley Patton: The Conscience of the Delta," *The Voice of the Delta: Charley Patton and the Mississippi Blues Traditions; Influences and Comparisons*, ed. Robert Sacre (Liège, Belgium: Presses Universitaires Liège, 1987) 158–59.

136. Quoted in Gayle Dean Wardlow, "Ledell Johnson Remembers His Brother, Tommy . . . ," *78 Quarterly* 1.1 (1967): 65.

137. In recent years, African Americans have been returning to the South in greater numbers. For an analysis of this return migration pattern to the Yazoo-Mississippi Delta region, see Robert Norman Brown II, "Coming Home: Black Return Migration to the Yazoo-Mississippi Delta," Ph.D. diss., Louisiana State U, 2001 (Ann Arbor: UMI, 2001).

138. W. E. B. Du Bois, "The Migration of Negroes," *Crisis* June 1917: 63, 65. Historian Steven Hahn argues that African Americans, as early as the 1890s, had already established a trend of migration to the North. Steven Hahn, *A Nation under Our Feet: Black Political Struggles in the Rural South from Slavery to the Great Migration* (Cambridge: Harvard UP, 2003) 466.

139. Jack Temple Kirby, "The Southern Exodus, 1910–1960: A Primer for Historians," *Journal of Southern History* 49.4 (1983): 591.

140. James N. Gregory, *How the Great Migrations of Black and White Southerners Transformed America* (Chapel Hill: U of North Carolina P, 2005) 330.

141. Segrest and Hoffman 98.

142. Edwards 150.

143. For example, James "Son" Thomas worked various labor-intensive jobs from sharecropping to grave digging. See Ken Cazalas, "Bluesman Lives Simple Life Today," *Delta Democrat Times* 23 May 1988: 1A, 10A.

144. Kirby, 585. As Kirby's statistics suggest, whites also left the region as well (594).

145. J. Todd Moye, *Let the People Decide: Black Freedom and White Resistance Movements in Sunflower County, Mississippi, 1945–1986* (Chapel Hill: U of North Carolina P, 2004) 43.

146. Pete Daniel, *Lost Revolutions: The South in the 1950s* (Chapel Hill: U of North Carolina P, 2000) 21.

147. Moye 41.

148. Brown v. Board of Education of Topeka, Shawnee County, Kan., no. 347, Supreme Ct. of the US, 17 May 1954, 691–92. The Court argued that separating students based on race, particularly at the secondary level, "generates a feeling of inferiority," impacting "their hearts and minds in a way unlikely ever to be undone."

149. Erle Johnson, *Mississippi's Defiant Years 1953–1973: An Interpretive Documentary with Personal Experiences* (Forest, Miss.: Lake Harbor, 1990) 369.

150. Quoted in Johnson 377.

6. Public Memory, Historical Amnesia, and the Shack Up Inn

1. W. Scott Poole, "Memory," *Myth, Manners, and Memory: The New Encyclopedia of Southern Culture (Vol. 4)*, ed. Charles Reagan Wilson (Chapel Hill: U of North Carolina P, 2006) 104.

2. Stephen Frenkel and Judy Walton, "Bavarian Leavenworth and the Symbolic Economy of a Theme Town," *Geographical Review* 90.4 (2000): 559.

3. John Bodnar, *Remaking America: Public Memory, Commemoration, and Patriotism in the Twentieth Century* (Princeton: Princeton UP, 1992) 15.

4. Barbie Zelizer, "Reading the Past against the Grain: The Shape of Memory Studies," *Critical Studies in Mass Communication* 12.2 (1995): 217.

5. Edward S. Casey, "Public Memory in Place and Time," *Framing Public Memory*, ed. Kendall R. Phillips (Tuscaloosa: U of Alabama P, 2004) 17–18.

6. In this study, I use the terms "public" and "collective" memory interchangeably. Many scholars have done likewise, although some scholars, such as Casey, clearly delineate the differences among individual, social, public, and collective memory. See Casey 20–32. Meanwhile, some scholars argue that individual memory does not exist, charging that all memory is social in nature. See, e.g., Michael Schudson, "Dynamics of Distortion in Collective Memory," *Memory Distortion: How Minds, Brains, and Societies Reconstruct the Past*, ed. Daniel L. Schacter (Cambridge: Harvard UP, 1995). 346–64.

7. Casey 32–36.

8. Casey 18.

9. Kendall R. Phillips, introduction to *Framing Public Memory*, ed. Kendall R. Phillips (Tuscaloosa: U of Alabama P, 2004) 2–3.

10. Stephen H. Browne, "Reading, Rhetoric, and the Texture of Public Memory," *Quarterly Journal of Speech* 81.2 (1995): 237.

11. Zelizer 221–34.

12. Benjamin Filene, *Romancing the Folk: Public Memory and American Roots Music* (Chapel Hill: U of North Carolina P, 2000) 5.

13. Bodnar 15.

14. Bernard J. Armada, "Memorial Agon: An Interpretive Tour of the National Civil Rights Museum," *Southern Communication Journal* 63.3 (1998): 237.

15. Zelizer 214.

16. David W. Blight, "Epilogue: Southerners Don't Lie; They Just Remember Big," *Where These Memories Grow: History, Memory, and Southern Identity*, ed. W. Fitzhugh Brundage (Chapel Hill: U of North Carolina P, 2000) 349.

17. Barbara A. Biesecker, "Remembering World War II: The Rhetoric and Politics of National Commemoration at the Turn of the 21st Century," *Quarterly Journal of Speech* 88.4 (2002): 393–409.

18. Paul A. Shackel, "The Making of the American Landscape," introduction to *Myth, Memory, and the Making of the American Landscape*, ed. Paul A. Shackel (Gainesville: UP of Florida, 2001) 3.

19. Poole 104–5; Charles Reagan Wilson, *Baptized in Blood: The Religion of the Lost Cause, 1865–1920* (Athens: U of Georgia P, 1980) 1–17.

20. David W. Blight, *Race and Reunion: The Civil War in American Memory* (Cambridge: Belknap, 2001) 77.

21. Poole 105.

22. Jennifer Ritterhouse, "Reading, Intimacy, and the Role of Uncle Remus in White Southern Social Memory," *Journal of Southern History* 69.3 (2003): 589.

23. Charles W. Capps Jr., interview with Charles Bolton, 9 August 1999, Charles W. Capps Jr. Oral History, OH246, Delta State University Archives, Cleveland, Miss.

24. "Race Issues Likely to Follow Barbour," *Commercial Appeal* 13 Sept. 2010; DeSoto ed.: DSA1.

25. J. Todd Moye, *Let the People Decide: Black Freedom and White Resistance Movements in Sunflower County, Mississippi, 1945–1986* (Chapel Hill: U of North Carolina P, 2004) 105.

26. Quoted in Margaret Talev, "Barbour Recalls Rights Era Fondly," *Commercial Appeal* 13 Sept. 2010: A1–A2.

27. Quoted in Emily Wagster Pettus, "States Cling to Southern Tradition," *Commercial Appeal* 25 Apr. 2009; DeSoto ed.: DSA1, DSA5.

28. Clarksdale and Coahoma County, "The Land Where the Blues Began . . ." Clarksdale, Miss.: Coahoma County Tourism Commission, n.d.

29. "The Path Finder: A Guide to Clarksdale and Coahoma County," Clarksdale, Miss.: Sunflower River Trading Company, 1999.

30. Lorry Heverly, "The Mississippi Blues Trial, Where Legends Begin," *City Social*, July 2009, 11 July 2010, p. 24, http://www.visitclevelandms.com/city_social.pdf.

31. Clarksdale and Coahoma County.

32. "Greenville on the Mississippi," Greenville, Miss.: Washington County Convention and Visitors Bureau, n.d. [brochure 1].

33. Neal Moore, "Livin' the Blues with James 'Super Chikan' Johnson—II," CNN.com, 29 Oct. 2009, 17 Apr. 2010, http://www.ireport.com/docs/DOC-347817.

34. Coahoma County Tourism Commission, "The Blues," 10 Sept. 2010, http://www
.clarksdaletourism.com/theblues.htm.

35. "Clarksdale, Mississippi," Clarksdale, Miss.: Clarksdale Downtown Development
Association/Memphis Convention and Visitors Bureau, n.d.

36. "The Path Finder."

37. See, e.g., Michael D. Cary, "Political Dimensions of the Blues," *Popular Music and
Society* 14.2 (1990): 37–48.

38. "Cleveland: Crossroads of Culture in the Mississippi Delta," Cleveland, Miss.:
Cleveland–Bolivar County Chamber of Commerce, n.d.

39. Quoted in Barbara Wright, "Delta Blues Grew Up on Plantation," *Greenwood
Commonwealth* 25 June 1978: 10.

40. Mississippi Development Authority, Dockery Farms, 10 Sept. 2010, http://www
.visitmississippi.org/groups_marketing/Itineraries/EDTour_Delta2.pdf.

41. Ted Gioia, *Delta Blues: The Life and Times of the Mississippi Masters Who Revolutionized American Music* (New York: W. W. Norton, 2008) 46.

42. Gioia 47.

43. Keith Somerville Dockery McLean with Deborah C. Fort, *Wanderer from the Delta*
(Xlibris, 2002) 121. *Wanderer from the Delta* describes the plantation as an important social and economic structure that "bound black and white Deltans together in a complex
web and created the social structures from which the blues grew and the world which it
reflects" (18). The "complexity" of that web, and the power structure between the powerful plantation owners and the black field hands, is absent from the authors' discussion of
Mississippi's plantation culture.

44. Gioia 46–47.

45. Robert Gordon, *Can't Be Satisfied: The Life and Times of Muddy Waters* (Boston:
Little, Brown, 2002) 8.

46. Giles Oakley, *The Devil's Music: A History of the Blues*, 2nd ed. (London: Da Capo,
1997) 53.

47. Quoted in Robert Palmer, *Deep Blues: A Musical and Cultural History of the Mississippi Delta* (1981; New York: Penguin, 1982) 56.

48. Skip Henderson, telephone interview, 19 Mar. 2008.

49. Quoted in Emily Yellin, "Homage at Last for Blues Makers; Through a Fan's Crusade, Unmarked Graves Get Memorials," *New York Times* 30 Sept. 1997: E6.

50. Mississippi, Believe It!, "No Black. No White. Just the Blues," 4 Mar. 2010, http://
www.mississippibelieveit.com/ads/4COLXII/JustTheBlues4Col.pdf.

51. Paul Garon, "Speak My Mind," editorial, *Living Blues* May–June 1993: 53.

52. Greg Tate, "Nigs R Us, or How Blackfolk Became Fetish Objects," *Everything but
the Burden: What White People Are Taking from Black Culture*, ed. Greg Tate (New York:
Broadway, 2003) 14.

53. Harry Boschert, "Singing in the Field," *Life in the Delta* Sept. 2008: 15.

54. Wyatt Emmerich, "Embrace the Uniqueness of the Delta," *Delta Magazine* Sept.–
Oct. 2003: 96.

55. "Landmarks, Legends, and Lyrics: African-American Heritage Guide," Greenville,
Miss.: Greenville–Washington County Convention and Visitors Bureau, n.d.

56. "Bug's Blues Lounge," Rosedale, Miss.: n.d. In contrast to other portrayals of the
blues as being songs of infidelity, Bug mentions that self-deprecating humor is prominent

in Delta blues music. He also proudly proclaims that his club, which is dedicated to Robert Johnson, is in fact "the only remaining club from Johnson's days."

57. Quoted in "Cleveland: Crossroads of Culture." In another example, Columbus—located on the eastern part of the state—advertised its Seventh Annual Heritage Festival by remembering that African American musicians were once denied entry into white-owned hotels, as part of the state's segregation practices. See "Block by Block . . . ," advertisement, Columbus Convention and Visitors Bureau, *Bolivar Commercial Advertiser* 18 Sept. 2007: 2.

58. Shack Up Inn, advertisement, *Oxford American* Winter 2009: 17.

59. James E. Thweatt, "Hopson Plantation History," Hopson Preservation Company, 30 June 2009, http://www.hopsonplantation.com/history.html.

60. Rebecca Hood-Adams, "Group Lands $400K Grant," *Clarksdale Press Register* 30 Oct. 2001: 1.

61. Quoted in "Delta Blues Revival Draws Pilgrims to U.S. South," *Blues News* 18 Nov. 2001, 26 July 2007, http://wwshackupinn.com/press/Blues%20News%20Internation al%20News.htm.

62. Jennifer Spencer, "Shacks to Rent, $40–$60," *Commercial Appeal* 28 Oct. 2001: E7.

63. Bill Talbot, personal interview, 17 Aug. 2003.

64. Quoted in Walt Grayson, "Look around Mississippi," 9 Apr. 2004, 1 Oct. 2010, http://www.wlbt.com/Global/Story,asp?S=17757227.

65. Quoted in Becky Gillette, "Shack Up Inn Draws Visitors from around the World," *Mississippi Business Journal* 13–19 Jan. 2003: 16. The owners' initial financial investment included purchasing the shacks from local farmers, transporting the structures to the plantation, and renovating the shacks to satisfy the tourists' need for electricity and running water. For example, the owners purchased the Robert Clay shack for $600 but spent an additional $2,500 in transportation fees. Once moved to the plantation, a shack is pressure-cleaned and repaired before being made available to the public. According to Talbot, each shack represents a sizable investment, ranging from $10,000 to $20,000.

66. Following in the footsteps of the Shack Up Inn, another blues tourist attraction, Tallahatchie Flats, features six shacks located on a cotton plantation. It is located on the banks of the Tallahatchie River approximately three miles north of Greenwood, Mississippi.

67. The Shack Up Inn, 1 Oct. 2010, http://www.shackupinn/main.html.

68. The Shack Up Inn.

69. Guy Malvezzi, personal interview, 27 Sept. 2002.

70. Bill Talbot, "Interview: Bill Talbot of the Hopson Plantation in Mississippi Dis cusses His Plans to Rent out Sharecropper Shacks to Tourists," National Public Radio, Weekend Edition Saturday, 2 Dec. 2001, http://ezproxy.deltastate.edu:2128/citation. asp?tb=1&_ug=dbs+0%2C1%2C4%2C8%2C9.

71. Quoted in Shack Up Inn, flyer, n.d.

72. "Shack Up Inn—Cotton Gin Inn Receive 2009 'Keeping the Blues Alive' Award," *Clarksdale Press Register* 11 Feb. 2009: 1A.

73. Jim Auchmutey, "Shacks Are Chic in Clarksdale, the Crossroads of the Delta Blues," *Atlanta Journal-Constitution* 29 July 2001: K1.

74. Malvezzi, personal interview.

75. Quoted in Michael Rowland, "Mississippi Delta Feels the Blues," *ABC News* 31 Aug. 2007, http://abc.net.au/news/stories/2007/08/16/2006665.htm?section=world.

76. Hopson Plantation, "Hopson Plantation: The Past and the Present," n.d.

77. Shack Up Inn, "FAQ/The Shackmeister Files," 31 Jan. 2003, http://www.shack upinn.com/faq.html.

78. "Shack Up Inn Gets Honor from State," *Clarksdale Press Register* 31 July 2009: 2A.

79. Ayesha Court, "Ten Great Places to Rent a Cottage, or a Lookout," *USA Today* 12 Jan. 2007: 3D.

80. Charles Shaar Murray, "Highway 61 Revisited," *Guardian* 28 Sept. 2001: 2.

81. "Delta Blues Revival."

82. Andy Ross, "Shack Up Inn Named 'Top Place to Stay,'" *Clarksdale Press Register* 28 Mar. 2008: 1A.

83. National Geographic Traveler, "U.S.A—Central," Apr. 2008, 22 Oct. 2010, http://traveler.nationalgeographic.com/2008/04/stay-list/usa-central-text.

84. Bill Minor, "Poor Sharecropper Shacks See New Life in Delta Tourism Trade," *Clarion-Ledger* 20 Jan. 2002: 3G.

85. "Clarksdale Group Gets Grant for Arts Center," *Clarion-Ledger* 6 Mar. 2002: 4B.

86. Murray 3.

87. Nicholas Lemann, *The Promised Land: The Great Black Migration and How It Changed America* (New York: Knopf, 1991) 49.

88. Paul Oliver, *The Story of the Blues* (1969; Boston: Northeastern UP, 1998) 10.

89. Talbot, personal interview.

90. Thweatt.

91. Eddie Boyd, "*Living Blues* Interview: Eddie Boyd (Part I)," interview with Jim O'Neal and Amy O'Neal, *Living Blues* Nov.–Dec. 1977: 13.

92. James C. Cobb, *The Most Southern Place on Earth: The Mississippi Delta and the Roots of Regional Identity* (New York: Oxford UP, 1992) 105.

93. Ted Ownby, *American Dreams in Mississippi: Consumers, Poverty, and Culture 1830–1998* (Chapel Hill: U of North Carolina P, 1999) 62–63.

94. Hilliard Lackey, "Shack Up Inn Conjures Up Memories," editorial, *Clarksdale Press Register* 14 Jan. 2004: 4A.

95. The Mississippi Blues Trail honored Perkins with a blues marker on May 3, 2008. The marker is located on Highway 49 in Belzoni, Mississippi.

96. Quoted in Emily Le Coz, "Pinetop Comes Home," *Clarksdale Press Register* 3 May 2003: 1A.

97. James Butler, personal interview, 27 Sept. 2002.

98. Talbot, "Interview: Bill Talbot."

99. Quoted in Cynthia Howle, "'Hard Times' and the Blues," *Commercial Appeal* 24 Mar. 2007: M4.

100. "American Roots Music: Oral Histories," interview with B. B. King, PBS, 1 Oct. 2010, http://www.pbs.org/americanrootsmusic/pbs_arm_oralh_bbking.html.

101. David Honeyboy Edwards with Janis Martinson and Michael Robert Frank, *The World Don't Owe Me Nothing: The Life and Times of Delta Bluesman Honeyboy Edwards* (Chicago: Chicago Review, 1997) 8.

102. Jeff Todd Titon, *Early Downhome Blues: A Musical and Cultural Analysis* (Urbana: U of Illinois P, 1977) 10–11.

103. Malvezzi, personal interview.

104. It was not until the mid-1960s that the United States started to track official poverty thresholds. Originally created by Mollie Orshansky (an employee of the Social Security Administration) in 1963–64 and first published in 1965, the report on poverty

thresholds was subsequently extended back to 1959. See Linda Barrington and Gordon M. Fisher, "Poverty," *Historical Statistics of the United States: Earliest Times to the Present*, Vol. 2, Part B, ed. Susan B. Carter, Scott Sigmund Gartner, Michael R. Haines, Alan L. Olmstead, Richard Sutch, and Gavin White (New York: Cambridge UP, 2006) 625–51.

105. Tommy W. Rogers, *A Demographic Analysis of Poverty in Mississippi* (Jackson: Governor's Office of Human Resources and Community Services, 1979) 368.

106. Minor 3G.

107. Lemann 17.

108. Hopson Preservation Company, 1 Oct. 2010, http://clarksdale.com/hpc.

109. Before the shack was purchased in the late 1990s, Robert Clay worked as a farmhand near Lula, Mississippi, raising seven sons in the eight-hundred-square-foot wooden dwelling without the benefit of running water or electricity. Despite his sons' efforts to relocate their father from his shack into more comfortable housing, Clay died there in 1998.

110. Elizabeth Hoover, "Happy Hour at the Shack Up Inn," Feb. 2004, 1 Oct. 2010, http://www.americanheritage.com.

111. Erik Cohen, "Tourism as Play," *Religion* 15.3 (1985): 298.

112. Bodnar 13.

7. Assessing Tourism Goals: Money, Image, and Reconciliation

1. The first epigraph comes from Jim O'Neal, e-mail communication, Mar. 29, 2008. As O'Neal remembered the event: "In fact, I vividly remember a tourist from Australia meeting us after having dined at a downtown restaurant where he said the older white owner asked him in disbelief, 'You mean you came all that way to hear a n—— play a guitar?' Apparently that wasn't the end of the conversation, and the Australian guy was just livid and red in the face when he told us about it."

2. *Fannie Lou Hamer: Courage and Faith*, Mississippi Public Broadcasting, 20 Feb. 2006, exec. producer Linda C. Coles.

3. B. B. King, no title, *Living Blues* Mar.–June 2004: 11.

4. Quoted in Joe Klein, "The Emancipation of Bolton, Mississippi," *Esquire* Dec. 1985: 260.

5. Michael Barone and Richard E. Cohen, *The Almanac of American Politics 2008* (Washington, D.C.: National Journal Group, 2008) 931.

6. "Bennie Thompson," *Black Americans in Congress, 1870–2007* (Washington, D.C.: Government Printing Office, 2008) 736.

7. Quoted in Klein 259.

8. Morgan Freeman, "My Mississippi Delta Story," foreword to *Highway 61: Heart of the Delta*, ed. Randall Norris (Knoxville: U of Tennessee P, 2008) x.

9. Freeman, "My Mississippi" x; Morgan Freeman, no title, *Living Blues* Mar.–June 2004: 9.

10. Freeman lived in Charleston as a child as well as other locations, including Chicago. Freeman currently owns a home in Charleston.

11. Katya Wachtel, "HuffPost Review: Prom Night in Mississippi," 20 July 2009, 14 Apr. 2010, http://www.huffingtonpost.com/katya-wachtel/huffpost-review-em-prom-n_b_241066.html.

12. Becky Gillette, "Banking on the Blues: Can Blues Tourism Be the Cure?," *Delta Business Journal* July 2010: 24–27.

13. "Mississippi Sings the Blues: Music Tourism Soars in State," CNN, 19 July 2010, 25 Oct. 2010, http://www.youtube.com/watch?v=fboPTYLM_9I.

14. Mississippi Development Authority/Tourism Division, "Fiscal Year 2009 Economic Contribution of Travel and Tourism in Mississippi, February 2010," pp. 4–5, 4 Oct. 2010, http://www.visitmississippi.org/resources/FY2009_Economic_Contribution_Report_and_Cover.pdf; Mississippi Development Authority/Tourism Division, "Fiscal Year 2004 Economic Impact for Tourism in Mississippi, February 2005," pp. v–vi, 4 Oct. 2010, http://www.visitmississippi.org/press_news/docs/08_Final_Economic_Contribution_Report.pdf.

15. Jim O'Neal, telephone interview, 22 Feb. 2008.

16. Danny McKenzie, "Delta Blues Museum Spreads Tuneful Tale across the World," *Clarion-Ledger* 27 Mar. 1992: 1B.

17. Billy Johnson, telephone interview, 19 Nov. 2004.

18. Quoted in Felix Ybarra, "'A Suburb of Mississippi: Talkin' Great Migration Blues with Mississippi Trail Boss, Alex Thomas," *Big City Rhythm and Blues* Oct.–Nov. 2009: 11.

19. Bill Seratt, telephone interview, 17 June 2008.

20. Susan Dwyer, "Reconciliation for Realists," *Ethics and International Affairs* 13.1 (1999): 82.

21. See, e.g., John B. Hatch, "Beyond Apologia: Racial Reconciliation and Apologies for Slavery," *Western Journal of Communication* 70.3 (2006): 189–90; David A. Frank and Mark Lawrence McPhail, "Barack Obama's Address to the 2004 Democratic National Convention: Trauma, Compromise, Consilience, and the (Im)possibility of Racial Reconciliation," *Rhetoric and Public Affairs* 8.4 (2005): 583.

22. Hatch 190.

23. "'Toughest Job' Ably Done in Winter's Four Years," *Commercial Appeal* 8 Jan. 1984: B2.

24. Andrew P. Mullins Jr., ed., *The Measure of Our Days: Writings of William F. Winter* (Jackson, Miss.: William Winter Institute for Racial Reconciliation, UP of Mississippi, 2006) xiii–xx, 92.

25. Mullins xxviii.

26. Mullins xxxii.

27. Gwen Wright, "Mississippi Communities Build on Democracy, Inclusion, and Racial Reconciliation," *Nation's Cities Weekly* 29 Aug. 2005: 1.

28. William Winter Institute for Racial Reconciliation, Mission Statement, 1 Oct. 2009, http://www.winterinstitute.org.

29. William Winter Institute for Racial Reconciliation, Position Statement on Reconciliation, 4 Oct. 2010, http://www.winterinstitute.org/pages/position-paper.htm.

30. Larry J. Griffin, "Race, Memory, and Historical Responsibility: What Do Southerners Do with a Difficult Past?," Sammy O. Cranford Memorial Lecture in History, Delta State University, Cleveland, Miss., 21 April 2008.

31. Adam Gussow, *Journeyman's Road: Modern Blues Lives from Faulkner's Mississippi to Post-9/11 New York* (Knoxville: U of Tennessee P, 2007) 157.

32. "He's Come Home," *Delta Democrat Times* 6 June 1980: 1.

33. Kappi Allen, personal interview, 3 Feb. 2003.

34. Neal Moore, "Politics Meets the Blues with Mississippi's Bill Luckett." CNN.com, 26 Oct. 2009, 12 Apr. 2010, http://www.ireport.com/docs/DOC-346661.

35. Bill Gresham, telephone interview, 4 Feb. 2003.

36. Wanda Clark, telephone interview, 23 Apr. 2008.

37. Bill Perry, personal interview, 11 Dec. 2007.

38. James Johnson, personal interview, 7 Dec. 2004.

39. Mississippi Slim, telephone interview, 2 Dec. 2004.

40. Emanuel de Kadt, "The Encounter: Changing Values and Attitudes," *Tourism: Passport to Development?*, ed. Emanuel de Kadt (New York: Oxford UP, 1979) 51.

41. Quoted in Shelia Hardwell Byrd, "Mississippi: Can the Delta's Blues Reel in Tourists?," *USA Today* 25 Sept. 2004, 8 Oct. 2007.

42. Patricia Hill Collins, *Fighting Words: Black Women and the Search for Justice* (Minneapolis: U of Minnesota P, 1998) 281.

43. Donna J. Haraway, *Simians, Cyborgs, and Women: The Reinvention of Nature* (New York: Routledge, 1991) 183.

44. Sandra Harding, *Is Science Multicultural? Postcolonialisms, Feminisms, and Epistemologies* (Bloomington: Indiana UP, 1998) 89.

45. Karl Dach-Gruschow and Ying-yi Hong, "The Racial Divide in Response to the Aftermath of Katrina: A Boundary Condition for Common Ingroup Identity Model," *Analyses of Social Issues and Public Policy* 6.1 (2006): 128.

46. Julia T. Wood, *Communication Theories in Action* 3rd ed. (Belmont, Calif.: Wadsworth, 2004) 212.

47. Wood 216.

48. Wood 216.

49. Nancy C. M. Hartsock, "The Feminist Standpoint: Developing the Ground for a Specifically Feminist Historical Materialism," *Discovering Reality: Feminist Perspectives on Epistemology: Metaphysics, Methodology, and Philosophy of Science*, ed. Sandra Harding and Merrill B. Hintikka (Dordrecht, Holland: D. Reidel, 1983) 285.

50. "Now They're Arguing in Greenwood about Where Robert Johnson Died . . . ," *Folo*, 15 Oct. 2010, http://www.folo.us.

51. Deacon Sylvester Hoover, "Robert Johnson Trail of Blues Tour," Delta Blues Tour, 4 Oct. 2010, http://home.earthlink.net/~robertjohnsonblues/id3.html.

52. Delta Blues Legend Tour, "The Back in the Day Museum," 4 Oct. 2010, http://hoovertours.homestead.com/backinday.html.

53. Sylvester Hoover, personal interview, 18 Jan. 2008.

54. Mitchell Pacelle, "Johnson Snapshots Lead to Tug of War," *Greenwood Commonwealth* 23 Mar. 2005: 12.

55. Susan Montgomery, "Blues Historian Is Opening a Museum Full of Information and Objects Concerning Robert L. Johnson," *Greenwood Commonwealth* 2 Sept. 2001: 9A.

56. Pacelle 12.

57. Steve LaVere, personal interview, 18 Jan. 2008.

58. LaVere, personal interview.

59. Quoted in David Monroe, "Blues Promoters Spar over Charge for Tour," *Greenwood Commonwealth* 14 June 2006: 1.

60. The Hoovers' restaurant has changed names and locations over the years. The Hoovers have operated the restaurant in Baptist Town (214 Young Street) and in Greenwood's downtown area (607 Main Street).

61. Hartsock 285.

62. Charlie Smith, "LaVeres to Close Eateries, Relocate," *Greenwood Commonwealth* 1 Apr. 2010, 12 Nov. 2010, http:www.gwcommonwealth.com.

63. Beverly J. Stoeltje, "Festival," *Folklore, Cultural Performances, and Popular Entertainments: A Communications-Centered Handbook*, ed. Richard Bauman (New York: Oxford UP, 1992) 268.

64. James Steven Sauceda, "Aesthetics as a Bridge to Multicultural Understanding," *Intercultural Communication: A Reader*, ed. Larry A. Samovar and Richard E. Porter, 8th ed. (Belmont: Wadsworth, 1997) 417–18.

65. Mae Smith, personal interview, 27 Sept. 2002.

66. Nancy Kossman, personal interview, 6 Sept. 2002. Dela's Stackhouse was originally called the Stackhouse Mississippi Arts and Gifts/Delta Record Mart.

67. Donald E. Wilcock, "From the Editor's Desk," *King Biscuit Times* Oct. 1998: 7.

68. David Nelson, no title, *10th Annual Sunflower River Blues and Gospel Festival* Aug. 1997: n.p.

69. Barry Bays, personal interview, 22 Mar. 2001.

70. *The 21th Annual Sunflower River Blues and Gospel Festival* Aug. 2008: n.p.

71. The Sunflower Musicians Relief Fund, *11th Annual Sunflower River Blues and Gospel Festival* Aug. 1998: n.p.

72. "Few Understand the Legend Behind the KBBF," *14th Annual King Biscuit Blues Festival* Oct. 1999: 10.

73. Quoted in Michael Richardson, "Helena, Arkansas: First Big City of the Blues," *Big City Blues* Dec. 1999/Jan. 2000: 18.

74. Rebecca Hood-Adams, "Concert to Benefit Burned Musician," *Clarion-Ledger* 16 Feb. 1987: 1B.

75. For example, the mission of the Leland Blues Project, according to the 2002 Highway 61 Blues Festival program, is to "honor the mid-Mississippi Delta Bluesmen and to educate the public on their contribution to the music." See "Leland Blues Project," *3rd Annual Highway 61 Blues Festival* June 2002: n.p. At the 2008 Leland festival, organizers celebrated the musicianship of David "Honeyboy" Edward, who at ninety-two performed a bracing set of traditional down-home blues.

76. "Four Nominated for Early Wright Blues Heritage Award," *Comin' Home for the 17th Sunflower River Blues and Gospel Festival* Aug. 2004: 8.

77. Fiat Lux, "Not from Around Here, Are Ya?," *8th Annual Sunflower River Blues and Gospel Festival* Aug. 1995: n.p.

78. Stoeltje 268.

79. Rebecca Brandt, "Iowa Visitor Not Impressed with Still Segregated Society," letter, *Clarksdale Press Register* 20 Jan. 2004: 4A.

80. James Johnson, personal interview.

81. Perry, personal interview.

82. Peggy McIntosh compares white privilege to an "invisible weightless knapsack of special provisions, maps, passports, codebooks, visas, clothes, tools and blank checks." For example, McIntosh lists twenty-six *unearned* privileges she possesses as a white woman that are not automatically granted to minorities, from being able to move into a neighborhood without the fear of violent reprisal to finding bandages that match her skin. See Peggy McIntosh, "White Privilege: Unpacking the Invisible Knapsack," *Race, Class, and Gender in the United States: An Integrated Study*, ed. Paula S. Rothenberg, 4th ed. (New York: St. Martin's, 1998) 165–69.

As scholars have pointed out, whiteness maintains its hegemony because it has assumed the character of objectivity and neutrality, projecting the standard by which all other groups are judged. Because racial privilege is conferred, made invisible, often unrecognized and even denied, "privilege is rarely seen by the holder of the privilege." See Stephanie M. Wildman with Adrienne D. Davis, "Making Systems of Privilege Visible," *Critical White Studies: Looking behind the Mirror*, ed. Richard Delgado and Jean Stefancic (Philadelphia: Temple UP, 1997): 316.

83. John Sherman, personal interview, 26 Oct. 2007.

84. Quoted in Terry Williams and Wesley Jefferson, "They Jukin' Hard: A Conversation with Big T. Williams and Wesley Junebug Jefferson," interview with Mark Coltrain, *Living Blues* Apr. 2008: 34.

85. Patty Johnson, telephone interview, 29 Apr. 2008.

86. Mickey Rogers, personal interview, 10 June 2003.

87. Mississippi Slim, telephone interview, 2 Dec. 2004.

88. Barbara Looney, personal interview, 10 Mar. 2003.

89. Terry Bean, telephone interview, 23 Apr. 2008.

90. Perry, personal interview.

91. James Johnson, personal interview.

92. Neal Moore, "Livin' the Blues with James 'Super Chikan' Johnson—I," CNN.com 29 Oct. 2009, 12 Apr. 2010, http://www.ireport.com/docs/DOC-347855.

93. Ken Cazalas, "Bluesman Lives Simple Life Today," *Delta Democrat Times* 23 May 1988: 1A.

94. Jay Kirgis, personal interview, 18 Nov. 2004.

95. David Evans, reader's report, July 2010.

96. Robert Jr. Lockwood, "*Living Blues* Interview: Robert Jr. Lockwood," interview with William Cummerow, *Living Blues* Spring 1973: 18.

97. Sade Turnipseed, personal interview, 21 Sept. 2007.

98. Robert Nicholson, *Mississippi: The Blues Today!* (New York: Da Capo, 1998) 58–61.

99. When I arrived for the interview, Ford was not at home. Subsequent efforts to reschedule the interview were unsuccessful.

100. *You See Me Laughin': The Last of the Hill Country Bluesmen*, dir. and prod. Mandy Stein (Plain Jane Productions/Fat Possum, 2003/5).

101. Kirgis, personal interview.

102. Quoted in J. Peder Zane, "From the Heart of Blues Country," *New York Times* 22 Jan. 1995, sec. 2: 30.

103. Sherman, personal interview.

104. Billy Johnson, telephone interview.

105. Scott Barretta, telephone interview, 28 Feb. 2008.

106. Gussow 156.

107. Alan W. Barton, *Attitudes about Heritage Tourism in the Mississippi Delta: A Policy Report from the 2005 Delta Rural Poll*, Policy Paper No. 05-02 (Delta State University: Center for Community and Economic Development, 2005) 22.

108. Skip Henderson, telephone interview, 19 Mar. 2008.

109. Quoted in Cynthia Howle, "Juke Joint Weekend," *Commercial Appeal* 10 Apr. 2007: M1.

110. Cheryl Line, personal interview, 10 May 2001.

111. Seratt, telephone interview.

112. Gresham, telephone interview.

113. Richard West and Lynn H. Turner, *Introducing Communication Theory: Analysis and Application*, 4th ed. (Boston: McGraw-Hill, 2010) 507.

114. Mullins 98.

BIBLIOGRAPHY

Books

Adams, Samuel C., Jr. "Changing Negro Life in the Delta." *Lost Delta Found: Rediscovering the Fisk University–Library of Congress Coahoma County Study, 1941–1942*. Ed. Robert Gordon and Bruce Nemerov. Nashville: Vanderbilt UP, 2005. 225–74.

Atkins, E. Taylor. *Blue Nippon: Authenticating Jazz in Japan*. Durham: Duke UP, 2001.

Baraka, Amiri (LeRoi Jones). "Blues People: *Looking* Both Ways." Introduction. *Blues People: Negro Music in White America*. 1999. By Baraka. New York: Harper-Perennial, 2002. vii–xii.

Barker, Hugh, and Yuval Taylor. *Faking It: The Quest for Authenticity in Popular Music*. New York: W. W. Norton, 2007.

Barker, Martin, and Roger Sabin. *The Lasting of the Mohicans: History of an American Myth*. Jackson: UP of Mississippi, 1995.

Barlow, William. *Voice Over: The Making of Black Radio*. Philadelphia: Temple UP, 1999.

Barone, Michael, and Richard E. Cohen. *The Almanac of American Politics 2008*. Washington, D.C.: National Journal Group, 2008.

Barry, John M. *Rising Tide: The Great Mississippi Flood of 1927 and How It Changed America*. New York: Simon and Schuster, 1997.

Barthes, Roland. *Mythologies*. Trans. Annette Lavers, 1957. New York: Noonday, 1972.

"Bennie Thompson." *Black Americans in Congress, 1870–2007*. Washington, D.C.: Government Printing Office, 2008. 736–37.

Berry, Mary Frances, and John W. Blassingame. *Long Memory: The Black Experience in America*. New York: Oxford UP, 1982.

Blackmon, Douglas A. *Slavery by Another Name: The Re-enslavement of Black Americans from the Civil War to World War II*. New York: Doubleday, 2008.

Blight, David W. *Race and Reunion: The Civil War in American Memory*. Cambridge: Belknap, 2001.

———. "Epilogue: Southerners Don't Lie; They Just Remember Big." *Where These Memories Grow: History, Memory, and Southern Identity*. Ed. W. Fitzhugh Brundage. Chapel Hill: U of North Carolina P, 2000. 347–53.

Bodnar, John. *Remaking America: Public Memory, Commemoration, and Patriotism in the Twentieth Century*. Princeton: Princeton UP, 1992.

Boorstin, Daniel J. *The Image: A Guide to Pseudo-events in America*. 1961. New York: Harper Colophon, 1964.

Brooks, Tim. *Lost Sounds: Blacks and the Birth of the Recording Industry, 1980–1919*. Urbana: U of Illinois P, 2004.

Broonzy, Big Bill, with Yannick Bruynoghe. *Big Bill Blues: William Broonzy's Story*. London: Cassell, 1955.

Calt, Stephen. *I'd Rather Be the Devil: Skip James and the Blues*. Chicago: Chicago Review, 1994.

Campbell, Joseph. *Myths to Live By*. New York: Viking, 1972.

———, with Bill D. Moyers. *The Power of Myth*. New York: Doubleday, 1988.

Cantor, Louis. *Wheelin' on Beale: How WDIA-Memphis Became the Nation's First All-Black Radio Station and Created the Sound That Changed America*. New York: Pharos, 1992.

Carlin, Richard. "Handy, W. C." *American National Biography*. Ed. John A. Garraty and Mark C. Carnes. Vol. 10. New York: Oxford UP, 1999. 4–5.

Casey, Edward S. "Public Memory in Place and Time." *Framing Public Memory*. Ed. Kendall R. Phillips. Tuscaloosa: U of Alabama P, 2004. 17–44.

Charters, Samuel. Preface. *The Country Blues*. 1959. By Charters. New York: Da Capo, 1975.

———. *The Roots of the Blues: An African Search*. Boston: Marion Boyars, 1981.

———. *Walking a Blues Road: A Blues Reader, 1956–2004*. New York: Marion Boyars, 2004.

———. "Workin' on the Building: Roots and Influences." *Nothing but the Blues: The Music and the Musicians*. Ed. Lawrence Cohn. New York: Abbeville, 1993. 13–31.

Cheseborough, Steve. *Blues Traveling: The Holy Sites of Delta Blues*. 2nd ed. Jackson: UP of Mississippi, 2004.

———. *Blues Traveling: The Holy Sites of Delta Blues*. 3rd ed. Jackson: UP of Mississippi, 2008.

Clynes, Tom. *Music Festivals: From Bach to Blues*. Detroit: Visible Ink, 1996.

Cobb, James C. *The Most Southern Place on Earth: The Mississippi Delta and the Roots of Regional Identity*. New York: Oxford UP, 1992.

Cohen, Rich. *The Record Men: The Chess Brothers and the Birth of Rock & Roll*. New York: W. W. Norton, 2004.

Cohn, David L. *Where I Was Born and Raised*. Boston: Houghton Mifflin, 1935/1948.

Coleman, Mark. "The Blues Brothers." *Rolling Stone Album Guide*. Ed. Anthony DeCurtis and James Henke with Holly George-Warren. New York: Random House, 1992. 70–71.

Collins, Patricia Hill. *Fighting Words: Black Women and the Search for Justice*. Minneapolis: U of Minnesota P, 1998.

Cowley, John. "West Indies Blues: An Historical Overview, 1920–1950s; Blues and Music from the English-Speaking West Indies." *Nobody Knows Where the Blues Come From: Lyrics and History*. Ed. Robert Springer. Jackson: UP of Mississippi, 2006. 187–263.

Craik, Jennifer. "The Culture of Tourism." *Touring Cultures: Transformations of Travel and Theory*. Ed. Chris Rojek and John Urry. London: Routledge, 1997. 113–36.

Cutler, James Elbert. *Lynch-Law: An Investigation into the History of Lynching in the United States*. London: Longmans, Green, 1905.

Daniel, Pete. *Lost Revolutions: The South in the 1950s*. Chapel Hill: U of North Carolina P, 2000.

Davis, Francis. *The History of the Blues: The Roots, the Music, the People from Charley Patton to Robert Cray*. New York: Hyperion, 1995.

de Kadt, Emanuel. "The Encounter: Changing Values and Attitudes." *Tourism: Passport to Development?* Ed. Emanuel de Kadt. New York: Oxford UP, 1979. 50–67.

Dickson, Harris. *The Story of King Cotton*. New York: Funk and Wagnalls, 1937.

Dixon, Robert M. W., and John Godrich. *Recording the Blues*. London: Studio Vista, 1970. In Oliver, Paul, Tony Russell, Robert M. W. Dixon, John Godrich, and Howard Rye. *Yonder Come the Blues: The Evolution of a Genre*. Cambridge: Cambridge UP, 2001. 243–329.

Dixon, Willie, with Don Snowden. *I Am the Blues: The Willie Dixon Story*. New York: Da Capo, 1989.

Doty, William G. *Myth: A Handbook*. Tuscaloosa: U of Alabama P, 2004.

———. *Mythography: The Study of Myths and Rituals*. Tuscaloosa: U of Alabama P, 1986.

Downs, Tom. *Lonely Planet Road Trip: Blues and BBQ*. Australia: Lonely Planet, 2005.

Du Bois, W. E. B. *Black Reconstruction in America: An Essay toward a History of the Part Which Black Folk Played in the Attempt to Reconstruct Democracy in America, 1860–1880*. 1935. New York: Atheneum, 1975.

———. "The Black Codes." *Race, Class, and Gender in the United States: An Integrated Study*. Ed. Paula S. Rothenberg. 4th ed. New York: St. Martin's, 1998. 408–16.

Edwards, David Honeyboy, with Janis Martinson and Michael Robert Frank. *The World Don't Owe Me Nothing: The Life and Times of Delta Bluesman Honeyboy Edwards*. Chicago: Chicago Review, 1997.

Evans, David. "African Elements in the Blues." *L'Oceano dei Suoni: Migrazioni, Musica e Razze nella Formazione delle Societa Euroatlantiche*. Ed. Pierangelo Castagneto. Torino: Otto Editore. 3–16.

———. *Big Road Blues: Tradition and Creativity in the Folk Blues*. Berkeley: U of California P, 1982.

———. "The Birth of the Blues." *American Roots Music*. Ed. Robert Santelli, Holly George-Warren, and Jim Brown. New York: Abrams, 2001. 34–55.

———. "Charley Patton: The Conscience of the Delta." *The Voice of the Delta: Charley Patton and the Mississippi Blues Traditions; Influences and Comparisons*. Ed. Robert Sacre. Liège, Belgium: Presses Universitaires Liège, 1987. 111–214.

———. "Goin' Up the Country: Blues in Texas and the Deep South." *Nothing but the Blues: The Music and the Musicians*. Ed. Lawrence Cohn. New York: Abbeville, 1993. 33–85.

———. "High Water Everywhere: Blues and Gospel Commentary on the 1927 Mississippi River Flood." *Nobody Knows Where the Blues Come From: Lyrics and History*. Ed. Robert Springer. Jackson: UP of Mississippi, 2006. 3–75.

———. *The NPR Curious Listener's Guide to Blues*. New York: Perigee, 2005.

Farmar, William J. *The Delta Prisons: Punishment for Profit*. Atlanta: Southern Regional Council, 1968.

The Federal Writers' Project, 1936–38. *Mississippi Slave Narratives: A Folk History of Slavery in Mississippi from Interviews with Former Slaves*. Bedford, Mass.: Applewood, n.d.

Ferris, William. *Give My Poor Heart Ease: Voices of the Mississippi Blues*. Chapel Hill: U of North Carolina P, 2009.

Filene, Benjamin. *Romancing the Folk: Public Memory and American Roots Music*. Chapel Hill: U of North Carolina P, 2000.

Finn, Julio. *The Bluesman: The Musical Heritage of Black Men and Women in the Americas*. New York: Interlink, 1991.

Fisher, Walter R. *Human Communication as Narration: Toward a Philosophy of Reason, Value, and Action*. Columbia: U of South Carolina P, 1987.

Foner, Eric. *Reconstruction: America's Unfinished Revolution, 1863–1877.* New York: Harper and Row, 1988.

Freeman, Morgan. "My Mississippi Delta Story." Foreword. *Highway 61: Heart of the Delta.* Ed. Randall Norris. Knoxville: U of Tennessee P, 2008. ix–xii.

Gage, Melissa, and Justin Gage. *Memphis and the Delta Blues Trail.* Woodstock, Vt.: Countryman, 2009.

Gates, Henry Louis, Jr. *The Signifying Monkey: A Theory of Afro-American Literary Criticism.* New York: Oxford UP, 1988.

George, Nelson. *The Death of Rhythm and Blues.* 1988. New York: Penguin, 2004.

Gibson, Chris, and John Connell. *Music and Tourism: On the Road Again.* Clevedon, Eng.: Channel View, 2005.

Gillett, Charlie. *The Sound of the City: The Rise of Rock and Roll.* New York: Outerbridge and Dienstfrey, 1970.

Gioia, Ted. *Delta Blues: The Life and Times of the Mississippi Masters Who Revolutionized American Music.* New York: W. W. Norton, 2008.

Gordon, Robert. *Can't Be Satisfied: The Life and Times of Muddy Waters.* Boston: Little, Brown, 2002.

———. *It Came from Memphis.* New York: Pocket, 1995.

Gray, William F. "Reconstruction." *Imperial Bolivar.* Ed. William Gray. Cleveland, Miss.: n.p., 1923. 14–16.

Grazian, David. *Blue Chicago: The Search for Authenticity in Urban Blues Clubs.* Chicago: U of Chicago P, 2003.

Gregory, James N. *The Southern Diaspora: How the Great Migrations of Black and White Southerners Transformed America.* Chapel Hill: U of North Carolina P, 2005.

Groom, Bob. *The Blues Revival.* London: Studio Vista, 1971.

Gussow, Adam. *Journeyman's Road: Modern Blues Lives from Faulkner's Mississippi to Post-9/11 New York.* Knoxville: U Tennessee P, 2007.

———. *Seems like Murder Here: Southern Violence and the Blues Tradition.* Chicago: U of Chicago P, 2002.

Hahn, Steven. *A Nation under Our Feet: Black Political Struggles in the Rural South from Slavery to the Great Migration.* Cambridge: Harvard UP, 2003.

Hamilton, Marybeth. *In Search of the Blues.* New York: Basic, 2008.

Handy, W. C. *Father of the Blues: An Autobiography.* 1941. New York: Da Capo, 1991.

Haraway, Donna J. *Simians, Cyborgs, and Women: The Reinvention of Nature.* New York: Routledge, 1991.

Harding, Sandra. *Is Science Multicultural? Postcolonialisms, Feminisms, and Epistemologies.* Bloomington: Indiana UP, 1998.

Hartsock, Nancy C. M. "The Feminist Standpoint: Developing the Ground for a Specifically Feminist Historical Materialism." *Discovering Reality: Feminist Perspectives on Epistemology, Metaphysics, Methodology, and Philosophy of Science.* Ed. Sandra Harding and Merrill B. Hintikka. Dordrecht, Holland: D. Reidel, 1983. 283–310.

Holley, Donald. *The Second Great Emancipation: The Mechanical Cotton Picker, Black Migration, and How They Shaped the Modern South.* Fayetteville: U of Arkansas P, 2000.

Hooker, John Lee. Foreword. Paul Trynka. *Portrait of the Blues.* 1996. New York: Da Capo, 1997. 7.

Hunter, Lloyd A. "The Immortal Confederacy: Another Look at Lost Cause Religion." *The Myth of the Lost Cause and Civil War History.* Ed. Gary W. Gallagher and Alan T. Nolan. Bloomington: Indiana UP, 2000. 185–218.

Jackson, Broadus B. *Civil War and Reconstruction in Mississippi: Mirror of Democracy in America*. Jackson, Miss.: Town Square, 1998.

Jackson, Kenneth T. *The Ku Klux Klan in the City, 1915–1930*. New York: Oxford UP, 1967.

Jagger, Mick. "Mick Jagger." Interview with Jonathan Cott. *The Rolling Stone Interviews: Talking with the Legends of Rock and Roll, 1967–1980*. Ed. Peter Herbst. New York: St. Martin's/Rolling Stone, 1981. 44–50.

Jewett, Clayton E., and John O. Allen. *Slavery in the South: A State-by-State History*. Westport, Conn.: Greenwood, 2004.

Johnson, Erle. *Mississippi's Defiant Years 1953–1973: An Interpretive Documentary with Personal Experiences*. Forest, Miss.: Lake Harbor, 1990.

Johnson, Patricia. No title. *Highway 61: Heart of the Delta*. Ed. Randall Norris. Knoxville: U of Tennessee P, 2008. 52–56.

Jones, LeRoi (Amiri Baraka). *Blues People: Negro Music in White America*. 1963. New York: Harper Perennial, 2002.

Karenga, Maulana. "Black Art: Mute Matter Given Force and Function." *The Norton Anthology of African American Literature*. Ed. Henry Louis Gates Jr. and Nellie Y. McKay. New York: W. W. Norton, 1997. 1972–77.

Keil, Charles. *Urban Blues*. Chicago: U of Chicago P, 1966.

King B. B. with David Ritz. *Blues All around Me: The Autobiography of B.B. King*. New York: Avon, 1996.

Komara, Edward. "Blues." *Encyclopedia of the Blues*. Ed. Edward Komara. Vol. 1. New York: Routledge, 2006. 105–29.

Kubik, Gerhard. *Africa and the Blues*. Jackson: UP of Mississippi, 2008.

Lemann, Nicholas. *The Promised Land: The Great Black Migration and How It Changed America*. New York: Knopf, 1991.

Lieb, Sandra R. *Mother of the Blues: A Study of Ma Rainey*. Amherst: U of Massachusetts P, 1981.

Loewen, James W. et. al., *Mississippi: Conflict and Change*. Ed. James W. Loewen and Charles Sallis. Rev. ed. New York: Pantheon, 1980.

Lomax, Alan. *The Land Where the Blues Began*. 1993. New York: New Press, 2002.

McGee, David. "Robert Johnson." *Rolling Stone Album Guide*. Ed. Anthony DeCurtis and James Henke with Holly George-Warren. New York: Random, 1992. 376–77.

McIntosh, Peggy. "White Privilege: Unpacking the Invisible Knapsack." *Race, Class, and Gender in the United States: An Integrated Study*. Ed. Paula S. Rothenberg. 4th ed. New York: St. Martin's, 1998. 165–69.

McLean, Keith Somerville Dockery, with Deborah C. Fort. *Wanderer from the Delta*. Xlibris, 2002.

Moore, Robert B. "Racism in the English Language." *Race, Class, and Gender in the United States: An Integrated Study*. 4th ed. Ed. Paula S. Rothenberg. New York: St. Martin's, 1998. 465–75.

Morgan, Kathleen O'Leary, and Scott Morgan, eds. *State Rankings 2008: A Statistical View of America*. Washington, D.C.: CQ Press, 2008.

———. *State Rankings 2009: A Statistical View of America*. Washington, D.C.: CQ Press, 2009.

Moye, Todd J. *Let the People Decide: Black Freedom and White Resistance Movements in Sunflower County, Mississippi, 1945–1986*. Chapel Hill: U of North Carolina P, 2004.

Muir, Peter C. *Long Lost Blues: Popular Blues in America, 1850–1920*. Urbana: U of Illinois P, 2010.

Mullins, Andrew P., Jr., ed. *The Measure of Our Days: Writings of William F. Winter.* Jackson, Miss.: William Winter Institute for Racial Reconciliation/UP of Mississippi, 2006.

Nager, Larry. *Memphis Beat: The Lives and Times of America's Musical Crossroads.* New York: St. Martin's, 1998.

Nardone, Jennifer. "Juke Joints." *Encyclopedia of the Blues.* Ed. Edward Komara. Vol. 1. New York: Routledge, 2006. 552–55.

———. "Roomful of Blues: Jukejoints and the Cultural Landscape of the Mississippi Delta." *Constructing Image, Identity, and Place: Perspectives in Vernacular Architecture.* Ed. Alison K. Hoagland and Kenneth A. Breisch. Knoxville: U of Tennessee P, 2003. 166–75.

Neal, Larry. "The Black Arts Movement." *The Norton Anthology of African American Literature.* Ed. Henry Louis Gates Jr. and Nellie Y. McKay. New York: W. W. Norton, 1997. 1960–72.

Nicholson, Robert. *Mississippi: The Blues Today!* New York: Da Capo, 1998.

Oakley, Giles. *The Devil's Music: A History of the Blues.* 2nd ed. London: Da Capo, 1997.

Oliver, Paul. "Blues." *The New Grove Dictionary of Music and Musicians.* Ed. Stanley Sadie. 2nd ed. Vol. 3. London: Macmillan, 2001. 730–37.

———. *Blues Fell This Morning: Meaning in the Blues.* 2nd ed. Cambridge: Cambridge UP, 1990.

———. *Conversation with the Blues.* 1965. London: Cassell, 1967.

———. *Savannah Syncopators: African Retentions in the Blues.* London: Studio Vista, 1970. In Oliver, Paul, Tony Russell, Robert M. W. Dixon, John Godrich, and Howard Rye, *Yonder Come the Blues: The Evolution of a Genre.* Cambridge, Eng.: Cambridge UP, 2001. 11–112.

———. *The Story of the Blues.* 1969. Boston: Northeastern UP, 1998.

O'Neal, Jim. *Delta Blues Map Kit.* Kansas City, Mo.: BluEsoterica, 2004.

———. "I Once Was Lost, but Now I'm Found: The Blues Revival of the 1960s." *Nothing but the Blues: The Music and the Musicians.* Ed. Lawrence Cohn. New York: Abbeville, 1993. 347–87.

Oshinsky, David M. *"Worse than Slavery": Parchman Farm and the Ordeal of Jim Crow Justice.* 1996. New York: Free Press, 1997.

Ownby, Ted. *American Dreams in Mississippi: Consumers, Poverty, and Culture 1830–1998.* Chapel Hill: U of North Carolina P, 1999.

Palmer, Robert. "Black Snake Moan: The History of Texas Blues." *Blues and Chaos: The Music Writing of Robert Palmer.* Ed. Anthony DeCurtis. New York: Scribner, 2009. 53–59.

———. *Deep Blues: A Musical and Cultural History of the Mississippi Delta.* 1981. New York: Penguin, 1982.

Pearson, Barry Lee. "Wasn't Only My Songs, They Got My Music Too." *Write Me a Few of Your Lines: A Blues Reader.* Ed. Steven C. Tracy. Amherst: U of Massachusetts P, 1999. 377–81.

———, and Bill McCulloch. *Robert Johnson: Lost and Found.* Urbana: U of Illinois P, 2003.

Percy, William Alexander. *Lanterns on the Levee: Recollection of a Planter's Son.* 1941. New York: Alfred A. Knopf, 1966.

Peterson, Richard A. *Creating Country Music: Fabricating Authenticity.* Chicago: U of Chicago P, 1997.

Phillips, Kendall R. Introduction to *Framing Public Memory*. Ed. Kendall R. Phillips. Tuscaloosa: U of Alabama P, 2004. 1–14.

Poole, W. Scott. "Memory." *Myth, Manners, and Memory: The New Encyclopedia of Southern Culture (Vol. 4)*. Ed. Charles Reagan Wilson. Chapel Hill: U of North Carolina P, 2006. 104–7.

Richards, Keith, with James Fox. *Life*. New York: Little, 2010.

Rogers, Tommy W. *A Demographic Analysis of Poverty in Mississippi*. Jackson: Governor's Office of Human Resources and Community Services, 1979.

Rotella, Carlo. *Good with Their Hands: Boxers, Bluesmen, and Other Characters from the Rust Belt*. Berkeley: U of California P, 2002.

Russell, Tony. *Blacks, Whites and Blues*. London: Studio Vista, 1970. In Oliver, Paul, Tony Russell, Robert M. W. Dixon, John Godrich, and Howard Rye, *Yonder Come the Blues: The Evolution of a Genre*. Cambridge: Cambridge UP, 2001. 143–242.

Sanjek, David. "Marketing." *Encyclopedia of the Blues*. Ed. Edward Komara. Vol. 2. New York: Routledge, 2006. 654–58.

Sauceda, James Steven. "Aesthetics as a Bridge to Multicultural Understanding." *Intercultural Communication: A Reader*. Ed. Larry A. Samovar and Richard E. Porter. 8th ed. Belmont: Wadsworth, 1997. 417–26.

Schroeder, Patricia R. *Robert Johnson, Mythmaking, and Contemporary American Culture*. Urbana: U of Illinois P, 2004.

Schudson, Michael. "Dynamics of Distortion in Collective Memory." *Memory Distortion: How Minds, Brains, and Societies Reconstruct the Past*. Ed. Daniel L. Schacter. Cambridge: Harvard UP, 1995. 346–64.

Schwartz, Roberta Freund. *How Britain Got the Blues: The Transmission and Reception of American Blues Style in the United Kingdom*. London: Ashgate, 2007.

Segrest, James, and Mark Hoffman. *Moanin' at Midnight: The Life and Times of Howlin' Wolf*. New York: Thunder's Mouth, 2005.

Shackel, Paul A. "The Making of the American Landscape." Introduction. *Myth, Memory, and the Making of the American Landscape*. Ed. Paul A. Shackel. Gainesville: UP of Florida, 2001. 1–16.

Sillars, Malcolm O., and Bruce E. Gronbeck. *Communication Criticism: Rhetoric, Social Codes, Cultural Studies*. Prospect Heights, Ill.: Waveland, 2001.

Sillers, Walter, Sr. "Historical." *Imperial Bolivar*. Ed. William F. Gray. Cleveland, Miss.: n.p., 1923. 7–10.

Spencer, Jon Michael. *Blues and Evil*. Knoxville: U of Tennessee P, 1993.

Starr, Larry, and Christopher Waterman. *American Popular Music: From Minstrelsy to MTV*. New York: Oxford UP, 2003.

Stoeltje, Beverly J. "Festival." *Folklore, Cultural Performances, and Popular Entertainments: A Communications-Centered Handbook*. Ed. Richard Bauman. New York: Oxford UP, 1992. 261–71.

Tate, Greg. "Nigs R Us, or How Blackfolk Became Fetish Objects." *Everything but the Burden: What White People Are Taking from Black Culture*. Ed. Greg Tate. New York: Broadway, 2003. 1–14.

Taylor, William Banks. *Down on Parchman Farm: The Great Prison in the Mississippi Delta*. Columbus: Ohio State UP, 1999.

Thamas, James F. "The Mississippi Prison System." *Proceedings of the 55th Annual Congress of the American Prison Association, Jackson, Mississippi, November 7th to 14th, 1925*. New York: Central Office, 1925. 77–90.

Theroux, Paul. *Dark Star Safari: Overland from Cairo to Cape Town*. Boston: Houghton Mifflin, 2003.

Tipaldi, Art. *Children of the Blues: 49 Musicians Shaping a New Blues Tradition*. San Francisco: Backbeat, 2002.

Titon, Jeff Todd. *Early Downhome Blues: A Musical and Cultural Analysis*. Urbana: U of Illinois P, 1977.

———. "Reconstructing the Blues: Reflections on the 1960s Blues Revival." *Transforming Tradition: Folk Music Revivals Examined*. Ed. Neil V. Rosenberg. Urbana: U of Illinois P, 1993. 220–40.

Tracy, Steven C. Introduction. *Write Me a Few of Your Lines: A Blues Reader*. Ed. Steven C. Tracy. Amherst: U of Massachusetts P, 1999. 1–7.

van Rijn, Guido. *Roosevelt's Blues: African-American Blues and Gospel Songs on FDR*. Jackson: UP of Mississippi, 1997.

Wald, Elijah. *Escaping the Delta: Robert Johnson and the Invention of the Blues*. New York: Harper Collins, 2004.

Walton, Anthony. *Mississippi: An American Journey*. New York: Vintage, 1996.

Walton, Ortiz M. *Music: Black, White, and Blue: A Sociological Survey of the Use and Misuse of Afro-American Music*. New York: William Morrow, 1972.

Ward, Brian. *Just My Soul Responding: Rhythm and Blues, Black Consciousness, and Race Relations*. Berkeley: U of California P, 1998.

Wardlow, Gayle Dean. *Chasin' That Devil Music: Searching for the Blues*. Ed. Edward Komara. San Francisco: Backbeat, 1998.

Waters, Muddy. "Muddy Waters." Interview with Jim O'Neal and Amy van Singel. *The Voice of the Blues: Classic Interviews from Living Blues Magazine*. Ed. Jim O'Neal and Amy van Singel. New York: Routledge, 2002. 155–201.

West, Richard, and Lynn H. Turner. *Introducing Communication Theory: Analysis and Application*. 4th ed. Boston: McGraw-Hill, 2010.

Whitfield, Stephen J. *A Death in the Delta: The Story of Emmett Till*. New York: Free Press, 1988.

Wildman, Stephanie M., with Adrienne D. Davis. "Making Systems of Privilege Visible. *Critical White Studies: Looking behind the Mirror*. Ed. Richard Delgado and Jean Stefancic. Philadelphia: Temple UP, 1997. 314–19.

Willis, John C. *Forgotten Time: The Yazoo-Mississippi Delta after the Civil War*. Charlottesville: UP of Virginia, 2000.

Wilson, Charles Reagan. *Baptized in Blood: The Religion of the Lost Cause, 1865–1920*. Athens: U of Georgia P, 1980.

Wilson, Christine. *All Shook Up: Mississippi Roots of American Popular Music*. Jackson: Mississippi Department of Archives and History, 1995.

Wolfe, Charles. "A Lighter Shade of Blue: White Country Blues." *Nothing but the Blues: The Music and the Musicians*. Ed. Lawrence Cohn. New York: Abbeville, 1993. 233–63.

Wood, Julia T. *Communication Theories in Action*. 3rd ed. Belmont, Calif.: Wadsworth, 2004.

Woods, Clyde. *Development Arrested: The Blues and Plantation Power in the Mississippi Delta*. London: Verso, 1998.

X, Malcolm, with Alex Haley. *The Autobiography of Malcolm X*. 1965. New York: Ballantine, 1990.

Journals

Abbott, Lynn, and Doug Seroff. "'They Cert'ly Sound Good to Me': Sheet Music, Southern Vaudeville, and the Commercial Ascendancy of the Blues." *American Music* 14.4 (1996): 402–54.

Adams, Samuel C., Jr. "The Acculturation of the Delta Negro." *Social Forces* 26 (1947): 202–5.

Adamson, Christopher R. "Punishment after Slavery: Southern State Penal Systems, 1865–1890." *Social Problems* 30.5 (1983): 555–69.

Adelt, Ulrich. "Trying to Find an Identity: Eric Clapton's Changing Conception of 'Blackness.'" *Popular Music and Society* 31.4 (2008): 433–52.

Armada, Bernard J. "Memorial Agon: An Interpretive Tour of the National Civil Rights Museum." *Southern Communication Journal* 63.3 (1998): 235–43.

Armstrong, Edward G. "Eminem's Construction of Authenticity." *Popular Music and Society* 27.3 (2004): 335–55.

Auslander, Philip. "Seeing Is Believing: Live Performance and the Discourse of Authenticity in Rock Culture." *Literature and Psychology* 44.4 (1998): 1–26.

Barlow, William. "'Fattening Frogs for Snakes': Blues and the Music Industry." *Popular Music and Society* 14.2 (1990): 7–35.

Bermanzohn, Sally Avery. "Violence, Nonviolence, and the Civil Rights Movement." *New Political Science* 22.1 (2000): 31–48.

Biesecker, Barbara A. "Remembering World War II: The Rhetoric and Politics of National Commemoration at the Turn of the 21st Century." *Quarterly Journal of Speech* 88.4 (2002): 393–409.

Brackett, David. "The Politics and Practice of 'Cross-Over' in American Popular Music, 1963 to 1965." *Musical Quarterly* 78.4 (1994): 774–97.

Bromell, Nick. "'The Blues and the Veil': The Cultural Work of Musical Form in Blues and '60s Rock." *American Music* 18.2 (2000): 193–221.

Brown, Robert N. "Traveling Riverside Blues: Landscapes of Robert Johnson in the Yazoo-Mississippi." *Focus on Geography* 49.3 (2006): 22–28.

Browne, Stephen H. "Reading, Rhetoric, and the Texture of Public Memory." *Quarterly Journal of Speech* 81.2 (1995): 237–65.

Bruner, Edward M. "The Maasai and the Lion King: Authenticity, Nationalism, and Globalism in African Tourism." *American Ethnologist* 28.4 (2001): 881–909.

Calt, Stephen, with Gayle Dean Wardlow. "Paramount's Decline and Fall (Part 5)." *78 Quarterly* 1.7 (1992): 7–29.

Cary, Michael D. "Political Dimensions of the Blues." *Popular Music and Society* 14.2 (1990): 37–48.

Cohen, Erik. "Authenticity and Commoditization in Tourism." *Annals of Tourism Research* 15.3 (1988): 371–86.

———. "A Phenomenology of Tourist Experiences." *Sociology* 13.2 (1979): 179–201.

———. "Tourism as Play." *Religion* 15.3 (1985): 291–304.

———. "Toward a Sociology of International Tourism." *Social Research* 39.1 (1972): 164–82.

———. "Who Is a Tourist? A Conceptual Clarification." *Sociological Review* 22.4 (1974): 527–55.

Connell, John, and Chris Gibson. "Music and Tourism: The Blues, the Bizarre, and Big Business." *Geodate* 17.2 (2004): 1–5.

Crocker, David A. "Reckoning with Past Wrongs: A Normative Framework." *Ethics and International Affairs* 13.1 (1999): 43–64.

Dach-Gruschow, Karl, and Ying-yi Hong. "The Racial Divide in Response to the Aftermath of Katrina: A Boundary Condition for Common Ingroup Identity Model." *Analyses of Social Issues and Public Policy* 6.1 (2006): 125–41.

Dallas, Jerry W. "The Delta and Providence Farms: A Mississippi Experiment in Cooperative Farming and Racial Cooperation, 1936–1956." *Mississippi Quarterly* 40.3 (1987): 283–308.

Daniels, Douglas Henry. "The Significance of Blues for American History." *Journal of Negro History* 70.1–2 (1985): 14–23.

Dwyer, Susan. "Reconciliation for Realists." *Ethics and International Affairs* 13.1 (1999): 81–98.

Evans, David. "An Interview with H. C. Speir." *JEMF Quarterly* 8.27 (1972): 117–21.

Ferris, William R., Jr. "Racial Repertoires among Blues Performers." *Ethnomusicology* 14.3 (1970): 439–49.

Fox, Jesse W. "Beale Street and the Blues." *West Tennessee Historical Society Papers* 13 (1959): 128–47.

Frank, David A., and Mark Lawrence McPhail. "Barack Obama's Address to the 2004 Democratic National Convention: Trauma, Compromise, Consilience, and the (Im)possibility of Racial Reconciliation." *Rhetoric and Public Affairs* 8.4 (2005): 571–94.

Frenkel, Stephen, and Judy Walton. "Bavarian Leavenworth and the Symbolic Economy of a Theme Town." *Geographical Review* 90.4 (2000): 559–84.

Gardner, Robert Owen. "Tradition and Authenticity in Popular Music." *Symbolic Interaction* 28.1 (2005): 135–44.

Gehmann, Ulrich. "Modern Myths." *Culture and Organization* 9.2 (2003): 105–19.

Gibson, James L. "Does Truth Lead to Reconciliation? Testing the Causal Assumptions of the South African Truth and Reconciliation Process." *American Journal of Political Science* 48.2 (2004): 201–17.

Goulding, Christina. "The Commodification of the Past, Postmodern Pastiche, and the Search for Authentic Experiences at Contemporary Heritage Attractions." *European Journal of Marketing* 34.7 (2000): 835–53.

Govenar, Alan. "Blind Lemon Jefferson: The Myth and the Man." *Black Music Research Journal* 20.1 (2000): 7–21.

Grazian, David. "The Production of Popular Music as a Confidence Game: The Case of the Chicago Blues." *Qualitative Sociology* 27.2 (2004): 137–58.

Hamilton, Marybeth. "The Blues, the Folk, and African-American History." *Transactions of the Royal Historical Society* 11 (2001): 17–35.

———. "Sexuality, Authenticity, and the Making of the Blues Tradition." *Past and Present* 169 (2000): 132–60.

Hatch, John B. "Beyond Apologia: Racial Reconciliation and Apologies for Slavery." *Western Journal of Communication* 70.3 (2006): 186–211.

Haynes, Robert V. "Territorial Mississippi, 1798–1817." *Journal of Mississippi History* 64.4 (2002): 283–317.

Hunt, Larry L., Matthew O. Hunt, and William W. Falk. "Who Is Headed South? U.S. Migration Trends in Black and White, 1970–2000." *Social Forces* 87.1 (2008): 95–119.

Hutchins, Fred L. "Beale Street as It Was." *West Tennessee Historical Society Papers* 26 (1972): 56–63.

Johnson, Guy B. "Double Meaning in the Popular Negro Blues." *Journal of Abnormal and Social Psychology* 22.1 (1929): 12–20.

Jones, J. H. "Penitentiary Reform in Mississippi." *Publications of the Mississippi Historical Society* 6 (1902): 111–28.

Kelley-Romano, Stephanie. "Mythmaking in Alien Abduction Narratives." *Communication Quarterly* 54.3 (2006): 383–406.

Kirby, Jack Temple. "The Southern Exodus, 1910–1960: A Primer for Historians." *Journal of Southern History* 49.4 (1983): 585–600.

Kloosterman, Robert C., and Chris Quispel. "Not Just the Same Old Show on My Radio: An Analysis of the Role of Radio in the Diffusion of Black Music among Whites in the South of the United States of America, 1920 to 1960." *Popular Music* 9.2 (1990): 151–64.

Lawson, R. A. "The First Century of Blues: One Hundred Years of Hearing and Interpreting the Music and the Musicians." *Southern Cultures* 13.3 (2007): 39–61.

Leach, Elizabeth Eva. "Vicars of 'Wannabe': Authenticity and the Spice Girls." *Popular Music* 20.2 (2001): 143–67.

Lieberfeld, Daniel. "Million-Dollar Juke Joint: Commodifying Blues Culture." *African American Review* 29.2 (1995): 217–21.

Lipsitz, George. "Remembering Robert Johnson: Romance and Reality." *Popular Music and Society* 21.4 (1997): 39–50.

Lornell, Kip. "The Cultural and Musical Implications of the Dixieland Jazz and Blues Revivals." *Arkansas Review: A Journal of Delta Studies* 29.1 (1998): 11–21.

MacCannell, Dean. "Staged Authenticity: Arrangements of Social Space in Tourist Settings." *American Journal of Sociology* 79.3 (1973): 589–603.

McDowell, Fred, and Roosevelt Sykes. "Blues People: Fred and Roosevelt." Interview with Valerie Wilmer. *Jazz Journal* 1966: 22–24.

McGinley, Paige. "Highway 61 Revisited." *TDR: The Drama Review* 51.3 (2007): 80–97.

McLeod, Kembrew. "Authenticity within Hip-Hop and Other Cultures Threatened with Assimilation." *Journal of Communication* 49.4 (1999): 134–50.

Moore, Mark P. "Rhetorical Criticism of Political Myth: From Goldwater Legend to Reagan Mystique." *Communication Studies* 42.3 (1991): 295–308.

Newman, Kathy M. "The Forgotten Fifteen Million: Black Radio, the 'Negro Market,' and the Civil Rights Movement." *Radical History Review* 76 (2000): 115–35.

Oliver, Paul. "Interview with Paul Oliver." Interview with David Horn. *Popular Music* 26.1 (2007): 5–13.

Ottenheimer, Harriet. "Blues in the Heartland: African-American Music and Culture in the Middle West." *Black Heartland: African American Life, the Middle West, and the Meaning of American Regionalism.* Occasional Papers Series, 1.2 (1997): 16–36.

———. "Prewar Blues in St. Louis." *Popular Music and Society* 14.2 (1990): 87–95.

Osborn, Michael. "Archetypal Metaphor in Rhetoric: The Light-Dark Family." *Quarterly Journal of Speech* 53.2 (1967): 115–26.

Peabody, Charles. "Notes on Negro Music." *Journal of American Folk-Lore* 16.62 (1903): 148–52.

Pearce, Philip L., and Gianna M. Moscardo. "The Concept of Authenticity in Tourist Experiences." *Australian and New Zealand Journal of Sociology* 22.1 (1986): 121–32.

Pearson, Barry Lee. "'If I Couldn't Make a Quarter in a City, I Was Gone': Blues Stories of Life on the Road." *Arkansas Review: A Journal of Delta Studies* 34.3 (2003): 219–28.

Peterson, Richard A. "In Search of Authenticity." *Journal of Management Studies* 42.5 (2005): 1083–98.

Ragains, Patrick. "Blues: An Assessment of Scholarship, Reference Tools, and Documentary Sources." *References Services Review* 21.4 (1993): 13–28.

Redd, Lawrence N. "Rock! It's Still Rhythm and Blues." *Black Perspective in Music* 13.1 (1985): 31–47.

Redfoot, Donald L. "Touristic Authenticity, Touristic Angst, and Modern Reality." *Qualitative Sociology* 7.4 (1984): 291–309.

Richard, Melissa J. "The Crossroads and the Myth of the Mississippi Delta Bluesman." *Interdisciplinary Humanities* 23.2 (2006): 19–26.

Ritterhouse, Jennifer. "Reading, Intimacy, and the Role of Uncle Remus in White Southern Social Memory." *Journal of Southern History* 69.3 (2003): 585–622.

Rotenstein, David S. "The Helena Blues: Cultural Tourism and African-American Folk Music." *Southern Folklore* 49.2 (1992): 133–46.

Rothenbuhler, Eric W. "Myth and Collective Memory in the Case of Robert Johnson." *Critical Studies in Media Communication* 24.3 (2007): 189–205.

Rowland, Robert C. "On Mythic Criticism." *Communication Studies* 41.2 (1990): 101–16.

Rudinow, Joel. "Race, Ethnicity, Expressive Authenticity: Can White People Sing the Blues?" *Journal of Aesthetics and Art Criticism* 52.1 (1994): 127–37.

Silver, Ira. "Marketing Authenticity in Third World Countries." *Annals of Tourism Research* 20.2 (1993): 302–18.

Smith, Ayana. "Blues, Criticism, and the Signifying Trickster." *Popular Music* 24.2 (2005): 179–91.

Soper, Anne K. "Developing Mauritianness: National Identity, Cultural Heritage Values, and Tourism." *Journal of Heritage Tourism* 2.2 (2007): 94–109.

Stauffer, John. "Interspatialism in the Nineteenth-century South: The Natchez of Henry Norman." *Slavery and Abolition* 29.2 (2008): 247–63.

Stein, Daniel. "The Things That Jes' Grew? The Blues 'I' and African American Autobiographies." *Interdisciplinary Humanities* 23.2 (2006): 43–54.

Stewart, James B. "Message in the Music: Political Commentary in Black Popular Music from Rhythm and Blues to Early Hip Hop." *Journal of American History* 90.3 (2005): 196–225.

Suisman, David. "Co-workers in the Kingdom of Culture: Black Swan Records and the Political Economy of African American Music." *Journal of American History* 90.4 (2004): 1295–1324.

Taylor, John P. "Authenticity and Sincerity in Tourism." *Annals of Tourism Research* 28.1 (2001): 7–26.

Titon, Jeff Todd. "The New Blues Tourism." *Arkansas Review: A Journal of Delta Studies* 29.1 (1998): 5–10.

Wallis, Robert J., and Jenny Blain. "Sites, Sacredness, and Stories: Interactions of Archaeology and Contemporary Paganism." *Folklore* 114.3 (2003): 307–21.

Wang, Ning. "Rethinking Authenticity in Tourism Experience." *Annals of Tourism Research* 26.2 (1999): 349–70.

Wardlow, Gayle Dean. "Godfather of Delta Blues: H. C. Speir." Interview with Pat Howse and Jimmy Phillips. *Monitor (Peavey)* 13.2 (1994): 34–44.

———. "Ledell Johnson Remembers His Brother, Tommy . . ." *78 Quarterly* 1.1 (1967): 63–65.

———. "The Talent Scouts: H. C. Speir (1895–1972)." *78 Quarterly* 1.8 (1993): 11–33.

Young, Martin. "The Social Construction of Tourist Places." *Australian Geographer* 30.3 (1999): 373–89.

Yurchenco, Henrietta. "'Blues Fallin' Down like Hail': Recorded Blues, 1920s–1940s." *American Music* 13.4 (1995): 448–69.

Zelizer, Barbie. "Reading the Past against the Grain: The Shape of Memory Studies." *Critical Studies in Mass Communication* 12.2 (1995): 214–39.

Magazines

Aschoff, Peter R. "The 1988 Delta Blues Festival." *Living Blues* Jan.–Feb. 1989: 17–18.

Austin, Farrah. "A Visit with Delta Royalty." *Southern Living* Aug. 2006: 24.

Barnaby, Laura. "Sid Graves' Field of Dreams." *Here's Clarksdale!* Aug. 2007: 6–11.

"B. B. on the Blues." *Humanities* May–June 1999: 4–8, 44–45.

"Biggest Negro Station." *Time* 11 Nov. 1957: 85–86.

"Bill Creates Mississippi Blues Commission." *Jet* 17 May 2004: 15.

"Blues Commission Awarded $25,000 by AT&T; Plans to Invest in Mississippi Blues Trail Mobile Technology." *Delta Business Journal* Dec. 2008: 10.

"Blues Joint." *Guitar Player* Sept. 2003. 15 Aug. 2003. http://www.guitarplayer.com/0903_I02.htm.

"Bluesville." *Living Blues* May–June 1998: 9.

"Bobby Rush: The King of Soul Blues." *Living Blues* Nov.–Dec. 2003: n.p.

Boschert, Harry. "Singing in the Field." *Life in the Delta* Sept. 2008: 15.

Bonner, Brett J. Editorial. *Living Blues* Jan.–Feb. 2004: 2.

Boyd, Eddie. "*Living Blues* Interview: Eddie Boyd (Part I)." Interview with Jim O'Neal and Amy O'Neal. *Living Blues* Nov.–Dec. 1977: 11–15.

Brown, Luther. "Blues Sites to See Before You Die." *Delta Magazine* July–Aug. 2005: 50–52.

Carr, Sam. "The Drums Got to Be Heard Just Right." Interview with Margo Cooper. *Living Blues* Jan.–Feb. 2004: 10–25.

Cazalas, Ken. "Bluesman Lives Simple Life Today." *Delta Democrat Times* 23 May 1988: 1A, 10A.

"Clarksdale, Tunica Form Partnership to Hike Tourism." *Memphis Business Journal* 18 Feb. 2000: 18.

Cobb, Charles E., Jr. "Traveling the Blues Highway." *National Geographic* Apr. 1999: 42–69.

Cohn, Lawrence. "Son House—Delta Bluesman." *Saturday Review* 28 Sept. 1968: 68–69.

Conforth, Bruce Michael. "Ike Zimmerman: The X in Robert Johnson's Crossroads." *Living Blues* Feb. 2008: 68–73.

Cusic, Eddie. "'Sound So Good': The Eddie Cusic Story." Interview with Barry Lee Pearson. *Living Blues* Nov.–Dec. 2006: 22–29.

Dawkins, Jimmy. "*Living Blues* Interview: Jimmy Dawkins." Interview with William Cummerow. *Living Blues* Sept.–Oct. 1978: 47–48.

Dawson, Walter. "Beale Street: Memphis Razes Blues Landmark." *Rolling Stone* 2 Aug. 1973: 20.

DeCurtis, Anthony. "Rocking My Life Away: The Blues Will Pour Down like Rain This Year." *Rolling Stone* 30 Apr. 2003. 3 May 2003. http://www.rollingstone.com/news/newsarticle.asp?nid=17985.

"Delta Blues Revival Draws Pilgrims to U.S. South." *Blues News* 18 Nov. 2001. 26 July 2007. http://www.shackupinn.com/press/Blues%20News%20International%20News.htm.

Dorris, Henry B. "Little Milton: 'The Blues Is Alright.'" *Mahogany Magazine* Feb.–Mar. 2003: 18–20.

"Down Home and Dirty." *Time* 9 Aug. 1971: 46.

Du Bois, W. E. B. "The Migration of Negroes." *Crisis* June 1917: 63–66.

Eddy, Sherwood. "The Delta Cooperative's First Year." *Christian Century* 3 Feb. 1937: 139–40.

Emmerich, Wyatt. "Embrace the Uniqueness of the Delta." *Delta Magazine* Sept.–Oct. 2003: 96.

Erlewine, Michael. "Ann Arbor Blues Festival: The First of Its Kind." *Living Blues* Mar.–Apr. 2006: 36–39.

Evans, David. "Alan Lomax: An Appreciation." *Living Blues* June–Aug. 2003: 48–55.

———. "Booker White—Part 2." *Blues Unlimited* Oct. 1966: 7–9.

———. "Blues on Dockery's Plantation: 1895 to 1967 [Part I]." *Blues Unlimited* Jan. 1968: 3–4.

———. "Blues on Dockery's Plantation: 1895 to 1967 [Part II]." *Blues Unlimited* Feb. 1968: 14–15.

"The Forgotten 15,000,000." *Sponsor* 10 Oct. 1949: 23–24.

Ford, T-Model. "I'm Hanging; I'm Happy." Interview with Margo Cooper. *Living Blues* Nov.–Dec. 2006: 10–21.

Freeman, Morgan. No title. *Living Blues* Mar.–June 2004: 9.

Garon, Paul. "Speak My Mind." Editorial. *Living Blues* May–June 1993: 53.

Gillette, Becky. "Banking on the Blues: Can Blues Tourism Be the Cure?" *Delta Business Journal* July 2010: 24–27.

———. "Blues Tourists Steady, Keep the Delta Green." *Mississippi Business Journal* Nov. 26–Dec. 2, 2001: 18, 28.

———. "Out of Suffering, the Blues Rose from the Mississippi Delta." *Mississippi Business Journal* 18–24 Aug. 2003: 8.

———. "Shack Up Inn Draws Visitors from around the World." *Mississippi Business Journal* 13–19 Jan. 2003: 16–17.

Golkin, Pete. "Blacks Whites and the Blues: The Story of Chess Records" (Part One)." *Living Blues* Sept.–Oct. 1989: 22–32.

Goodwin, Michael. "Son House: 'You Can't Fool God.'" *Rolling Stone* 27 Dec. 1969: 14–16.

Greenville–Washington County Convention and Visitors Bureau. Advertisement. *Oxford American* Winter 2009: 16.

Greenwood Convention and Visitors Bureau. Advertisement. *Living Blues* Oct. 2009: 52.

Guralnick, Peter. "I Do Not Play No Rock 'n' Roll: Malaco Records—the Last Soul Company." *Living Blues* Jan.–Feb. 1989: 36–46.

Harvey, Hank. "Growing Up with the Blues." *Living Blues* July–Aug. 1986: 25–28.

Haynie, Holli. "Super Chikan and the River Rat." Advertisement. *Memphis Spoon* Spring 2010: 102–3.

Heverly, Lorry. "The Mississippi Blues Trial, Where Legends Begin." *City Social.* July 2009. 11 July 2010. http://www.visitclevelandms.com/city_social.pdf.

Hoffman, Lawrence. "At the Crossroads." Editorial. *Guitar Player* Aug. 1990: 18.

Hood-Adams, Rebecca. "The Delta Blues Museum: A Happy Harmony." *Delta Scene* Fall 1980: 8–9, 24.

House, Son. "I Can Make My Own Songs." *Sing Out!* July 1965: 38–45.

Hunter, Kris. "'America's Blues Alley' Campaign Expanding to Lure German Visitors to Mississippi." *Memphis Business Journal* 4 Mar. 1996: 40.

Jacobson, Mark. "Down to the Crossroads." *Natural History* Sept. 1996: 48–55.

Jones, Calvin "Fuzz." "Calvin 'Fuzz' Jones: I Love the Blues; The Blues Is Everything I Was Raised Up With." Interview with Margo Cooper. *Living Blues* Feb. 2008: 24–31.

Jones, LeRoi. "Blues, Black, and White America." *Metronome* Mar. 1961: 11–15.

King, B. B. No title. *Living Blues* Mar.–June 2004: 11.

Kinnon, Joy Bennett. "Are Whites Taking or Are Blacks Giving Away the Blues?" *Ebony* Sept. 1997: 86–92.

Klatzko, Bernard. "Finding Son House." *Blues Unlimited* Sept. 1964: 8–9.

Klein, Joe. "The Emancipation of Bolton, Mississippi." *Esquire* Dec. 1985: 258–62.

Lauterbach, Preston. Editorial. *Living Blues* Mar.–June 2004: 6.

Leadbitter, Mike. "Bring It on Home." *Blues Unlimited* Jan. 1973: 4–13.

Lockwood, Robert Jr. "*Living Blues* Interview: Robert Jr. Lockwood." Interview with William Cummerow. *Living Blues* Spring 1973: 18–19.

Lofton, Lynn. "Cigar Company Promoting Hand-Rolled Products, Delta Blues." *Mississippi Business Journal* 8–14 Jan. 2007: 3.

"Looking for the Blues." *Newsweek* 13 July 1964: 82–83.

Milton, Little. "*Living Blues* Interview: Little Milton." Interview with Lynn S. Summers and Bob Scheir. *Living Blues* Autumn 1974: 17–24.

"Mississippi Turning." *Economist* 6 Jan. 2007: 27–28.

Moon, Thomas D. "Part I: We and Big Joe." *Living Blues* Nov.–Dec. 2004: 72–79.

Murray, Charles Shaar. "Highway 61 Revisited." *Guardian* 28 Sept. 2001: 2–4.

"The New Blues." *Newsweek* 24 June 1968: 112.

Niebuhr, Reinhold. "Meditations from Mississippi." *Christian Century* 10 Feb. 1937: 183–84.

Northway, Wally. "Blues Continue to Draw Tourists to Towns around the State." *Mississippi Business Journal* 2 May 2005: 18.

Obrecht, Jas. "Deep Down in the Delta: The Adventures of Son House, Willie Brown, and Friends." *Guitar Player* Aug. 1992: 67–81, 98.

———. "Sam Chatmon: The Last of the Mississippi Sheiks." *Living Blues* Feb. 2009: 68–73.

O'Keefe, Kinchen. "A Letter from Our Publisher." *Here's Clarksdale!* Apr. 2007: 5.

O'Neal, Amy. "King Biscuit Time 1971." *Living Blues* Summer 1971: 4–5.

O'Neal, Jim. "Blues for the Tourists at Blues Alley in Memphis." *Living Blues* Nov.–Dec. 1978: 28–29.

———. "The Continuing Wellspring of the Blues." *Living Blues* Mar.–June 2004: 16–32, 124–45.

Phillips, Esther. "'Baby I'm for Real': Esther Phillips." Interview with Jim O'Neal and Amy O'Neal. *Living Blues* Summer 1974: 13–17.

Pope, Victoria. "Still Singing the Blues in the Mississippi Delta." *U.S. News and World Report* 23 Apr. 2001: 66–68.

Ray, Craig. "Come One, Come All." Interview with Leslie Galloway. *Mississippi Business Journal* 6–12 July 2009: 50.

"Rebirth of the Blues." *Newsweek* 26 May 1969: 82–85.

Richardson, Michael. "Helena, Arkansas: First Big City of the Blues." *Big City Blues.* Dec. 1999–Jan. 2000: 16–18.

Robertshaw, Nicky. "Beale Street Survivor: Rum Boogie Hangs On, Reaps Rewards." *Memphis Business Journal* 15 May 1995. 24 Feb. 1999.

Rush, Bobby. "Bobby Rush." Interview with William Cochrane, Bill Ferris, Peter Lee, and Jim O'Neal. *Living Blues* Jan.–Feb. 1989: 23–32.

Sampson, Tim. "72 Miles to Clarksdale." *Memphis* June 2001: 43–47.

Shack Up Inn. Advertisement. *Oxford American* Winter 2009: 17.

Shines, Johnny. "The Deep Blues of Johnny Shines." Interview with Jas Obrecht. *Guitar Player* Apr. 1989: 40–48.

Stackhouse, Houston. "*Living Blues* Interview: Houston Stackhouse." Interview with Jim O'Neal. *Living Blues* Summer 1974: 20–36.

Snyder, Howard. "Traits of My Plantation Negroes." *Century* July 1921: 367–76.

Stolle, Roger. "Juke Joint Festival." *Blues Revue* Sept.–Oct. 2010: 48–49.

Taylor, Hound Dog. "Hound Dog Taylor." Interview with Jim O'Neal and R. T. Cuniff. *Living Blues* Winter 1970–71: 4–7.

"Tourism Boost Foreseen." Editorial. *Memphis Business Journal* 17–21 Feb. 1997: 4.

"Tune in Mississippi." *Life in the Delta* Nov. 2007: 38.

Vincent, Ted. "The Social Context of Black Swan Records." *Living Blues* May–June 1989: 34–40.

West, Hollie I. "Can White People Sing the Blues? *Ebony* July 1979: 140–42.

Walker, T-Bone. "*Living Blues* Interview: T-Bone Walker." Interview with Jim O'Neal and Amy O'Neal, *Living Blues* Winter 1972–73: 20–26.

Wilcock, Donald E. From the Editor's Desk. *King Biscuit Times* Oct. 1998: 7.

Williams, Terry, and Wesley Jefferson. "They Jukin' Hard: A Conversation with Big T. Williams and Wesley Junebug Jefferson." Interview with Mark Coltrain. *Living Blues* Apr. 2008: 30–35.

Ybarra, Felix. "'A Suburb of Mississippi': Talkin' Great Migration Blues with Mississippi Trail Boss, Alex Thomas." *Big City Rhythm and Blues* Oct.–Nov. 2009: 11–12.

Young, Stephen Flinn. "Looking for the Blues in Inverness, Mississippi." *Southern Reader* Fall 1989: 20–25, 71–72.

Newspapers and Newsletters

Abernathy, Harry. "'New World' Scorned by Clarksdale Elite." *Clarksdale Press Register* 14–15 Aug. 1982: 4B.

Alberts, Sheldon. "Delta Blues Fans Are Living the Music They Love." *Montreal Gazette.* CanWest News Service. 9 Oct. 2007. 10 Oct. 2007.

Arkansas Vacation and Destination brochure. Advertisement supplement. *Commercial Appeal* 30 Sept. 2007.

Atkins, Joe. "Born-and-Bred Yankee in Oxford Best Friend Bluesman Ever Had." *Clarion-Ledger* 16 Oct. 1994: 3G.

Auchmutey, Jim. "Shacks Are Chic in Clarksdale, the Crossroads of the Delta Blues." *Atlanta Journal-Constitution* 29 July 2001: K1.

Bangs, Gregg B. "Blues Festival Celebrates 'Dying Art.'" *Clarion-Ledger/Jackson Daily News* 22 Oct. 1978: 3A, 6A.

Barbieri, Landry. "King of the Delta Blues Opens Doors to Museum." *Bolivar Commercial Advertiser* 16 Sept. 2008: 2.

"Block by Block . . ." Advertisement. Columbus Convention and Visitors Bureau. *Bolivar Commercial Advertiser* 18 Sept. 2007: 2.

Bragg, Rick. "The Blues Is Dying in the Place It Was Born." *New York Times* 22 Apr. 2001: A1, A26.

Brakefield, Jay. "Birthplace of the Blues Draws Tourists to Clarksdale." *Milwaukee Sentinel* 23 Jan. 1991, sec. 5: 2.

Brandt, Rebecca. "Iowa Visitor Not Impressed with Still Segregated Society." Letter. *Clarksdale Press Register* 20 Jan. 2004: 4A.

Brown, Charles M. "Little Zion Split over Johnson." *Greenwood Commonwealth* 6 June 2004: 1A, 14A.

Brown, Luther. "Guest Commentary." Editorial. *Cleveland Current* 22 Mar. 2009: A4, A6.

Burnham, Maria. "Will the Blues Bring Bucks?" *Clarion-Ledger* 1 May 2001: 1C, 8C.

Byrd, Shelia Hardwell. "Deltans Find Hope in Blues." *Bolivar Commercial Advertiser* 28 Sept. 2004: 1–2.

———. "Mississippi: Can the Delta's Blues Reel in Tourists?" *USA Today* 25 Sept. 2004, 8 Oct. 2007.

———. "Music Heritage May Be Next Cash Crop." *Commercial Appeal* 22 Mar. 2010; DeSoto ed.: DSA1, DSA3.

———. "Perhaps Fewer Musicians Will Sing the Blues." *Commercial Appeal* 5 Mar. 2010; DeSoto ed.: DSA2.

Cazalas, Ken. "Bluesman Lives Simple Life Today." *Delta Democrat Times* 23 May 1988: 1A, 10A.

"Clarksdale Group Gets Grant for Arts Center." *Clarion-Ledger* 6 Mar. 2002: 4B.

"The Corinth Burning." Editorial. *Daily Clarion-Ledger* 2 Oct. 1902: 4.

Court, Ayesha. "Ten Great Places to Rent a Cottage, or a Lookout." *USA Today* 12 Jan. 2007: 3D.

Dean, Eddie. "Skip James' Hard Time Killing Floor Blues." *Washington City Paper* Nov. 25–Dec. 1 1994: 24–34.

"Delta Blues Festival Set for Sept. 8." *Clarion-Ledger/Jackson Daily News* 19 Aug. 1979: 3G.

Donahue, Michael. "Blues Traveler: Taking the Long Road for the Real Thing." *Commercial Appeal* 5 Oct. 2003: D1, D6.

Douglas, Ellen. "Delta Beat." *Washington Post* 23 Oct. 1978: B1, B3.

"Early Wright." Advertisement. *Clarksdale Press Register* 23 Feb. 1988: 12.

Evans, David. "Revise History of the Blues." Letter. *Commercial Appeal*. Clarksdale, Miss.: Carnegie Public Library.

Ewing, Jim. "Wade Walton: The Singing Barber of Blues Fame." *Clarion-Ledger/Jackson Daily News* 22 Nov. 1981: F1.

Farish, Jennifer. "Mississippi Looks for Ways to Cash In on the Growing Interest of Historic Music Culture." *Daily Journal* 27 June 2004: 1A, 5A.

"Festival Provides Showcase for National, Regional Talent." *Clarion-Ledger* 19 Sept. 1985: 1G, 4G.

"Fifth Annual Delta Blues Festival." *Jackson Advocate* 11–17 Nov. 1982: A8.

Goldstein, Patrick. "The Bluest Voice on the Delta." *Washington Post* 19 Mar. 1989: G1, G4-G5.

"Greenville Flooded When City Levee Is Topped by Torrent." *Commercial Appeal* 22 Apr. 1927: 1, 6.

Hammond, John. "John Hammond: A Life for the Record." Interview with Neville L. Johnson. *L.A. Weekly* 11–17 Jan. 1985: 60– 63.

Harris, John. "Plantation for Sale." Advertisement. *Hinds County Gazette* 14 Feb. 1855: n.p.

Harrington, J. Winston. "Work or Die of Hunger Is Dixie Order." *Chicago Defender* 4 June 1927, sec. 1: 1–2.

Havighurst, Craig. "B. B. King's Hometown Museum." *Wall Street Journal* 16 Oct. 2008: D7.

Herring, Lori. "Mississippi Has the Blues." *Clarion-Ledger* 9 June 2002: 1A.

———. "Mississippi Has the Blues." *Clarion-Ledger* 10 June 2002: 1D, 3D.

"He's Come Home." *Delta Democrat Times* 6 June 1980: 1.

"Highway 61 Scores New Name." *Bolivar Commercial* 14 May 2009. 17 May 2009. http://www.bolivarcom.com.

"Home for Blues." *Commercial Appeal* 10 May 2009; DeSoto ed.: DSA2.

Hood-Adams, Rebecca. "Concert to Benefit Burned Musician." *Clarion-Ledger* 16 Feb. 1987: 1B–2B.

———. "Group Lands $400K Grant." *Clarksdale Press Register* 30 Oct. 2001: 1–2.

Howle, Cynthia. "'Hard Times' and the Blues." *Commercial Appeal* 24 Mar. 2007: M1, M4.

———. "Juke Joint Weekend." *Commercial Appeal* 10 Apr. 2007: M1, M4.

Johnson, Rheta Grimsley. "Guiding Pilgrims to Holy Land of the Blues." *Clarion-Ledger* 20 Feb. 1995: 1D.

Jones, Yolanda. "Nesbit's Callicott Honored with Blues Trail Marker." *Commercial Appeal* 12 Mar. 2010; DeSoto ed.: DSA1–DSA2.

———. "Still Wheelin'." *Commercial Appeal* 18 Oct. 2005: M1, M4.

Katz, Larry. "Don't Miss Mississippi Delta, Birthplace of Blues." *Boston Sunday Herald* 31 Mar. 1991: 58–62.

"King Museum Still Drawing Crowds." *Commercial Appeal* 13 Sept. 2009; DeSoto ed.: DSA1.

Lackey, Hilliard. "Shack Up Inn Conjures Up Memories." Editorial. *Clarksdale Press Register* 14 Jan. 2004: 4A.

Le Coz, Emily. "Pinetop Comes Home." *Clarksdale Press Register* 3 May 2003: 1A–2A.

Lush, David. "Pianist from Holland Fascinated by the Blues." *Bolivar Commercial Advertiser* 30 Jan. 2001: 1–2.

Mayfield, Panny. "Blues Festival Is Saturday." *Clarksdale Press Register* 2 Aug. 1989: 3A.

———. "Busy Weekend Includes Blues and Beauties." *Clarksdale Press Register* 4 Aug. 1989: 3A.

———. "Keeping Blues 'Authentic' Goal of Delta Music Lovers." *Clarion-Ledger* 25 Feb. 2001: 33.

———. "Library Head Sid Graves Resigns Post." *Clarksdale Press Register* 15 Mar. 1995: 1A–2A.

———. "Sunflower River Blues Festival Draws Fine Music, Many Smiles and Visitors." *Clarksdale Press Register* 8 Aug. 1990: 1B.

McIntire, Carl. "Blues Had Birth in Mississippi Delta." *Clarion-Ledger* 30 Sept. 1979: 1F–2F.

McKenzie, Danny. "Delta Blues Museum Spreads Tuneful Tale across the World." *Clarion-Ledger* 27 Mar. 1992: 1B.

McLaurin, C. "Bargains to Be Had! Sale of Land, Negroes, &C." Advertisement. *Mississippi State Gazette* 27 Jan. 1858: 1.

McWilliams, Andy. "Why Does City Lack Major Blues Attraction?" Letter. *Clarksdale Press Register* 21 Oct. 1989: 5A.

Mehr, Bob. "Delta and Its King Interpreted." gomemphis.com. *Commercial Appeal* 12 Sept. 2008: 8–9.

Mikell, Ray. "Singing Blues No Sweat for Eugene Powell." *Delta Democrat Times* 11 Sept. 1989: 2A.

Minor, Bill. "Poor Sharecropper Shacks See New Life in Delta Tourism Trade." *Clarion-Ledger* 20 Jan. 2002: 3G.

"Miss. Schools Ordered to End Racial Imbalance." *Commercial Appeal* 17 Apr. 2010, DeSoto ed.: DSA3.

Monroe, David. "Blues Promoters Spar over Charge for Tour." *Greenwood Commonwealth* 14 June 2006: 1.

Montgomery, Susan. "Blues Historian Is Opening a Museum Full of Information and Objects Concerning Robert L. Johnson." *Greenwood Commonwealth* 2 Sept. 2001: 1A, 9A.

Nixon, Bruce. "The Landscape of the Mississippi Blues." *Dallas Herald Times* 29 Jan. 1984: 13–21, 24–28.

Pacelle, Mitchell. "Johnson Snapshots Lead to Tug of War." *Greenwood Commonwealth* 23 Mar. 2005: 1, 12.

Pettus, Emily Wagster. "States Cling to Southern Tradition." *Commercial Appeal* 25 Apr. 2009; DeSoto ed.: DSA1, DSA5.

"Protective Agencies Are Massed on River." *Commercial Appeal* 14 Apr. 1927: 1, 5.

"Purpose of the Law." Editorial. *Daily Clarion-Ledger* 2 Oct. 1902: 2.

Quinn, Archie. "Let's Move beyond the Blues." *Commercial Appeal* 24 Feb. 1985: J7.

"Race Issues Likely to Follow Barbour." *Commercial Appeal* 13 Sept. 2010; DeSoto Ed.: DSA1.

Rawls, D. L. "Land and Negroes for Sale." Advertisement. *Vicksburg Whig* 5 Oct 1859: n.p.

Robinette, Aimee. "Tourism Big Business in Cleveland." *Bolivar Commercial* 19 May 2006: 1, 8.

Ross, Andy. "Shack Up Inn Named 'Top Place to Stay.'" *Clarksdale Press Register* 28 Mar. 2008: 1A, 6A.

———. "Two New Blues Trail Markers Placed." *Clarksdale Press Register* 14 Feb. 2008: 1A, 6A.

Rushing, Robin. "Revisit Tourism Board's Mission." Editorial. *Clarksdale Press Register* 12 Feb. 2004: 4A.

Ruskey, John. "Blues Fan Plans to Return." Letter. *Clarksdale Press Register* 2 Aug. 1990: 12.

Scruggs, Afi-Odelia E. "Making Sounds in the Silence." *Clarion-Ledger* 29 Nov. 1988: 1C, 5C.

"Shack Up Inn—Cotton Gin Inn Receive 2009 'Keeping the Blues Alive' Award." *Clarksdale Press Register* 11 Feb. 2009: 1A, 6A.

"Shack Up Inn Gets Honor from State." *Clarksdale Press Register* 31 July 2009: 2A.

Smith, Charlie. "LaVeres to Close Eateries, Relocate." *Greenwood Commonwealth* 1 Apr. 2010. 12 Nov. 2010. http:www.gwcommonwealth.com.

"Speir to Record Mississippi Talent." *Jackson City News* 30 Nov. 1930: 18.

Spencer, Jennifer. "Shacks to Rent, $40–$60." *Commercial Appeal* 28 Oct. 2001: E1, E7.

"State Can Aid Efforts to Promote the Blues." Editorial. *Clarksdale Press Register*. 20 Jan. 2004: 4A.

"Sunflower River Blues Festival Is a True Gem." *Clarksdale Press Register* 29 May 2008. 15 July 2008. http://www.sunflowerfest.org/index.cfm?page=news&newsid=52.

Taff, Carol. "Stackhouse, Friends Sing the Delta Blues Tomorrow." *Clarion-Ledger* 7 Sept. 1979: 1C, 5C.

Talev, Margaret. "Barbour Recalls Rights Era Fondly." *Commercial Appeal* 13 Sept. 2010: A1–A2.

"There Are $ in Blues, Tourism." *Clarksdale Press Register* 29 Aug. 1991: 1B.

"Today's Radio Programs and Highlights." *Commercial Appeal* 8 Nov. 1949: 12.

Toler, Kenneth. "Smoldering 'Suspicions' Flare over Farm Project Activities." *Commercial Appeal* 1 Oct. 1955: 28.

"'Toughest Job' Ably Done in Winter's Four Years." *Commercial Appeal* 8 Jan. 1984: B2.

"Travel: Ten Top Places to Hear Authentic American Music." *USA Weekend* 18 May 2008. 14 July 2008. http://www.usaweekend.com/08_issues/080518/080518summer-travel.html.

Walton, Steve. "Tour Map Marks the Spots Where Blues Were Birthed." *Clarion-Ledger* 30 July 1992: 3E.

Watkins, Billy. "B. B. King Isn't Singing the Blues over Museum." *USA Today* 15 Sept. 2008, 29 Jan. 2009.

Weldon, Jeremy S. "ZZ Top Kicks Off Fund-Raising for Delta Blues Museum." *Daily Mississippian* 27 Apr. 1988: 11.

West, Phil. "Gov. Addresses Delta Summit." *Commercial Appeal* 17 June 2010; DeSoto ed.: DSA1, DSA6.

———. "'Trail' to Honor Country Music Heritage." *Commercial Appeal* 13 Feb. 2009; DeSoto ed.: DSA1, DSA7.

Wilcock, Donald E. "From the Editor's Desk." *King Biscuit Times* Oct. 1998: 7.

Williamson, Nigel. "In Search of the Blues." *Observer* 28 Jan. 2007. 22 Aug. 2009. http://www.guardian.co.uk/travel/2007/jan/28/culturaltrips.usa.escape.

Wright, Barbara. "Delta Blues Grew Up on Plantation." *Greenwood Commonwealth* 25 June 1978: 10.

Wright, Gwen. "Mississippi Communities Build on Democracy, Inclusion, and Racial Reconciliation." *Nation's Cities Weekly* 29 Aug. 2005: 1, 8.

WROX. *Clarksdale Daily Register and Daily News* 9 Feb. 1948: 4.

WROX. *Clarksdale Press Register* 25 June 1954: 8.

Wynn, Ron. "Museum Not Singing Blues." *Commercial Appeal* 13 Jan. 1991: G1–G2.

Yellin, Emily. "Homage at Last for Blues Makers; Through a Fan's Crusade, Unmarked Graves Get Memorials." *New York Times* 30 Sept. 1997: E1, E6.

Zane, J. Peder. "From the Heart of Blues Country." *New York Times* 22 Jan. 1995, sec. 2: 30–33.

Theses and Dissertations

Brown, Robert Norman II. "Coming Home: Black Return Migration to the Yazoo-Mississippi Delta." Diss. Louisiana State U, 2001. Ann Arbor: UMI, 2001.

Hutson, Marvin Lee. "Mississippi's State Penal System." Thesis. U of Mississippi, 1939.

Special Collection Documents

American Folk Blues Festival '65. Subject Files (Events and Festivals), no. 7. Blues Archives and Special Collections. University of Mississippi, Oxford, Miss.
American Folk Blues Festival '66. Subject Files (Events and Festivals), no. 8. Blues Archives and Special Collections. University of Mississippi. Oxford, Miss.
American Folk Blues Festival '68. Subject Files (Events and Festivals), no. 10. Blues Archives and Special Collections. University of Mississippi. Oxford, Miss.
Bass, A. J. Slave contract. 27 Oct. 1853. Bacon-Messenger Family Papers. Collection M138. Box 1 (Folder 1). Delta State University Archives. Cleveland, Miss.
Capps, Charles W., Jr. Interview with Charles Bolton. 9 August 1999. Charles W. Capps, Jr. Oral History. OH246. Delta State University Archives. Cleveland, Miss.
"Dr. Sherwood Eddy's Co-operative Farm." Jerry Dallas Delta Cooperative Farm Collection. Manuscript 109. Delta State University Archives. Cleveland, Miss.
No name. Slave contract. 7 Dec. 1858. Bacon-Messenger Family Papers. Collection M138. Box 2 (Folder 1). Delta State University Archives. Cleveland, Miss.
Oliver, Sylvester W. "Local Folk Singer—an Unsong Legend." Clarksdale, Miss.: Carnegie Public Library, 1980.
Race Parody Sheet Music. Box 1 (6–12). Blues Archives and Special Collections. University of Mississippi. Oxford, Miss.
"Some Basic Principles of the Delta Cooperative Farm." Jerry Dallas Delta Cooperative Farm Collection. Manuscript 109. Delta State University Archives. Cleveland, Miss.
Waterman, Dick. "Dick Waterman Speaks at Brown Bag Lunch." 7 Nov. 1984. Subject File (producer), no. 2288. Blues Archives and Special Collections. University of Mississippi. Oxford, Miss.
Williams, Nat D. "Oral History Interview with Nat D. Williams." Interview with Ronald Anderson Walter. 13 Sept. 1976. Memphis Public Library (Central).
Winter, William F. Mississippi Executive Department Jackson. "A Proclamation by the Governor." Blues Archives and Special Collections. University of Mississippi. Oxford, Miss.
Wright, Early. No title. 1993. Subject Files (miscellaneous), no. 2423. Blues Archives and Special Collections. University of Mississippi. Oxford, Miss.

Policy Papers

Barton, Alan W. *Attitudes about Heritage Tourism in the Mississippi Delta: A Policy Report from the 2005 Delta Rural Poll.* Policy Paper No. 05-02. Delta State University: Center for Community and Economic Development, 2005.
———. *Attitudes and Perceptions of Heritage Tourism in the Mississippi Delta.* Paper Policy No. 06-01. Delta State University: Center for Community and Economic Development, 2006.
———. *Visitation to Heritage Tourism Sites by Residents of the Mississippi Delta.* Policy Paper No. 07-01. Delta State University: Center for Community and Economic Development, 2007.

Government and Legal Documents

Barrington Linda, and Gordon M. Fisher. "Poverty." *Historical Statistics of the United States: Earliest Times to the Present.* Vol. 2. Part B. Ed. Carter, Susan B., Scott Sigmund

Gartner, Michael R. Haines, Alan L. Olmstead, Richard Sutch, and Gavin White. New York: Cambridge UP, 2006. 625–51.

Brown v. Board of Education of Topeka. Shawnee County, Kansas. No. 347. Supreme Ct of the US. 17 May 1954.

General Population Census (Mississippi). Geospatial and Statistical Data Center, U of Virginia Library. 1 Mar. 2010. http://fisher.lib.virginia.edu/collections/stats/histcensus/php/newlong3.php.

Mississippi Department of Employment. Labor Market Information Department. 18 Feb. 2008, p. 11. http://www.mdes.ms.gov.

Mississippi Department of Employment Security. Labor Market Information Department. July 2010. Unemployment Rates. 11 Sept. 2010. http://www.mdes.ms.gov.

Mississippi Development Authority. *2004–2007 State of Mississippi Delta Region Development Plan*. Jackson, Miss.: Mississippi Development Authority, 2004.

Mississippi Development Authority/Tourism Division. "Fiscal Year 2009 Economic Contribution of Travel and Tourism in Mississippi, February 2010." 4 Oct. 2010. http://www.visitmississippi.org/resources/FY2009_Economic_Contribution_Report_and_Cover.pdf.

———. "Fiscal Year 2004 Economic Impact for Tourism in Mississippi, February 2005." 4 Oct. 2010. http://www.visitmississippi.org/press_news/docs/08_Final_Economic_Contribution_Report.pdf.

———. Marketing Plan FY 2009. 4 Oct. 2010. http://www.visitmississippi.org/resources/09_fy09_advertising_marketing_plan.pdf.

"Mississippi: Poverty Rate by Race/Ethnicity, States (2005–2006), U.S. (2006)." statehealthfacts.org. 17 July 2008. http://www.statehealthfacts.org/profileind.jsp?rgn=26&cat=1&ind=14.

"Mississippi: Poverty Rate by Race/Ethnicity, States (2007–2008), U.S. (2008)." statehealthfacts.org. 20 Aug. 2010. http://www.statehealthfacts.org/comparebar.jsp?ind=14@cat=1.

Slave Population Census (Mississippi). Geospatial and Statistical Data Center. U of Virginia Library. 1 Mar. 2010. http://fisher.lib.virginia.edu/collections/stats/histcensus/php/newlong3.php.

U.S. Census Bureau. "The 2010 Statistical Abstract: State Rankings," 7 June 2010. http://www.census.gov/compendia/statab/rankings.html.

U.S. Department of Labor. Bureau of Labor Statistics. "Employment Status of Civilian Noninstitutionalized Population by Sex, Race, Hispanic or Latino Ethnicity, and Detailed Age, 2007 Annual Averages." 17 July 2008. http://www.bls.gov/lau/pat able14fill2007.pdf.

U.S. Department of Labor. Bureau of Labor Statistics. "Employment Status of the Civilian Noninstitutionalized Population by Race, Hispanic or Latino Ethnicity, Sex, and Age." 17 July 2008. http://www.bls.gov/web/cpseea15.pdf.

U.S. Department of Labor. Bureau of Labor Statistics. Unemployment Rates for States. 15 Oct. 2010. http://www.bls.gov/web/laus/laumstrk.htm.

Brochures, Pamphlets, Programs, Reports, Press Releases, and Fliers

"Blues and More." Cleveland, Miss.: Cleveland–Bolivar County Chamber of Commerce, n.d.

"Bug's Blues Lounge." Rosedale, Miss., n.d.

"Chasin' the Ghost of the Crossroads." Clarksdale, Miss: Clarksdale Revitalization, n.d.

Clarksdale and Coahoma County. "The Land Where the Blues Began . . ." Clarksdale, Miss.: Coahoma County Tourism Commission, n.d.

"Clarksdale, Mississippi." Clarksdale, Miss.: Clarksdale Downtown Development Association/Memphis Convention and Visitors Bureau, n.d.

"Cleveland: Crossroads of Culture in the Mississippi Delta." Cleveland, Miss.: Cleveland–Bolivar County Chamber of Commerce, n.d.

Fifth Annual Peavine Awards. Delta State University. Cleveland, Miss. 15 Oct. 2002.

"From the Mississippi Delta to the Chicago Blues Festival—Juke Joints Are Still Alive." Press Release. 19 May 2006.

"Greenville on the Mississippi." Greenville, Miss.: Greenville–Washington County Convention and Visitors Bureau, n.d. [brochure 1].

"Greenville on the Mississippi." Greenville, Miss.: Greenville–Washington County Convention and Visitors Bureau, n.d. [brochure 2].

Ground Zero Blues Club. Advertisement, n.d.

Hopson Plantation. "Hopson Plantation: The Past and The Present." n.d.

"Landmarks, Legends and Lyrics: African-American Heritage Guide." Greenville, Miss.: Greenville–Washington County Convention and Visitors Bureau, n.d.

Mississippi Action for Community Education. Press Release. 21 June 1985.

"Mississippi Blues Trail." Flyer, n.d.

"Mississippi Delta and the Blues." Advertisement. *Tunica Mississippi 2009 Visitor's Guide*, p. 19. Tunica, Miss.: Tunica Convention and Visitors Bureau, 2009.

"The Mississippi Delta: Where the Music Meets the Soul." Greenville, Miss.: Mississippi Delta Tourism Association, n.d.

"The Path Finder: A Guide to Clarksdale and Coahoma County." Clarksdale, Miss.: Sunflower River Trading Company, 1999.

Randall Travel Marketing. *Mississippi Millennium Blues Trail: Strategic Marketing Plan for Travel and Tourism*. Mooresville, N. C., 2001.

Shack Up Inn. Flyer, n.d.

Festival Programs and Guides

"Few Understand the Legend Behind the KBBF." *14th Annual King Biscuit Blues Festival* Oct. 1999: 10.

"Four Nominated for Early Wright Blues Heritage Award." *Comin' Home for the 17th Sunflower River Blues and Gospel Festival* Aug. 2004: 8.

Juke Joint Festival Guide. April 2006, n.p.

"Leland Blues Project." *3rd Annual Highway 61 Blues Festival* June 2002: n.p.

"Live from the Birthplace of American Music." Advertisement. Visitmississippi.org. *Juke Joint Festival Guide*. Apr. 2006.

Lux, Fiat. "Not from Around Here, Are Ya?" *8th Annual Sunflower River Blues and Gospel Festival* Aug. 1995: n.p.

Nelson, David. No title. *10th Annual Sunflower River Blues and Gospel Festival* Aug. 1997: n.p.

9th Annual Highway 61 Blues Festival. June 2008.

O'Neal, Jim. "We've Got the Blues." Editorial. *10th Annual Mississippi Delta Blues Festival,* Sept. 1987, n.p.

"The 16th Annual Sunflower Rover Blues and Gospel Festival." Flyer. 2003.

Summer, [E. H.] Dok. "Selective Memories of Festivals Past." *8th Annual Sunflower River Blues and Gospel Festival* Aug. 1995: n.p.

———. "Shake Your Moneymaker." *The 10th Annual Sunflower River Blues and Gospel Festival* Aug. 1997: n.p.

The Sunflower Musicians Relief Fund. *11th Annual Sunflower River Blues and Gospel Festival* Aug. 1998: n.p.

The 21th Annual Sunflower River Blues and Gospel Festival. Aug. 2008.

24th Annual Mississippi Delta Blues and Heritage Festival. Sept. 2001.

Internet Sources

"American Roots Music: Oral Histories." Interview with B. B. King. PBS. 1 Oct. 2010. http://www.pbs.org/americanrootsmusic/pbs_arm_oralh_bbking.html.

"Avalon Cigars." 22 Aug. 2009. http://www.avalon.cigars.com/about/html.

Beldin, Fred. "The Blues Brothers: Made in America." allmusic. 10 Mar. 2010. http://www.allmusic.com/cg/amg.dll?p=amg&sql=10:3ifixqq5ldhe.

The Blues Highway Association. 20 Feb. 2008. http://www.blueshighway.org/bha.htm.

———. 11 Sept. 2009. http://www.blueshighway.org/bluesnews.htm.

———. "Registry of Blues and Blues Heritage Sites." 24 Feb. 2010. http://www.blueshighway.org/registry.htm.

———. Senate Bill 2082. 3 Sept. 2010. http://www.blueshighway.org/commissionlegislation.htm.

The Blues Highway Association and the Mississippi Blues Commission. 20 Feb. 2008. http://www.blues highway.org/synergies.htm.

"Broadcasting the Blues." Mississippi Blues Trail. http://www.msbluestrail.org/_webapp_1301186/ Broadcasting_the_Blues.

Center for the Study of Southern Culture. History of Southern Studies. 10 May 2008. http://www.olemiss.edu/depts/south/history.html.

Coahoma County Tourism Commission. "The Blues." 10 Sept. 2010. http://www.clarksdaletourism.com/theblues.htm.

———. "Clarksdale and Coahoma County." 10 Sept. 2010. http://www.clarksdaletourism.com.

"A Conversation on the Blues." 14 Mar. 2001. http://www.bluesworld.com/Lornell.htm.

Crossroads Blues Society. 8 July 2009. http://www.rosedaleblues.com.

Cruickshank, Douglas. "Mississippi Delta: A Trip up the Mississippi Delta, the Bittersweet and Poignantly Beautiful Birthplace of the Blues." SFGate.com. 14 Mar. 1999. 16 Apr. 2010. http://www.sfgate.com/cgi-bin/article.cgi?file=/e/a/1999/03/14/MAGAZINE16138.dtl&type=printable.

"Dead Blues Guys," 20 Aug. 2009. http://www.deadbluesguys.com.

Delta Blues Legends Tour. "The Back in the Day Museum." 4 Oct. 2010. http://hoovertours.homestead.com/backinday.html.

Delta Blues Museum. "Mission Statement." 23 Oct. 2009. http://www.deltabluesmuseum.org.

"The Delta Communities: The Diary of a Delta Traveler." Mississippi Delta Tourism Association. 31 July 2009. http://www.visitthedelta.com/communities.

Delta Music Experience. 2 Nov. 2007. http://www.deltamusicexperience.com.

Dockery Farms. "History." 10 Sept. 2010. http://www.dockeryfarms.org/History.html.

Erlewine, Stephen Thomas. "Stevie Ray Vaughan: Biography." allmusic. 10 Mar. 2010. http://www.allmusic.com/cg/amg.dll?p=amg&sql=11:wzftxqegldke-T1.

"FAQ/The Shackmeister Files." Shack Up Inn. 26 June 2007. http://www.shackupinn.com/faq. html.

"Fatal Flood." PBS American Experience. 1 Oct. 2006. http://www.pbs.org/wgbh/amex/flood/index.html.

"Festival and Related Events, April 16–18, 2010." STLBlues.net. 15 Sept. 2010. http://www.stlblues.net/jjf_2010.htm.

Garon, Paul. "White Blues." 5 Feb. 2010. http://raceraitor.org/blues.html.

Gass, Glenn. "A Trip through the Delta Blues." 10 Sept. 2010. http://www.music.indiana.edu/som/courses/rock/delta.html.

Gatchet, Roger. "Interview and Review: The Blues Brothers." 10 Mar. 2010. http://www.austinsound.net/author/roger-gatchet/page/2.

Grayson, Walt. "Look around Mississippi." 9 Apr. 2004. 1 Oct. 2010. http://www.wlbt.com/Global/Story.asp?S=17757227.

Greenwood Convention and Visitor's Bureau. "Back in the Day." 10 Sept. 2010. http://www.gcvb.com/back_museum.php.

Greenville-Washington County Convention and Visitors Bureau. "Greenville on the Mississippi." 10 Sept. 2010. http://www.visitgreenville.org.

Ground Zero Blues Club. 15 Sept. 2010. http://www.groundzerobluesclub.com.

Hewston, Curtis. "The Blues Highway." 15 Sept. 2010. http://thebluehighway.com/links.html.

Hoover, Deacon Sylvester. "Robert Johnson Trail of Blues Tour." Delta Blues Tour. 4 Oct. 2010. http://home.earthlink.net/~robertjohnsonblues/id3.html.

Hoover, Elizabeth. "Happy Hour at the Shack Up Inn." Feb. 2004. 1 Oct. 2010. http://americanheritage.com.

Hopson Preservation Company. 1 Oct. 2010. http://www.clarksdale.com/hpc/7.

House of Blues. "About the House of Blues." 10 Sept. 2010. http://www.houseofblues.com/aboutHOB.

Jordan, Mark. "Music Notes." *Memphis Flyer*. 18 Feb. 2010. http://www.memphisflyer.com/backissues/issue416/mus416.htm.

Millennium Trails. Program Overview. 19 May 2003. http://www.millenniumtrails.org/MT_active_pages/overview/b-right.asp.

Mississippi Action for Community Education. "History: Mississippi Delta Blues and Heritage Festival." 3 Sept. 2010. http://www.deltablues.org/index.php?id=9.

Mississippi, Believe It! 15 July 2009. http://mississippibelieveit.com.

———. "No Black. No White. Just the Blues." 4 Mar. 2010. http://www.mississippibelieveit.com/ads/4COLX11/JustTheBlues4Col.pdf.

Mississippi Blues Commission. 9 Mar. 2008. http://www.msbluestrail.org/commission.html.

———. Mississippi Blues Trail. 9 Mar. 2008. http://www.msbluestrail.org/blues_trail.

———. 9 Mar. 2008. http://www.msbluestrail.org/index.htm.

Mississippi Blues Trail. "Experiencing the Blues Where They Were Born." 28 Aug. 2010. http://www.msbluestrail.org.

Mississippi Delta Graveyard Dirt. 22 Aug. 2009. http://www.deltablues.net/dirt.html.
Mississippi Delta Tourism Association. 16 Apr. 2008. http://www.visitthedelta.com/.
———. 15 Oct. 2010. http://www.visitthedelta.com/.
Mississippi Development Authority. "The Birthplace of America's Music." 10 Sept. 2010.
    http://www.visitmississippi.org.
———. Dockery Farms. 10 Sept. 2010. http://www.visitmississippi.org/groups_market
    ing/Itineraries/EDTour_Delta2.pdf.
———. "Featured City—Clarksdale." 10 Sept. 2010. http://www.visitmississippi.org/
    features/clarksdale.html.
———. "Soulful Sounds," 25 June 2006. http://www.visitmississippi.org.
Mississippi Tourism Association. 10 Sept. 2010. http://www.mstourism.com.
Moore, Neal. "Livin' the Blues with James 'Super Chikan' Johnson—I." CNN.com 29
    Oct. 2009. 12 Apr. 2010. http://www.ireport.com/docs/DOC-347855.
———. "Livin' the Blues with James 'Super Chikan' Johnson—II." CNN.com 29 Oct.
    2009. 17 Apr. 2010. http://www.ireport.com/docs/DOC-347817.
———. "Politics Meets the Blues with Mississippi's Bill Luckett." CNN.com, 26 Oct.
    2009. 12 Apr. 2010. http://www.ireport.com/docs/DOC-346661.
Morgan, Michele A. "Lower Mississippi Delta." 4 Aug. 2003, pp. 84–89. http://morgan
    graphicstakoma.com/T57ADeltaOverview.pdf.
MS River Blues." Mississippi Blues Trail. 28 Feb. 2010. http://www.msbluestrail
    . org/_webapp_2718877/Miss._River_Blues.
"Music Trail Marker to Be Unveiled." *Daily World*. 10 Dec. 2009. 14 Mar. 2010. http://
    www.helena-arkansas.com/entertainment/x1669483201/Music-trail-marker-to-be-
    unveiled.
National Geographic Traveler. "U.S.A—Central." Apr. 2008. 22 Oct. 2010. http://traveler
    .nationalgeographic.com/2008/04/stay-list/usa-central-text.
"Now They're Arguing in Greenwood About Where Robert Johnson Died . . ." *Folo*. 15
    Oct. 2010. http://www.folo.us.
Oshinsky, David. "Forced Labor in the 19th Century South: The Story of Parchman
    Farm." 28 Feb. 2010, pp. 1–19. http://www.yale.edu/glc/events/cbss/Oshinsky.pdf.
"Otha Turner Kept Fife-and-Drum Tradition Alive." Blues Music Now! 15 Sept. 2010.
    http://www.bluesmusicnow.com/otha_obit.html.
Plant, Robert. News. "Mississippi Blues Trail Marker Dedication Honoring W. C.
    Handy—RP Interview." 26 Nov. 2009. 15 Feb. 2010. http://www.robertplant.com/
    news/mississippi-blues-trail-marker-dedication-honoring-wc-handy-rp-interview.
Resource Entertainment Group. "Celebrity Industry Profile Featuring Howard Stovall." 18
    Feb. 2010. http://www.regmemphis.com/index.cfm?page=newsArticle&newsID=13.
"Roots of Rhythm." 2 Nov. 2007. http://www.rootsofrhythm.com/tours.html.
Rowland, Michael. "Mississippi Delta Feels the Blues." *ABC News*. 31 Aug. 2007. http://
    abc.net.au/news/stories/2007/08/16/2006665.htm?section=world.
The Shack Up Inn. 1 Oct. 2010. http://www.shackupinn.com.
———. "FAQ/The Shackmeister Files." 31 Jan. 2003. http://www.shackupinn.com/faq
    .html.
Stovall, Howard. MySpace. 18 Feb. 2010. http://www.myspace.com/howardstovall.
Sunflower River Blues and Gospel Festival. "About Awards." 12 Feb. 2010. http://www
    .sunflowerfest.org/index.cfm?page=awards&sub=awards.
———. "History." 13 July 2008. http://www.sunflowerfest.org/index.cfm?page=history.
Sweet Magnolia Tours. "Nuttin' but the Blues Vacation Holiday." 24 Feb. 2010. http://
    www.sweetmagnoliatours.com/P_FlyDrive_NuttinButBlues.php.

"Three Icons of the Delta: The River, the Plantation, and the Juke." Blues Highway Association. 10 Sept. 2010. http://www.blueshighway.org/icons.htm.

Thweatt, James E. "Hopson Plantation History." Hopson Preservation Company. 30 June 2009. http://www.hopsonplantation.com/history.html.

Trip Advisor. "Red's Lounge." 17 July 2008. http://www.tripadvisor.com/ShowUserRe views-g43722-d626776-r116721827-Red_s_Lounge-Clarksdale_Mississippi.html.

"2006 Sunflower River Blues and Gospel Festival." Discussion Board. Nikonians.org. 17 July 2008. http://www.nikonians.org/forums/dcboard.php?az=show_topic& forum=168&topic_id=1434.

Vanderheyden, Nathalie. "Traveling to the Holy Ground of the Delta Blues." BlogCritics. Org. 1 Dec. 2008. 1 June 2009. http://www.crossroadshotel.tv/PDF/Dec1_08BCM.pdf.

Voodoo Girls' Blues Pilgrimage. "Mississippi Delta Day 2." 1998. 15 Dec. 2006. http://www.p1.com/mp/Delta%20-%20Day%202.htm.

Wachtel, Katya. "HuffPost Review: Prom Night in Mississippi," 20 July 2009. 14 Apr. 2010. http://www.huffingtonpost.com/katya-wachtel/huffpost-review-em-prom-n_b_241066.html.

William Winter Institute for Racial Reconciliation. Mission Statement. 1 Oct. 2009. http://www.winterinstitute.org.

———. Position Statement on Reconciliation. 4 Oct. 2010. http://www.winterinstitute.org/papers/position-paper.htm.

The Year of the Blues. "Official Proclamation." 20 Aug. 2007. http://www.yearoftheblues.org/officialProclamation.asp.

Audio and Video Media

Blues in the Mississippi Night. Cambridge: Rounder, 2003.

Deep Blues: A Musical Pilgrimage to the Crossroads. Dir. Robert Mugge. Oil Factory/Radio ActiveFilms, 1991.

Fannie Lou Hamer: Courage and Faith. Mississippi Public Broadcasting. 20 Feb. 2006. Exec. Producer Linda C. Coles.

Johnson, Robert. *King of the Delta Blues Singers.* Columbia, 1961.

King, Willie, and the Liberators. *Living in a New World.* Rooster Blues, 2002.

"Mississippi Sings the Blues: Music Tourism Soars in State." CNN. 19 July 2010. 25 Oct. 2010 http://www.youtube.com/watch?v=fboPTYLM_9I.

"Red, White, and Blues." *The Blues: A Musical Journey (Part 6).* Dir. Mike Figgis. Executive prod. Martin Scorsese. PBS. Jackson, Miss. 4 Oct. 2004.

Talbot, Bill. "Interview: Bill Talbot of the Hopson Plantation in Mississippi Discusses His Plans to Rent Out Sharecropper Shacks to Tourists." National Public Radio. Weekend Edition Saturday. 22 Dec. 2001.

WXVT-TV. Newscast. Greenville, Miss. 20 Apr. 2006.

You See Me Laughin': The Last of the Hill Country Bluesmen. Dir. and Prod. Mandy Stein. Plain Jane Productions/Fat Possum, 2003/5.

Lectures, Symposiums, and Speeches

Ellis, Greg. Lecture. "WROX Early Years." Clarksdale, Miss. 8 Aug. 2003.

Griffin, Larry J. "Race, Memory, and Historical Responsibility: What Do Southerners Do with a Difficult Past?" Sammy O. Cranford Memorial Lecture in History. Delta State University, Cleveland, Miss. 21 Apr. 2008.

Lester, Bill. "The Dockery Farms Restoration Project." First Tuesday Program. Delta State University, Cleveland, Miss. 4 May 2010.

McKee, Margaret. Speech, ts. Carnegie Public Library. Clarksdale, Miss. 20 Apr. 1983.

Payne, Sonny. Interview with Jim O'Neal. Living Blues Symposium. Oxford, Miss. 19 Feb. 2005.

Rush, Bobby. "Blues Music Today." Blues Today: A *Living Blues* Symposium. University of Mississippi, Oxford, Miss. 22 Feb. 2003.

Interviews and E-mails

Allen, Kappi. Personal interview. 3 Feb. 2003. Telephone interview. 5 Oct. 2007.

Barretta, Scott. Telephone interview. 28 Feb. 2008.

Bays, Barry. Personal interview. 22 and 29 Mar. 2001.

Bean, Terry. Telephone interview. 23 Apr. 2008.

Blues Highway Association. Minutes from September 10, 2002 meeting. Luther Brown, e-mail communication.

Brown, Luther. Personal interview. 20 Mar. 2001, 7 Sept. 2007. Telephone interview. 23 Aug. 2006.

Brown, Rob. Personal interview. 18 June 2001.

Butler, James. Personal interview. 27 Sept. 2002.

Clark, Wanda. Telephone interview. 23 Apr. 2008.

Czech, Tony Czech. Personal interview. 1 July 2002.

Evans, David. Reader's report. December 2008 and July 2010.

Ferris, William. Telephone interview. 3 June 2008.

Gresham, Bill. Telephone interview. 4 Feb. 2003.

Gussow, Adam. Reader's report. June 2010.

Henderson, Skip. Telephone interview. 19 Mar. 2008.

Hines, George. Personal interview. 18 Oct. 2004.

Hoover, Sylvester. Personal interview. 18 Jan. 2008.

Hurwitt, Elliott. E-mail communication. 7–16 July 2010.

Johnson, Billy. Telephone interview. 19 Nov. 2004.

Johnson, James. Personal interview. 7 Dec. 2004.

Johnson, Patty. Telephone interview. 29 Apr. 2008.

Kirgis, Jay. Personal interview. 18 Nov. 2004.

Kossman, Nancy. Personal interview. 6 Sept. 2002.

LaVere, Steve. Personal interview. 18 Jan. 2008.

Line, Cheryl. Personal interview. 10 May 2001. Telephone interview. 3 Oct. 2007 and 13 Mar. 2008.

Looney, Barbara. Personal interview. 10 Mar. 2003.

Malvezzi, Guy. Personal interview. 27 Sept. 2002.

Mitchell, Don Allen, Personal interview. 31 Jan. 2008.

O'Keefe, Kinchen. Personal interview. 18 Oct. 2004.

O'Neal, Jim. Telephone interview. 22 Feb. 2008. E-mail communication. 29 Mar. 2008.

Pennington, Bill. Personal interview. 29 Apr. 2008.

Perry, Bill. Personal interview. 11 Dec. 2007.

Ratliff, Frank. Personal interview. 30 Aug. 2003.

Ritter, Shelly. Personal interview. 7 Sept. 2004.

Rogers, Mickey. Personal interview. 10 June 2003.

Rush, Bobby. Personal interview. 8 June 2002.

Ruskey, John. Personal interview. 20 Apr. 2001. Telephone interview. 10 July 2008.

Seratt, Bill. Telephone interview. 17 June 2008.

Shawhan, Dorothy. E-mail communication. 29 Apr. 2008.

Sherman, John, Personal interview. 26 Oct. 2007.

Slim, Mississippi (Walter Horn). Telephone interview. 2 Dec. 2004.

Smith, Mae. Personal interview. 27 Sept. 2002; Telephone interview. 11 July 2008.

Stolle, Roger. Personal interview. 1 Sept. 2004.

Talbot, Bill. Personal interview. 17 Aug. 2003.

Thomas, Alex. Telephone interview. 27 Mar. 2008. E-mail communication. 12 Oct. 2010.

Thompson, Dave. Personal interview. 22 May 2003.

Tillis, Melville. Personal interview. 26 Oct. 2007.

Turnipseed, Sade. Personal interview. 21 Sept. 2007.

Walsh, Carmen. E-mail communication. 15 Oct. 2007.

SELECTIVE DISCOGRAPHY

asual blues fans are certainly familiar with the music of Charley Patton and B. B. King, among other well-known Mississippi Delta blues artists. Yet other, more obscure Mississippi Delta musicians have not received the full attention they deserve. The following is a selective discography by artists who were born and/or lived in the Mississippi Delta.

Roosevelt "Booba" Barnes and the Playboys: *The Heartbroken Man* (Rooster Blues, 1995). A consummate performer, Barnes rocks the house with an impassioned set of originals ("How Long This Must Go On") and cover songs ("Rocking Daddy"). This music was made for juke house dancing. Originally released in 1990.

T-Model Ford: *She Ain't None of Your'n* (Fat Possum, 2000). Chainsaw electric guitar and authoritative blues singing powers T-Model's third release from Fat Possum. His screams on the lead cut, "She Asked Me So I Told Her," prepare the listener for thirty-seven minutes of down-and-dirty Delta blues.

Willie Foster: *Live at Airport Grocery* (Mempho, 2000). I had the opportunity to see Willie Foster perform at the Airport Grocery and at other venues in the Delta. Although legally blind and confined to a wheelchair (both legs were amputated), Foster was a heck of a harmonica player and singer. Foster's music is a wonderful blend of Delta and Chicago influences (he lived in Chicago for a spell and played with Muddy Waters). After listening to this live set, it's obvious why Willie often said, "I was born in the blues, I've lived the blues, and I'm *still* living the blues."

Big Jack Johnson and the Oilers: *Roots Stew* (M.C., 2000). A versatile set from the Clarksdale native and former member of the Jelly Roll Kings. Standard blues rockers ("Going Too Far") and slide guitar pieces ("Since I Met

You Baby") seamlessly mix with softer, acoustic numbers ("Cherry Tree") that sometimes include Johnson's tasteful work on the mandolin.

Jelly Roll Kings: *Rockin' the Juke Joint Down* (Earwig, 1993). Originally released in 1979, this record demonstrates why the Jelly Roll Kings were one of Mississippi's most popular blues bands from the 1960s to the 1980s. *Rockin'* shows off the considerable skills of the members—Frank Frost (vocal, harmonica, organ), Jack Johnson (vocals, guitar), and Sam Carr (drums)—as the band moves from loping, slow blues ("Mighty Long Time") to fast-paced, organ- and guitar-driven songs ("Have Mercy Baby").

M for Mississippi: A Road Trip through the Birthplace of the Blues (Music from the Motion Picture) (Broke and Hungry/Cat Head Delta Blues and Art/Mudpuppy, 2008). The sound track from the award-winning documentary. Many of Mississippi's legendary blues artists are dead, but the blues is certainly not dead in the Mississippi Delta. The soundtrack features local and regional acts, including the Wesley Jefferson Blues Band, Pat Thomas, T-Model Ford, and L. C. Ulmer. A second CD from the movie is also available from Broke and Hungry Records (*M for Mississippi: A Road Trip through the Birthplace of the Blues (More Music from the Motion Picture)*).

The Rough Guide to Delta Blues (World Music Network, 2002). An effective sampler of well-known (Robert Johnson, Skip James) and more obscure (Blind Joe Reynolds, Robert Belfour) Mississippi blues music.

Super Chikan: *Chikadelic* (Bluestown, 2009). James Johnson (a.k.a. Super Chikan) sings about juke joints, catfish, dollar stores, and cotton fields, and his songs are mostly up-tempo electric blues with an occasional R&B-flavored tune ("Ain't Nobody") thrown in for good measure. His scorching slide guitar work on "Front Porch Boogie" beats ZZ Top at their own game.

Dave Thompson: *Little Dave and Big Love* (Fat Possum, 1995). Although Lil' Dave would release three additional albums before his death in 2010, his 1995 debut album arguably remains his best. Under the direction of blues writer and producer Robert Palmer, Thompson's guitar fire and virtuosity are evident throughout, especially in songs such as "Standing Up on My Own," "You Took My Baby," and "Instrumental #7."

Terry "Big T" Williams: *Jump Back Big T's in the House* (Blumert, 2010). Recorded in Clarksdale, Big T's third album may be his finest musical offering. Williams is a ferocious guitarist who possesses both technique and emotion, and he rarely overplays onstage or in the studio. The band is tight and swinging, and Williams's guitar and voice are in fine form, especially on "The Night Doctor" and the title track. He even gets funky on "Booty Wild." Slower acoustic numbers ("Devil in the Cottonfield," "Bound for Clarksdale") demonstrate his range and influence. Excellent production values.

Noteworthy albums from other Mississippi, Arkansas, and Alabama blues artists include Terry "Harmonica" Bean, *Two Sides of the Blues* (no label, 2007); Big George Brock, *Club Caravan* (Cat Head, 2006); Kenny Brown, *Stingray* (Fat Possum, 2003); R. L. Burnside, *Too Bad Jim* (Fat Possum, 1994); CeDell Davis, *Feel Like Doin' Something Wrong* (Fat Possum, 1994); Odell Harris, *Searching for Odell Harris* (Broke and Hungry, 2006); Jessie Mae Hemphill, *Feelin' Good* (HMG, 1987); Jimmy "Duck" Holmes, *Ain't It Lonesome* (Broke and Hungry, 2010); Junior Kimbrough, *All Night Long* (Fat Possum, 1992); Willie King and the Liberators, *Freedom Creek* (Rooster Blues, 2000), *Living in a New World* (Rooster Blues, 2002); North Mississippi Allstars, *Polaris* (ATO, 2003); Bobby Rush, *Folkfunk* (Deep Rush, 2004); Otha Turner and the Afrossippi Allstars, *From Senegal to Senatobia* (Birdman, 1999).

INDEX

African American. *See* black
Alligator Records, 61
Allison, Mose, 150
American Folk Blues Festival (AFBF), 44–46
America's Blues Alley, 68
Ann Arbor Blues Festival, 53
Arkansas Blues and Heritage Festival. *See* King Biscuit Blues Festival
authenticity, 18–19, 42, 45–48, 166, 207n152; blues and race, 104–6; difficulty defining, 102; rhetorical construction of, 103–4, 116; types of, 102–3. *See also* blues festivals

Back in the Day Museum, 87, 95, 175
Baptist Town, 174, 177
Baraka, Amiri (LeRoi Jones), xiii, 24, 50
Barbour, Haley, 6, 73, 82, 144
Barnes, Roosevelt "Booba," 67
Barnett, Ross, 144, 169
B. B. King Blues Club, 60
B. B. King Day, 170
B. B. King Homecoming Festival, 112, 180
B. B. King Museum and Delta Interpretive Center, 17, 138, 167
Beale Street, 14, 56, 59, 60, 67
Bean, Terry "Harmonica," xiv, 107, 109, 132, 184
Bentonia Blues Festival, 57
birthplace myth, 19, 81–91, 99, 150, 166; corrective to, 87; defending claims of, 81–82; and Dockery Farms, 85–87; and W. C. Handy, 84–85; media, 84; origins

of, 81; and privileged memory, 90–91; to promote the state's image, 90; reinforcement of "pure" blues culture, 87–89
black codes, 122
black disc jockeys, 36–37
black migration: out-migration, 19, 112, 156; reverse migration, 111, 228n137
black poverty, 10, 90, 115, 161, 190
Bland, Bobby "Blue," 50, 61, 70, 162
Blues: A Musical Journey, The (film), 3
blues: black interest in, 12–13, 50–51, 208–9n177; co-optation of, xiii–xiv, 193n4; country, xiv, 29–32, 41–43, 46–47, 81; declining interest in, xi, 193n1; Delta (*see* Delta Blues); emotions associated with, 23; impact on American and British white musicians, 48–50; and myth, 78–79; origin of music, 24–27, 85–86; origin of term, 23; popularity of, 3–4, 14, 39, 67–68; primitive, 24, 29, 38, 46; as protest music, xiii, 24, 141, 147, 149, 221n46; radio (*see* radio); record companies, 28–33; recording in the South, 29, 31–32; soul-blues, 21, 101, 108–10; urban, 50, 52; vaudeville, 28–29; viewed as evil, 12, 91, 98–99; white consumers of, 29; white influence on, xiii–xiv
Blues Aid, 181
Blues Alley, 16, 107, 112, 115
Blues Brothers, The, 13, 74
blues festivals (Mississippi), 7, 44–46, 52–53, 56–58; assisting aging musicians, 180–82; and black audiences, 101, 190; illusion of racial harmony, 177–78,

182–83, 188; law enforcement presence at, 63–64; local musicians v. headliners, 188; pay disparity, 183–84; positive outcomes, 181–82; and poverty, 114–15; promoting racial harmony, 57, 177–79; questionable profitability, 187, 189; reconciliation themes, 180–82; settings of, 111–12; and soul-blues, 108–10; white perceptions of authenticity, 101, 104–5; and white tourists, 101, 105, 110
Blues Highway Association, 72, 86
Blues Homecoming Festival, 58
Blues Hound Flat, 16
blues lodging. *See* Blues Hound Flat; Riverside Hotel; Shack Up Inn
blues museums, 7, 18. *See also* Delta Blues Museum; Greenwood Blues Heritage Museum and Gallery; Highway 61 Blues Museum; WROX Museum
blues musicians: arrest of/imprisonment of, 126–30; complaints of economic exploitation, 32–33, 178, 186; employment outside musical career, 185–87; and lynching, 124–25; mobility as resistance to white oppression, 134; Second Great Migration, 137; segregation impacting, 135–36; serving in World War II, 137–38; white interest in, 136–37; white violence towards, 133–34
blues radio. *See* radio
blues tourism (Mississippi): and casinos, 70; centralization/decentralization of promotional efforts, 69–77; changing attitudes of local population regarding, 141, 145; cross-promotion of, 76; economic impact of, 5–6, 166–67, 189; goal—economic growth, 5–9; goal—improve image of Mississippi, 9–11, 90, 168; goal—racial reconciliation, 11, 170–73; history of, 54–77; intra-town conflict, 70; local interest in, 8–9; as a modern-day form of sharecropping, 189–91; perceptions of white exploitation, 19, 189–91; press coverage of, 62
blues tourism: New Blues Tourism, 68; scholarship in, 18

blues tourists: definition, 195n10; profile of, 11–14
Boyd, Eddie, 133, 157, 160
Bracey, Ishmon, 31–32, 203n53
Brock, Big George, 160
brokerage compensation system (radio), 37
Broonzy, Big Bill, 45, 47, 126, 133, 160
Brown, Luther, 72
Brown, Willie, 30–32, 84–86, 92, 94, 212n76
Brown v. Board of Education, 133, 138, 229n148
Bug's Blues Lounge, 151
Burnside, R. L., 29, 67, 137, 187

Callicott, Joe, 75, 207n132
Carr, Leroy, 28
Carr, Sam, 74, 106, 133
Carter, Bo, 31
Cat Head Delta Blues and Folk Art, 16, 68, 72–73
Charters, Samuel, 39–40, 81
Chatmon, Sam, 57
Chess Records, 38
Clapton, Eric, 47–49
Clarksdale Station, 16, 107, 112, 199n77
classic blues. *See* vaudeville blues
collective memory. *See* public memory
Complete Recordings, The (album), 67, 175
Confederate Memorial Day, 144
Congress of Racial Equality (CORE), 138
convict-leasing, 125–26
coon songs, 25
Cotton, James, 74–75
Country Blues, The (book & LP), 39–40, 206n113, 206n116
Cray, Robert, 70, 108, 198n69
"Crazy Blues" (Smith), 28
"Cross Road Blues" (Johnson), 93, 97
Crossroads (film), 94, 212n76
Crossroads Blues Festival, 106, 112
Crossroads Blues Society, 95, 104
crossroads myth, 91–99; and black community, 92; and Robert Johnson, 91–99; and Tommy Johnson, 92; negative imagery, 97–99; use in tourism materials, 94–97

Crudup, Arthur, 24, 44, 75–76, 207n141
cultural tourism, 4, 69, 76, 115, 140
Cusic, Eddie, 107, 133

Dawkins, Jimmy, 51
Deep Blues: A Musical Pilgrimage to the Crossroads (film), 65, 67, 187
Delta blues: development of term, 30; style, 29–30. *See also* blues
Delta Blues Legend Tour, 8, 174
Delta Blues Museum, 7, 16, 58–59, 62–63, 66, 70, 73, 95, 112, 167, 210n22, 216–17n66
Delta Blues Room, 16
Delta Cooperative Farm (DCF), 131–32
Diddley, Bo (Ellas Otha Bates), 38, 48, 108, 149
disc jockeys. *See* black disc jockeys
Dixon, Willie, 32, 38, 45, 49, 76, 118, 124, 126, 137
Dockery, Joe Rice, 147–48, 156
Dockery, Will, 147–48, 156
Dockery Farms, 75, 85–87, 96, 140, 147–48
"Dry Spell Blues" (House), 41

Early Wright Award, 181
Edwards, David "Honeyboy," xi, 30, 78, 97, 106, 117, 126–27, 131, 137, 160, 174
Estes, Sleepy John, 43, 46
Esu Elegbara, 91, 217n80

Fat Possum Records, 61, 68
Ferris, William, 40, 53, 55–56, 60, 132
First Great Migration, 137
Floyd, "Harmonica" Frank, 150
Ford, James "T-Model," xi, 133, 186–87
Foster, Willie, 37, 137, 180
Freedom Village, 56, 111
Freeman, Morgan, 9, 15, 65, 83, 112–13, 165–66
Frost, Frank, 106

Graves, Sid, 58, 66–67
gravesites, xi, 15, 140
Great Depression, 33, 131, 188
Great Flood of 1927, 129–31

Greenwood Blues Heritage Museum and Gallery, 16, 18, 95, 176
Ground Zero Blues Club, 15–16, 65, 73, 83, 112–14
Guy, Buddy, 44, 52, 184, 193n1, 197n41

Handy, W. C., 3, 15, 20, 26–27, 48, 59, 60, 78, 84–85, 124, 149
Harris, William, 31–32
"Hellhound on My Trail" (Johnson), 93, 97
Hemphill, Jessie Mae, 104, 180
Henderson, Skip, 66–67, 148
High Water Records, 61
Highway 61, xi–xii, 15, 75, 82–83, 94–96, 115, 136, 149, 151
Highway 61 Blues Festival, 106–7, 112, 180, 187, 237n75
Highway 61 Blues Museum, 15, 18
Hill, Z. Z., 61
Hooker, John Lee, 32, 46, 66, 108, 113, 135, 137, 147, 149, 181
Hoover, Mary Ann Edwards, 174–75
Hoover, Sylvester, 8, 87, 174–77
Hopson, H. Howell, 152–53, 156, 158
Hopson Plantation, 152–53, 156, 162
Horton, John, 107, 185
House, Son (Eddie James), 13, 16, 30–32, 37, 39, 41–42, 44, 46, 79, 86, 91–93, 118, 123, 129, 145, 160, 209n4, 218n94
House of Blues, 89
Howlin' Wolf. *See* Wolf, Howlin'
Hurt, Mississippi John, 8, 13, 39, 42, 44

"I Can't Be Satisfied" (Waters), 38
"I Feel Like Going Home" (Waters), 38

James, Elmore (Elmore Brooks), xi, 137, 174
James, Skip (Nehemiah Curtis), 29–32, 37, 39, 42–44, 46, 57, 91
Jefferson, Blind Lemon, 29, 131
Jefferson, Wesley, 180, 183
Jim Crow Laws, 9–10, 55, 90, 112, 124, 135, 138, 144, 151, 156, 161, 181, 183, 185
Johnson, Big Jack, 185

Johnson, James "Super Chikan," 146, 172, 182, 185

Johnson, Patty, 63, 65–67, 183

Johnson, Robert, xi–xiii, 4, 8–9, 13, 16, 24, 29–30, 33, 47, 49, 55, 62, 67, 70, 78, 83, 91–100, 106, 134, 140, 149, 152, 162, 174–77, 218n94, 218n97; as amateur musician, 92–93; birth of, 92; birthplace of, 93; Brown and, 92–93; death of, 93; House and, 92–93; promotion of, 174–77; recording career of, 96–97; use of in tourism materials, 94–97, 174–77

Johnson, Tommy, 20, 29, 31–32, 79, 86, 92, 137

Jones, Calvin "Fuzz," 34–35

Jones, LeRoi. See Baraka, Amiri

Jones, Paul, 136

Jordan, David, 9, 73, 75, 174

Juke Joint Festival, 14, 100, 104

Kimbrough, David "Junior," 29, 67–68, 187

King, Albert, 70, 108

King, B. B. (Riley B.), xi, 4, 9, 24, 36–37, 46, 48, 50–52, 59, 61–62, 78, 81, 118, 124, 134, 145, 149, 160, 165, 170

King, Martin Luther, Jr., 138

King, Willie, 164, 180

King Biscuit Blues Festival, 35, 62, 106

King Biscuit Boys, 34, 135, 204n79

King Biscuit Flour, 34

"King Biscuit Time," 33–38

King of the Delta Blues Singers (album), 33, 47, 175

Kirgis, Jay, 186–87

Ku Klux Klan, 10, 129–30, 132, 138, 164, 226n93

LaSalle, Denise, 61

"Last Fair Deal Gone Down" (Johnson), 47

LaVere, Steve, 16, 43, 174–77

Leadbelly (Huddie Ledbetter), 32, 147

levee camps, 123

Lewis, Furry (Walter), 59

Little Milton. See Milton, Little

"Little Red Rooster" (Dixon; Rolling Stones), 49

Little Walter. See Walter, Little

Little Zion Missionary Baptist Church, 94, 176

Lockwood, Robert, Jr., 34, 97, 186

Lomax, Alan, xi, 39, 55–56, 88, 148, 203n56, 209n4

Looney, Barbara, 184

Lost Cause story, 143–44

Luckett, Bill, 65, 83, 112–13, 167, 171

lynching, 124–25

M for Mississippi: A Road Trip through the Birthplace of the Blues (film), 73

Malaco Records, 56, 61

Malvezzi, Guy, 37, 152–53, 160, 167

Mayfield, Panny, 132

McClennan, Tommy, 33

McCoy, Prince, 85

McDowell, Fred, 39, 43–44

McKune, James, 30, 81

"Me and the Devil Blues" (Johnson), 47, 96

migration. See black migration; First Great Migration; Second Great Migration

Milton, Little (James Milton Campbell), 37, 51–52, 61, 132–33, 149

Mississippi: poverty, 5, 10; unemployment rates, 5, 10

Mississippi Action for Community Education (MACE), 54, 56, 76, 101, 108, 188

Mississippi, Believe It!, 9, 149

Mississippi Blues Commission, 17, 24, 27, 73–74, 79, 81, 100, 136, 213n101

Mississippi Blues Trail, 17, 27, 35, 74–77, 81–82, 87; positive memory-building practices, 145, 151, 163; unveiling ceremonies, 74–75, 171

Mississippi Blues Trail markers, 27, 31, 35, 48, 74–76, 87, 127, 130, 136, 151, 233n95

Mississippi Delta: black migration to, 123; Civil War, 121–22; cotton production, 121; deforestation of, 122; demographic changes, 88–89; disease, 119; Native American removal from, 119; "Negro Rule," 122; slavery in, 119–21; social changes, 88–89; white romanticism of, 118

Mississippi Delta Blues and Heritage Festival, 56, 61–62, 83, 104, 106–8, 110–11, 188
Mississippi Delta Tourism Association, 4, 69, 71, 98
Mississippi Sheiks, 30, 32
Mount Zion Memorial Fund, 148
Musselwhite, Charlie, 150, 206n116
myth, 18–19, 78, 79–81; characteristics, 79–80; definition, 79–80; goals, 80–81; misconceptions, 80. See also birthplace myth; crossroads myth

Nelson Street, 15
New Blues Tourism, 68
New World District, 16, 199n80
Night Hawks, The, 35
Nighthawk, Robert (Robert Lee McCollum), 24, 35, 135
1960s Blues Revival, 13, 38–53; authenticity, 45–48; decline of, 53–55; festivals, 44–46, 52–53; impact on blues tourism, 39; impetus for, 39–41; record collectors, 41–42; search for blues musicians, 42–43
"No Black, No White, Just the Blues" (slogan), 149–50, 178, 180
Northeast Mississippi Blues and Gospel Music Folk Festival, 57

official culture, 143
OKeh Records, 28, 31, 32
Oliver, Paul, 50, 53, 98
O'Neal, Jim, 17, 63, 65, 75, 87, 167, 234n1
Owens, Jack, 29

Paramount Records, 33, 38
Parchman Farm (prison), 127–29, 226n83
Patton, Charley, xi, 20, 29, 31, 75, 84–86, 106, 113, 131, 136–37, 140, 145, 147–48
Payne, Sonny, 34–35, 181
Peabody, Charles, 26
Perkins, Pinetop (Willie Perkins), 35, 151–52, 158
Perry, Bill "Howl-N-Madd," 172, 182, 184
Phillips, Esther, 134–35
pig law, 126
Pitchford, Lonnie, 106
Plant, Robert, 48, 154

plantation commissary, 161
Plessy v. Ferguson, 124, 138
Poor Monkey's (juke joint), xi, 7
Powell, Eugene, 136, 180
"Preachin' Blues (Up Jumped the Devil)" (Johnson), 96
Presley, Elvis, 9, 49, 82, 150
Prom Night in Mississippi (film), 166
public memory, 18–19; definition, 141–42, 229n6; and forgetting, 142, 172; and privileged memory, 90–91, 166; and rhetoric, 142; and southern culture, 140, 143–45; vernacular v. official communities, 142–43

race records, 28–29, 33
racial reconciliation, 163, 168–69, 172, 191
radio, 33–38, 205n95; KFFA, 34; WDIA, 35–36; WROX, 35–37
Rainey, Ma (Gertrude Pridgett), 28, 46
Randall Travel Marketing Group, 68–69
Ratliff, Frank, 63, 135, 181
reconciliation, 11, 169, 172
Reconstruction, 121–22, 129
record collectors, 41–42
Red's Lounge, 114
Reed, Jimmy, 137
Riverside Hotel, 15, 63, 135, 151, 181
Rodgers, Jimmie, 17, 82, 150
Rogers, Mickey, 184
Rolling Stones, 13, 46, 49, 65, 68, 194n11
Rooster Blues Records, 61, 65
Rum Boogie Café, 60
Rush, Bobby (Emmet Ellis, Jr.), 21, 70, 108–9, 135
Ruskey, John, 58–59, 66

Sarah's Kitchen, 16
Second Great Migration, 37, 117, 137, 146
segregation, 10, 12, 19, 63, 67, 88, 90, 114, 118, 124, 132, 134–35, 138, 141, 144, 146–47, 151, 161, 164–65, 172, 182, 190, 228n128, 232n57
Selvidge, Sid, 59
Seratt, Bill, 71–72, 190
Shack Up Inn, 15, 74, 95, 141, 232n65; authenticity of, 153–54; awards received

by, 155; Cotton Gin Inn, 153; critique of, 155–63; customer feedback, 158–59; diversity of patrons, 154; history of, 153; Hopson Plantation, 152–53, 155–56; media coverage of, 155; and nostalgia, 158–59, 161; owners' rejection of black exploitation claims, 154, 159; owners' response to criticism, 154, 156, 159; preservation goals, 154–55; Robert Clay Shack, 153–54, 162, 232n65, 234n109; use of blues artifacts and imagery, 152, 161–63

sharecropping, 19, 123, 132–34, 157

Shaw Blues Festival, 109

Shines, Johnny, 30, 127

slave contracts, 120

slavery, 119–21

Slim, Memphis (John Len Chatman), 23, 45, 118, 123, 133

Slim, Mississippi (Walter Horn, Jr.), 105, 135, 172, 184

Smith, Bessie, 27–28, 32, 46, 92, 136

Smith, Mamie, 20, 28

Sonny Boy Blues Society, 181

Sovereignty Commission (Mississippi), 10, 113, 139

Speir, H. C., 31–32, 203n53

Spottswood, Dick, 41

"St. Louis Blues" (Handy), 60

Stackhouse, Houston (Houston Goff), 34, 62, 136

Stackhouse Mississippi Arts and Gifts/Delta Record Mart, 65–66, 72, 212n69

standpoint theory, 173–74, 177, 191

Stolle, Roger, 68, 72–73, 109, 167, 178

Stovall, Howard, 64–65, 83, 112, 171

Stovall Plantation, 64, 152

Student Nonviolent Coordinating Committee (SNCC), 138

Sumlin, Hubert, 75

Sunflower River Blues and Gospel Festival, 37, 63–64, 70, 73, 101, 104, 106–7, 111–12, 115, 180–81, 183, 187

Sunflower River Blues Association, 109, 180–81

Taylor, Hound Dog (Theodore Roosevelt), 8, 50

Taylor, Johnnie, 61

Taylor, Koko (Cora Walton), 12, 38, 183

"Terraplane Blues" (Johnson), 93, 162

"32-20 Blues" (Johnson), 47

Thomas, James "Son," 57, 75, 107, 137, 181, 185–86, 229n143

Thomas, Pat, 72, 107, 185

Thompson, Bennie, 165

Thompson, Dave, 108–9

Till, Emmett, 138

tourism, 172. See also blues tourism

tourist: definition, 194n4; types, 11–12, 198n59, 219–20n10

"Traveling Riverside Blues" (Johnson), 95, 106

Turner, Ike, 135

Turner, Othar, 107

Turner, Shardee and the Rising Star Fife and Drum Band, 107

United States Colored Troops, 121

Walker, T-Bone (Aaron Thibeaux), 51, 228n128

Walter, Little (Marion Walter Jacobs), 38, 137

Walton, Wade, 58, 62, 64, 181

"Wang Dang Doodle" (Dixon; Taylor), 38

Wardlow, Gayle Dean, 41, 148

Waterman, Dick, 42–44, 207n141

Waters, Muddy (McKinley Morganfield), xi, 4, 8, 24, 37–38, 46, 48–50, 59, 64–65, 79, 81–83, 107–8, 113, 135, 137, 145, 147, 149, 152, 162, 194n11, 199n77, 211n50

Wheatstraw, Peetie (William Bunch), 92, 97, 131

White, Bukka (Booker T. Washington), 8, 13, 30, 42–43, 49, 59, 129

White, Josh, 147

White Citizens' Council, 10, 138–39

white privilege, 10, 183, 191, 237–38n82

William Winter Institute for Racial Reconciliation, 169–70

Williams, Big Joe, 46
Williams, Nat D., 36, 59
Williams, Robert Pete, 43–44
Williams, Terry "Big T," 167, 183, 185
Williamson (II), Sonny Boy (Aleck
    "Rice"), 15, 27, 34–36, 48–49, 71, 133,
    135, 140, 174
Willie Clay Homecoming Festival, 110
Winter, William F., 61, 169–70, 192
Wolf, Howlin' (Chester Burnett), 24, 30,
    37, 51, 62, 70, 75, 85, 91, 135, 137, 149
Wright, Early, 16, 36–37, 181
WROX Museum, 37, 190

Year of the Blues, 3, 73, 194n1

Zimmerman, Ike, 93
ZZ Top, 62–63, 211n50

CPSIA information can be obtained
at www.ICGtesting.com
Printed in the USA
BVHW082248270819
556983BV00001B/20/P